Economic Valuation with Stated Preference Techniques: A Manual

Department
for **Transport**

Economic Valuation with Stated Preference Techniques

A Manual

Ian J. Bateman, Richard T. Carson, Brett Day,
Michael Hanemann, Nick Hanley, Tannis Hett,
Michael Jones-Lee, Graham Loomes, Susana Mourato,
Ece Özdemiroḡlu, David W. Pearce OBE,
Robert Sugden and John Swanson

Edward Elgar
Cheltenham, UK • Northampton, MA, USA

Published for the Department for Transport, under licence from the Controller of her Majesty's Stationery Office by

Edward Elgar Publishing Limited
Glensanda House
Montpellier Parade
Cheltenham
Glos GL50 1UA
UK

Edward Elgar Publishing, Inc.
136 West Street
Suite 202
Northampton
Massachusetts 01060
USA

Following the reorganisation of the government in May 2002, the responsibilities of the former Department of the Environment, Transport and the Regions (DETR) and latterly the Department for Transport, Local Government and the Regions (DTLR) in this area were transferred to the Department for Transport.

A catalogue record for this book is available from the British Library

Library of Congress Cataloguing in Publication Data
Economic valuation with stated preference techniques : a manual / Ian Bateman ... [et al.].
    p. cm.
   Includes bibliographical references and index.
    1. Environmental economics—Handbooks, manuals, etc. 2. Environmental
auditing—Handbooks, manuals, etc. I. Bateman, Ian.

HC79.E5 E275 2002
333.7—dc21

2002019501

ISBN 1 84064 919 4

Printed in the UK on material comprising approximately 90% post-consumer waste and 10% TCF pulp.

Typeset by Manton Typesetters, Louth, Lincolnshire, UK.
Printed and bound in Great Britain by MPG Books Ltd, Bodmin, Cornwall.

Contents

Figures

Tables

Boxes

The authors

Ian J. Bateman is Professor of Environmental Economics at the School of Environmental Sciences, and Senior Research Fellow at the Centre for Social and Economic Research on the Global Environment (CSERGE), University of East Anglia and University College London, UK.

Richard T. Carson is Professor of Economics at the University of California, San Diego, Research Director for International Environmental Policy at the UC Institute for Global Conflict and Cooperation, and a Senior Fellow at the San Diego Supercomputer Center, US.

Brett Day is Senior Research Fellow at CSERGE, University of East Anglia, UK.

Michael Hanemann is Chancellor's Professor of Agricultural and Resource Economics and Public Policy, University of California at Berkeley, US.

Nick Hanley is Professor of Environmental Economics, University of Glasgow, UK.

Tannis Hett worked as a consultant for Economics for the Environment Consultancy Ltd (EFTEC), London, UK. She is currently an independent environmental economics consultant based in Canada.

Michael Jones-Lee is Professor of Economics, University of Newcastle, UK.

Graham Loomes is Professor of Economic Behaviour and Decision Theory at the University of East Anglia, UK.

Susana Mourato is Lecturer in Environmental Economics in the Department of Environment Science and Technology at Imperial College of Science, Technology and Medicine, London, UK.

Ece Özdemiroğlu is a Director of Economics for the Environment Consultancy Ltd (EFTEC), London, UK.

David W. Pearce OBE is Professor of Environmental Economics at University College London, and Honorary Professor in the Department of Environmental Science and Technology, Imperial College of Science, Technology and Medicine, London, UK.

Robert Sugden holds the Leverhulme Personal Research Professorship in Economics at the Department of Economics, University of East Anglia, UK.

John Swanson works for Steer Davies Gleave, an independent transport planning consultancy based in London, UK.

Alexandra Howarth, a Director of Economics for the Environment Consultancy Ltd (EFTEC), London, UK, has also contributed to finalising the book.

Acronyms

ASC	Alternative specific constants
BT	Benefits transfer
CAPI	Computer-assisted personal interview
CATI	Computer-assisted telephone interview
CBA	Cost–benefit analysis
CDF	Cumulative density function
CE	Choice experiment
CEA	Cost-effectiveness analysis
CM	Choice modelling
CRA	Comparative risk assessment
CV	Contingent valuation
DC	Dichotomous choice
EIA	Environmental impact assessment
ERA	Environmental risk assessment
GIS	Geographical information system
HHA	Health-health assessment
HP	Hedonic pricing
HRA	Health risk assessment
IIA	Independence from irrelevant alternatives
LCA	Life-cycle analysis
MCA	Multi-criteria analysis
MNL	Multi-nomial logit model
MTPR	Marginal time preference rate
NATA	New approach to appraisal
NUV	Non-use value (also known as passive use value)
OLS	Ordinary least squares
PAVA	Pooled adjacent violators algorithm
PDF	Probability density function
PSU	Primary sampling unit
QALY	Quality adjusted life year
RAD	Restricted activity day
RDD	Random digit dialling
RIA	Regulatory impact assessment
RCS	Randomised card sorting
RP	Revealed preference
RPL	Random parameters logit
RRA	Risk-risk assessment

SP	Stated preference
TC	Travel cost
TDM	Total design method
TEV	Total economic value
TSCA	Turnbull's self-consistency algorithm
VOSL	Value of statistical life
WTA	Willingness to accept compensation
WTP	Willingness to pay

Foreword

Sound appraisal is at the heart of good policymaking, and robust valuation of impacts in money terms helps decision makers to take proper account of them. Some of the costs and benefits of policy decisions can be readily valued because they impact directly on markets. But some cannot, and measures therefore have to be constructed or obtained from complementary markets. It will never be possible in practice to value all impacts, but we should aim to extend valuation to as many as we can. Valuation is implicit in most policy decisions, and it is preferable to make it explicit where possible to improve quality and transparency, whatever objections some may have.

Of the various valuation techniques available, stated preference (SP) techniques are being used to an increasing extent. Indeed they are the only kind of technique suitable in many circumstances. This volume, together with its companion 'Summary Guide' (published by the Department for Transport, Local Government and the Regions at http://www.dtlr.gov.uk/about/economics/index.htm), was commissioned by the Department of the Environment, Transport and the Regions in order to increase the accessibility of SP techniques and to set out what the literature tells us about best practice. We hope that they will both promote the use of SP techniques and, most importantly, improve the quality of studies that are undertaken. There are many methodological and procedural pitfalls in implementing such techniques which, if not avoided, can easily discredit the results, thus not only failing to help the policymaker but also bringing the techniques into disrepute.

The material we have put together is addressed to two main groups of people. This volume will be most helpful for students and those who themselves undertake SP studies. They need to be aware of latest developments and the requirements of good practice. The companion 'Summary Guide' is targeted mainly at those in the policy community, including people who may need to commission or manage valuation studies, who have to understand the nature and quality of the results in order to inform decisions. Policy managers need to be able to challenge work commissioned from practitioners and to ensure that it can withstand critical examination when required to support policy. This cannot be done well without some knowledge of the techniques involved.

SP valuation is a rapidly developing field, and this book provides up-to-date information about the latest techniques and approaches. It has been prepared by a top class team of experts, led by Prof. David Pearce and including many of the leading figures in stated preference on both sides of the

Atlantic. I'm very grateful to all those involved in getting this material into the public domain.

Appraisal can be contentious and difficult. It is not solely the preserve of economists, although good appraisal is largely underpinned by analysis of costs and benefits. Cost–benefit analysis aims for a degree of objectivity and impartiality when comparing the relative merits of feasible options. Nevertheless, the potentially all-embracing nature of good appraisal means that many disciplines have contributions to make, both in the social sciences as part of the decision process and in the natural sciences by providing the necessary evidence as inputs for decisions. Cost–benefit analysis reaches its limits when some significant impacts cannot in practice be given money values, and in such cases other techniques may help, such as multi-criteria decision analysis (see, for example, DETR's guidance).

But my aim is to promote actively the use of valuation where it is a practical proposition. Valuation techniques are frequently used for measuring environmental impacts. They also have a long history of use in the health and safety field, where willingness to pay studies of changes to risk of illness, injury or death have informed many policy and investment decisions. In transport they are used for valuing time savings, and hence congestion costs. I hope that by making stated preference techniques more accessible, this book and accompanying guidance will enable more policy areas to take advantage of them, using best practice techniques.

Chris Riley
Chief Economist
Department for Transport
January 2002

Introduction

1 PURPOSE OF THIS MANUAL

This volume is a detailed statement of how to carry out economic valuation using 'stated preference techniques'. Economic valuation refers to the assignment of monetary values to non-market goods and services, where the monetary values have a particular and precise meaning. Any economy provides a mix of marketed and non-marketed goods and services. A marketed good involves an explicit exchange between buyers and sellers and prices are 'posted' in the market place. A non-marketed good has no market, or it may have a limited, or 'incomplete', market. But, provided the relevant good contributes positively to human wellbeing, it has *economic value*. Similarly, a disservice or 'bad' has negative economic value – it detracts from human wellbeing. Broadly, there are two ways of uncovering the economic values attached to non-marketed goods and services and to bads: by seeing if they influence actual markets for some other good (known as *revealed preference techniques*) and by asking people what economic value they attach to those goods and services (known as *stated preference techniques*). This volume is concerned with the latter approach for eliciting economic values.

Examples of non-marketed goods and services are widespread: cleaner air, cleaner water, the provision of public open space, healthcare that is not sold through private markets, risk reduction policies and investments not provided privately, the provision of information as with the recorded heritage, the protection of cultural assets and so on. In the same vein, 'bads' would be instanced by such things as polluted air and water, loss of biological diversity, global warming, any activity inducing ill-health, and the destruction of cultural and recorded heritage.

The essence of the notion of economic value is that it measures the change in human wellbeing arising from the provision of a good or service. The notion of 'wellbeing' in turn reflects what individuals prefer. Wellbeing is therefore a preference-based concept. As this manual makes clear, wellbeing emanates from preference satisfaction, and preferences are regularly revealed in market places. Hence there is a logical link from preferences to *willingness to pay*. Essentially, willingness to pay (WTP) can be shown to be a measure of preference satisfaction and hence a measure of wellbeing. This link is explored in more detail in Chapter 1, but the historical background to it is that of the sub-discipline of *welfare economics*. More detail about the foundations

1

and contents of welfare economics can be found in any number of modern texts (see, for example, Johansson, 1991; Boardman et al., 1996).

What is the justification for trying to assign economic values to such goods and services? This is the subject of a very large literature. The current volume is not intended to debate the question but, rather, to answer the question of how one carries out economic valuation once it has been decided that it is something that will aid rational decision-making. Nonetheless, some idea of the driving forces for engaging in this valuation activity is required.

2 JUSTIFICATION FOR ASSIGNING ECONOMIC VALUES TO NON-MARKET EFFECTS

All decision-making involves choices and all choices involve a sacrifice. If A is chosen, B cannot be, if only because the resources allocated to A cannot now be allocated to B. This notion of *opportunity cost* is fundamental to decision-making. Opportunity cost is defined as the value of the thing that is sacrificed by making a particular choice. The value of the resources allocated to the option chosen (a policy, a project or a programme of action) is conventionally measured in money terms. Money is *fungible*: it can be used for many different things, it is divisible, and it can be used in *discrete* amounts. Expressed as the cost of a particular action, a money value that reflects what that money could secure in a market place also has another property: it is an approximation of the economic value of that forgone choice. Hence choices involve a comparison of the 'worth' of a given choice and the value of the sacrificed choice, where the latter is usually expressed in terms of the cost of making the given choice. The worth of the choice is therefore being compared to the economic value of the alternative use of resources.

There are clearly many ways in which choices could be made. Choices about alternative ways of saving lives, for example, could be made by comparing how many lives are saved with the cost of saving those lives. If policy A saves 100 lives per year, policy B saves 50 lives per year and each policy costs £1 million, the choice appears to be clear: A would be chosen because it saves more lives or, put another way, the 'cost per life saved' is less under A than it is under B. This would be an example of *cost-effectiveness analysis*, and cost-effectiveness is fundamental to efficient decision-making. Resources should not be allocated to a particular scheme for saving lives if more lives could be saved by allocating the resources in a different way. But perhaps not all lives are 'equal'. Society may think that saving the lives of infants is more important than saving the lives of old people. If so, different lives would have to be 'weighted' to reflect this importance. The choice may be between saving lives now or saving lives in the future. Again, lives may or may not be equally weighted according to when they are saved. The choice may also be between saving lives with different 'qualities of living' attached to them. Perhaps extending the life of person X by one year is regarded as being less important than extending the life of person Y by one year because person X's extended life-year would have a low quality of existence.

While cost-effectiveness is a critical ingredient of sensible decision-making, it can be seen that it quickly enters the realm of 'weighting', of assigning different degrees of importance to the indicator of effectiveness, in the above case to life-years.[1]

The 'saving life-years' example is an instance of an *instrumental* approach to decision-making. The goal of policy is also related to some human objective, the procedure is *anthropocentric*. The notion of economic value is clearly anthropocentric and instrumental. An alternative philosophy might instead assign values to things 'in themselves' rather than because those things serve some human-oriented end (extending life, wellbeing and so on). There is a rich array of philosophical writing that argues for the assignment of *intrinsic values* to things. Intrinsic values might be attached to all things, living or otherwise, just to living things, to living sentient things, or to some sub classification of living sentient things, for example, animals.

Notions of intrinsic value are especially debated in the context of conserving biological diversity. For some, biodiversity – the 'web of life' – is so important that its value transcends the value of other things. Without biological diversity there can be no human existence. Hence the idea of 'trading' biodiversity against other things – which is explicit in instrumental approaches to value – is not acceptable to some people. But some form of 'trade' is unavoidable in a world of limited resources. Perhaps what those who refuse to consider such trades are saying is that the issue they are concerned with (for example, biodiversity) is extremely important and that its profile needs to be raised in public debate. Most people accept that hard choices have to be made, but even with that acceptance very fierce debates take place about how much diversity to save and which diverse areas of the planet should be conserved first.

Environmental philosophers who accept that there is a limited 'conservation budget' opt for some form of cost-effectiveness criterion. Thus, Norton (1987) argues that a cost-effectiveness criterion could be adopted based solely on what he calls *formal* criteria. Formal criteria involve rankings of species that do not have to refer to characteristics of the species in question (for example, their 'attractiveness' or 'importance'). An index of species richness would be a formal ranking, but an index of richness where each species was weighted by some indicator of importance or its own characteristics (such as longevity) would be a *substantive* criterion. The essential difference, Norton argues, is that formal criteria involve no controversial value judgements, whereas substantive criteria do. A ranking of species by richness and endangerment would similarly be formal, not substantive, assuming that everyone can agree on what the indicators of threat are. A process of prioritising species conservation could therefore be 'value free'. Norton suggests that rankings would remain value free even if they included taxonomic status. Human values would not enter the analysis because such measures of species distinctiveness are 'scientific'. The goal of conservation would be to maintain the most diverse gene pool possible, which Norton sees as an end in itself, rather than as a means to an end such as human survival or human wellbeing. Norton regards this approach as being based solely on 'ecological value', a scientific measure of value.

In fact, this approach may not be very distinct from the cost-effectiveness approach. The goal could be restated as one of maximising the expected value of diversity, where 'value' refers to ecological value. The term 'expected value' denotes the probability-weighted value of species, where the probabilities in question are those of extinction of a given species. Such a goal is strongly identified in the economics literature as one of maximising *option value*, which refers to the value that a species might have for humankind in the future. Individuals would be willing to pay to conserve that species not because they make 'use' of it now but because they (and future generations) may make use of it later on. It seems more likely that a set of species containing more genetic distance than another set will have a higher option value. Survival probabilities are also maximised because species that are genetically similar are likely to have similar resistance to threats.

One other reason for supposing that approaches based on intrinsic value may not differ substantively from approaches based on economic value is that preferences may themselves be influenced by intrinsic values. Individuals may confer value on something for its own sake. If that something does not have a 'voice' in decision-making, individuals may opt to act as that voice. One attractive feature of stated preference techniques to determining economic value is that they permit the *motives* for preferences to be uncovered. In the biodiversity context, those motives often appear to be consistent with some notion of intrinsic value. Some environmental philosophers acknowledge this fact by referring to *weak anthropocentrism*, human-oriented values that reflect motivations that include concerns for other species and living systems.

If intrinsic values are regarded as the 'right' notion of value, and if it is not accepted that their reflection in human preferences is, in some sense, 'enough', then the question arises as to how intrinsic values can be entered into a decision-making rule. Since intrinsic values are not measurable, they tend to take on a zero-one characteristic. Something either has intrinsic value or it doesn't – there are no gradations of intrinsic value (although note the discussion of biodiversity value above). The answer to 'how much' of the good possessing intrinsic value should be provided could be approached in various ways. It might be as much as can be afforded – a notion that does imply trade-offs, it could be as much as there is and no less,[2] as much as is consistent with the political process, or it could be some amount consistent with a notion like the precautionary principle or 'safe minimum standards'.[3] Since such rules are actually embodied in some legislation, they are not 'academic' concerns. Some of the rules have an 'objective' element, that is, there is some attempt to provide criteria for what should be achieved, but some stress the acceptability of the *process* of decision-making, so that whatever emerges from that 'right' process is itself right. Some rules are consistent with a preference-oriented system (for example, a process-based rule that stresses public participation), some may not be (for example, how much precaution to take may be left to expert judgement).

Clearly, there are differences of view about how best to approach decision-making, and the extent to which formal procedures, such as economic valuation, should be embodied in that decision-making. It is not part of this manual to debate these alternative views, nor to pronounce on the 'right' approach in such a debate. The manual deals with the economic approach (and then only that part relying on stated preferences) because it does have several attractions. The resulting measure of value can be compared to the notion of resource cost, which itself is an approximation of economic value. The approach is explicit in addressing the issue of opportunity cost, whereas notions of intrinsic value face more difficulty in this respect since intrinsic value may reside in the option that is sacrificed through choice – offending the view of some that trade-offs cannot be made. Economic value also permits a choice to be made as to whether any of the available alternatives is acceptable (the economic value of the gains from the choice must exceed the cost), whereas cost-effectiveness approaches do not permit this option to be taken. Economic value is preference-determined, and preferences matter in any democratic society.

But others may take a different view. Perhaps individuals are not always good judges of their own wellbeing. Economic values reflect not only preferences but also the wealth/income of those expressing the preferences, as in any market system. Perhaps some things cannot be dealt with by the measuring rod of money. Perhaps some policies and actions are simply 'right' and are not to be judged by their consequences for human wellbeing. The debate has continued for many hundreds of years and it will not be resolved in this manual, if at all. This manual takes as its starting point the argument that preference-oriented instrumental value is important.

3   A GUIDE TO THE MANUAL

The structure of the manual is set out in the 'map' in Figure 0.1. The manual is organised in three parts:

- Part I: Concepts
- Part II: Stated Preference Techniques
- Part III: Further Issues.

Before the main elements of the manual on stated preference are presented, Part I sets out the conceptual background to economic or monetary valuation of non-market effects (Chapter 1) and some guidelines that those who commission valuation studies should follow (Chapter 2). Because the conduct of professional stated preference studies involves considerable expertise, it is important that those who commission the studies are able to identify that expertise and ensure that it is embodied in the design of questionnaires and in the econometric processing of the results. Many of the recommendations are common to the commissioning of any consultancy, but some are specific to stated preference studies because of the need to minimise biases in individuals' responses and to maximise validity and reliability. Chapter 2 concludes with an outline of the typical workplan for a stated preference study.

The eight chapters in Part II of the manual follow the order of the workplan presented in Chapter 2. Chapter 3 begins with the issue of which technique to apply to which problem. There are no very clear rules because stated preference techniques can, in principle, be applied to any object of valuation. But certain techniques are likely to be more successful in some applications than in others and Chapter 3 suggests some general guidance. The issue of 'standing' is also discussed. Standing refers to the establishment of whose preferences count in an economic valuation study, for example, nationals only or nationals and overseas residents? The answer to this question can greatly affect the final results, as the sample responses are aggregated over the population with standing. The issues of standing and sampling are the first steps in any study and must be established clearly at the outset. Finally, Chapter 3 looks at the selection of the sample to be given the questionnaire.

The manual then divides with the next chapters (Chapters 4 and 5) being allocated to contingent valuation and later chapters (Chapters 6 and 7) being devoted to choice modelling. It is important to recognise that the design of a

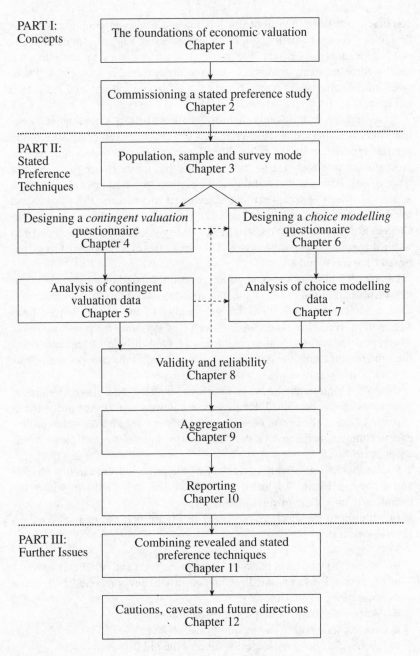

Figure 0.1 The 'map' of the manual

contingent valuation questionnaire has many features in common with the design of a choice modelling questionnaire, so that Chapter 6, for example, is not independent of Chapter 4. Similarly, when it comes to analysing the results, there are many common features to the required econometrics. These links from Chapter 4 to Chapter 6 and from Chapter 5 to Chapter 7 are shown in Figure 0.1 with dotted arrows.

Assessing the validity and reliability of the results of a contingent valuation study is addressed in Chapter 8. This is a detailed chapter because of the central importance of the issue. Stated preference techniques are applied precisely because there are no 'real' markets to refer to. Hence the important issue of just how much credibility can be given to stated answers has to be addressed. Much of Chapter 8 is also relevant to assessing the validity and reliability of choice modelling, hence the sequential arrow from Chapter 7 to Chapter 8 in Figure 0.1. Note that most validity issues need to be considered when designing the questionnaire. Therefore, there are some overlaps between Chapters 4 and 8.

Chapter 9 addresses the issue of aggregation. In significant part, aggregation involves returning to the issue of sampling, since biases in sampling will have considerable implications for the validity of the results derived from aggregation. But other issues arise as well (for example, the population over which positive non-use values might be expected to hold). Chapter 10 outlines the requirements for state-of-the-art reporting of the process and results of a stated preference study.

Chapter 11 presents the ways in which revealed and stated preference techniques can be combined. Finally, some cautions and caveats presented in Chapter 12 are at the centre of some of the current debate over stated preference techniques and some readers may find it helpful to read parts of this chapter early on.

Each chapter begins with a summary of the issues covered in that chapter and a copy of Figure 0.1 to highlight where the chapter fits in within the overall structure of the manual.

In addition to the chapters presented in Figure 0.1, the manual contains several annexes:

- Annex 1.1: the links between stated preference and benefits transfer; ·
- Annex 1.2: use of stated preference in UK environmental policy: the case of the aggregates levy;
- Annex 1.3: basic principles of discounting;
- Annex 4.1: writing survey questions;
- Annex 5.1: econometric estimation of the bid function;
- Annex 5.2: estimating mean and median WTP; and

- Annex 11.1: random utility models combining stated preference and revealed preference data.

The list of references and the glossary can be found at the end of the manual. Terms that appear in the glossary are written in italic throughout the manual.

NOTES

1. The extensive literature on QALYS (quality adjusted life years) and DALYS (disability adjusted life years) deals with this issue of how to weight life years. In each case a life year is weighted by a factor representing how individuals assess the quality of that life year.
2. The 'no less than there is' rule is familiar in environmental economics as 'strong sustainability'.
3. The precautionary principle has many interpretations but it would basically urge protection of any resource with unknown but potentially high value (however measured), sometimes irrespective of cost, sometimes at some acceptable cost. The safe minimum standards approach argues that the object with unknown value should be conserved unless the social cost of conservation is, in some sense, 'too high'.

PART I

Concepts

1. The foundations of economic valuation

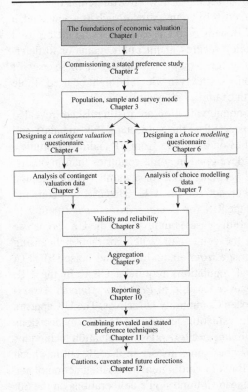

SUMMARY

This chapter outlines the foundations of economic valuation techniques. The background is set by examining the potential and actual uses of economic valuation in the UK and internationally. It then defines costs and benefits, their interpretation in the context of economic efficiency and their connection to the concepts of willingness to pay (WTP) and willingness to accept compensation (WTA) which are used in economic valuation. An overview of arguments for and against economic valuation is provided.

The remainder of the chapter outlines the economic theory underlying economic valuation in the context of welfare economics, including measures of changes in welfare. The concept of 'total economic value' is defined, with a discussion of which components of value can be measured using various valuation techniques. Aggregation issues in using valuation to measure total economic value are overviewed. Finally, the role of valuation in public participation methods of appraisal is examined. The chapter concludes with annexes on benefits transfer, an example of using stated preference techniques in policy-making, and discounting.

1.1 THE USES OF ECONOMIC VALUATION

This manual describes techniques for assigning money values to the outcomes of choices about policies, projects and programmes. One of the most

13

important contexts for these choices is that of *cost–benefit analysis* (CBA) or *benefit analysis* or *damage analysis*. CBA seeks to measure the benefits and costs of a policy measure, such as setting a new environmental quality or food standard; or the benefits and costs of an investment such as a new road, a dam or release of a new drug. Benefit or damage analysis might be used simply to demonstrate that a policy secures major public gains or to determine costs in the case of liability for a major accident. But these uses of economic valuation are not the only contexts in which it might be used. Table 1.1 lists the various contexts, with examples relevant to the UK.

Three broad categories of economic valuation are distinguished: revealed preference (RP), stated preference (SP – the subject of this manual) and benefits transfer (BT), which relies on estimates from SP and/or RP studies. Some applications are far more developed in some countries than in others. Thus, monetised *green national accounts* exist for a number of developing countries, the US and Japan, but not for the UK. The use of economic valuation has been standard in the US for *damage assessment* (mainly to assess the scale of damages in liability cases) but less so in the UK. Some use of valuation has been made in the context of water abstraction licensing decisions and in valuing the damage from air pollution and noise (EFTEC, 1998a). In the US many federal regulations require a CBA. In the UK, monetary valuation is used whenever feasible in *Regulatory Impact Assessment* (RIA) of national and European Community Directives. The UK appears to be unique in using economic valuation techniques to inform decisions about the *rates for potential environmental taxes*. Using valuation techniques to help determine *policy priorities* has some history in the UK but has been used fairly widely by the World Bank in guiding environmental action plans, and has played a role in the European Commission's deliberations on the 6th Environmental Action Plan.

Economic valuation therefore has a very wide potential application. The focus in this manual on CBA arises in the main from the concerns of the commissioning agencies (government departments, and DEFRA and DTLR in particular). The appraisal of policies, programmes and public investments is already the subject of systematic guidance from HM Treasury (HM Treasury, 1997) – the 'green book'. Treasury advice is that, where possible, benefits and risks from policies should be valued in money terms, and that those which cannot be valued in this way must at least be described and may also be measured in non-monetary terms. Treasury guidance is explicit that 'non-marketed goods are generally best valued in terms of people's willingness to pay for marginal changes in supply' (HM Treasury, 1997, p. 46). The green book makes reference to both revealed and stated preference techniques, noting that the reliability of the estimates requires careful scrutiny.

Table 1.1   Applications of economic valuation techniques

Context	Comment	Type of valuation likely to be relevant
Cost–benefit analysis: projects and programmes	This is the context in which CBA was originally developed. Usually public investment projects in public or quasi-public goods	RP, SP, BT
Cost–benefit analysis: policies, including regulations	A more recent focus in the UK but RIA now required for all regulations. Traditional for mainly RIA in the US	RP, SP, BT
'Demonstration' of the importance of an issue	Usually used to estimate economic damage from some activity, e.g. behaviour towards health, pollution, noise	Usually BT only
Setting priorities within a sectoral plan	Used for prioritising road investments	Usually BT only
Setting priorities across sectors	Rare	Mainly BT
Establishing the basis for an environmental tax or charge	Recent UK experience appears to be unique, e.g. landfill tax, possible pesticides tax, aggregates tax	Mainly BT but can include original RP and SP
'Green' national income accounting	Only utilised in a minor way in the UK	Usually BT only
Corporate green accounting	A few studies exist, but even fewer are public	BT only
Legal damage assessment	Not used in the UK but extensively used in the US	RP, SP and BT
Estimating discount rates	Used in health literature and to derive discount rates in developing countries	SP

Notes:
RIA = Regulatory Impact Assessment
RP = revealed preference
SP = stated preference
BT = benefits transfer

In large part, then, this manual takes as its starting point the existing Treasury guidance on appraisal and evaluation in government.

1.2   THE NATURE OF ECONOMIC VALUATION AND ECONOMIC EFFICIENCY

Benefits and costs are defined in terms of *individuals' preferences*. An individual receives a benefit whenever he receives something in return for which he is willing to give up something else that he values. To measure how large that benefit is, we measure how much he is willing to give up to get it. Conversely, an individual incurs a cost whenever she gives up something that she would willingly give up only if she was given something else that she valued as compensation. To measure how large that cost is, we measure how much would compensate her for incurring it.

These formulations define benefits and costs in terms of one another. The measure of any benefit is that cost which, in the preferences of the individual who benefits, would exactly offset it. And, conversely, the measure of any cost is that benefit which, in the relevant individual's preferences, would exactly offset it. This is not a circularity. It reflects a crucial feature of economic valuation: there is no absolute measure of value, there are only equivalences of value between one thing and another. By not claiming that any particular dimension of human life – health, material wealth, happiness, achievement or whatever – has absolute value, economic valuation avoids taking any substantive position about what is good for people. It simply uses whatever relative valuations are revealed in people's preferences.

This approach allows all costs and benefits to be measured in a single dimension if, *as a matter of convention*, we choose one particular type of benefit to use as a standard. We can then express all other benefits and costs in terms of that standard, using individuals' own preferences to determine equivalences of value.

If we are to use the same standard of measurement for all individuals, the standard has to be a good that everyone prefers to have more of rather than less, and that individuals treat as a potential substitute[1] for the array of benefits and costs that we want to measure. And it has to be finely divisible. In economics, the usual convention is to use *money* as the standard of measurement. Money, obviously, is finely divisible. It represents general purchasing power – that is, the power to buy from the vast range of goods that are sold on markets. Because money can be put to so many different uses, it is a safe generalisation that most people prefer more money rather than less, irrespective of their specific preferences among goods. For the same reason, money is a particularly effective substitute good. However, as we shall explain in Section 1.6, there are some special cases in which money may not be the best standard of measurement.

If money is used as the standard to measure welfare, the measure of benefit is *willingness to pay* (WTP) to secure that benefit, or *willingness to accept* compensation (WTA) to forgo the same. Similarly, the measure of cost is WTA to suffer that cost, or WTP to avoid the same.

These measures of benefit and cost underlie the concept of *economic efficiency*. A reallocation of resources increases economic efficiency if the sum of the benefits to those who gain by that reallocation exceeds the sum of the costs to those who lose. In other words, there is an increase in economic efficiency if the sum of WTP for the gainers exceeds the sum of WTA for the losers, that is, if (in principle) the gainers could compensate the losers without becoming losers themselves. This test is the *efficiency criterion* (or *compensation test*). CBA typically uses this criterion to appraise specific proposals.

There is a significant connection between the concept of economic efficiency and what happens in markets. Economic efficiency rests on the theories of *welfare economics*. It is a theorem of welfare economics that, in any equilibrium state of a competitive economy, resources are allocated in such a way that no further gains of economic efficiency are possible. Also, in a perfectly competitive economy, each person increases economic efficiency whenever she acts in accordance with her own preferences. It is important to see why this is so. Obviously, by acting according to her own preferences, a person maximises benefit to herself; but we have to take account of the effects of her actions on other people. It is not true (as is sometimes thought) that each person's actions in a competitive market have no effects on other people. What is true is that these effects, when measured by WTP and WTA, *cancel out*. For example, suppose that Joe, who has previously drunk beer, decides to switch to mineral water. In a competitive market, the effect is to reduce the price of beer and to increase the price of water, with consequent costs and benefits for producers and consumers of the two goods. Although these price changes are very small, they affect a very large number of people; the gross costs and benefits imposed on other people are of the same order of magnitude as Joe's switch of expenditure. However, producers of water gain exactly as much as consumers of water lose, and consumers of beer gain exactly as much as producers of beer lose.[2] Thus, to the extent that real markets approximate to the competitive model, everyday economic transactions satisfy the efficiency criterion.

Given that the allocation of resources among private consumption goods *is* generally determined through markets, it is highly desirable that the methods of valuation that are used to guide public decision-making should underwrite the allocations of resources that are generated by markets, wherever it is uncontroversial that markets should be relied on. The efficiency criterion has this desirable property.

Thus, CBA is redundant when markets work well. Its main use is in situations in which markets do not exist, or in which they fail to generate economic efficiency. In particular, it is useful when policy is concerned with *public goods*. A good is public to the extent that consumption of it is *non-rival*, that is, one person's consuming it does not reduce the amount available to others, and *non-excludable*, that is, it is not possible to supply the good only to those who choose to pay for it, and to exclude everyone else. Many environmental goods, such as species diversity, sea level and the effect of the ozone layer in screening out ultraviolet radiation, are classic examples of public goods.

The concepts of cost, benefit, WTP, WTA and economic efficiency are not specific to private consumption goods or to markets. As explained above, these concepts are defined in terms of individuals' preferences. They are applicable wherever individuals' preferences are adequately comprehensive, stable and coherent. By 'comprehensive', we mean that individuals must be able to make meaningful preference comparisons between the specific costs or benefits under consideration and the standard of measurement (normally money). By 'stable', we mean that preferences must not vary arbitrarily over time, and that different theoretically valid methods of eliciting a person's preferences should yield the same results. By 'coherent', we mean that the preferences that are elicited for any person must be internally consistent, as viewed in the light of some acceptable theory of preference. In economics, it is normally assumed that individuals have comprehensive, stable and coherent preferences, and we shall make this assumption in the rest of this chapter. The validity of this assumption is considered in Chapters 8 and 12. If individuals have preferences about public goods which satisfy these conditions, then WTP and WTA are meaningful concepts and decisions about the provision of such goods can be appraised by using the efficiency criterion. This manual describes some techniques which can be used to identify WTP and WTA.

1.3 ECONOMIC VALUATION AND OTHER VALUES

Any analyst must expect to meet a range of moral arguments against economic valuation. Some of these were discussed briefly in the Introduction. Consideration of these arguments helps to sharpen up the rationale for the techniques discussed in this manual.

Some critics of economic valuation find its emphasis on opportunity cost morally objectionable. It is often argued, especially in the healthcare context, but also in safety and environmental contexts, that certain outcomes of policies should not be subject to budget considerations. Patients, it is said, should be treated with the best healthcare available regardless of cost; road and rail safety should be an absolute priority regardless of cost; and environmental protection is an absolute moral imperative and cannot be subject to rationing by cost. The main difficulty with these views is that they ignore the meaning of cost. The proper measure of cost is the benefit that is forgone by allocating expenditure to a chosen project or policy. If money is spent on A it cannot be spent on B. While A may have some of the characteristics of being 'moral goods', like health and safety, so might B. Money spent on road safety cannot be spent on cancer research or hospice care. The principle can be extended. If funds are raised to finance a risk reducing expenditure, the effect may be to impose risks on the people who are taxed to raise the funds.[3] The essential point is that cost is not 'just money': it is an expression of resources that could be used for all kinds of other, perhaps equally deserving, purposes.

More fundamentally, some critics object that, by focusing on the preferences of *individuals*, economic valuation takes account only of self-interest. If an individual has a preference for or against something, it might appear that the preference will be formed on the basis of what that individual judges to be best for himself. A short way of expressing this point is to say that the individual acts out of *self-interest*. Indeed, this is how 'consumer sovereignty' or 'economic rationality' is often characterised. But the issues for which economic valuation will be used will often be those where the *public interest* is the issue, that is, what is best for society as a whole.

Whether or not the public interest is the same thing as the sum of individuals' self-interests is a controversial question in political philosophy. So too is the question of whether it is better if, when acting in the political arena, individuals act in pursuit of their private interests, constrained only by rules of procedural fairness, or if they act on the basis of 'public spirited' or 'citizens'' preferences. Viewed in some philosophical perspectives, it is wrong to reach collective decisions by adding up self-interested preferences. The proper procedure is to ensure that the context of decision-making is one where citizens' preferences are expressed. That context would appear to be the political arena, not the outcome of a process where experts collect questionnaires from respondents who are asked for their stated preferences.[4] We say 'appear' because, as a matter of plain fact, it is far from clear that preferences revealed in the political process are less self-interested and more public-spirited than those revealed by the same people in the market.

As a first response to this criticism, we emphasise that CBA is not a substitute for the political process; it merely provides information to the actors in that process. Someone who believes that a particular policy is morally required, or is morally prohibited, can properly try to persuade other political actors to share this belief and to act on it, whatever the results of a CBA. For example, if Jane believes that everyone has a moral obligation to accept a certain increase in taxation in order to pay for a programme to conserve endangered species, the fact that the programme fails to satisfy the CBA test does not require her to change her belief: she is entitled to conclude that other people are evading their moral obligations. But the CBA results remain meaningful information about what people really are willing to pay for the programme.

However, it is a mistake to think that CBA takes account only of self-interested preferences. It takes account of whatever preferences people have, for whatever reasons they have them. For example, a person may want an environmental asset to continue in existence even though he makes no direct use of it, nor intends ever to make any use of it. To the extent that he is willing to forgo other things that he values in order to conserve the asset, he has a preference for its conservation and its conservation is a benefit to him. He might be motivated by the fact that without the asset's continued exist-ence; he could not enjoy it vicariously through television or film. This motive might be described as self-interested. But he might also be motivated simply by wanting the asset to continue in existence for its own sake, or because he sees himself as a 'steward' of the environment, or because he wants it for his children or future generations to enjoy. In short, there is nothing in the concept of preference that tells us that preferences have to be motivated by self-interest. One of the attractions of stated preference techniques is that they can include separate questions about motives to help understand the stated preference responses. As discussed in Chapter 12, such 'other-regarding' considerations may be an important issue in the elicitation of values, and may also pose a number of problems for the design of surveys and for the interpretation of the data they generate.

1.4 ECONOMIC VALUATION WHEN THERE ARE NO MARKETS

This manual is concerned with one major set of techniques for eliciting economic valuations. These are known as *stated preference* (SP) techniques. We use this term generically, to refer to any questionnaire-based technique which seeks to discover individuals' preferences, 'preference' being understood in the sense outlined in Section 1.1. We are particularly concerned with techniques which, directly or indirectly, elicit individuals' money valuations of costs and benefits. For compactness, we shall generally refer to these valuations as 'WTP', but we are also concerned with preference-related monetary valuations, such as WTA and equivalent gain (the latter is defined in Section 1.6).

SP techniques elicit WTP directly by asking questions of the form 'What are you willing to pay?' or 'Are you willing to pay £x?', or by asking respondents to express preferences across some set of alternatives. Typically, these techniques are used when we do *not* have relevant information which has been generated by markets. Other techniques, known as *revealed preference* (RP) techniques, use information from markets that are associated with the good or service that is being evaluated.

There is a strong case for using RP techniques whenever the *relevant* WTP information can be inferred from individuals' actual decisions. As explained in Section 1.1, the principles underlying economic valuation are ones which tend to endorse the outcomes of markets where they exist. It is consistent with this general approach to accept, as a working rule, that decisions actually made in markets are reliable indicators of preference: if a person actually pays £x to buy something, we can infer that his WTP for that thing is at least £x. Although inferring current actions is a relatively straightforward process, predicting actions (by using RP techniques) under a new set of conditions not yet experienced is not so simple.

SP techniques become necessary when the WTP information that is needed cannot be inferred from markets. However, they are not restricted to market contexts. What matters is that answers to questionnaires are intended to *simulate* the behaviour of individuals in the marketplace. A great deal of care needs to be taken to ensure that questionnaires mimic the relevant features of the marketplace, the guidance for which is provided in Part II of this manual.

There are various reasons why markets may fail to provide the data necessary for WTP to be inferred. The most obvious is that no markets exist for the benefit or cost in question, as in the case of many public goods. In such cases, RP techniques have to rely on information from markets for *proxy* private goods, consumption of which is a precondition for benefiting from the relevant public goods. For example, we might try to infer WTP for a national park by studying the costs that people are willing to pay in order to visit it; or we might try to infer WTP for the absence of traffic noise by studying the difference in prices between houses affected by different levels of noise. But this approach is liable to understate the value of public goods, by not capturing all of the ways in which people benefit from them.

In particular, some important measures of WTP are associated with individuals who would not buy a good or service even if there was a market. Such people may want the product to be available even though they do not purchase it at the moment, or they may simply want it to be available even though they have no intention at all of purchasing it at any time. These are the so-called *option users* and *non-users*. In the case of the national park, for example, people who have no specific intention to visit it may still be willing to pay something in order to preserve that option for themselves in the future. Or they may be willing to pay merely to preserve the park itself, whether they visit it or not.

Even where relevant proxy markets exist, they may fail to provide adequate information about WTP. For any given individual at any given time, observations of her behaviour in markets can only set limits to WTP. For example, suppose it would cost a person £10 to travel to a national park. If she decides to go, we can infer that the benefit of the trip – though not necessarily of the park itself – to her is *at least* £10. If she decides not to go, we can infer that the benefit is *less than* £10. In order to be able to infer actual values of benefit it is necessary to have data from a cross-section of cases in which similar individuals have faced a sufficiently wide range of different prices. Such data are not always available.

SP techniques are undoubtedly resource-intensive because they involve the collection of substantial original data. However, once a reasonable number of such studies has been carried out, it may be possible to discern some uniformity in the expressions of WTP, or to discern some rules that would enable us to adopt certain WTP estimates without going to the trouble of carrying out another survey. This is the goal of *benefits transfer*. Benefits transfer may involve taking an estimate of mean WTP from an existing study of one site and transferring it to another site, or it may involve taking a whole WTP *function* from one site and inserting relevant parameter values at a new site to estimate the WTP at that new site. This manual is not primarily concerned with benefits transfer, but it is important to understand that it is one of the goals of repeated studies. Annex 1.1 therefore provides a brief overview of benefits transfer. A simple illustration of how a SP study was undertaken and the results then applied in the policy process is given in Annex 1.2.

1.5   ECONOMIC VALUATION AND THE DEMAND CURVE

WTP has a formal relationship to the notion of a demand curve. Figure 1.1 shows the usual depiction of a demand curve for an individual.[5] The horizon-

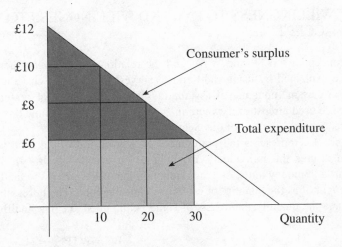

Figure 1.1   Demand and willingness to pay

tal axis measures the total number of units that can be bought and the vertical axis measures the price per unit. Points on the individual's demand curve show, for each quantity purchased, how much that individual is willing to pay for that last (or *marginal*) unit. For example, the individual is willing to pay £10 each for the first ten units, £8 each for the next ten units, £6 each for the following ten units and so on. The *total* WTP for thirty units is £[(12 – 6) × 30 × 0.5 + (6 × 30)] = £270. Hence marginal WTP is given by points on the demand curve and total WTP is given by the area under the demand curve up to the amount purchased. Suppose the market price settles at £6 per unit, then we see that total expenditure is 30 × £6 = £180 and this is less than total WTP of £270. The difference between total WTP and actual expenditure, that is £270 – £180 = £90, is the *consumer's surplus*. Consumer surplus is therefore a measure of the net benefit to the consumer of buying 30 units at the market price since he or she pays out £180 but 'gets back' £270 in the form of wellbeing as measured by WTP. The £270 in this case is a measure of the *gross* change in wellbeing (or welfare, or utility) from buying 30 units, and the £90, the consumer surplus, is a measure of the net change in wellbeing (welfare or utility).

A basic formula, then, is:

Total WTP = Market Price + Consumer's Surplus

1.6 WILLINGNESS TO PAY AND WILLINGNESS TO ACCEPT

The concepts of WTP and WTA, and the relationships between them, can best be explained by using indifference curves. Indifference curve analysis rests on certain fundamental assumptions about the nature of preferences, which are used almost everywhere in economics. We shall follow this standard practice until the end of this Section.

Figure 1.2 represents the preferences of a given individual. The vertical axis measures the individual's expenditure on private goods (y). This is measured in money units, on the assumption that prices are given, and it can be thought of as the quantity of a single composite good. The horizontal axis measures the quantity that exists of some public good (x). The indifference

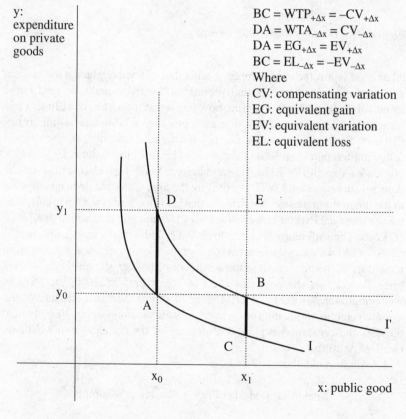

Figure 1.2   Measure of change in human welfare

curves I and I′ link combinations of the two goods between which the individual is indifferent. Each curve can be thought of as corresponding to a level of welfare, utility or well-being, with I′ corresponding to the higher level.[6] In this scenario, as the indifference curves move up and to the right, the welfare of the individual increases.

There are four measures of the value of a change in the quantity of a public good. First, consider the value to the individual of an *increase* in the quantity of the public good from x_0 to x_1. Suppose that initially the individual has y_0 private consumption, and so is at A. Compare point C. At C the individual can enjoy x_1 of the public good but his private consumption is less by the amount BC. Since A and C are on the same indifference curve I, we can infer that his WTP for the increase in the public good is BC. In welfare economics, the negative of this amount is called the *compensating variation* for the *increase* in the public good, since the loss of BC in private consumption exactly compensates for that increase.

Second, consider the opposite case, in which the individual, again starting with y_0 private consumption, faces a *decrease* in the public good from x_1 to x_0. Now the initial position is B. Compare point D. At D, the individual enjoys only x_0 of the public good, but his private consumption is greater by DA. Since B and D are on the same indifference curve I′, we can infer that his WTA for the reduction in the public good is DA. This is the *compensating variation* for the *reduction* in the public good.

Third, it is useful to consider two other measures of the value to the individual of the increase in the public good from x_0 to x_1. Suppose that the individual starts off with y_0 private consumption and x_0 of the public good: he is at A. We may ask what additional amount of private consumption would be just as preferable as an increase in the public good to x_1. This is the *equivalent gain* measure of the value of the change in the public good. Since D is on the same indifference curve as B, equivalent gain is equal to DA. In the language of welfare economics, DA is the *equivalent variation* for the *increase* in the public good. Notice that equivalent gain and WTA are both equal to DA. The equality of these two measures is an implication of the standard economic theory of preference. In terms of stated preference questionnaires, however, equivalent gain and WTA are distinct concepts, elicited by different types of question. ('How much money would just compensate you for losing X?' is a different question from 'How much money would be just as good as gaining X?') The theory tells us to expect that these two types of question will yield the same answers.

To arrive at the fourth measure, suppose the individual starts off with y_0 private consumption and x_1 of the public good, that is, at B. We may ask what loss of private consumption would be just as preferable as a decrease in the public good to x_0. This is the *equivalent loss* measure of the change in the public good; since C and A are on the same indifference curve, equivalent loss is equal to BC. In the language of welfare economics, the negative of BC is the *equivalent variation* for the *decrease* in the public good. Notice that equivalent loss and WTP are both equal to BC. As in the case of equivalent gain and WTA, this is a theoretical implication about the equivalence of what, in stated preference terms, are two different methods of eliciting valuations.

These fine distinctions are significant only to the extent that different measures yield different valuations. In the diagram, DA > BC. That is, WTA is greater than WTP (and likewise, equivalent gain is greater than equivalent loss). It can be shown theoretically that this inequality holds whenever the indifference curves are convex to the origin and the public good is 'normal', that is, if the good could be bought at constant prices, the amount consumed would increase with income. It should be clear from the diagram that the ratio between WTA and WTP will tend to be greater, the more convex the indifference curves are, that is, the less substitutability there is between private consumption and the public good, and the greater the difference between x_0 and x_1. These qualitative conclusions are derived formally by Hanemann (1999).

However, in most of the cases in which SP techniques are used, the divergence between WTA and WTP, as predicted by the theory, should be very small. To see why, consider the case in which the individual starts with private consumption of y_1. In this case, WTP for an increase in the public good from x_0 to x_1 is EB. EB is greater than BC: if the individual is richer, he can afford to spend more in order to increase the public good. But notice that EB = DA. Thus, the difference between WTA and WTP (when both are evaluated in relation to an initial private consumption level of y_0) is exactly the same as the difference between the two measures of WTP – one evaluated in relation to y_0, the other in relation to y_1. Notice also that the difference between y_1 and y_0 is WTA, that is, a measure of the individual's money valuation of the change in the public good. The size of the difference between WTP and WTA hinges on the magnitude of the income elasticity of WTP, that is, the responsiveness of WTP to changes in income. Economic theory shows that this elasticity depends on the elasticity of substitution between money and the good in question. But, whether this elasticity is large or small is an empirical question.

In empirical studies it is common to find that *stated* WTA is greater than *stated* WTP. However, the WTP/WTA disparity issue is not specific to SP techniques. For example, a recent review article (Horowitz and McConnell, 1999) shows that there are large differences between WTP in both SP and RP data. The size of the difference does not appear to be related to the SP versus

RP distinction. For a recent theoretical paper that postulates why there should be differences between WTP and WTA, see Kolstad and Guzman (1999). One possible explanation is that these disparities are artefacts of the ways in which stated preference questions have been asked – the implication being that such disparities could be greatly reduced by improved survey design. A rather different possibility is that the disparity reflects fundamental limitations in the standard theoretical underpinnings. Variants of these alternative possibilities are discussed in more detail in Chapter 12.

In the rare cases in which a policy has such a large impact on individual welfare as to cause a large divergence between WTA and WTP, there are grounds for questioning whether money is an appropriate standard of value (compare Section 1.1). For example, suppose we are trying to value the benefits of a costly medical treatment which, for a small number of identifiable individuals, would eliminate a 20 per cent risk of immediate death. We might expect such an individual to be willing to pay a significant part of her expected lifetime income to gain this benefit; but WTP is inevitably constrained by income. Now suppose the same individual has an entitlement to the treatment. What is her WTA for giving up this entitlement and accepting a 20 per cent risk of death? She might well be unwilling to accept *any* amount of money as compensation for this risk. In other words, WTA may be infinitely greater than WTP. Clearly, however, it would be wrong to conclude that a 20 per cent risk of death is infinitely bad. Some things (like a 40 per cent risk of death) are a lot worse. A more appropriate conclusion is that in this case, money is not a satisfactory standard of value, since it is not seen as a substitute for the benefit in question.

To illustrate this point, consider a person of retirement age who might face either of two highly undesirable outcomes. The first is a 20 per cent risk of immediate death. The second is that her pension scheme will collapse, taking with it all her savings (say £200,000). It is quite possible that she would think the second outcome even less preferable than the first one. Yet, while her WTA for the risk may be infinite, her WTA for the second is presumably £200,000. The explanation of this apparent paradox is that a large sum of money is a good substitute for a lost pension entitlement, but not for a large risk of death.

This example does not count against the economic concept of cost and benefit, or against stated preference techniques. It merely points to the need to choose a suitable standard of value. In the case of very large[7] risks of death or injury, for example, a standard of value based on years of life expectancy might be more appropriate than a money standard. This is part of the logic of using quality adjusted life years (QALYs) as a standard in the evaluation of policies concerning healthcare.

The cases considered in the three preceding paragraphs are exceptional. In principle, the question of whether WTP or WTA valuations should be used in any instance should be addressed by taking one policy option (usually the 'do nothing' scenario) as the datum in relation to which costs and benefits are defined. Then benefits, that is, changes that are more preferred than the datum, should be measured by WTP, while costs, that is, changes that are less preferred than the datum, should be measured by WTA.

1.7   TOTAL ECONOMIC VALUE AND AGGREGATION

The total gain in wellbeing arising from a project or policy and for any one individual is given by that individual's WTP or WTA for the change in question (WTP if the individual prefers the change to the *status quo*, WTA if the *status quo* is preferred). Two forms of aggregation are now required: aggregation across all individuals, and aggregation over time. The types of economic value or the motivations underlying WTP or WTA statements affect the aggregation process. Therefore, the first sub-section below outlines these types or motivations.

1.7.1   Total Economic Value

The net sum of all the relevant WTPs and WTAs defines the *total economic value* (TEV) of any change in wellbeing due to a policy or project. TEV can be characterised differently according to the type of economic value arising. It is usual to divide TEV into *use* and *non-use* (or *passive use*) values. Use values relate to actual use of the good in question (for example, a visit to a national park), planned use (a visit planned in the future) or possible use. Actual and planned uses are fairly obvious concepts, but possible use could also be important since people may be willing to pay to maintain a good in existence in order to preserve the *option* of using it in the future. *Option value* thus becomes a form of use value. Non-use value refers to willingness to pay to maintain some good in existence even though there is no actual, planned or possible use. The types of non-use value could be various, but a convenient classification is in terms of (a) existence value, (b) altruistic value, and (c) bequest value. Existence value refers to the WTP to keep a good in existence in a context where the individual expressing the value has no actual or planned use for himself or herself *or for anyone else*. Motivations here could vary and might include having a feeling of concern for the asset itself (for example, a threatened species) or a 'stewardship' motive whereby the valuer feels some responsibility for the asset. *Altruistic value* might arise when the individual is concerned that the good in question should be available to others in the current generation. A *bequest value* is similar but the concern is that the next and future generations should have the option to make use of the good.

Figure 1.3 shows the characterisation of TEV by types of value. SP techniques are suited to eliciting all these kinds of value, although in practice it is usually not possible to disaggregate individual types of non-use value, nor is it usually relevant to a decision to secure that breakdown. But differentiating use and non-use values can be important because, as will be seen, the latter can be large relative to the former, especially when the good in question has few substitutes and is widely valued. In addition, non-use value remains controversial, so that it is important to separate it out for presentational and strategic reasons.

How do stated preferences relate to the concept of TEV? Figure 1.4 shows how the various valuation techniques apply to the major component parts of TEV. Several observations are in order.

First, non-use values, which are likely to be especially important in contexts where the good being valued has few or no substitutes, can only be estimated using stated preference techniques. Since non-use values tend not to leave a 'behavioural trail', that is, some behavioural change which affects a price or quantity which can be observed, revealed preference techniques are unlikely to elicit non-use values. But since use of a service or good leaves a behavioural trail, both revealed and stated preference techniques can be used to elicit use values.

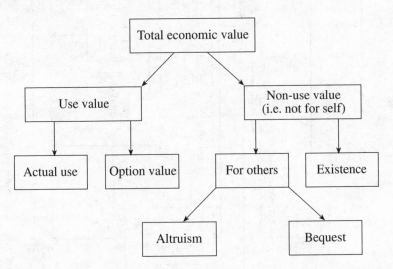

Figure 1.3   Total economic value

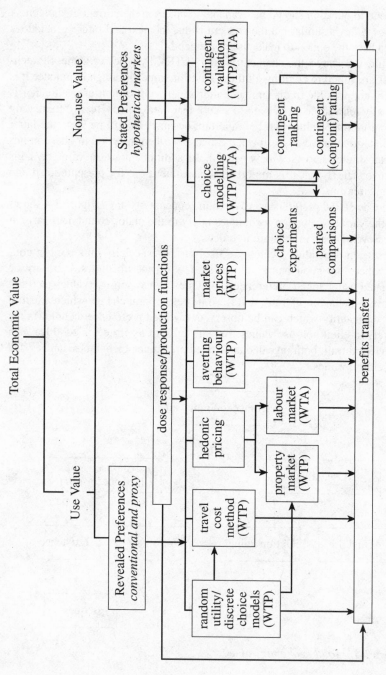

Figure 1.4 Economic valuation techniques

Second, the central role of 'dose-response functions' or 'production functions' is observed. These functions link some change in the state of nature or a policy measure to some response. For example, air pollution would be a 'dose' and a response might be an increased number of chronic bronchitis cases. Or there may be some change in medical care that improves patient wellbeing: the link is between the productive activity (medical care) and the output (patient wellbeing). These functions will invariably need to be estimated or derived from various kinds of literature. Economists have no particular expertise in this area and it will be important to ensure that research or policy analysis involving the use of such functions involves the relevant experts (epidemiologists, clinicians, technologists and so on).

Third, the lower part of the diagram suggests that *benefits transfer* is one of the 'goals' of valuation. Certainly, the more 'primary research' there is on valuation the more we can learn about benefits transfer. But benefits transfer is a subject within itself and an overview of the links between stated preferences and benefits transfer is given in Annex 1.1.

How is TEV related to the notion of *intrinsic value*? Intrinsic value is often regarded as being a value that resides 'in' the asset in question, and especially environmental assets, but which is independent of human preferences. By definition, TEV relates to the preferences of individual human beings, so that if intrinsic value is defined to be independent of those preferences, TEV cannot encompass intrinsic values. However, notions of intrinsic value may well *influence* WTP, and SP techniques are particularly useful in eliciting such influences. SP questionnaires always seek to obtain information on the *motives* for stated WTP. These motives vary and may well include notions such as 'a right to exist' for the asset in question. This is a fairly common motive when the asset is, for example, a living creature. Hence, TEV cannot embrace a *measure* of intrinsic value, but SP does help to make the motivations for WTP explicit, and those motives may well involve a concern 'on behalf' of the object being valued.

1.7.2   Aggregating Across Individuals: Stakeholder Analysis

The simplest procedure for aggregating gains and losses across individuals is to add up the relevant WTP (or WTA) across all *affected* individuals. An affected individual is essentially anyone who is willing to pay or accept an amount greater than zero for the outcome of the project or policy. Careful choice of the *population sample* should help determine who those affected individuals are. Thus, if the sample chosen is representative of the entire population, then the sample results can be aggregated across the whole population. This issue is discussed in detail in Chapters 3, 5 and 9. But there may be reasons for treating particular groups of individuals differently. For example, a group of affected persons may be vulnerable in a number of ways, and a CBA that ignored this vulnerability might not be acceptable. It is important therefore to define the various stakeholders at the outset and to monitor the results of a CBA in terms of the gains and losses to different socio-economic groups, perhaps to different geographical units, and to people at different points in time. It follows that the same should be done with the stated preference valuation procedure. This is often done and is readily facilitated by the fact that SP techniques always derive information on the socio-economic characteristics of the respondents.

Particular problems arise when dealing with categories of persons who reside outside of national boundaries but who may be affected individuals in the sense defined above. The treatment of foreign nationals, for example, can be very important when dealing with transportation projects and environmental or heritage assets, since foreign visitors may benefit from these.

Certain rules of thumb may be adopted for deciding who has *standing* in CBA. First, for UK studies, all residents within the UK should be assumed to have standing. Second, where the UK is a signatory to an international agreement, all individuals within the participating nations and who are affected by a project or policy should have standing. Thus, beneficiaries of an acid rain control policy in the UK would include other European citizens in so far as they are affected by acidifying emissions from the UK.

Thereafter, clear rules on standing are more difficult to state. As an example, no nation exhibits the same concern for geographically distant individuals as it exhibits for its own residents. Whether it should or not is a moral issue, the outcome of which could affect some CBAs quite dramatically.[8]

Table 1.2(a) sets out a 'spreadsheet' showing two alternative policy options, A1 and A2. The individuals affected by this policy are listed in the first column. Each cell in the spreadsheet then records the individual's WTP and WTA as found from a stated preference survey. The WTPs are assumed to relate to gains and the WTAs to losses. Hypothetical numbers are inserted simply to illustrate the process. Note that time is ignored, as are any resource costs of the policy, just to make the example simple. Aggregation is then shown as the sum of the WTPs and WTAs in each column. The sum total having the highest net gain, that is, the sum of WTPs minus the sum of WTAs, is the preferred policy. The meaning of each sum total can be made clearer by reorganising the spreadsheet to group together all those who gain and all those who lose. This is done in the second part of the spreadsheet 1.2(b).

First, policy A1 is seen to be better than policy A2 because it has higher net benefits, 23 compared to 3. One way of thinking about these net benefits is that

Table 1.2(a)   Aggregating gains and losses across individuals

	WTP (+) or WTA (−)	
Individual	Policy A1	Policy A2
1	+10	+8
2	+9	−4
3	+22	+11
4	−2	−7
5	−16	−5
Sum	+23	+3

Table 1.2(b)   Aggregating gains and losses across grouped individuals

	WTP (+) or WTA (−)	
Individuals	Policy A1	Policy A2
1, 3 (gain from both policies)	+32	+19
2 (gains from A1, loses from A2)	+9	−4
4, 5 (lose from both policies)	−18	−12
Sum	+23	+3

those who gain (individuals 1, 2, 3 in A1, and individuals 1, 3 in A2) could compensate those who lose (4, 5 in A1, and 2, 4, 5 in A2) and still have net gains left over. Thus, for A1 gains are 41 and losses are 18, so 18 could be transferred to the losers and the gainers would still have 23 left over. In A2, gainers could transfer 16 to the losers and still have net gains of 3. In both cases, transfers could take place such that no-one is worse off and at least some people are better off. This is the economic efficiency or compensation test (explained in Section 1.2). However, unless transfers are *actually* made, some people gain and some people lose. Since the identity of gainers and losers may matter, the cost–benefit results should be presented in the form taken by Table 1.2(b) rather than simply presenting the total net gains of the two policies.

Table 1.2(b) would mark the beginning of a *stakeholder analysis*, that is, a CBA in which those who gain and those who lose are clearly identified. Such a stakeholder analysis may still be required in the event that actual compensation occurs. A stakeholder analysis represents the first step in an analysis of the *distributional implications* of the policy or project.

Because SP techniques provide information *both* about respondents' WTP (WTA) *and* about respondents' socio-economic characteristics, it is ideally suited to stakeholder analysis. For it means that WTP information can be correlated with socio-economic information to see who the gainers and losers are.[9] This richness of information often contrasts with other valuation techniques.

1.7.3   Aggregating Across Individuals: Distributional Adjustments

Generally, the economic efficiency criterion weights each person's money units of WTP or WTA equally. If compensation is not actually paid, this criterion tends to favour people who are relatively well-off. Recall that WTP is constrained by income, so that we might expect WTP to be high for individuals with high incomes and low for individuals with low incomes. Thus, a policy which benefited a small number of wealthy individuals might be favoured over an alternative policy which provided similar kinds of benefit to a larger number of poorer people.

One way of testing for this effect of the program on the distribution of income is to recompute gains and losses using an adjustment factor. A general formula for such an adjustment is to multiply benefits and costs accruing to the *i*th individual (or, more likely, stakeholder group) by:

$$a_i = \left(\frac{Y_m}{Y_i} \right)^b, \tag{1.1}$$

where Y_i is the average income of the *i*th group, Y_m is the average income across all groups, and *b* is a positive parameter which allows benefits and costs to be weighted differently for different income groups. Groups with incomes higher than the average will have their benefits and costs scaled down. Groups with incomes below the average will have their benefits and costs scaled upwards. For example, if *b* = 1, a WTP of £20 by an individual with an income of £20,000 per year is given the same weight as a WTP of £40 by an individual with an income of £40,000 per year.

This kind of 'equity weighting', or variants of it, was popular in the early days of CBA, especially in developing country contexts.[10] It is not usually incorporated in modern cost–benefit studies. A common view is that individual policies and projects are not the appropriate medium for delivering an equity goal. Rather, equity is better served by looking at the overall set of

BOX 1.1 USING STATED PREFERENCE
TECHNIQUES TO VALUE DIFFERENT
NOTIONS OF EQUITY

A study by Atkinson, Marchado and Mourato (1999) suggests
that stated preference techniques can be used to evaluate trade-
offs between efficiency and equity, and can also produce insights
into the values attached to different concepts of equity. The
scenario presented to respondents is an urban air quality programme, which is assumed to have benefits in excess of costs.
The issue is how to distribute the costs of the programme across
the city's residents. Residents are assumed to vary in their characteristics with a threefold classification: whether they cause the
pollution, the extent to which they benefit from the programme,
and their ability to pay. A *contingent ranking* study was conducted in Lisbon. In a 'dummy variable model' respondents were
first asked to rank different groups of individuals according to the
respondent's view of who should pay first for the programme.
The combinations are shown below, where blanks are interpreted as meaning does not benefit and is not responsible.
Respondents are asked to say which of these groups should pay
first (ranked 1), which next (ranked 2) and so on.

Group/characteristics	A	B	C	D	E	F
Health state	Benefits			Benefits		
Income level	Low	High	Low	High	Low	High
Responsibility		Pollutes	Pollutes			

A second experiment, the 'continuous variables model', focused
on ranking individuals. It first assumed that income was the
same across the six individuals, so that respondents were asked
to rank individuals by benefits and responsibility alone. This time
the responsibility characteristic had three levels, low, medium
and high. The aim here was to focus on the property rights issue.
Another question assumed benefits were equal and individuals
were ranked according to income and responsibility alone. This
permits an analysis of property rights and concern for the distribution of income. Roughly 250 people were sampled with the
dummy variable model and another 250 with the continuous

variables models. The results suggested the following conclusions, based on the econometric processing of the rankings:

Dummy variable model: Responsibility for pollution was regarded as the single most important attribute, that is, respondents appeared to embody the 'polluter pays principle' in their answers. If the benefit and income coefficients are added together, the sum exceeds the value for responsibility. This suggests that there is a trade-off between responsibility and a combination of income and benefits. Those with high income and high benefits should pay more than someone who is responsible for pollution but who has low income and low benefits. These findings are not altered when the results are adjusted for selfish behaviour, that is, high-income people biasing their answers away from assigning responsibility to themselves.

If individuals refuse to trade-off between the various attributes, their responses are said to be 'lexical', that is, they decide on the basis of one attribute alone regardless of the values taken by the other attributes. Lexicality is potentially important because it would strike at the heart of the cost–benefit assumption that people are willing to make trade-offs. Initial analysis suggested that some 20 per cent of respondents appeared to rank lexically on the basis of responsibility alone being the determinant of who should pay. But such rankings have been shown to be consistent with underlying preferences that simply place a very high value on the attribute in question. Trade-offs still occur (Foster and Mourato, 1998).

The continuous variables model: The continuous variables model was tested to see if it bore out the results of the initial model. The two are not directly comparable because the second model deals with only two attributes at a time, rather than the full three attributes in the first model. Nonetheless, the researchers found that the second model confirms the findings of the first model: responsibility matters most and people do trade-off attributes.

The research suggests some important lines of inquiry. The net benefits of the hypothetical programme were taken to be positive and the focus was on who should pay for the costs. The success of the models suggests that they could be extended to see if equity and efficiency (net benefits) themselves have trade-offs from the point of view of individual respondents.

policies and projects and making the appropriate adjustments via the tax and social security system. Nonetheless, the approach illustrates one fairly simple way in which equity concerns could be accounted for if it was thought necessary. Box 1.1 illustrates a novel approach to taking equity concerns into account by using stated preference techniques.

1.7.4 Aggregation Over Time

Just as WTP and WTA need to be aggregated across individuals, so they must also be aggregated across time. Time aggregation involves two considerations:

1. the choice of a time horizon, and
2. the choice of a discount rate.

The choice of a time horizon for a *project* is usually determined by the life of the investment itself (for example, a dam, a road, a forest rotation and so on). But many projects have effects well after the estimated physical life. If so, a *terminal value* can be added in the cost–benefit calculation. Terminal value is essentially the value of the flow of costs and benefits after the period over which the present value is calculated. Various rules of thumb exist for approximating terminal value.[11] The choice of time horizon for a *policy* is less determinate. In theory, policies may exert effects over very long time horizons so that adopting infinite time horizons may have some justification. However, political time horizons and periods over which, in practice, effects are likely to be pronounced will be far shorter.

The choice of a discount rate remains the subject of extensive debate in economics.[12] Official UK guidance on the choice of a discount rate is given in HM Treasury (1997), although this is currently the subject of some reappraisal. The 'core' discount rate according to HM Treasury has been 6 per cent in real terms since 1989, but is subject to review. Others, for example Pearce and Ulph (1999), have suggested very much lower rates of the order of 2.5–3.0 per cent.

Aggregation of benefits and costs over time can be shown as follows:

$$\sum_t \sum_i \frac{(B_{i,t} - C_{i,t})}{(1+s)^t}. \tag{1.2}$$

Aggregating over time should also allow for potential *relative price effects*. If the good in question is likely to experience a rising relative value over time and in real terms, this should be built into the CBA. The simplest way is to allow future benefits to have unit values which are higher than current unit values. Thus a unit benefit in year t, b_t, would be given by $b_t = b_o(1 + p)^t$, where p is the percentage growth in the relative price. Relative price effects are likely to be important for goods in already fixed supply, such as national built and recorded heritage and environmental assets. A variant of this rule is to deduct any growth in the relative price from the discount rate to give a 'net' discount rate. Annex 1.3 provides a general model for determining discount rates.

The full cost–benefit formula taking into account the various forms of aggregation now appears as follows:

$$\sum_t \sum_i \frac{a_i(B_{i,t} - C_{i,t})}{(1 + s - p)^t} > 0. \tag{1.3}$$

Where a_i is the distributive weight applicable to stakeholder group i, s is the discount rate and p is the relative price effect. The economic efficiency criterion is met when the above aggregation results in a figure greater than zero, that is, the sum of benefits is greater than the sum of the costs. This criterion is also valid for the first aggregation formula above.

1.8 STATED PREFERENCES AND PUBLIC PARTICIPATION

Modern approaches to project and policy appraisal rightly stress the need for public participation in the process of appraisal. While participation is often seen as an end in itself, it is also a necessary ingredient for economic efficiency. The reason for this is that lack of participation can easily engender opposition to a project or policy, making it difficult to implement and costly to reverse. Participation may also produce better policy and project design since those most affected are closer to the issue than analysts and decision-makers. In the economic development literature, it is well established that development projects are more likely to succeed if communities and gender groups are involved in the process (Davis and Whittington, 1997). Appraisal techniques are often criticised because they may omit this participatory feature of decision-making. SP techniques, however, have an important role to play in securing participation, a role that emanates directly from the fact that techniques elicit all kinds of information about attitudes, motivations, preferences and willingness to pay.

The literature is not always clear on the meaning of the term 'participation'. At least three versions of the term appear: (i) participation as consultation, that is, taking account of the preferences of affected parties; (ii) participation as influence, that is, ensuring that affected parties influence the direction and form of the project or policy; and (iii) participation as benefit-sharing, that is,

---

BOX 1.2   COMMUNITY MEETINGS 'VERSUS' CONTINGENT VALUATION IN LUGAZI, UGANDA

Lugazi in Uganda is a town of about 20,000 people which, at the time of the study, had no piped water supply and no sewerage collection scheme. The issue was whether it was worth installing such schemes and, if so, what kind of scheme should be developed. The researchers conducted both a contingent valuation study and community meetings to discuss the alternatives. The community meetings involved pictorial presentations of the various alternatives and random participants were asked to rank them. One of the problems with community meetings is that individuals may be influenced by what their peers, their elders or their landlords might say. Attempts were therefore made to enable votes to be made 'in secret' by having votes expressed through the handing of a kernel of corn to a facilitator, both hands being held out such that no-one else could see which hand held the kernel. If it was held in the right hand it would signify one form of preference, if in the left hand it signified another. The various costs of the different water systems were also presented.

The results of the two approaches differed in some respects. For example, the contingent valuation study found 80 per cent of the population willing to pay around $0.5 for a public water supply, whereas the community meetings found that only 50 per cent were willing to pay at this price. But the proportions willing to pay for private water connections were similar, and they were closer still for the provision of a public latrine system. Which approach was better? In a country with better information one initial test would be to see which approach reflected sample characteristics that were representative of the population as a whole. In the Lugazi case, unfortunately, no population data existed so it was not possible to say which approach was more representative.

ensuring that affected parties receive a share of the resulting benefits. In any of these contexts great care needs to be taken that all genuine stakeholders are consulted. As we have seen earlier in this chapter, stakeholders may include non-users, so that limiting the focus of participatory processes to directly affected parties only can be inefficient. This reinforces the need to ensure that proper sampling of opinion is undertaken. Simply working with a *focus group* of a handful of people is unlikely to meet the requirement that a reasonable sample of opinion be surveyed. Even in the context of wider 'community meetings', participants may be far from being a random sample. Meetings may be dominated by activists, by those who can afford the time to attend such meetings, and may be subject to strategic behaviour because of the potential for any one individual deliberately to influence what others say. The more discursive approach to participation can, however, enhance the amount and perhaps the quality of information provided because responses tend to be more open-ended and not restricted to the questions that a SP tends to ask.

Surprisingly little research has been done to *compare* SP and other participatory approaches. In the developing world the issue is better researched than it is in the richer countries. A notable example is the study by Davis and Whittington (1997) in Uganda – see Box 1.2. The study could not show which approach was 'best' in the sense of being more representative, but it did show that contingent valuation has all the potential to act as a public participation exercise. The two approaches are not exclusive, of course, so that the argument should not really be one of which is exclusively better or worse than the other. However, the evidence does suggest that questionnaire-based approaches should not be rejected in favour of community participation procedures, and questionnaire approaches have a number of advantages over more traditional consultative procedures.

NOTES

1. 'Substitute' is used here in a subjective sense: with respect to the preferences of a given individual, two goods are substitutes for one another to the extent that that individual is willing to accept a gain of one as compensation for a loss of the other.
2. Strictly, these equalities hold exactly only in the limit, as the size of the price change tends to zero. We are taking it to be part of the definition of a competitive economy that each individual's decisions have infinitesimal effects on prices.
3. This aspect is explored in the literature on 'risk-risk' analysis. See Viscusi (1998).
4. This is the view taken, for example, by Sagoff (1988).
5. At this stage we are not concerned to specify the exact nature of the demand curve needed for valuation techniques. For simplicity, this example uses a linear demand curve.
6. The absence of any word which satisfactorily describes what these 'levels' are levels of is a consequence of the fact, explained earlier, that the economic analysis of preference does

not invoke any absolute standard of value. Terms such as 'welfare', 'utility' and 'well-being' are used in philosophical discussions to refer to particular aspects of an individual's life which can be asserted to have value. In contrast, an indifference curve simply describes an individual's willingness to accept some things in exchange for others. Strictly speaking, it is not a level *of* anything.

7. If, for each individual, the incremental risks associated with a policy option are small, the theory implies that the divergence between WTA and WTP will also be small. The argument against a monetary standard applies only to large risks.

8. For a discussion on the issue of standing, see Pearce et al. (1994), Ch. 4.

9. The links between WTP and, say, income and education are formally estimated in stated preference studies primarily to test the reasonableness of the results – see Chapters 5 and 8. We are suggesting an additional use of this information.

10. See, for example, Squire and van der Tak (1975), Ch. 7 for a discussion of 'consumption distribution weights'. In the case discussed there our 'b' is the elasticity of a function linking the marginal utility of consumption to consumption levels.

11. See Boardman et al. (1996), Ch. 4 and, on buildings and land, HM Treasury (1997), Annex F.

12. The most extensive discussions on discounting can be found in Lind (1982) and Portney and Weyant (1999).

ANNEX 1.1 Benefits transfer and stated preference techniques

This manual is not concerned in any detail with benefits transfer – the process of taking information about benefits from one context (the 'study site') and applying it to another context (the 'policy site'). Nonetheless, benefits transfer (BT) is the subject of a rapidly growing literature. The reason is obvious. If BT is a valid procedure, then the need for original (or 'primary') studies of the kind discussed in this manual would be vastly reduced. In the limit, values could be taken 'off the shelf' and applied to new contexts. Ironically, this is in fact how a great many cost–benefit studies or other contexts in which economic valuation is used proceed, and have proceeded for some considerable time. But it is only in the last decade that the question has been properly raised as to whether this procedure is valid. It seems fair to anticipate the interim conclusion (interim, because so much research is currently under way on this issue) that, currently, *BT is unreliable* (Loomis et al., 1995; Downing and Ozuna, 1996; Kirchoff et al., 1997; Brouwer, 1998: Bateman, Langford and Kerr, 1999). This conclusion needs to be qualified to some extent. BT seems to work in some contexts better than in others, for reasons that are not very clear at the moment.

This annex looks briefly at the basic elements of BT and then at the issue of whether SP techniques fare any better or worse than other valuation techniques in terms of transferability. Thus, the essential problem with benefits transfer is its reliability. How can the transferred value be validated? There are three broad procedures:

1. Transfer a value and then carry out a primary study at the policy site as well. Ideally, the transferred value and the primary estimate should be similar. If this exercise is repeated until a significant sample of studies exists in which primary and transferred values are calculated for policy sites, then there would be a justification for assuming that transferred values could be used in the future without the need to validate them with primary studies.

2. Conduct a *meta-analysis* on existing studies to explain why studies result in different mean (or median) estimates of WTP. At its simplest, a meta-analysis might simply take an average of existing estimates of WTP, provided the dispersion about the average is not found to be substantial, and use that average in policy site studies. Or, average values might be weighted by the dispersion about the mean, the wider the dispersion the lower the weight the estimate would receive. A more sophisticated ap-

proach takes a set of n primary studies and uses $n-1$ of the studies to estimate the value at the nth site. That 'transferred' value can then be compared with the original primary value at that site.

3. Benefits transfer could be tested by estimating WTP before an actual project is implemented and then revisiting the area later when the project is complete to see if people behaved according to their stated WTP.

In benefits transfer, it is possible to (i) transfer an average WTP estimate from one primary study, (ii) transfer WTP estimates from meta-analyses, and (iii) transfer a WTP function. The requirements for the latter are discussed in Chapter 5; the others are discussed below.

TRANSFERRING AVERAGE WTP FROM A SINGLE STUDY TO ANOTHER SITE WHICH HAS NO STUDY

One elementary procedure is to 'borrow' an estimate of WTP in context i (the study site) and apply it to context j (the policy site). The estimate may be left unadjusted, or it may be adjusted in some way. Transferring unadjusted estimates is clearly hazardous, although it is widely practised. Reasons for differences in average WTP include differences in the:

- socio-economic characteristics of the relevant populations;
- physical characteristics of the study and policy site;
- proposed change in provision between the sites of the good to be valued; and
- market conditions applying to the sites (for example, variation in the availability of substitutes) (Bateman, Nishikawa and Brouwer, 1999).

As a general rule, there is little evidence that the conditions for accepting unadjusted value transfer hold in practice. Effectively, those conditions amount to saying that the various conditions listed above all do not hold, that is, sites are effectively 'identical' in all these characteristics. An alternative is therefore to adjust the WTP estimates in some way.

A widely used formula for adjusted transfer is :

$$WTP_j = WTP_i (Y_j / Y_i)^e, \tag{1}$$

where Y is income per capita, WTP is willingness to pay, and e is the 'income elasticity of WTP', that is, an estimate of how the WTP for the environmental attribute in question varies with changes in income. The typical practice in benefit transfers between countries has been to use the ratio of income in the two countries. For an income elasticity of WTP that is less than one (the typical case), the usual practice will underestimate WTP$_j$ when transferring the estimate from a developed to a developing country (Flores and Carson, 1997). In this case, the feature that is changed between the two sites is income, perhaps because it is thought that this is the most important factor resulting in changes in WTP. But it should also be possible to make a similar adjustment for, say, changes in age structure between the two sites, changes in population density and so on. Making multiple changes of this kind amounts to transferring benefit functions (see below).

Bateman, Nishikawa and Brouwer (1999) distinguish various forms of adjusted transfer:

- expert judgement;
- re-analysis of existing study samples to identify sub-samples of data suitable for transfer; and
- 'meta-analyses' of numbers of previous estimates permitting the estimation of cross study benefit functions applicable to policy sites.

The first two are discussed below. The use of meta-analysis is addressed later.

In the early days of cost–benefit analysis, experts frequently adopted unit values (for example, for the value of a recreation day). Adjusted unit value approaches have also been applied to the valuation of health impacts and values of statistical life. Alberini et al. (1996) conducted a study of WTP to avoid the common cold. The study was conducted in Taiwan, but validation of its findings was secured by comparing income adjusted results with those derived from two studies carried out in the US. In other words, the formula given above was used. For colds which result in one 'restricted activity day' (RAD), Alberini et al. (1996) produce a value of around $24 and a confidence interval of about $14 to $34. Several US studies for identical episodes yielded values in this range.

A second approach to adjusted transfer involves the selection of a sub-sample from the original study site and then transferring that result to the policy site on the grounds that the policy site is more like the sub-sample than the complete study site sample. Unit values can then be estimated for these sub-samples for transfer purposes. This may work in some contexts but subdividing samples may render the transferred values less reliable due to small sample size.

TRANSFERRING BENEFIT FUNCTIONS: META-ANALYSIS

A more sophisticated approach is to transfer the *benefit function* (or *bid function*) from *i* and apply it to *j*. Thus if it is known that $WTP_i = f(A,B,C,Y)$ where *A,B,C* and *Y* are factors affecting WTP at site *i*, then WTP_j can be estimated using the coefficients from this equation but using the values of *A,B,C,Y* at site *j*.

An alternative is to use *meta-analysis* to take the results from a number of studies and analyse them in such a way that the variations in WTP found in those studies can be explained. This should enable better transfer of values since we can find out what WTP depends on. In the meta-analysis case, whole functions are transferred rather than average values, but the functions do not come from a single study but from a collection of studies.

Interest in the application of meta-analysis to the field of economic valuation has expanded rapidly in recent years. Studies have taken place in respect of urban pollution, outdoor recreation, the ecological functions of wetlands, values of statistical life, noise and congestion, and the local income generation effects of tourism (see, for example, Rosenberger and Loomis, 2000 and Smith et al., 1996).

Meta-analysis on Stated Preference Studies: An Example

Brouwer, Langford, Bateman and Turner (1999) conducted a meta-analysis of wetland values; 30 studies were finally used, producing over 100 estimates of WTP derived from stated preference studies.

In order to make the money valuation amount compatible between survey dates and across national boundaries, all national currencies were expressed in terms of their countries' 1990 purchasing power expressed in units of Special Drawing Rights (SDRs). Average WTP across all studies was 62 SDRs, while the median was considerably lower at 34 SDRs. Table A1.1.1 illustrates how the original WTP estimates varied. Statistical regressions were run relating WTP to factors judged to be potentially influential on WTP. Table A1.1.2 reports the variables which were statistically significant at the 0.10 level.

The estimated coefficients in the semi-log function represent the constant proportional rate of change in the dependent variable per unit change in the independent variables. Hence, the coefficient estimated for the dummy variable 'payment vehicle' in the basic model reflects, *ceteris paribus*, an almost twice as high average WTP for an increase in income tax than for any other payment vehicle. It is possible that people were willing to pay more via

Table A1.1.1   WTP estimates in wetland studies (SDR, 1990)

	Mean (SDRs)	Standard Error	n^a	$\chi^2 (p<)^b$
Value type				6.1 (0.05)
use value	68.1	8.4	50	
non-use value	35.5	4.8	13	
use and non-use values	63.8	12.9	40	
Wetland function				7.8 (0.05)
flood control	92.6	24.4	5	
water generation	21.5	6.8	9	
water quality	52.5	5.9	43	
biodiversity	76.1	12.8	46	
Relative wetland size				13.1 (0.01)
very large	86.9	17.6	8	
large	70.3	21.6	16	
medium	67.0	8.9	58	
small	29.5	13.2	13	
very small	53.4	13.8	6	
Country				−3.0 (0.003)[c]
US and Canada	70.8	7.8	80	
Europe	32.8	8.4	23	
Payment mode				27.4 (0.001)
income tax	121.3	18.1	22	
private market[d]	28.6	5.7	28	
product prices	47.8	8.9	22	
combination of income tax and product prices	42.8	6.3	26	
trip expenditures	102.9	6.8	3	
not specified	237.5	106.2	2	
Elicitation format				10.1 (0.01)
open-ended	37.4	6.5	35	
dichotomous choice	91.2	17.1	29	
iterative bidding	78.5	14.9	20	
payment card	47.1	8.4	19	
Response rate[1]				4.3 (0.11)
less than 30%	47.5	14.6	10	
between 31 and 50%	46.9	9.2	25	
more than 50%	78.3	9.9	59	

Notes:
[a]   The number of observations does not sum up to 103 in all cases as a result of missing values.
[b]   Outcome of the non-parametric Kruskal–Wallis test statistic which has approximately a Chi-squared distribution under the null hypothesis of equal average WTP in all groups.
[c]   Outcome of the non-parametric Mann–Whitney test statistic for two independent samples which has approximately a standard normal distribution under the null hypothesis of equal average WTP in all groups.
[d]   Private fund/entrance fee.

Source: Brouwer, Langford, Bateman and Turner (1999)

Table A1.1.2   WTP for wetlands: regression results for the basic and extended model

Fixed Effects		Basic Model		Extended Model	
Parameter	Parameter definition	Estimate	Standard Error	Estimate	Standard Error
Constant	Intercept	3.356***	0.100	3.311***	0.247
Payment vehicle	dummy: 1 = income tax 0 = other	1.880***	0.265	1.576***	0.362
Elicitation format	dummy: 1 = open-ended 0 = other	–0.411**	0.130	–0.376*	0.183
Country	dummy: 1 = North America 0 = other	1.861***	0.217	1.629***	0.363
Response rate (1)	dummy: 1 = 30–50 per cent 0 = other	–2.253***	0.326	–1.722***	0.451
Response rate (2)	dummy: 1 = > 50 per cent 0 = other	–1.904***	0.333	–1.461**	0.450
Flood control	dummy: 1 = flood control 0 = other	1.477***	0.240	1.134*	0.456
Water generation	dummy: 1 = water generation 0 = other	0.691*	0.342	0.441	0.479
Water quality	dummy: 1 = water quality 0 = other	0.545[†]	0.282	0.659*	0.327
Pseudo R-squared		0.365		0.380	
N		92		92	

Notes:
[†]   = significant at 0.10
*   = significant at 0.05
**   = significant at 0.01
*** = significant at 0.001

Source: Brouwer, Langford, Bateman and Turner

income tax than via other payment vehicles because tax indicated the social relevance of the problem. But the general understanding that most people will pay, avoiding possible feelings of unfairness or injustice and hence avoiding lower bid amounts or even protest bids, could have been relevant, as might the greater certainty or trust placed in this payment vehicle as an indication that the promised environmental services will be provided. The open-ended elicitation format is seen to produce a significantly lower WTP, by about 40 per cent, than other formats. This may be due to the uncertainty experienced in answering an unfamiliar question in an open-ended format. The dichotomous choice format yields the highest average WTP, followed by the iterative bidding procedure.

The basic model also indicates that study location has a significant impact on average WTP. The dummy variable has a value 1 if the research took place in North America and zero if in Europe. Average WTP appears to be substantially higher in North America than in Europe. In low response rate studies only those who are really interested in the good, and thereby also have a high WTP, make the effort to respond. Therefore mean WTP is high in such cases. Conversely, higher response rates, a rough indicator of overall study quality, appear to result in significantly lower average WTP because people with low WTP are also responding. Although Table A1.1.1 suggests that WTP increases overall with increasing relative wetland size, the statistical analysis does not bear this presumption out.

More interesting is the role played by the wetland functions themselves since they have a statistically significant role in explaining variance in average WTP. The average WTP is highest for flood control, followed by the function of supplying or supporting biodiversity, then water generation and lowest for water quality.

The suitability of the meta-analysis for benefits transfer is again the subject of some cautionary remarks by Brouwer, Langford, Bateman and Turner (1999). But the authors suggest that if low variance reflects the quality of the estimate for purposes of benefit transfer, then studies using income taxation as a payment vehicle are better suited than other payment vehicles, and studies valuing wetland biodiversity are more reliably transferred than estimates of the value of wetlands in their capacity of generating water or maintaining water quality.

BENEFITS TRANSFER AND STATED PREFERENCE

The previous sections have illustrated the various ways in which BT might be practised. Is BT affected in any particular way by the nature of the valuation studies that are included? For example, is there any reason to suppose that SP studies will perform better or worse than revealed preference studies?

The first approach to answering this question is an intuitive one. Certain conditions probably have to be met for a valid transfer of value to take place. These are widely recognised to be:

- the studies included in the analysis must themselves be sound;
- the studies should contain WTP regressions, that is, regressions showing how WTP varies with explanatory variables;
- the study and policy sites must be similar in terms of population and population characteristics or differences in population must be accounted for;
- the change in the provision of the good being valued at the two sites should be similar;
- site characteristics should be the same, or differences should be accounted for; and
- property rights should be the same across the sites.

On this intuitive test there is no particular reason to suppose that SP studies would fare any worse than any other form of study, although care will need to be taken to ensure that views about who has effective property rights are fully accounted for. Otherwise, the tests are very much a matter of carefully scrutinising the accuracy and professionalism of the original studies.

The intuitive approach is a beginning but still leaves considerable room for doubt about the sensitivity of transfers to the nature of the studies included. A second test might therefore be one of seeing how far the transferred values are accurate. If transferred value from SP studies have more error than transferred values from revealed preference studies, then there may be a legitimate concern about the validity of SP transfers. Brouwer (1998) observes that there are comparatively few studies that test for the validity of BT, on whatever basis the original estimates were obtained. Some general findings are that:

- transferring benefit functions is more accurate than transferring average values;
- contingent valuation studies appear to perform no worse than revealed preference studies in terms of transfer error;
- transfer error can be quite large, 1–75 per cent if 'outliers' are ignored, but up to 450 per cent if they are included;
- there is some reason to suppose that individuals' attitudes are important determinants of WTP in SP studies, yet most BT makes little effort

to test for variability in attitudes across sites. This suggests that BT would have to be supplemented by social surveys at the policy site;

- meta-analysis of contingent valuation studies can explain a reasonable proportion of the variation in the original studies, but the original studies do not include sufficient information to test whether more information would have increased the explanatory power of the meta-analysis; and

- the missing information may well be of the motivational type, that is, why people adopt the value stances they do. This conclusion fits well with the current focus in economics on the analysis of motives for preferences.

The new focus on motives does not invalidate economic valuation. It does suggest that more attention should be paid to motives in SP studies so that there is a better chance of explaining WTP variation between studies. Study context may also be important (for example, the historical factors affecting a particular site, or the 'causes' of the problem that is being valued). Efforts to conduct SP studies in a context-free environment should help to resolve this issue, although care must be taken not to render the questions meaningless to respondents.

Overall, and as a general proposition, BT cannot, at the moment, be relied upon to produce valuation estimates which are statistically indistinguishable from the 'true' values. As discussed above, results tend to differ by up to 75 per cent if outliers are excluded, and by up to 450 per cent if they are included. However, whether this margin of error is considered 'large' or 'too large' depends on the use of the results. For some project and policy applications it is probably acceptable, and uncertainty of the final results can be dealt with through sensitivity analysis. Indeed, it is not uncommon to find demand studies for market goods and services where, depending on the method of estimation, the functional form, and the selection of observations, the results can vary by a factor of five or more.

It may be that values are transferable but that much more information is required before meta-analyses can explain the variation in WTP across studies. On this view, more research will improve the reliability of BT at some stage in the future. Another view is that values are inherently not transferable because what is valued is site specific and because the characteristics of those engaging in valuation are site specific too. At the moment, there is no consensus on these issues. This points the way towards (i) continued reliance on primary studies, and (ii) conducting those primary studies in a manner that is consistent with future BT tests. These points notwithstanding, details of primary studies can be found at the EVRI database from Environment Canada at www.evri.ec.gc.ca and the UK Department of Environment, Food and Rural Affairs reference list (www.defra.gov.uk/environment/evslist/index.htm).

NOTE TO ANNEX 1.1

1. These data do not conflict with the assertion that high response rates result in low WTP, because the table reports raw subgroup means. When we control for all the other explanatory factors via a multiple regression, the relationship reverses (lower response rates give higher WTP). This relationship is statistically significant.

ANNEX 1.2 Use of stated preference in UK environmental policy: the case of the aggregates levy

The UK's Budget 2000 announced the introduction of an aggregates levy of £1.60 per tonne from April 2002, to ensure that the environmental impacts of aggregates production not already addressed in regulation are more fully reflected in prices. To appraise the policy proposal, a contingent valuation study on the disamenities of quarrying, entitled 'The External Costs and Benefits of the Supply of Aggregates: Phase II' was commissioned by the then DETR and published in 1999 (available at www.planning.odpm.gov.uk/ecb/index.htm). This built upon earlier research, also commissioned by the Department.

The purpose of the study was to help inform the decision-making on whether there should be a tax on aggregates, and if so, at what level. The study was designed to ascertain the value that people place on the damage caused to the environment by the quarrying of aggregates, such as crushed rock, sand and gravel. This would help to inform the most appropriate level of a tax in order for it to fully reflect the value of the environmental damage caused by quarrying.

Ten thousand respondents were picked at random from within a 5-mile radius of 21 representative sample quarries and other extraction sites. They were asked how much they would be willing to pay in the form of increased taxes over a five year period in order for the government to shut down the local quarry, restore the site in keeping with the surrounding landscape and ensure that the workers found new employment.

A further 1,000 respondents were chosen randomly by postcode from around England, and were asked what they would be willing to pay to close a quarry in a National Park (the Peak District and the Yorkshire Dales were used as examples). These surveys were carried out to show the value attributed to the environmental damages of quarrying by those who are not directly affected.

The environmental effects which people were asked to value included:

- adverse effects on nature, such as loss of biodiversity;
- noise from quarry transport and blasting;
- increase in traffic and dust levels; and
- visual intrusion.

Respondents were shown one of three payment cards, each stating four possible amounts that it might cost households to close the quarry. They were then asked whether they would be willing to pay each of the amounts written on the card sequentially. If the respondent stated that they were willing to pay the highest value on the card, they were then asked an open-ended question about the *maximum* they would be willing and able to pay to get the quarry closed. Using three cards with different amounts on each enabled a check to be made for the existence of any anchoring bias to the amounts given.

From the results of the surveys, national estimates for the average amount that people were willing to pay for the environmental benefits obtained from early closure of a quarry were calculated. These are shown in Table A1.2.1.

Table A1.2.1   The results of the aggregates survey

Case study sites	£/tonne
Hard rock	0.34
Sand and gravel	1.96
Quarries in National Parks	10.52

Source: *www.planning.odpm.gov.uk/ecb/index.htm*

The national average amount which individuals were willing to pay for the closure of *all* types of quarry sites, weighted by the type of output, was calculated to be £1.80 per tonne of output.

These results are more likely to be understatements than overstatements of people's true valuation of the environmental impacts of quarrying, as the study was designed specifically to produce conservative figures. For example:

- WTP figures were ascertained rather than willingness to accept, as these are generally accepted as being the lower of the two measures;
- a payment card approach was used to aid people in deciding their own WTP;
- the WTP of people living more than 5 miles from each of the sample sites was omitted due to resource constraints, although they may still have a WTP greater than the values obtained from the national survey; and
- the WTP of respondents in relation to quarrying in special landscapes other than National Parks (such as Areas of Outstanding Natural Beauty) was also omitted.

Overall, the results showed a positive value for the environmental costs imposed by quarrying activities for each category of output and therefore supported the case for introducing a tax on aggregate production. These conclusions played an important role in helping to inform the decision over the introduction of an aggregates levy, and in Budget 2000 it was announced that a levy would be introduced at a rate of £1.60 per tonne from April 2002.

ANNEX 1.3   Discounting

A generalised formula for discounting is:

$$W_t = 1/(1+r)^{\alpha(t)}, \tag{1}$$

where W_t is the weight to be attached to a cost or benefit in year t, and is known as the *discount factor* and r is the discount rate, and $\alpha(t)$ is function of the perception of the speed at which time passes. For conventional ('exponential') discounting $\alpha t = t$, so $\alpha = 1$, so that:

$$W_t = 1/(1+r)^t. \tag{2}$$

This is the discount factor formula that can be found in all CBA textbooks. But there is in fact no particular reason to suppose that discounting should proceed in this way. We need to distinguish money goods from goods other than money.

If the good in question is money, the existence of positive rates of interest in the economy does imply exponential discounting. Essentially, if the market rate of interest is i, then £1 next year is not worth the same as £1 now because £1 now can be invested at i per cent to become £(1 + i) next year. Conversely, then, £1 next year must be worth £1/(1 + i) now. If there is a constant market rate of interest, discounting on this argument implies an exponential discount rate. At the level of the economy as a whole, individuals' time preferences help to determine the market interest rate. Individuals adjust their consumption and savings so that, *at the margin*, they discount at the interest rate. Just as prices are measures of marginal valuation, so interest rates are measures of the marginal time preference for money.

When the good in question is not money, then, given that money is nonetheless the standard of value, there is no measure of the discount rate that is independent of the money valuations of the good in the relevant periods. Suppose that X is willing to pay £1 for a unit of clean air today and £0.99 for clean air to be enjoyed next year, the marginal time preference rate (MTPR) for clean air is 1 per cent. If the MTPR in money is 5 per cent, we can say that the money value of clean air is increasing at 4 per cent per year. In general, the MTPR for different goods will be different, simply because money valuations for goods change over time. It is a *convention* that we use money as the unit for MTPR and treat everything else as changes in money valuations. But having adopted this convention, we have to use the MTPR for money (which equals the interest rate in a well functioning market) as the discount rate for *all* costs and benefits *once these have been measured in units of money.*

But if the focus is on the way in which individuals discount the future there are no *a priori* restrictions on the nature of discounting. Indeed, it is possible that people may discount the future differently for different goods and that they may even discount the future at a negative rate (for example, preferring to 'get the worst over now').

A generalised function is given by:

$$W_t = 1/(1+r)^{\alpha(t)} = 1/(1+gt)^{h/g}, \tag{3}$$

where h measures the speed of an individual's time perception. If $h = 0$, time periods pass infinitely quickly. If $h = \infty$ time is perceived as not passing at all. g measures the degree of departure from the standard (exponential) discounting model. As g tends to 0, so W_t approaches the conventional discount function.

Cross multiplying:

$$(1+r)^{\alpha(t)} = (1+gt)^{h/g}, \tag{4}$$

and hence:

$$\alpha(t) = h.\ln(1+gt)/g.\ln(1+r). \tag{5}$$

From this general formula various *hyperbolic* discount factors can be derived, for example:

$$g = 1 \Rightarrow W_t = 1/(1+gt)^{h/g} = 1/(1+t)^h, \tag{6}$$

and:

$$\alpha(t) = h.\ln(1+gt)/g.\ln(1+r) = h.\ln(1+t)/\ln(1+r), \tag{7}$$

$$h/g = 1 \Rightarrow W_t = 1/(1+gt)^{h/g} = 1/(1+gt) \tag{8}$$

and:

$$\alpha(t) = h.\ln(1+gt)/g.\ln(1+r) = \ln(1+t)/\ln(1+r). \tag{9}$$

Note also that:

$$h = 0 \Rightarrow W_t = 1, \tag{10}$$

which means that the same weight is applied to each period. In this case, the individual is said to be 'timing indifferent', that is, $r = 0$ and:

$$h = \infty \Rightarrow 1/(1+r)^t = 0, \tag{11}$$

which means that there can be no value for future consequences (note this is quite different to saying the discount *rate* is zero – see (10)).

BOX A1.3.1   DISCOUNTING AND SAFETY

In the case of future safety effects, it seems reasonable to assume that an individual's anticipated utility loss associated with the prospect of premature death (or injury of given severity) remains effectively *constant* over time. If this is so, then the individual's WTP (in real terms) for a given reduction in the risk of death (or injury) will grow at more or less the same rate as the rate at which the marginal utility of income declines over time with increasing real income. In view of this, the growth in future WTP-based real monetary values of safety will, to all intents and purposes, be *exactly offset* by the 'diminishing marginal utility' component, µg, of the social discount rate. Thus, rather than making predictions about future monetary values of safety and then subjecting the latter to the full social discount rate, it is equally legitimate (and somewhat more straightforward) to value future safety effects on the basis of *current* monetary values of safety and then subject the resultant safety benefits *only* to the pure utility discount rate δ (see, for example, Jones-Lee and Loomes, 1997 or Rowlatt et al., 1998). Economists dispute the size of δ. Some argue that it is irrational to discount utility at all, so that δ = 0. Others argue that δ > 0 but that it will be small and of the order of 1–2 per cent per year (Rowlatt et al., 1998).

In comparison to the conventional model, hyperbolic discounting produces *lower discount factors* in the near term, but *higher discount factors* for periods of time further into the future. An example of the use of SP to elicit personal time preference rates is given in Box A1.3.1.[1] A *social discount rate* based on individuals' time preference takes the form:

$$s = \delta + \mu.g, \tag{12}$$

where δ is the rate at which individuals discount future *utility*, μ is the elasticity of the marginal utility of consumption[2] and g is the rate of growth of consumption per head.

Pearce and Ulph (1999) decompose δ into $\rho - L$, where ρ is the 'pure utility discount rate' and L is the rate of change in the risk of death. Rowlatt et al. suggest that ρ will be no more than 2 per cent and closer to 1 per cent. Pearce and Ulph suggest a value of δ of around 0.5 per cent. L can be estimated by the number of deaths in the UK in a year, divided by the population, giving a value of about 1 per cent.

The expression $\mu.g$ relates to the discounting of future consumption. While estimates of μ have traditionally been put in the range 1–2, Pearce and Ulph (1999) show that, for the UK, a value of 0.8 is more likely. Long-term growth rates of consumption per head in the UK have been 1.3 per cent per annum from 1885 to the 1990s, and 2.2 per cent from 1951 to the 1990s. Overall, then, a social discount rate has a probable value of:

$$s = \delta - L + \mu.g \Rightarrow 1.0 + 1.0 + (0.8)(1.3 \text{ to } 2.2) \Rightarrow, \tag{13}$$

between 2.0 and 3.8 per cent per year (note that L is negative). Box A1.3.2 illustrates how discount rates might be derived from SP techniques.

BOX A1.3.2   INDIVIDUALS' DISCOUNT RATES IN THE UK: EVIDENCE FROM STATED PREFERENCE TECHNIQUES

There is some evidence that individuals do discount the future 'hyperbolically' rather than 'exponentially'. The evidence comes from several psychological and medical studies. Thus, Cairns and van der Pol (2000) found that the hyperbolic model fitted better than the exponential model when applied to individuals' stated preferences for non-fatal health impacts on individuals' own health and the health of others. The SP techniques involved an open-ended and a dichotomous choice approach (see Chapter 4). The open-ended approach posed a question of the following kind: imagine you will be ill at some point in the future, and that this spell of ill-health can be postponed for several years through a minor one-off treatment. By allowing the number of days in the year in which ill-health is experienced to be varied, respondents were asked to indicate the maximum number of days of ill-health in the later period at which it would still be worthwhile receiving the treatment. For example, someone might say they would 'swap' 40 days of ill health if they were postponed by x years, compared to 20 days of ill-health in the near-term future. Let y be the maximum number of days in the distant future, let the near-term future be two years with a period of ill-health of x days, and s be the number of years the ill-health is postponed, then by definition the present values of the two eventualities must be the same:

$$x/(1+r)^2 = y/(1+r)^{s-2}$$

and

$$r = (y/x)^{1/s-2} - 1.$$

In the dichotomous choice context, respondents were presented with two alternative treatments. For the first treatment individuals would be ill early on for x days, and for the second treatment individuals would be ill later on but with more days of illness. Respondents were then asked to indicate their preferences.

The Cairns and van der Pol (2000) study suggests a number of provisional conclusions:

- there is evidence that discount rates decline with time: the longer the delay in the onset of ill-health, the lower the discount rate. This phenomenon of 'decreasing timing aversion' fits the hyperbolic model better than the conventional exponential model;
- median discount rates ranged from 3.8 per cent to 6.4 per cent;
- median discount rates were perhaps higher using the open ended method than the dichotomous choice technique (there were only a few cases where the difference was statistically significant); and
- time preference for own health is similar to that for the health of others.

NOTES TO ANNEXE 1.3

1. A similar exercise for several developing countries and economies in transition is given in Poulos and Whittington (1999). As might be expected, discount *rates* in poor economies are high: around 40 per cent for a period of 5 years.
2. That is, the elasticity of a function showing how marginal utility falls as consumption increases.

2. Commissioning a stated preference study

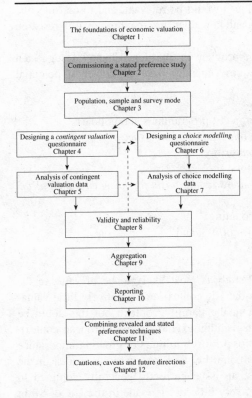

The foundations of economic valuation
Chapter 1

Commissioning a stated preference study
Chapter 2

Population, sample and survey mode
Chapter 3

Designing a *contingent valuation* questionnaire
Chapter 4

Designing a *choice modelling* questionnaire
Chapter 6

Analysis of contingent valuation data
Chapter 5

Analysis of choice modelling data
Chapter 7

Validity and reliability
Chapter 8

Aggregation
Chapter 9

Reporting
Chapter 10

Combining revealed and stated preference techniques
Chapter 11

Cautions, caveats and future directions
Chapter 12

SUMMARY

This chapter is designed to provide guidance for those charged with commissioning a stated preference study, both in terms of when a study might be desirable and what to expect from the consultants delivering the work.

The current and potential uses of valuation studies are reviewed, with examples of the sorts of questions they are useful in addressing.

Criteria for deciding whether any economic valuation is necessary are proposed, with an overview of alternative appraisal techniques and their suitability to different contexts.

Because mixed valuation and non-valuation approaches are desirable in some instances, an overview of these approaches is provided in this chapter, along with a selection of appropriate examples.

For those contexts in which a stated preference study is required, this chapter provides guidance on which techniques are best suited to which problems. Guidance is also given regarding judgement of the required level of accuracy of a study, and to social considerations such as distributional effects, the issue of 'standing', the role of expert advice, the anticipated costs of a study, and assessment of the consultants.

The chapter concludes with an outline of the steps for implementing a stated preference study, which is intended to set the basis for the structure of Chapters 3 to 10.

2.1   DEFINING THE CONTEXT

While the dominant part of this manual concerns the detailed issues of how to carry out stated preference (SP) studies, it is important at the outset to define the contexts in which SP techniques would be relevant, and to consider the stages of commissioning a study and how to ensure that high quality research is carried out.

The first issue is to define the problem in question. Chapter 1 suggested that economic valuation techniques generally have a number of potential uses:

- cost–benefit analyses of projects, programmes and policies;
- *the 'demonstration' of the importance of an issue*;
- *priority-setting within a sector*;
- priority-setting across sectors;
- *determining marginal damages as the basis for an environmental tax or charge*;
- green national income accounting;
- *legal damage assessment (liability)*; and
- *determining discount rates.*

Within this list, a 'primary' SP study is most likely to be of value in the applications shown in italics. In the UK context, comparatively little valuation work has been carried out in the liability context, but this could be expected to change as liability legislation extends in the European context. The use of valuation techniques for priority setting is of growing importance and, in principle, SP techniques could be used to secure some idea of the public's perception of priorities, an issue currently generally confined to public opinion polls. In practice, very little use is made in the UK of SP in this respect. Setting priorities across sectors is, as Chapter 1 noted, extremely unusual. Typically, priority-setting will occur within a sector, say health, rather than across sectors, say health and transport. Finally, it is extremely unlikely that modified national accounting would require original, primary studies, although the possibility cannot be ruled out. Typically, however, these issues are dealt through the use of benefits transfer estimates (see Annex 1.1).

The questions that are being answered through the use of valuation techniques will take the following forms:

- *Investment and policy expenditure issues*
  Is project A, policy B or programme C 'worthwhile'?

How might a choice be made between alternative policies and projects?
How might compatible projects and policies be ranked in order of 'worth'?
How might the constituent parts of a programme be chosen so as to
maximise net benefits?
How large should a given project or programme be?
On what scale should a policy be implemented? Or, what is an appro-
priate standard or target for a policy measure?

- *Taxation issues*
  How large should a given environmental tax be?

- *Prioritisation issues*
  How important is a given issue (for example, work days lost through
  illness, air pollution)?

Policy analysts emphasise the need to establish at the outset some framework
for the comparison of the criteria of a 'good' policy (project, programme and
so on) and the alternative options that are open. A typical example is shown
in Table 2.1, which reveals the nature of the trade-offs in all choices.

The alternative policy (speed limit) options are shown at the top right of
the matrix. The criteria by which the desirability of changes in the speed
limits could be judged are shown to the left of the matrix. The criteria might
be the number of serious accidents, travel time saved and the cost of operating vehicles. The cells of the matrix then show estimates of the effect of the
change in speed limits on each of the criteria used. Illustrative numbers are
provided. The second matrix, Table 2.2, shows the same information but this
time 'normalised' on reference base, for example, 80 km/hour. Since injuries
and cost increase with higher speed, but time spent travelling falls, there is a
trade-off between the criteria.

Table 2.1   Criteria/alternatives matrix: original data

Criteria	Alternative speed limit options, km/h			
	70	80	90	100
Serious injuries per million vehicle kms	5.0	5.4	5.9	6.5
Time spent travelling: years per million vehicle kms	3.3	3.1	2.9	2.7
Vehicle operating costs £ million per million vehicle kms	12.6	12.8	13.2	13.8

Table 2.2   Criteria/alternatives matrix: normalised on 80 km/h

	Alternative speed limit options, km/h			
Criteria	70	80	90	100
Serious injuries per million vehicle kms	−0.4	0	+0.5	+1.1
Time spent: years travelling per million vehicle kms	+0.2	0	−0.2	−0.4
Vehicle operating costs: £ million per million vehicle kms	−0.2	0	+0.4	+1.0

Table 2.3   Criteria/alternatives matrix: monetised outcome

	Alternative speed limit options, km/h			
Criteria	70	80	90	100
Money value of serious injuries: £ million	+0.4	0	−0.5	−1.1
Money value of time spent: £ million	−0.2	0	+0.2	+0.4
Money value of vehicle operating costs: £ million	+0.2	0	−0.4	−1.0
Aggregated net benefit £ million	+0.4	0	−0.7	−1.7

Tables 2.1 and 2.2 make it clear that the choice of the 'right' speed limit depends on factors over and above the 'basic' information provided about the effects of speed limits. What is required is some mechanism for trading-off the time, cost and injuries, that is, we need to know at what rate the benefits of saving time can be traded for increased cost and increased injuries. Economists adopt preferences, as revealed through WTP, as the means of making the trade-off. To illustrate, Table 2.3 shows what happens if we adopted the following WTP figures: each injury is valued at £1 million and a year of saving time is also valued at £1 million. Then the computation is simple, as Table 2.3 shows. The highest net benefit would be for a change in the speed limit downwards to 70 km/hour.

Table 2.3 uses WTP as the weighting mechanism to inform the trade-off required for the policy options to be evaluated. In theory, any set of weights can be used provided there is sound rationale. For example, experts might place 'scores' on the various changes, the scores reflecting their judgement about the relative importance of the different impacts of the changes in speed limit.

2.2 IS ECONOMIC VALUATION NECESSARY AND CREDIBLE?

In order to decide whether *any* economic valuation is required, the following considerations need to be addressed:

- If economic valuation is not used, what alternative and appropriate procedures are available?
- What are the chances that credible economic value estimates will emerge?
- How much will the study cost?
- Could mixed economic valuation and other approaches be used to increase credibility?

2.2.1 What Alternative and Appropriate Procedures are Available?

Taking the classification above, it is important to recognise that investment and policy analysis decisions and priority assessment require measures of benefits *and* costs. SP techniques relate to benefits only (or damages). Hence choosing between economic valuation and other procedures needs to be done in the context of thinking about policy and project costs as well as benefits. On the assumption that costs can be estimated, at least broadly, then the choice becomes one from a number of techniques. These techniques are shown schematically in Figure 2.1. Some of the considerations relevant to choosing between them are discussed in outline below. More detail can be found in EFTEC (1998a), which should be consulted at this stage of choosing different approaches.

Four categories of gain and loss are shown in Figure 2.1: resource costs (for example, the money cost of a project), gains or losses in human health, gains and losses to the environment, and other gains and losses. The box 'LCA' shows *life-cycle analysis*, which refers to the requirement to assess all gains and losses over the whole life-cycle of the changes brought about by a policy or a project. LCA tends to be subsumed in CBA, which adopts the 'with/without' principle. In turn this principle requires that all impacts legitimately due to the relevant action (project or policy) be accounted for. Strictly, LCA applies to all the categories of gain or loss, although this rule is not always followed. Health risks can be formally evaluated with *health risk assessment* (HRA), which should involve the estimation of the probability of some adverse health conse-quence and some measure of the scale of that consequence (for example, numbers of persons). HRA should also incorporate the costs of reducing risks, that is the resource costs, but often does not do this.

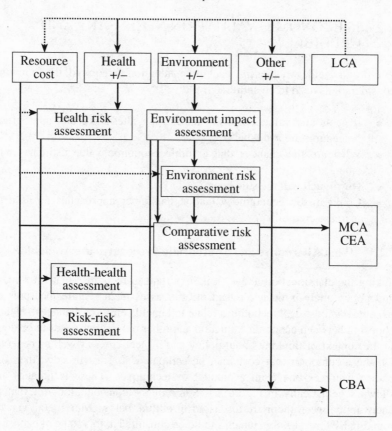

Figure 2.1   Appraisal techniques: health, safety and environment risks

Environmental impacts from a change in policy or project can be formally identified with *environmental impact assessment* (EIA). EIA does not in itself offer any decision rule about acceptance or rejection of a policy or project. Processing EIA into *environmental risk assessment* (ERA) goes one stage further in offering some guidance on decision-making. ERA estimates the likelihood of adverse environmental consequences and the scale of those consequences. While it should, like properly executed HRA, include the costs of reducing risks, it very often does not do this. *Comparative risk assessment* (CRA) extends risk analysis to choice contexts by comparing cost–risk reduction ratios between alternative policies or options. Thus a cost of saving one life under option A may be £10,000 and under option B £100,000. Option A would be chosen under CRA. CRA can involve just human health risks, just environmental risks, or both. When both are involved, however, there are problems of comparing the 'worth' of human health risks against environmental risks and this can only be done by some weighting procedure. Note that if the weights are WTP or WTA estimates, then CRA approximates cost–benefit analysis.

Multi-criteria analysis (MCA) may involve estimates of health risks, environmental risks, resource costs and other gains or losses. In the initial stages of MCA, these will not be aggregated. Various combinations of the 'criteria' (risks and so on) will be compared to see if any sets of criteria dominate others. Dominated sets are then eliminated. Remaining sets can then be compared by some form of weighting. Again, if the weights are WTP prices, MCA reduces to CBA. However, CBA tends to focus on efficiency gains and losses whereas MCA is likely to embrace wider concepts of social goals, including distributive incidence, employment impacts and so on. Many MCAs may also appear as *cost-effectiveness analyses* (CEA). Under CEA there tends to be one composite but non-monetary unit of effectiveness, and this is compared to the resource cost, usually in the form of a ratio. MCA will approximate CEA if the various criteria can be 'collapsed' through some form of equivalence weighting into a single measure of effectiveness. For an account of MCA, see the manual published by DETR at www.dtlr.gov.uk/about/multicriteria/index.htm.

Health-health assessment (HHA) involves estimating changing health risks from a policy or project. The risks in question arise from the impacts of the policy or project but also from the expenditures required to implement the measure. Expenditures coming from, say, taxes on households could lead to reduced expenditures on other risk reduction. The 'unit' of comparison is usually lives saved so that the cost of the regulation (lives lost due to diverted risk reduction expenditures) is compared to the benefit of the regulation (lives saved by the measure). HHA appears not to be in significant use in the UK.

Risk-risk assessment (RRA) has similarities to HHA in that it compares the risks reduced by a policy or project and asks what the risks would be if the policy was not implemented. A ban on saccharin because of cancer fears, for example, might be counterproductive in risk-risk terms if the ban results in increased sugar consumption with all the attendant risks.

How does economic valuation fit with the schema of Figure 2.1?

Only MCA, CEA (potentially) and CBA can capture all the elements of gain and loss. Other techniques are partial in the sense of focusing on one aspect of risk or in ignoring cost altogether. Any technique ignoring cost must, by definition, pose serious questions concerning resource mis-allocation. MCA can extend beyond CBA to embrace goals other than efficiency as measured by the sum of consumer surpluses. MCA may often not involve reference to individuals' choices and tends to involve more 'expert' opinion, but in principle can reflect individuals' choices. MCA is also close to CEA in not having a basis in welfare economics. Another way of saying this is that it can identify cost-efficient options but cannot indicate whether any action at all is warranted. This is because gains and losses are not calculated in the same units which, in turn, reflect an underlying conceptual structure.

2.2.2 How credible will the results be?

The credibility of an economic valuation study will depend on (i) the intrinsic merits of the technique chosen, (ii) the scientific and physical data, and (iii) the quality of the study itself. In respect of (i) the issue, often overlooked, is how credible the approach adopted is relative to the alternative procedures that are available. Much depends on the context. For example, if the issue is how to choose between two alternatives and the *sole criterion* is, say, lives saved, then economic valuation is not needed. The relevant approach is cost-effectiveness where 'lives saved per £ spent' is the appropriate criterion. The point of the criteria/alternatives matrix in Section 2.1 above is to first test whether a single goal, such as lives saved, is in fact the only criterion for choice. The matrix also reminds the decision-maker that, even for a single goal, he or she should confirm that the units of 'effectiveness' (lives saved) are intended to have equal weights (for example, irrespective of age, health state and so on). If the answers to these questions are in the affirmative, then cost-effectiveness is the right criterion. Finally, the choice context needs to be made clear. In the criterion/alternatives matrix the choices are clearly set out – leave things as they are or change to some new speed limit. Presenting a choice as being between two alternatives could be misleading if one of those alternatives is not the *status quo*, that is, leaving things as they are. Cost-effectiveness does not answer the question of whether any of a set of alternatives that differ from the *status quo* should be chosen. It simply says that, given that some change has to occur, choose the most cost-effective change. The attraction of decision rules that compare costs and benefits in like units is that they can provide an answer to that question.

Data considerations are very important. No amount of economic analysis will cast light on an issue if the underlying data are not available or cannot be generated by the study itself. An example might be assessing the costs and benefits of setting an environmental standard for a chemical that has not been subjected to a risk assessment. If there is no known relationship between the concentration of the chemical and risks to human health or to ecosystems, then there is no point in pursuing a CBA. In some circumstances a SP study could cast some light on this issue but only in terms of individuals' *perceptions* of risk. The study would provide information but since the perceptions would not be informed by any notion of objective risk, the extent to which those perceptions should be integrated into policy is debatable. How to achieve credibility with regard to the third issue above, namely the quality of the study itself, is the topic of Part II of this book.

2.2.3 The Cost of the Study

The issue of cost is important because those commissioning such studies tend to have very limited budgets. The costs of SP studies vary enormously. World Bank commissioned contingent valuations have cost £250,000, the US Environment Protection Agency has spent over £500,000 on some SP projects, and the cost of high-quality SP projects executed for litigation in the US often exceed £1 million. They have typically been carried out in considerable detail with mixes of contingent valuation and participatory approaches, large samples, face-to-face interviews and so on. On the other hand, many small-scale studies are executed for as little as £8–10,000. Size of budget is not necessarily any guarantee of quality, but studies costing as little as £8–10,000 should be regarded with caution.

A significant part of a study's cost is the survey itself. Survey costs will vary with (i) sample size, (ii) the nature of the interview process, (iii) who does the interviewing, (iv) the complexity of the questionnaire design and (v) the location of the sampling points. Unless there are very strong reasons to suppose otherwise, it is strongly recommended that professional interviewers familiar with the SP questionnaires are used. In some contexts where using, say, students for interviewers is unavoidable, training in general interview techniques as well as SP questionnaires are necessary.

Table 2.4   Typical survey costs in 2000

	Mailshot	Telephone	Face-to-face
£ per completed questionnaire	10–20	15–30	25–50

The costs of different interview processes (generally classified as mail, telephone and face-to-face plus some combinations of the three – see Chapter 3) are different due to the different time and effort requirements. Table 2.4

sets out some rough ranges for the different interview procedures and different sample sizes when a market research company is used. Using students would reduce the costs but this may have a potentially higher risk of unsuccessful implementation and will require additional training costs which are not included here.

Mail survey costs are based on the assumption of a 10-page questionnaire and include printing, postage (out and return) and reminder phone call. Multiple mailings are usually necessary to get a high response rate. The use of multiple mailings makes a high-quality mail survey usually take about two months to carry out. The cost does not include data entry.

Telephone survey costs are based on the assumption of a 20-minute interview based on a 10-page questionnaire, open eligibility for interview with age/sex quota, national spread using telephone directories or specific local directories (plus some random dialling for ex-directory numbers) and using own resources of the company. Note that the costs exclude printing of the questionnaires but include data entry. The cost of the face-to-face survey is based on the same assumptions about the length of the questionnaire as the telephone survey.

In addition to survey costs there will be the personnel time for questionnaire design and revisions, focus groups, pilot surveys, data entry and analysis, and other costs and expenses such as travel, overheads and reporting costs.

2.2.4   'Mixed' Valuation and Non-valuation Approaches

Data deficiencies may limit the extent to which all the significant impacts from a policy or project can be measured in monetary terms. In such contexts a 'mixed' approach would involve identifying and valuing all those impacts that can be credibly valued, and recording those which cannot be valued in money terms.

The reasons for the absence of monetary values tend to be:

- The underlying physical data do not exist. As noted previously, if no-one has carried out a risk assessment of, say, a given chemical, it will not be possible to say what the economic value of reducing that chemical in the environment is.
- The underlying physical data may exist but not be in a form suitable for monetisation. Recall that the money values reflect preferences. Now suppose the physical data take the form of 'a reduction of X tonnes in biochemical oxygen demand (BOD)' in a river. Individuals do not have measurable preferences for BOD. What they have preferences for is more or less water quality. The 'object' of preferences does

not correspond to the physical measure of the environmental change. This is the so-called correspondence problem.

- The relevant physical data may exist and may correspond to what people value, but the research may simply not have been done. Consider biological diversity. There are numerous studies of the willingness to pay to conserve *biological resources* (for example, endangered species) but hardly any that tell us what people's preferences are for *diversity* per se. ERM (1996) used 'diversity' as the subject of valuation for a study of forest management options in the UK. The study is important as one of the few attempts to value diversity rather than resources as such. When initially presented with the issue of biological diversity, focus groups had difficulty understanding what it was. Some even expressed a dislike for the term 'biodiversity'. Once explained, however, 'a majority of people grasp its structure quickly; they appreciate that uniform conifer plantations cannot be conducive to a variety of wildlife, and they see that there must be a cost penalty if forests are to be planted with more open space and a greater variety of trees.'

What should be done if some costs and/or benefits cannot be monetised?

Depending on the context, it may still be possible to reach a conclusion about the outcome of the CBA. Consider the matrix below:

	Bnm > 0	*Bnm < 0 or Cnm > 0*
Bm > Cm	Accept	?
Bm < Cm	?	Reject

Bm refers to monetised benefits and Bnm refers to non-monetised benefits. Similarly with costs, C. Suppose monetised benefits exceed monetised costs and that Bnm > 0. Then the project or policy should be accepted even though we do not know the size of non-monetary benefits because the non-monetary benefits will simply be additional to the monetised benefits which in turn already justify the project.

If, on the other hand, Bm > Cm but Bnm is negative, that is there are non-monetised costs, we do not know whether to accept or reject the project/ policy. But we can 'invert' the analysis and ask whether, judgementally, we think Bm-Cm is sufficient to compensate for the non-monetary costs. At the very least, the procedure forces the decision-maker to list costs and benefits and to ask searching questions about the non-monetised costs. The same procedure can be followed for the final row of the matrix.

Box 2.1 presents an example of how monetary and non-monetary approaches are combined for the appraisal of transport projects.

BOX 2.1   MIXED MONETARY AND NON-MONETARY APPROACHES: THE NATA FRAMEWORK

The UK Government's 1998 Transport White Paper set the agenda for the development of integrated transport at national, regional and local levels. While authorities in the development of local transport strategies have previously adopted many of the principles of integrated transport, the White Paper adapts and formalises these. The new policy provides a framework within which all means must be considered on a level playing field when pursuing a particular end. The ends themselves must also demonstrate coherence with higher order regional and national objectives as well as seeking to address local problems and opportunities.

The Government's five over-arching objectives set out in the White Paper are: to protect and enhance the built and natural environment; to improve safety for all travellers; to contribute to an efficient economy, and to support sustainable economic growth in appropriate locations; to promote accessibility to everyday facilities for all, especially those without a car; and to promote the integration of all forms of transport and land use planning, leading to a better, more efficient transport system. These objectives are to be treated independently with no attempt, at the technical level, to provide value comparisons between them.

The five primary objectives are the basis for appraisal and the first step is to develop sub-criteria against these for the appraisal framework. In the new approach to appraisal (NATA), sub-criteria are carefully selected and defined to avoid double counting of benefits. Where possible this discipline is adhered to in the development of appraisal frameworks though the overlaps and close relationships that exist between criteria need to be recognised and to a degree some double counting is inevitable.

When undertaking a NATA based appraisal, it is recognised that there are areas of appraisal that do not lend themselves to monetary valuation, but which nevertheless will be important in establishing a full understanding of a project's or plan's impact on meeting the five over-arching objectives (and associated sub-objectives). The use of well-established forecasting and valuation techniques allows for sensible quantification of economic costs and benefits and this is a requirement of NATA framework appraisals. The aspects included are capital and operating costs, time savings, and accidents when viewed as an element of overall non-user benefits. These are then used in the calculation of net present values and benefit to cost ratios.

Elsewhere (assessment in relation to the integration, accessibility, safety and environment objectives) the method of evaluation does not rely on monetary valuation, but rather establishing, and where possible quantifying, impacts and relationships using alternative methods. Consequently, the bulk of a NATA framework appraisal does not require or involve monetary valuation of impacts/effects. Given the breadth of objectives against which an appraisal is undertaken there are a number of differing techniques used in coming to an assessment. One is the assessment of impacts using a matrix based on quantification of the number of people affected and the scale and direction of effect, with textual scales used to describe where the impact falls within the matrix. Elsewhere a more descriptive approach, often revolving around the identification of key relationships, is used and coupled with judgement to arrive at an assessment using a textual scale. Textual scales are used to summarise the impact/effect of a project/plan/strategy, with this providing a common method of 'scoring' that can be adopted consistently across the appraisal framework.

Though the principles of NATA are well understood, the method of application inevitably varies according to the level at which appraisal is being undertaken. At the level of minor (low cost) schemes appraisal tends to put less emphasis on detailed evaluation. For major (high cost) schemes there tends to be an expectancy that a high degree of detailed assessment and evaluation will be carried out and that significant data collection and analysis to facilitate this is necessary. At plan or strategy level, a 'higher level' assessment involving the use of aggregate data may be acceptable so as to enable appraisal to be undertaken within reasonable timescales.

2.3   CHOOSING BETWEEN ECONOMIC VALUATION TECHNIQUES

The array of economic valuation techniques ranges across revealed preference and stated preference techniques as shown in Figure 1.4 in Chapter 1. Which techniques are best suited to which problems? Some general guidelines are set out below.

When using stated preferences, the main choice is between choice modelling (CM) and contingent valuation (CV). It is important to take account of the following:

- Generally, CV should be chosen when the WTP for the environmental good or service in total is needed, and CM when WTP for individual attributes is required. CM is also useful if information is needed on relative values for different attributes of an environmental good.
- The use of CM approaches in the context of environmental issues is more recent than that of CV. Therefore, a larger literature using CM approaches and further evidence about their results is required before we can be confident about implementing CM approaches.
- Not all CM techniques are consistent with underlying welfare theory. If welfare-consistent estimates are needed, then choice experiments (or, to a degree, contingent ranking) are preferable to, say, contingent rating.
- Questions such as 'What are you willing to pay?' are thought by some critics of CV to present cognitive problems. CM does not explicitly ask about money values so it is argued that CM is easier for people to understand.
- CM offers a more 'efficient' means of sampling than CV since, typically, more responses are obtained from each individual with CM than with CV.

2.3.1   Use and Non-use Values

One of the issues to be determined before commissioning a study is the extent to which non-use values (NUVs) are likely to be important. The reason is that NUV can only be detected by SP techniques. As a general rule, NUV will potentially be of importance where the object or impact being valued has few substitutes. The absence of substitutes will be an important characteristic of some environmental and cultural resources. This may be fairly obvious in the context of 'national' and fairly unique resources such as the Norfolk Broads or the Yorkshire Dales, but studies suggest that NUV is also important for resources that are held in local regard or which have attracted a wider media interest (for example, the Pevensey Levels, the River Darent). This is not only because substitution is a matter of individuals' subjective preferences but also because, if people believe in some principle such as avoiding the loss of a resource, then it would be wrong for the experts to assume that one resource is a perfectly good substitute for another. There are, therefore, no easy rules for determining at the outset that NUVs are likely to be significant. Focus groups may help test the likelihood of their relevance.

2.3.2 Attributes and Total Values

Choice modelling approaches allow a more direct route to the valuation of the *characteristics* or *attributes* of a good, and of marginal changes in these characteristics, rather than the value of the good *in toto*. This may matter because management decisions, project appraisals and policy appraisals are often mainly concerned with changes in the levels that these attributes take. For example, in the context of environmental resources, the following can be of interest:

- changing pollution levels in rivers, and the impacts on the economic value of health risks and ecosystem risks;
- changes in the appearance of the countryside, through agri-environmental policy initiatives;
- changes in outdoor recreation opportunities in rivers, forests and national parks; and
- changes in the attributes of travel modes.

Contingent valuation can, of course, be used to value such changes, but the number of scenarios that can be considered in any one study is limited. There will be a presumption, therefore, that choice modelling approaches will be preferred over contingent valuation approaches in contexts where it is important to value individual attributes. This advantage has to be traded against some of the weaknesses of choice modelling (see Chapter 6).

2.3.3 Hard versus Soft Data

Whether the perception is justified or not, there remains a fairly widespread view that revealed preference (RP) data are more credible than SP data. The reason for this is that WTP estimates from RP contexts show up in actual markets (housing, land, labour and so on) rather than in hypothetical markets, even if the actual market does not involve the good in question in any direct fashion. Ultimately, WTP responses from SP techniques are going to remain hypothetical and hence there is always a risk of hypothetical bias, and the size or direction of this bias may not be at all easy to determine.

This preference for 'hard' RP data is not confined to sceptics of SP techniques. Many economists simply prefer RP data because they are more used to observing behaviour and outcomes in real markets. But there may be subtle problems with RP techniques. Technically, for example, the hedonic property price approach estimates the value of a marginal change in the provision of the good in question. To value discrete changes, which are often of interest, requires the full 'two stage' approach to hedonic price estimation. This can be complex and the resulting estimates can be very uncertain. Estimates derived from the first stage only, that is, the change in property price with respect to the small change in the variable affecting the property price, are, however, thought to be upper bounds to the theoretically complete estimate if one assumes that there is variation on the extensive margin (for example, among alternative locations), not on the intensive margin (for example, alternative house sizes). Similar problems of interpreting WTP estimates from RP approaches arise with the averting behaviour approach where the good used to trade-off against some negative feature may have other benefits (for example, double glazing as a noise-reducing device has multiple outputs such as anti-burglary and energy conservation). Again, the suggestion is that such WTP estimates will be upper bounds rather than the estimates that may be required for policy purposes. SP approaches may therefore score over RP approaches in this respect.

2.3.4   Contexts where Given Techniques Cannot be Applied

One advantage of SP techniques is that they can, in principle, be applied to any context. In contrast, RP techniques are confined to those contexts where there is an associated market. Hedonic wage risk studies can only value those effects that relate to wages – accident risk is the most widely studied, but less obvious ones such as the value of a warmer climate is another.[1] Similarly, hedonic property studies are relevant only to those factors affecting property prices. As it happens the array of such factors is very wide, ranging from environmental factors to neighbourhood features, social and community factors, infrastructure and so on. Travel-cost approaches are self-evidently limited mainly to recreational contexts.

While SP can be applied to all contexts, special issues related to the cognitive ability of respondents to comprehend the nature of the good do arise. This is especially the case with small changes in risk and perhaps with complex goods with which the respondent is not very familiar.

2.3.5   Other Considerations

Although it may be desirable to recommend a specific technique for a specific impact, such a prescriptive approach is not possible since the site- and purpose-specific characteristics are crucial in the choice of valuation technique.

Time and data available for analysis
Availability of data about the physical measure of environmental impacts is a concern for all valuation techniques. The availability of economic valuation data is typically not a concern for SP studies since the necessary data are generated by the study itself. For this reason, SP studies can take between six months to a year depending on the complexity of the resource and the nature of the potential change to it. A SP study should be implemented as soon as possible after environmental impacts are assessed.

Provided that the necessary economic data are available, RP studies can take about six months to implement. But if such data do not exist, a RP study can take as long as a SP study. Data for travel cost method and random utility models can be collected using surveys. Since such surveys are likely to take similar time and effort as SP surveys, it would be more efficient to design a questionnaire that would enable the application of SP and travel cost and/or random utility models simultaneously. On the other hand, in the absence of data, hedonic pricing is unlikely to be feasible since the necessary data (especially time series) cannot be collected within the time scale of a study. Benefits transfer can, in principle, be applied in a matter of weeks.

Significance of the environmental resource impacted
The more important the resource and the more significant the impact, the greater the need for as comprehensive an analysis as possible. Benefits transfer is constrained, for example, by the limited coverage of all aspects of biodiversity damage in the literature and by its insensitivity to site-specific characteristics. RP techniques are limited to the use values associated with those resources that are reflected in actual markets. The scope of SP techniques is the largest in this context, given that potentially all impacts can be covered and both use and non-use values can be estimated.

Cost
The cost of the valuation exercise depends on the complexity of the proposed measure and its impacts, which affect the complexity of the questionnaire design, the size of the sample and the complexity of the data analysis. Benefits transfer is relatively inexpensive given that there is little need for

data collection and significantly less time input is required. SP studies can cost between £50,000 and £200,000 (although some studies have cost millions of dollars in the US; see Section 2.2.3 for more details on the costs of studies). A comprehensive RP study could also cost towards the higher end of this range if the necessary data are not readily available, and towards the lower end of this range (or may be even lower) if such data are ready. However, the crucial criterion is not the absolute cost of a valuation exercise but its incremental cost in terms of additional information it provides and the increased accuracy and reliability of the results produced. The cost of the valuation exercise should also be seen in the light of the total costs of an action. Even the most expensive form of SP study is a small amount relative to the total cost of a policy or project that can cost many millions of pounds. Spending more at the beginning of an assessment process is usually more cost-effective than spending to mitigate the outcome of a wrong decision afterwards.

Timing of the valuation exercise
It can be difficult for a SP study to elicit people's preferences for the environmental impacts of concern and distinguish these from strategic choices once the incident causing damage becomes a political issue. This is an empirical issue and one which can be dealt with by adjusting the questionnaire design. For example, the contingent valuation study undertaken for the Exxon Valdez oil spill asks the respondents how much they are willing to pay to avoid a similar incident in the future, rather than asking for WTP for restoration or WTA for damage (Carson, Mitchell, Hanemann, Kopp, Presser and Ruud 1992). This puts the valuation question in a more neutral setting. What is most important is to ensure that the respondents are given incentives to answer truthfully. This can be achieved if people care about the damage and believe that note will be taken of their responses.

Limitations of economic valuation techniques due to insufficient information or data on the nature of the non-market effect are covered in Section 2.2.4. Other potential limitations or caveats of economic valuation techniques are discussed in Chapter 12.

2.4   COMMISSIONING A VALUATION STUDY: A CHECKLIST

This section suggests some basic guidance for commissioning an economic valuation study that involves the use of stated preference techniques.

2.4.1 Social Goals and CBA

Using a structure such as Figure 2.1, determine whether economic valuation is likely to provide most, all, or only some of the guidance needed for the question in hand. Policy analysts continue to debate the comparative merits of structured approaches, such as CBA, and 'multidimensional' approaches. Multidimensional approaches might regard aspects of 'process' and 'participation' as being just as important as securing an economically efficient outcome. If so, a decision has to be made as to whether CBA can be 'moulded' to meet these wider concerns. If it cannot be moulded in this way, CBA will be only a part of the guidance required. The remaining guidance may come automatically from the political process itself, or it may be that the other goals have to be met by investing in particular institutions. Or it may be that CBA can be executed in a broader fashion. Thus SP techniques have far more potential for involving the public in a participatory mode because of the use of questionnaires, focus groups and so on. RP techniques effectively 'close off' the participatory mode.

Establish initially how important distributional considerations are likely to be. Rough guidance might be obtained by looking at household expenditure surveys to see how important certain expenditure items are in family budgets. Policies on motor vehicle use, for example, may be regressive within the vehicle owning population but not across the whole population (including non-owners of vehicles). Where distribution is likely to be important, the goal of distributive justice might be incorporated into the CBA at the very least by stakeholder assessment (see Chapter 1), but perhaps more formally by careful assessment of the cost and benefit incidence of the project or policy. Accept that quantitative consensus on distributional weights is unlikely to be forthcoming and may in turn produce a 'black box syndrome' whereby only the analysts understand what the weights mean.[2] Challenge the consultant to devise a methodology for highlighting distributional concerns. It should be noted, however, that *treating* distributional concerns is a political decision.

2.4.2 The Required Level of Accuracy

Make a judgement about just how accurate any estimates of economic values need to be for the question in hand as this would affect the sample size and questionnaire design (see Chapters 3 and 4). For projects and policies that are likely to have major consequences, accuracy in benefit estimation will matter. A rough guide to this magnitude is the cost of the measure itself. For projects this is usually known fairly accurately, for policies it is often not known in the absence of a detailed compliance cost assessment. While primary valuation studies may appear expensive when expressed in absolute terms, a different guideline is what the study will cost relative to the cost of the project or policy going wrong. Thus, a general guide is to ask what is at stake if the measure is unsuccessful, and to compare that judgement with the cost of undertaking the study. Where budgets really are tight, acknowledge that a good benefits transfer (BT) study is likely to be just as good, if not better, than a poor SP or RP study. But if the decision is to opt for BT, make sure the context is one where there are adequate primary studies for BT to be performed properly. Where sufficient previous studies exist, it is not unreasonable to expect some meta-analysis in a BT study. In many contexts, too few studies exist for any BT analysis (see Annex 1.1). Seek guidance from acknowledged experts who can advise very quickly on the number of studies in a given area.

Ensure that the valuation study can capture most of the likely costs and benefits or, if not, that it is capable of helping to determine which the most important costs and benefits are for measurement purposes. There is a risk that evaluating only part of the overall picture will give rise to the impression that the monetised impacts are more important that the non-monetised impacts. A particular problem may arise if measured benefits are less than measured costs but unmeasured benefits remain (see Section 2.2 above).

2.4.3   The Issue of 'Standing'

Make a clear decision at the outset as to *whose* values matter. If the judgement is that experts rather than citizens are in the best position to provide the relevant advice, there is no need for an SP approach, although imposing a cost–benefit structure to the expert assessment is still going to be useful. To avoid paternalism, where possible, secure a citizen-based CBA and some form of expert assessment together. It is now quite common to juxtapose citizen-based surveys with 'Delphi' procedures that seek consensus from experts. If it is the general public that matters, further decisions must be made. Be prepared for expert and citizen preferences to diverge.

Are only UK residents relevant or should overseas visitors and overseas residents be included? Considerations relevant to this question were briefly discussed in Chapter 1 and are elaborated upon in Chapter 3.

Is the policy or project likely to have long term consequences for future generations? If so, decide early on if it is satisfactory to adopt a conventional discounting approach to CBA or whether some supplementary procedure is required to account for sustainability considerations. Some analysts argue that CBA already incorporates much of this long-term impact through the way in which preferences are formed, through the discount rate (if this is open to independent estimation) and through relative price effects. Others argue that there may be some 'premium' to be applied to activities that serve long-term interests.

Are non-human interests at stake? All preference-oriented procedures are human-interest biased. If non-human wellbeing is involved, some form of ethical guidance from experts needs to be sought. However, be careful not to confuse the role of moral issues in the debate over the policy or project – where there is already a political or planning inquiry arena for that debate – and the role of moral issues in the CBA. The proper place for the moral debate is outside the CBA (see, for example, Quiggin, 1993; MacRae and Whittington, 1997).

Determine early on if non-use values are likely to be important. This is likely to be the case where some fairly unique asset is affected by the decision (for example, national parks, SSSIs, cultural and recorded heritage, skylines with fine views, threatened species). If NUV is likely to be important only SP techniques can be used (see Section 2.3.1).

2.4.4   Issues with Stated Preference Techniques

Where risks to human health from the project are very low, or where perceived changes in the environment are very small, seek early expert guidance on whether SP techniques are capable of 'detecting' small changes.

Be clear about what you expect to get from the survey. Chapters 4–7 indicate what can be expected and Chapter 10 provides guidelines as to how to present the results.

You may want to experience a SP questionnaire yourself. If you have time, put yourself in the place of a respondent and see how easy or difficult the questions are to answer.

Determine whether the SP technique is to be validated by the use of another valuation technique. If not, validation will be 'internal', that is, through the application of tests to see if the WTP estimates 'make sense'. The use of two valuation techniques at the same time helps to secure validation but may not be very relevant if there is a judgement that non-use values are important (remember, RP techniques cannot elicit non-use values). Of course, running two valuation studies will be more expensive and some reassurance that RP and SP techniques are consistent can be found in the extensive review of this kind of approach to validity – see Carson, Flores, Martin and Wright (1996). More on this discussion can be found in Chapter 11.

2.4.5 Using Expert Advice

As a general matter, and subject to the confidentiality that may surround discussions of such studies, seek external expert advice early on *before* the terms of reference are issued. One or two days' consultancy may avoid major mistakes that will cost many times this amount.

Ensure that acknowledged independent experts are appointed to membership of the steering group of the study.

If, for some reason, independent experts cannot be appointed to the steering group, appoint one or two peer reviewers. Try to involve peer reviewers *before* study drafts are at a stage where the consultant has no real flexibility to change a report in light of peer reviewer comments.

2.4.6 Assessing the Consultants

All contracts will be open to competitive tender. Encourage established groups to register their interest in tendering, rather than relying on those who seek registration, or on past consultants.

Ensure that consultants at least have access to 'state of the art' advice on how to carry out SP studies. Typically, this will mean involving one or more academics, and may also involve making use of experts from outside the UK and especially from North America. Seek advice from independent experts not involved in tendering as to who are the leading authorities in the relevant area of SP application. Ideally, the government could have a committee of outside independent experts (generally academics) to advise them on merits of accepting the contract proposals received. Ideally, the membership of such a committee should be rotating.

Inform the tendering consultants of the policy context of the SP study. This should include the possible uses to which the study may be put, indications of major disagreements within a department or across departments about the role that SP techniques (and CBA in general) may play, and the sensitivities concerning any likely outcome of the study. This provides the consultants with a chance to present information in a more helpful way, rather than discovering later that a lot of hard work is 'shelved' because of issues that could perhaps have been accommodated in the study design.

Always ask for a schedule and deadlines. However, consultants are probably best placed to know how long a given piece of work will take, and asking for excessively tight deadlines can compromise quality. Subject to what will often be serious time constraints on commissioning a study, invite tenderers to make comments about the terms of reference. *The most common weakness of terms of reference is asking for too much in too short a time.* SP studies take time because of the need to engage with focus groups, conduct pilot studies, engage in full interviewing and econometrically processing data. Attempting to get the consultants to do too much simply results in medium-grade research. Ultimately, if the research can be challenged by those stakeholders affected by the outcome, not only is more time taken up, delaying the policy process, but serious damage can be done to the credibility of the techniques being commissioned. Consultants will often have pressures of their own to agree to terms of reference and to time constraints that, in their better judgement, they might not wish to. Some flexibility in the terms of reference gives more scope for consultants to say what can be done in the time available, rather than responding in a 'take it or leave it' fashion.

Open government now favours the release of studies in public format, for example, as a priced or free document from government sources. Such a policy increases public exposure and hence should improve quality. Care has to be taken, however, that dissemination policy of this kind does not provide 'equal quality' status to all publications. Ultimately, some research will not be of the highest standard whatever safeguards are in place. One additional safeguard is to invite consultants to state their own plans for dissemination in the event that the document will be made public. Outlets that involve further peer review (for example, journal publication) again add to assurances about quality control.

Where possible, ensure that commissioning project officers and consultants are aware of any overall reviews of experience with stated preference techniques and CBA even if most of these are from the US (for example, MacRae and Whittington (1997), Bateman and Willis (1999), Carson, Flores and Meade (1996)). Newly developed and rapidly expanding economic valuation databases can also prove useful. These include the EVRI database from Environment Canada (www.evri.ec.gc.ca), the Envalue database from the New South Wales Environment Protection Agency (www.epa.nsw.gov.au/envalue) and the UK DEFRA reference list (www.defra.gov.uk/environment/evslist/index.htm).

If time permits, invite the consultants to present the results of the study to a seminar to which known adversaries are also invited. Ensure that actual questionnaires are routinely provided in the report and to seminar participants – this is a requirement for academic publication in many cases. Guidance on reporting is provided in Chapter 10.

2.5　A TYPICAL WORKPLAN FOR A STATED PREFERENCE STUDY

A typical workplan for a SP study and the questions that need to be answered in each stage are presented in Figure 2.2. Both contingent valuation and choice modelling studies follow this timetable, even though they differ in the questionnaire design and data analysis stages.

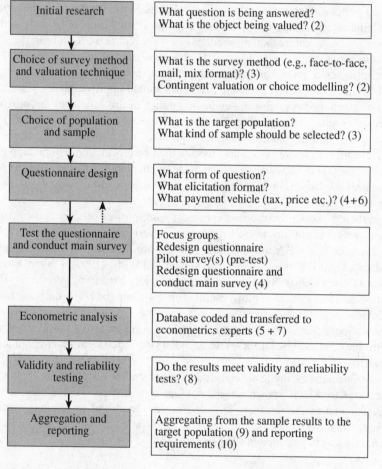

Note: The numbers in brackets in the boxes on the right hand side of the figure indicate the relevant chapter numbers in this manual.

Figure 2.2　A typical workplan for a stated preference study

NOTES

1. Wage rates have been found to vary inversely with a better climate as measured by temperature and/or rainfall, that is, wages are less for locations where climate is better.
2. A cautionary note: the official UK social discount rate incorporates a quite explicit quantitative distributional judgement in the form of the 'elasticity of the marginal utility of consumption'. Arguably, implicit distributional judgements across social groups now should be consistent with this parameter of inequality aversion.

PART II

Stated preference techniques

3. Population, sample and survey mode

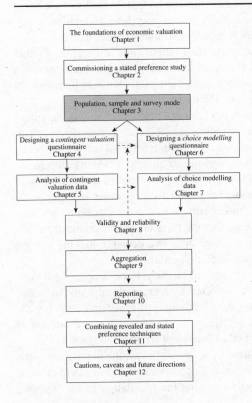

The foundations of economic valuation
Chapter 1

↓

Commissioning a stated preference study
Chapter 2

↓

Population, sample and survey mode
Chapter 3

↓

Designing a *contingent valuation* questionnaire
Chapter 4

Designing a *choice modelling* questionnaire
Chapter 6

Analysis of contingent valuation data
Chapter 5

Analysis of choice modelling data
Chapter 7

↓

Validity and reliability
Chapter 8

↓

Aggregation
Chapter 9

↓

Reporting
Chapter 10

↓

Combining revealed and stated preference techniques
Chapter 11

↓

Cautions, caveats and future directions
Chapter 12

SUMMARY

This chapter discusses the methods for identifying the target population for a valuation exercise and sampling from that population together with some of the problems or biases that may be encountered. The following are the important questions that need to be answered for the target population to be determined: (i) Who is likely to be affected by the change in question? (ii) Who is likely to have some knowledge of the issue or to have thought about it beforehand? and (iii) Who is it reasonable to think will pay (or ask compensation) for it?

Sampling methods covered in this chapter are non-probabilistic (convenience, judgement and quota samples) and probabilistic (simple random, systematic, stratified and cluster sampling).

The chapter also presents the different survey modes since this issue is closely linked to the choice and the size of the sample (which is also discussed). The main modes covered here are mail surveys, telephone interviews and face-to-face interviews. Combinations of these main methods such as drop-off, mail and telephone and computer-assisted surveys are also discussed.

3.1 DEFINING THE TARGET POPULATION

The target population consists of those who receive the benefits or the costs of the non-market effect in question. Ensuring that the population is defined accurately requires expert judgement, interrogation of available data sources and, potentially, the collection of new data. For geographically well-defined goods (for example, recreational areas) those who benefit will include users and those holding non-use values. Both groups may be geographically dispersed although sampling of users is in theory straightforward. The population bearing the costs of a good may be distributed quite differently to that benefiting from the good (for example, national parks are paid for on a national basis while those who benefit from their existence may be relatively more concentrated within and around the park).

In cases where the relevant population is not readily apparent, secondary sources may provide a useful input indicating who may benefit from or pay for the good in question. Examples might include: the use of tourist board information in studies of open-access goods; angling and boating club membership in water pollution incidents; maps of transmission line routes in respect of valuing associated disamenity; and lists of water rate payers in assessments of water improvement benefits. While access to such data may be restricted, it may well be the case that the relevant organisations are either directly involved in the valuation exercise or have a decision-making interest in its findings such that information is made available.

The 'user population' is relatively easy to identify. For example, the households living in the area that will be affected by increased noise due to a road scheme can be found by mapping the distribution of noise and counting the households living in that area. Similarly, if the population of interest is anglers at a lake whose recreational activity will be affected (possibly negatively) by the visual intrusion caused by a new highway, the population is the total number of anglers using that lake. Such population data could exist or could be collected either by simply counting the population or by sampling and extrapolation.

Determining the population holding non-use values is not as straightforward. There is no clear-cut rule to predict the existence or absence of non-use values. The resource could be nationally unique, in which case, the relevant population is likely to be the whole nation or locally unique or important, in which case the relevant population is the local one. In some cases, the resource could be of global importance such as a UNESCO recognised World Heritage Site, in which case whether the global population would be affected would be hard to predict in advance.

Many studies assume that if non-use value exists, it must exist for all non-users. This is the rationale for extrapolating mean non-use values to a whole population, usually the national population. It is more correct to sample the non-user population by geographical location. For example, for a site A, the presence of non-use value would be tested by sampling the population, say,

100 km from A, 200 km and so on. One hypothesis is that non-use values will decline with distance – a 'distance decay' notion. This hypothesis is borne out in a few studies, but others have found no effect of distance on non-use value. Accordingly, there are no *a priori* rules for determining the aggregation procedure. Geographical sampling must take place. This requirement imposes a limitation on benefits transfer (see Annex 1.1).

Factors to consider when determining user and non-user population(s) include:

- *Uniqueness or substitutability of the good or service in question.* Unique resources (whether at local, country or global scale) are more likely to attract non-use values and hence their valuation requires sampling beyond the user population.
- *Familiarity of respondents with the good or service.* Related to the uniqueness, the familiarity with certain resources can decline with the distance from them. It is conceivable that beyond a certain distance, the good or the service that is the topic of the survey will have no effect on the population. However, it may be difficult or misleading to decide where this 'cut-off' is prior to the survey.
- *Scale of the change in question.* The more significant a change is, the more likely that it will affect larger populations. For example, a small drop in the water level of a reservoir may affect bird populations there (requiring sampling of, say, birdwatchers only), while a larger decline can also affect boating (requiring sampling of both birdwatchers and boaters).
- *Context in which the valuation results will be used (related to the payment vehicle).* For example, a local tax can only be relevant to the local population and visitor fees to visitors, while for a national tax, a national sampling is likely to be more representative.

Table 3.1 provides some examples of user populations (see Chapter 9 for more discussion).

The question of whose costs and benefits count is also closely linked to the geographical boundaries of a CBA, and not only in terms of non-use values. Conventionally, any costs and benefits that accrue outside the nation of concern have been excluded from a CBA. Although this rule applies in most situations, in some cases the 'affected' population (especially that affected by environmental impacts) can be outside the national boundaries. For example:

- Where the environmental change in question relates to impacts which are the subject of binding international agreement, then the relevant

Table 3.1   Selected user populations for each non-market effect

Effect	User population
Public human risk	Those who live within the geographical range over which the pollution in question is effective or those who may be using a contaminated resource. Both the geographical range and population at risk from using contaminated resources should be identified by the scientific evidence on the effects of pollutants. All users of all modes of transport who face risk of accidents.
Ecosystem risks	Local residents, users of the affected environmental resources who are not local residents, and visitors to the area if open to recreation.
Disamenity	Local residents, visitors who should be grouped according to their recreational activity and the area they reside in, and if relevant, workers.
Nature conservation and management	Local residents, and visitors who should be grouped according to their recreational activity.
Time (present)	Whole population, visitors to the site(s) in question for leisure time, and users of the relevant mode(s) of transport for waiting and changeover time.
Workplace	Workers and other users of the workplace.
Information	Anyone to whom the said information is available including those who make direct use of the information in order to incorporate it into their service and product, e.g. makers of documentaries and those who use processed information, e.g. viewers of documentaries.

costs and benefits should be defined in terms of the signatories to that agreement. In the context of global warming or stratospheric ozone depletion, for example, the relevant benefits and costs would be global. In the context of acidifying pollutants, the relevant boundary for any European country would be the rest of Europe, or the European countries who may be affected by the emissions of acidifying pollutants from the country in question. Even without international legal agreements, any nation may feel a moral obligation to account for its impacts on others.

- Some changes may not be the concern of national property rights only. A cultural asset that is a World Heritage Site, for example, is, effectively, an asset over which the world as a whole might claim property rights in some form. It is then wholly appropriate to measure the benefits of conserving that site so as to include the benefits or costs to people outside national boundaries. This international property rights issue becomes of practical concern, if such transboundary benefits could be appropriated by pricing policies (for example, charging others for the conservation of cultural assets).

Following the guidance here for determining the correct target population is essential for avoiding *population choice bias* which has significant impacts for the aggregation of individual or household WTP or WTA over the population (see Chapter 9).

3.2 THE NEED FOR AND THE IMPORTANCE OF SAMPLING

Given the target population identified for the valuation study, an appropriate sample that represents this population must be obtained. The sample is the subset of the target population to whom the survey will be administered. A sample is used to save the time and, especially, the expense that would otherwise be required to survey the entire population.

Sample design involves deciding both which types of people to interview and how many of them. The guiding principle is to select a subset of the target population such that the results of the survey can accurately and reliably be extrapolated to the entire population. From the statistical perspective, this involves considerations of bias (whether the sample produces results that are unbiased and representative of the population) and variance (whether the sample is large enough to produce a sufficiently precise estimate of the mean or median WTP). From the survey research perspective, there are some other important aspects of survey reliability and quality that are further explored in Chapter 9.

The chief alternative modes of data collection are face-to-face interviews, telephone interviews, mail surveys and some combination thereof (see Section 3.5). The sampling design inherently interacts with the choice of survey mode, since different modes entail different degrees of access to given individuals, different costs of data collection, and different settings for the data collection. Thus, the final determination of a survey mode and a sampling design involves a trade-off between the costs and logistical practicalities of data collection, the statistical properties of the estimates derived from data thus collected, and survey research considerations regarding the quality and reliability of the data.

3.3   THE SAMPLING FRAME

Given the choice of a target population, the next step is to put together a list of the target population, known as the *sample frame population*, from which the sample will ultimately be drawn. Some examples of a sample frame population are: all the dwelling units within a city, all the voters registered in a city, all households with a telephone, all the residential and commercial customers of an electricity utility, all subscribers to a sportfishing magazine, all the members of an environmental group, or all the visitors to a particular beach. In many cases the sample frame is an explicit list (for example, a master list of residential addresses, or of registered voters, or of utility customers and so on). In the case of beach visitors, however, there is an implicit sample frame rather than an explicit list.

Choosing the sample frame requires some prior decision regarding survey mode: if one plans a telephone survey, for example, the voter list is likely to be a poor choice of sample frame, since not all voters may have phones and not all people who have phones may be voters. Above all, the sample frame must also be consistent with the target population. The ideal frame is one where every member of the target population is listed once and only once. This makes it possible to select a random sample from the frame (see Section 3.4) without having to worry about under- or over-sampling some particular subset of the target population. To the extent that the sample frame provides a biased or unreliable coverage of the target population, this is known in Groves' (1989) terminology as *coverage error* or *sampling frame bias*. Coverage error is one potential source of *survey error*, of which others will be identified below. The survey designer aims to minimise the overall survey error subject to budgetary limitations.

There is often some trade-off between the cost and coverage of a sample frame: lists of specific, smaller populations may be more readily available than a list of the general population. Unfortunately, few sample frames are perfect. Typical problems are that the frame omits certain members of the target population, includes them more than once, or includes people not of interest to the study. The survey designer must work around these problems as much as possible.

An example involving a general population list is using a telephone directory as the sample frame when the target population is all adult residents in a city. People without phones have no chance of being selected. People with unlisted numbers, or with new listings, will not appear in the telephone directory, although this source of coverage error can in principle be eliminated through *random digit dialling* (RDD). Some people with phones may not be adults or permanent residents of the city; these can be *screened out* at the beginning of the telephone survey. In addition, households with two or more phone numbers, or in which household members with different last names have separate listings, have a *greater* chance of being included in the sample than those with a single phone number and a single listing. To handle this, many phone surveys now include a question asking how many different phone numbers there are in the household (apart from fax numbers or lines used exclusively for access to the Internet), so that households with multiple entries in the sample frame can be appropriately down-weighted, that is, an estimate of fax and computer lines will need to be subtracted from the number of total phone lines. Omissions, duplicate entries and inaccuracies can also be a problem for sample frames based on lists of special populations (for example, the membership list for an environmental group may be out of date, incomplete or simply contain wrong information).

In some cases, it may be difficult or impossible to obtain a sample frame that lists the target population. In those cases, a surrogate procedure must be devised. Suppose, for example, that the target population is adults over 18 who have visited the Yorkshire Dales National Park during the preceding 12 months. There may be no lists for a population like this. Instead, one may have to resort to some more general sample frame and then use screening to narrow it down to the population of interest. Another example of non-list sampling is when the target population is visitors to a particular beach. In that case, one may need to go on site and sample people who show up at the beach. Such *intercept surveys* have their own complications, since there may be more than one entrance or exit, more people may show up at some times than others, and the composition of visitors may differ substantially during different times of the year (for example, school holidays versus other times). The best strategy for an intercept survey is generally to sample people either as they arrive or as they leave. A common way to implement this is to sample hours of the day or the week; during the sampled hours, one might sample every n^{th} person who arrives or who leaves. But to do this effectively requires having enough interviewers so that the same proportion of visitors is interviewed at every access point and during busy as well as slow times; the logistics and cost can become quite substantial.

3.4   CHOOSING THE SAMPLE

Given the sample frame population, the next step is to select a particular sample from the frame. Depending on how this is done, there could be sampling error and/or non-response error. *Sampling error* arises because the item of interest is measured on a subset of the population. To the extent that different subsets exhibit different characteristics with respect to the item of interest, the sample survey estimates will vary depending on which subset happens to be measured. *(Unit) non-response error*, including what is sometimes called *sample selection bias*, arises because some persons in the sample frame cannot be located or refuse the request for an interview. To the extent that they have different characteristics than those who are included in the sample, the survey statistics and the aggregation process can be affected (see Chapters 5 and 9). The aim in selecting a sampling approach is to minimise both sources of error subject, as always, to budgetary limitations.

The main sampling techniques are presented in Table 3.2. The main choice to be made is between probabilistic and non-probabilistic designs: the former is a sampling procedure in which each element of the population has a fixed probabilistic chance of being selected for the sample, while in the latter the sampling procedure relies on the personal judgement of the researcher. Non-probabilistic designs are simpler and cheaper to implement and are useful for exploratory research and pilot studies where findings are treated as preliminary. Probabilistic sampling is typically used for conclusive research where the results are to be extrapolated for the population of interest.

Table 3.2   Taxonomy of sampling designs

Non-probabilistic designs	Convenience samples
	Judgement samples
	Quota samples
Probabilistic designs	Simple random-sampling
	Systematic sampling
	Stratified sampling
	Cluster sampling

Probability sampling is typically more costly and less convenient than the various non-probability alternatives. Its major advantage is that it permits the use of statistical theory to derive the properties of the sample estimators. This makes it possible to correct for bias in sample selection and to construct confidence intervals for the population parameters using the sample data.

With non-probability sampling, no such theoretical development is possible. Some members of the population may have a strong chance of being chosen, others may have no chance at all, and there is no way to tell the specific probability in either case. Consequently, the researcher has to rely on her subjective evaluation of the survey results.

3.4.1 Non-probabilistic Design

Convenience samples are the most elementary, and least satisfactory, form of sampling: one assembles a sample haphazardly, at the convenience of the researcher and – by implication – with the minimal control over the selection process. An example would be when a professor recruits college students as subjects, or a newspaper conducts a straw poll and invites its readers to send in their vote on some issue. In a *judgement (or 'purposive') sample*, by contrast, a (typically small) panel of respondents judged to be representative of the target population is assembled. The selection is controlled but non-random. *Quota samples* emerged as the preferred sampling method in political opinion polls and market research in the 1930s. Here selection is controlled (in principle) by the interviewers, who are directed to ensure that the samples they survey contain given proportions (or quotas) of various types of re-spondents, designed to reflect the population of interest. For example, so many men, so many women, so many people aged 21–40, 41–60 and over 60. However, the ultimate selection of respondents is not made by a probability mechanism.

3.4.2 Probabilistic Design

Probability sampling was first proposed around the turn of the last century. However, it was not until the mid 1930s that the first systematic development of the statistical theory underlying probability sampling was provided. By about 1940, probability sampling was deemed to be the preferred method by mathematical statisticians. Probability sampling is now recognised as the gold standard for survey sampling. With probability sampling, each element in the population frame has a known and non-zero probability of being selected. The selection procedure involves the use of a randomised procedure, such as a computer-generated list of random numbers.

A number of probability sampling methods have been developed to serve various purposes. The most basic method is *simple random sampling* in which every element of the sample frame is given an equal chance of being selected. A related approach is *systematic sampling*, in which one selects every k^{th} element from a randomly-ordered population frame.

With *stratified sampling*, the sample frame population is divided into distinct subpopulations, or strata. A separate and independent sample is selected with each stratum, using random sampling with either the same sampling fraction for each of the strata (*proportionate stratification*) or different sampling fractions (*disproportionate stratification*). The data are used to develop separate within-stratum estimates. Finally, the separate stratum estimates are combined (weighted) to form an overall estimate for the entire population. One reason to use stratification is if the strata are themselves of independent interest, for example, because they represent key subgroups of the population for which the researcher wishes to obtain separate estimates. An example is where some subgroups of interest account for a small fraction of the population. In a beach study, for example, surfers may be believed to have different preferences than other beach goers, but they may account for only 5 per cent of the population of beach goers. A simple random sample of 1,000 beach users would therefore generate only about 50 surfers, far too small a sample for effective analysis. With stratified sampling, one is free to over-sample surfers in order to obtain a sufficient sample size for separate analysis. Another reason for stratification arises if variances differ between strata or if survey costs are different for different strata. In those cases, stratified sampling can greatly increase sampling efficiency for a given overall sample size or survey budget. Finally, the creation of strata permits the use of different sample designs for different portions of the population. An example is piecing together separate frames for different strata in the absence of a single frame that uniformly covers the entire population.

With *clustered sampling*, the population is divided into a set of groups or 'clusters' but, unlike stratified sampling, one selects only a random sample of the clusters. Strictly defined, cluster sampling involves sampling *all* the elements within the selected clusters, but the term is also used more loosely to cover multi-stage sampling, in which one selects only *a random sample* of the elements within the selected clusters. An example of cluster sampling would be to divide a city into zones, randomly select a set of zones, and then survey every household within the selected zones. In a multi-stage sample, by contrast, one would survey only a sample of households within the selected zones. In both cases, the sampling units in the first stage are different from those in the second stage (and similarly if there are more than two stages). The elements in the first stage are the clusters, commonly called the *primary sampling units* (PSUs), while the elements in the second stage are the elements of the particular clusters selected, referred to as *secondary units* or *subunits*.

This last step – selecting the respondent from within a household – must be emphasised because it is often overlooked. In some circumstances, *any* adult member of the household will suffice, because he or she can speak for the entire household and does not need to be chosen randomly or screened for any particular characteristic. In this case, the respondent can often be anyone over 18, and no further selection is needed. However, to the extent that the researcher is concerned with individual preferences, she cannot be satisfied with whoever answers the phone in a telephone survey, comes to the door in a face-to-face survey, or answers the mail in a mail survey. Moreover, this is likely to be highly non-random across members of the household. The typical experience is that older people and females are more likely to pick up the phone in telephone surveys, or be found at home in face-to-face surveys, than younger or male household members. In mail surveys, by contrast, there tends to be a preponderance of male as well as older household respondents. For higher quality SP surveys, it will probably be desirable to employ random selection of an adult household member. One way to do this in a telephone or face-to-face interview is to ask at the outset for the person 18 years of age or older, say, *who had the most recent birthday*. Another, more refined, procedure is for the interviewer to ask the initial respondent to list all the household members over 18 by gender and age, and then randomly select a person from this list with whom to continue the interview. In both cases, the selected individual may not be present at that moment, necessitating one or more callbacks to complete the interview. Box 3.1 presents an example of sampling design in Great Britain.

For surveys of large populations that possess some sort of hierarchical structure, *multi-stage sampling* is generally more convenient and more economical than one-stage simple random sampling. Such designs are extremely common for contingent valuation surveys of large populations. In face-to-face surveys of a widespread population, some clustering of interviews is a necessity because it would be impossibly expensive to scatter individual interviews across the entire population. Multi-stage sampling is also attractive when no overall sample frame is available. For example, if the target population is households in England, one could employ a two-stage design where the PSUs are census tracts; one first selects a sample of census tracts and then takes a sample of households within the selected census tracts. Similarly, if the target population is adults over 18, one might employ a three-stage design, with the same first two stages as above and a third stage in which one randomly samples adults within the selected households. Most good survey designs are multi-stage designs with initial stratification, some type of clustering, and then some type of respondent selection procedure.

BOX 3.1   SAMPLING DESIGN: SOME TRANSPORT SAFETY ILLUSTRATIONS

Examples of stratified, random sampling designed to produce representative samples of the adult population of Great Britain are provided by two SP road safety valuation studies by Jones-Lee (1989) and Jones-Lee et al. (1993).

The sample for the first study was selected by NOP Market Research Limited using their standard procedure, which essentially operated in three stages. At the first stage, a systematic sample of 90 parliamentary constituencies was selected under a procedure which ensures: (i) that constituencies are selected with probability proportional to their electorates (so that if second stage samples of electors of equal size are chosen from each selected constituency then all electors in Great Britain have equal probability of being selected); and (ii) the constituencies selected are representative of the regions of Great Britain and, within region, representative of type, that is metropolitan, other urban, mixed or rural, and, within region and type, representative of electoral voting behaviour, as reflected by the ratio of Conservative to Labour votes at the 1979 General Election.

At the second stage of sampling a cluster sample of 18 electors was selected from each of the 90 constituencies selected at the first stage. Finally, in the third stage of sampling one non-elector aged 16 or over was selected at random from each household containing a selected elector and other non-electors. In contrast to the desirable properties of the first stage of sampling, the second stage involved the economical but statistically less desirable technique of cluster sampling, while the third stage represented the only practical means of sampling non-electors.

The sample for the second study was selected by the Office of Population Censuses and Surveys, again using a three-stage stratified sampling procedure. At the first stage, 60 postal sectors were selected so as to be representative of Great Britain in terms of geographical region, social class and car ownership/non-ownership. At the second stage, within each sampled postal sector a systematic sample of postal addresses was selected with the number of addresses in each sector being proportional to the total number of addresses in the geographical region concerned. Finally, at the third stage, one person aged 17 or over was selected at random from each sampled postal address.

While this sampling procedure clearly had several desirable features, its one potential limitation was that at the first stage, if the sampled postal sector lay outside a 50-mile radius of the location of the nearest Transport Research Laboratory interviewer, then that postal sector was abandoned and another selected. However, in the event, it proved to be necessary to make only 70 selections in order to yield 60 postal sectors that met the 50-mile radius criterion.

3.5   CHOOSING THE SURVEY MODE

The main survey modes are:

- *Mail surveys*: sending to a sample of respondents a questionnaire by mail; respondents then complete the questionnaires themselves and send them back to the researchers;
- *Telephone interviews*: telephoning a sample of respondents and interviewing them; and
- *Face-to-face interviews*: respondents are asked questions by an interviewer, face-to-face:
  In-home survey: the interview takes place in the respondents' homes; or
  Intercept surveys: the interview takes place in a location outside the home (for example, on the street, in a park).

Each data collection method differs in terms of cost, time necessary to collect the data, quality of data, quantity of data, sample control, response rate and the degree of complexity and versatility allowed. Most importantly, the design of the questionnaire must take into account and be consistent with the chosen data collection method. For example, a questionnaire requiring the use of visual aids cannot be administered solely by telephone, and a mail SP survey must contain simple questions presented in an appealing way.

In terms of Groves' (1989) classification of survey error, these issues fall within his category of *measurement error*, defined as errors associated with inaccuracies in the responses recorded on the survey instruments. These can arise from:

- the effects of the interviewers on the respondents' answers to the survey questions;
- error due to the respondents, arising from their inability to answer questions, their lack of requisite effort to obtain the correct answer, or other psychological factors;
- error due to weaknesses in the wording of the survey questionnaire; and
- error due to effects of the mode of data collection.

Groves goes on to note that:

> Most methods that attempt to reduce these various errors have cost implications for the survey. This occurs because administrative features of a survey design can affect the size of these errors (e.g. interviewer training, sample design and size, effort at persuading sample persons to co-operate). Further, these errors can be linked to one another in practice – attempting to decrease one source of error may merely increase another (e.g. reducing non-response by aggressively persuading sample persons to co-operate may result in larger measurement errors in the survey data).

Thus, the sources of measurement error are by no means independent. In particular, there can be interactions between the survey mode and interviewer error or respondent error (more discussion on these issues can be seen in Chapters 4, 8 and 9).

The least ambiguous ranking of survey modes is with respect to *cost*. As shown in Chapter 2, mail surveys are by far the cheapest, since they avoid the expense of interviewers. Telephone surveys are intermediate in cost; there is the expense of the interviewer as well as the phone call, but these are often relatively short calls of perhaps 10–15 minutes' duration, and they take up far less time than if the interviewer had to travel to the respondent's home. Because of the travel requirements, face-to-face interviews are time consuming, logistically challenging and expensive.

Although experiences vary, the ranking of survey modes with respect to *response rates* tends to be inverse to the ranking of costs. Unless they are carefully managed, mail surveys of the general population tend to elicit the lowest response rates, sometimes on the order of 25–50 per cent, which would generally be considered unacceptable. Telephone surveys can typically elicit response rates in the order of 60–75 per cent, although some resistance is now appearing to participation in telephone surveys because of people's irritation at the heavy volume of telemarketing in the evenings and on weekends when families tend to be at home. On the other hand, high-quality face-to-face surveys achieve response rates of 70 per cent or higher.

Mail surveys of special populations (for example, the customers of an electricity utility) generate significantly higher response rates than mail surveys of the general population, and some steps can certainly be taken to boost the response rate to mail surveys of the general population by sending additional letters reminding subjects and coaxing them to respond. Professor Don Dillman, perhaps the most successful practitioner of mail surveys in the US, and their strong advocate, has published a book describing his techniques in some detail, which include an artful combination of flattery and moral suasion and culminate in the mailing of a registered letter to the remaining hold-outs (Dillman, 1978 and 2000). Nevertheless, compared to the other survey modes, mail has some inherent disadvantages with respect to response rate, including the fact that the address lists used as the sample frame for mail surveys are somewhat more likely to be affected by coverage error than frames used for the other survey modes. Mail surveys are also somewhat more likely to experience non-response error for reasons stemming from the absence of an interviewer conducting and controlling the survey, including problems of illiteracy or limited literacy, which in the US can run as high as 20 per cent or more of the adult population, and also the fact that people who receive a mail questionnaire have the chance to examine it before deciding whether to respond, and their attitude towards the topic may affect whether they respond.

The NOAA Panel (Arrow et al., 1993) recommended that face-to-face surveys be used for all major CV studies involved with litigation for natural resource damages. Professor Dillman had attempted to persuade the Panel to authorise the use of mail surveys, but it rejected this suggestion. Some researchers, concerned at the great expense of face-to-face surveys, believe that the Panel was being too conservative. Many of them would recommend the mail–telephone survey as an acceptable and considerably more affordable alternative. On the other hand, mail surveys are more likely to lead to *self-selection bias* since a large proportion of those who return the surveys is likely to be those who are interested in the topic of the survey. This may lead to unrepresentative samples (see Chapters 5 and 9).

The other crucial consideration is the *quality of data collection*. This can be affected both adversely and positively by the presence of an interviewer. On the one hand, the absence of an interviewer in a mail survey provides greater anonymity for giving information about income, political attitudes or other items that people may consider sensitive. Moreover, interviewers can sometimes bias survey responses, and respondents may give the answers that they think the interviewer wants to hear. Some elements of interviewer bias can be corrected through careful and rigorous training of the interviewers prior to the start of the survey. This should always be included in the planning of a survey, and the researchers should aim to attend the interviewer training in order to assure themselves that the surveys are being administered in accordance with their intentions. In telephone surveys, it is also possible to monitor interviewer performance while the survey is in progress by listening in remotely. Researchers should plan to do this, too, for the purpose of quality control. One can modify the wording of the questionnaire in order to lessen the likelihood of respondents acquiescing to what they think the interviewer wants to hear, for example by including 'reasons for saying no' after the voting question in a referendum CV survey, and one can conduct tests such as split-sample survey experiments to assess whether this type of bias has been controlled. An example is the ballot box experiment conducted by Carson, Hanemann, Kopp, Krosnick, Mitchell, Presser, Ruud and Smith (1994) to test whether different CV responses were obtained when respondents directly told the interviewers how they would vote on a referendum to contain future oil spills in Prince William Sound versus recording their vote on a secret ballot that the interviewer would not see; in that case, there was no observable difference in the responses.

The problem with a conventional telephone survey is that most people are unwilling to participate in cold-call interviews that last more than a few minutes. This limitation on survey length precludes most CV surveys, unless the respondents are already adequately informed or the issue can be presented very briefly and without visual aids.

There are several positive benefits from having an interviewer or the face-to-face survey mode. A well-trained interviewer functions as the agent of the researcher. The interviewer can ensure that the correct member of the household responds to the survey, something over which there is no control in a mail survey. The interviewer controls the unfolding of information during the interview, so that the researcher can tell what information was available to the respondent at each stage. The interviewer can assist if the respondent does not understand the question (subject to guidelines specified ahead of time by the researcher regarding what the interviewer should do in these circumstances and how she should answer frequently asked questions). The interviewer can correct the respondent if he overlooks a question or otherwise fails to follow the instructions in the questionnaire. The interviewer can motivate the respondent to keep going if his interest flags. The interviewer can be instructed to record verbatim comments made by the respondent, noting when they occurred. And, most importantly, the interviewer can monitor the respondent's demeanour and behaviour, recording whether he seemed attentive, or thoughtful or confident in his response to key questions. With the interviewer's assistance, the researcher can attempt to obtain a more complete picture of what transpired during the course of the survey.

There are many variations to the basic methods described above. For example, a *drop-off survey* combines features of mail surveys and personal interviews. This consists of a personally delivered questionnaire, say to a respondent's home, which is then self-completed by the respondent and returned by mail or collected by the surveyor at a later date. The initial personal contact encourages respondents to complete the questionnaire and gives the survey a 'human face'.

Gaining popularity amongst CV practitioners are *combined mail–telephone surveys*, where respondents are first telephoned to arrange an interview time, then sent a questionnaire/information pack by mail and then called back and interviewed over the telephone. If they agree and they provide their address, some materials are mailed to them and a time is set for calling them back to complete the survey over the phone – they themselves will *not* need to fill out or mail the questionnaire. It is important that, when subjects are recruited in the initial telephone contact, they are given minimal information about the specific subject of the survey in order to eliminate the possibility of selection bias. A common strategy is to describe the survey in general terms as involving some issues in the news or some issues concerned with the spending of government funds. The interviewer calls back at the pre-arranged time. If this turns out to be inconvenient, the interview is rescheduled for a later time; it is similarly rescheduled if the subject did not receive the mailed materials, or if he has not had an opportunity to review them. The experience is that when the interview does take place it can readily be continued for up to 20 or 30 minutes because the subjects are prepared and receptive. Although this arrangement costs more than a conventional one-shot telephone survey, it allows for a far more extensive interview than is normally feasible over the phone. The experience has been that one can obtain the quality of interaction usually associated with a face-to-face survey but at a much lower cost. The major sampling problem with combination mail–telephone surveys is that they can lead to high non-response rates, since total non-response consists of both the initial set of respondents not contacted plus those contacted who refuse to participate.

The use of *computer-assisted telephone interviewing* (CATI) and *computer-assisted personal interviewing* (CAPI) has also increased a lot in recent years, due to advances in computer technology. CATI makes use of a computerised survey instrument where interviewers read the questions from the screen and enter respondents' answers directly into the computer, while CAPI brings computers into people's homes and respondents are asked to record the answers to the questions that appear on the screen directly on the computer. This method allows questionnaires to be tailor-made for individual respondents and facilitates the use of complex questionnaires as skip

Table 3.3 Survey modes

Mode	Advantages	Disadvantages
Mail surveys	*Relatively inexpensive* Lack of interviewer bias Easier to answer sensitive questions Can be completed at respondent's own pace	*Low response rates 25–50%* Self-selection bias Time-consuming Little control over who fills the questionnaire Fixed question order No clarification or probing possible Restricts the use of visual aids Respondent can alter earlier responses
Telephone interviews	Complex questionnaire structures are possible *Cheaper than personal interviews* Permits probing and clarification Relatively quick to administer Easy to monitor *60–75% response rates*	No use of visual aids Restricts use of lengthy scales Respondent may get tired Respondents may not answer sensitive questions Non-telephone or non-listed respondents not sampled
Face-to-face interviews	Highly flexible Complex questions and questionnaire structures are possible Permits probing and clarification Larger quantity of data can be collected Potential for extensive use of visual and demonstration aids *High response rates 70%+* Greatest sample control	*Relatively expensive* Interviewer bias Intercept surveys: samples normally not representative and self-selection bias Intercept surveys: questionnaires have to be short
Mixed modes: Drop off survey (mail + face-to-face)	Initial personal contact gives survey a 'human face'	Survey may be lost in interval before calling back *Expensive*
Mail +telephone surveys	Respondent telephoned for interview time, gives personal touch Can complete mailed questionnaire in own time	Shares some of the limitations of mail surveys *Relatively expensive*
Computer-assisted interviews	Interviewer records responses directly on computer and/or respondent may respond to questions on computer screen, speeding up analysis Permits more complex interviews Permits use of e-mail and Internet	Possible rejection of 'computer technology' E-mail/Internet may preclude random sample unless wide coverage of PCs

patterns, that is sections of the questionnaire that are by-passed, are done automatically.

Finally, recent technological advances have led to the expansion of electronic survey methods such as *e-mail and Internet surveys*. The Internet offers the prospect of being able to conduct interviews at virtually zero marginal cost. However, there are concerns regarding the quality of Internet surveys. An Internet survey would tend to function more like a self-administered survey than an interviewer-administered survey. Even if an Internet survey were programmed to prevent respondents from looking ahead before answering questions, there still would not be the same degree of monitoring and control as with an interviewer-administered survey. There are also major concerns regarding coverage error (not everybody has access to the Internet) and sampling error, especially selection bias with respect to who participates in Internet surveys. It may eventually be possible to solve some of the sampling problems if Internet companies emerge that develop representative panels of respondents, analogous to the Nielsen families whose television viewing is monitored in order to measure trends in the general population. Table 3.3 summarises the survey modes discussed above and their advantages and disadvantages.

3.6   CHOOSING THE SAMPLE SIZE

The trade-offs involved in the selection of a sampling approach and a survey mode culminate in the determination of a sample size. Choosing the sample size is a balancing of cost versus precision. The optimal sample size depends essentially on three considerations:

1. The smallest subgroup within the sample for which estimates are needed.
2. The precision with which estimates are needed – how much sampling error can be tolerated.
3. How much variation there is in the target population with respect to the characteristic of interest.

Starting with the last item first, the greater the variation in the underlying population, the larger the sample required to estimate a parameter with a given degree of precision. If there were *no* variation, a single observation would suffice (for example, since all the blood cells in a person's body are of the same type, one blood cell would be adequate to determine blood type). Of course, there is a paradox in sampling. The reason for sampling the population is because one does not know the true distribution of the variable of interest; yet one would need to know this distribution in order to design the most efficient sample. The paradox is broken in practice either by guessing at the value of the unknown population variance or by relying on information from other studies in the literature.

The precision with which estimates are needed can be characterised in terms of the width of, say, the 95 per cent confidence interval estimated from the sample data, which can be thought of as equal to the sample mean *plus or minus twice the standard error*. Three features of the sample affect the size of the standard error. The first is the *sampling approach* since the standard error associated with simple random sampling is different from those associated with stratified sampling, cluster sampling or multi-stage sampling. For simplicity, we focus on the standard error of a proportion estimated from a simple random sample, which is given by:

$$se(p) = (pq/N)^{0.5}, \qquad (3.1)$$

where $se(p)$ is the standard error of a proportion; p and q are the proportions of the population that do (p) and do not (q) have the characteristic of interest; N is the size of the sample.

The second feature of the sample that influences the standard error, and therefore the width of the 95 per cent confidence interval, is *the variation within the population with respect to the characteristic of interest*, as has already been noted. The standard error is larger the closer p and q approach 0.5, which can be thought of as representing the maximum degree of variation within the population; as either p or q goes to zero (the minimum degree of variation), the standard error shrinks to zero. The third feature is the *sample size*, N. The standard error decreases with *the square root* of N. This induces a form of diminishing returns to sample size – while the *cost* of the sample is likely to increase linearly with sample size, the *benefit* (in terms of the width of the confidence interval) decreases at a diminishing rate as N increases.

Box 3.2 illustrates examples of sample sizes based on the size of the target population (25,000 and 1,000,000), proportions of the chosen characteristics in the sample (p and q in equation (3.1)) and required accuracy of standard error.

Similar advice regarding sample sizes and accuracy levels is given by Mitchell and Carson (1989). Equation (3.1) is based on the assumption that a simple random sampling is used. Typically, however, the researcher will be interested in the likely magnitude of the relative error (the percentage deviation from the true mean) rather than the absolute magnitude of the error. In this situation, the researcher needs to have a prior estimate of the coefficient of variation, V, where:

BOX 3.2 CHOOSING THE SAMPLE SIZE: AN ILLUSTRATION

95% confidence interval

Target population	1,000,000		25,000	
Proportion in true sample	0.5	0.2	0.5	0.2
Accuracy: standard error × 2	±3% ±5%	±3% ±5%	±3% ±5%	±3% ±5%
Sample size required:	1111 400	711 256	1066 384	682 246

Note: Sample size is estimated from equation (3.1). In this example, $p = 0.5$ and 0.2. Since the 95 per cent confidence interval can be approximated by sample mean $\pm 2 \times se$ of the sample mean, the value of *se* entering the equation is twice the required level of accuracy shown in the table. Population size determines the 'degrees of freedom' so that 25,000 is taken to mean that 3 per cent and 5 per cent are divided by 2, and 1,000,000 corresponds to dividing by 1.96.

$$V = \frac{\sigma}{\overline{TWTP}},$$ (3.2)

where σ is the standard deviation of WTP responses and $\overline{TWTP}$ is the true (or population mean) WTP. Mitchell and Carson (1989) give the following formula for the necessary sample size, N:[1]

$$N = \frac{Z\hat{\sigma}}{\delta \overline{RWTP}},$$ (3.3

where N is the sample size needed, $\overline{RWTP}$ is the mean of the estimated WTP bids, δ is the percentage difference between the true willingness to pay and RWTP, $\hat{\sigma}$ is the estimated standard deviation to the WTP response, and Z represents the critical values for t-statistics. Standard values for t are 1.96 (the 95 per cent confidence interval) and 1.69 (the 90 per cent confidence interval). Reasonable values for δ lie between 0.05 and 0.3.

Table 3.4 presents the indicated sample sizes for different combinations of relative error (V), confidence levels ($1 - \alpha$) and the percentage difference

Table 3.4 Sample sizes needed (usable responses)

V, α	δ						
	0.05	0.10	0.15	0.20	0.25	0.30	0.50
$V = 1, \alpha = 0.10$	1,143	286	127	72	46	32	12
$V = 1, \alpha = 0.05$	1,537	385	171	97	62	43	16
$V = 1.5, \alpha = 0.10$	2,571	643	286	161	103	72	26
$V = 1.5, \alpha = 0.05$	3,458	865	385	217	139	97	36
$V = 2.0, \alpha = 0.10$	4,570	1,143	508	286	183	127	46
$V = 2.0, \alpha = 0.05$	6,174	1,537	683	385	246	171	62
$V = 2.5, \alpha = 0.10$	7,141	1,786	794	447	286	199	72
$V = 2.5, \alpha = 0.05$	9,604	2,401	1,608	601	385	267	97
$V = 3.0, \alpha = 0.10$	10,282	2,570	1,143	643	412	286	103
$V = 3.0, \alpha = 0.05$	13,830	3,458	1,537	865	554	385	139

Notes:
V is the coefficient of variation ($\sigma / \overline{TWTP}$)
δ is the possible deviation as percentage of $\overline{RWTP}$
$\alpha = 0.05$ indicates that 95% of the time estimated WTP ($\overline{RWTP}$) will be within δ of true WTP ($\overline{TWTP}$)
$\alpha = 0.10$ indicates that 90% of the time estimated WTP ($\overline{RWTP}$) will be within δ of true WTP ($\overline{TWTP}$)

Source: Mitchell and Carson (1989)

between $\overline{TWTP}$ and $\overline{RWTP}$ that the researcher is willing to tolerate (δ). The researcher should be careful to inflate the sample size by the expected number of unusable WTP responses, such as non-respondents and protest zeros (see Chapter 5 for further details of how to deal with protest responses).

Based on such reasoning, it is common to recommend sample sizes of about 250–500 for open-ended CV surveys, and about 500–1,000 for closed-ended (referendum) CV surveys.

Having said this, one should immediately note at least three qualifications:

1. The survey budget may impose an absolute limitation on the size of the sample: cost and precision are traded-off.
2. These sample sizes must be expanded if one also wishes to obtain reliable estimates for subgroups of the population. Unfortunately, there is no free lunch with respect to obtaining estimates for subgroups. The required sample size increases linearly to a first approximation with the number of subgroups for which separate parameter estimates are re-

quired. If there are two subgroups, say, then a sample of about 250–500 *from each* is needed in the event of open-ended CV, or a sample of about 500–1,000 from each in the event of a closed-ended CV study. In the face of this, researchers often compromise by accepting a somewhat lower standard of precision for the subgroup estimates than for the overall group estimates.

3. Smaller sample sizes can be employed if one collects *more information* per respondent, for example in choice modelling where multiple choices or valuations are elicited from each respondent. However, some caution should be exercised before shrinking the sample size unduly in these cases. The available evidence suggests that, for both statistical and survey research reasons, there is *no* free lunch in reducing the sample size and increasing the amount of data collected from each respondent. The statistical concern arises from the possibility of positive correlation among successive responses from the same subject, which can arise from a variety of sources including fatigue or inattentiveness. To the extent that such correlation occurs, it reduces the amount of *statistical information* in the data obtained from each subject and entails that obtaining 10 responses, say, from each of 100 subjects is *not* as informative as obtaining one response from each of 1,000 subjects – although it undoubtedly is considerably cheaper. The survey research concern arises from the fact that eliciting multiple valuations from the same subject is likely to undermine the *realism* of each individual scenario and make it seem more hypothetical than if the respondent were confronted with a single valuation scenario. It is fair to say that the trade-offs in data collection cost and quality between single and multiple elicitations of value from survey respondents are still being investigated.

NOTE

1. The following formula links formulae (3.2) and (3.3):

$$\left[\frac{Z\hat{\sigma}}{\delta \overline{RWTP}}\right] = \left[\frac{Z\hat{V}}{\delta}\right]^2.$$

4. Designing a contingent valuation questionnaire

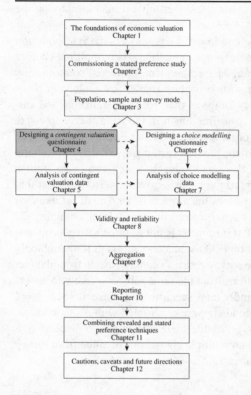

The foundations of economic valuation
Chapter 1

↓

Commissioning a stated preference study
Chapter 2

↓

Population, sample and survey mode
Chapter 3

↓

Designing a *contingent valuation* questionnaire
Chapter 4

Designing a *choice modelling* questionnaire
Chapter 6

↓

Analysis of contingent valuation data
Chapter 5

Analysis of choice modelling data
Chapter 7

↓

Validity and reliability
Chapter 8

↓

Aggregation
Chapter 9

↓

Reporting
Chapter 10

↓

Combining revealed and stated preference techniques
Chapter 11

↓

Cautions, caveats and future directions
Chapter 12

SUMMARY

The key element in a stated preference (SP) study, like other survey techniques, is a properly designed questionnaire. A questionnaire is a data-collection instrument that sets out, in a formal way, the questions designed to elicit the desired information.

This chapter introduces basics of contingent valuation (CV) questionnaire design, most of which also apply to choice modelling questionnaires (for specific details on choice modelling questionnaires, see Chapter 6).

Annex 4.1 provides guidelines on the actual wording and types of questions that can be used in a CV questionnaire to encourage respondents to think seriously about the topic of interest and to identify and state their monetary valuation.

The aim of a typical contingent valuation questionnaire is to elicit individual preferences, in monetary terms, for changes in the quantity or quality of a non-market good or service. The questionnaire intends to uncover individuals' estimates of how much having or avoiding the change in question is worth to them. Expressing preferences in monetary terms means finding out people's maximum WTP or minimum WTA for various changes of interest. In other words, a CV questionnaire is a survey instrument that sets out a number of questions to elicit the monetary value of a change in a non-market good. The change described can be the result of a hypothetical or actual policy or project. This implies that the way the change comes about can influence the results of the survey.

CV questionnaires should be designed to get respondents to think seriously about the topic of interest, to provide the necessary information for them to be able to make informed decisions and to encourage them to identify and reveal their monetary valuations.

Questionnaire design may seem to be a trivial task where all that is required is to put together a number of questions about the subject of interest. But this apparent simplicity lies at the root of many badly designed surveys that elicit biased, inaccurate and useless information, possibly at a great cost. In fact, even very simple questions require proper wording, format, content, placement and organisation if they are to elicit accurate information. Writing effective questionnaires in which scenarios and questions are uniformly, correctly and easily understood by respondents and which encourage them to answer in a considered and truthful manner is no easy task (Mitchell and Carson, 1989). Therefore, one of the best ways to assess a CV study is to read the questionnaire and determine whether it is a fair and accurate description of the good or service and the changes to it.

The chapter starts with an overview of the questionnaire design developments in other fields (especially social psychology and sociology) and focuses on three stages of CV questionnaire design: formulating the valuation problem, additional questions and pre-testing the questionnaire. The following elicitation formats are discussed in this context: open-ended, bidding game, payment card, single-bounded, one and a half bounded and double bounded dichotomous choice and randomised card sorting procedure.

4.1   USEFUL LESSONS FROM OTHER DISCIPLINES

Best practice CV questionnaires share many of the same design principles of questionnaires that are used for other purposes. Although there are no scientific principles that guarantee a single optimal questionnaire design, over the years researchers in many fields of social research such as marketing, transport, political science, psychology, sociology and economics have accumulated a wealth of knowledge about questionnaire design and implementation from which useful principles and lessons can be drawn. Cross-fertilisation between disciplines is therefore highly desirable.

Of particular interest are the *attitude-behavioural models* developed by cognitive psychologists and sociologists that look at the link between people's attitudes and intended behaviour as revealed by surveys, and subsequent actual behaviour. From a psychological point of view, WTP or WTA expressed in CV surveys are behavioural intentions. One such model, which is developed by Fishbein and Ajzen (1975), is a theory of reasoned action that

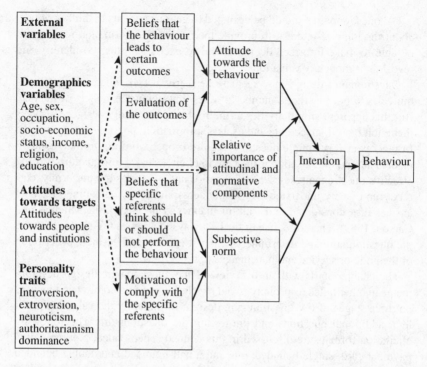

Source: Fishbein and Ajzen, 1975

Figure 4.1   Theory of reasoned action

comprises a well-known model of behavioural intentions, summarised in Figure 4.1.

According to this model, a particular behaviour, say an actual payment for an environmental improvement, is determined by an individual's behavioural intention, say hypothetical willingness to pay. In turn, behavioural intentions are a function of the personal attitudes held towards the behaviour and of perceptions held about what important others think the individual should do (subjective norm). For example, a person may have a positive WTP to save the black rhino if he considers rhinos to be worth saving and perceives that others think it is an important thing to do as well. Finally, attitudes and subjective norms can be seen to be determined by a person's beliefs, which are influenced by external individual characteristics.

The Fishbein and Ajzen framework has obvious design implications for CV surveys. Mitchell and Carson (1989) identify three important design considerations that follow from the attitude-behaviour model:

- *Correspondence*: asking questions about attitudes to public goods is not as powerful a predictor of underlying values as eliciting attitudes towards paying for public goods.
- *Proximity*: attitudes are poorer indicators of likely payment behaviour than are statements regarding valuation intentions, that is, willingness to pay.
- *Familiarity*: 'The more familiar the behaviour, the more likely the respondent's attitude and/or behavioural intention will predict that behaviour' (Mitchell and Carson, 1989, p. 186).

Also worth mentioning is the highly influential *total design method* (TDM) and the *tailored design method* developed by sociologist and survey expert Don Dillman (Dillman, 1978, 2000). The TDM is a system of interconnected design and implementation procedures for conducting high-quality mail surveys and achieving high response rates. Response rates of 70 per cent for surveys of the general population were consistently achieved using the TDM (Dillman, 1978).

The TDM has recently been updated with the introduction of a new approach, the tailored design, which is a standard set of design and implementation principles and procedures, generally applicable to all surveys and which takes into account the possibilities offered by current computer technology and the emergence of the internet (Dillman, 2000). The tailored design aims at 'creating respondent trust and perceptions of increased rewards and reduced costs for being a respondent, which take into account

Table 4.1   Some elements of the tailored design method

To establish trust	To increase rewards	To reduce social costs
<ul><li>provide token of appreciation in advance</li><li>sponsorship by legitimate authority</li><li>make the task appear important</li><li>invoke other exchange relationships</li></ul>	<ul><li>show positive regard</li><li>say thank you</li><li>ask for advice</li><li>support group values</li><li>give tangible rewards</li><li>make the questionnaire interesting</li><li>give social validation</li><li>communicate scarcity of response opportunities</li></ul>	<ul><li>avoid subordinating language</li><li>avoid embarrassment</li><li>avoid inconvenience</li><li>make questionnaire short and easy</li><li>minimise requests to obtain personal information</li><li>emphasise similarity to other requests</li></ul>

Note: Caution should be exercised with respect to giving tangible rewards as these have not been shown to be neutral with respect to elicited WTP amounts.

features of the survey situation and have as their goal overall reduction of survey error' (Dillman, 2000, p. 27) (see Chapter 3 for the implications of this for survey mode selection). Table 4.1 reviews some of the design and implementation procedures implied by the tailored design approach.

Like the attitude-behaviour model, the total and tailored design method can also be used to inform a CV questionnaire design and to reduce survey error (for further details on survey error, see Chapters 3 and 8).

4.2   THE STAGES OF DESIGNING A CONTINGENT VALUATION QUESTIONNAIRE

While similarities exist between CV surveys and the type of surveys conducted in other disciplines, CV questionnaires possess some distinguishing features that require special consideration. This is mainly for three reasons:

- CV questionnaires require respondents to consider how a change in a good or service that is typically not traded in markets might affect them. In contrast to most other types of surveys, the policy change is described in detail before respondents are asked to evaluate it. The policy described can be real or hypothetical; in either case it should be perceived as realistic and feasible.
- Although many policy changes involving mixed or public goods and services are well known and familiar to respondents (for example, an improvement of sanitation or drinking water provision, policies involving landscape changes), some types of mixed or public goods and services can be complex and unfamiliar (for example, changes in biodiversity, policies resulting in air quality changes leading to changes on mortality and morbidity patterns).
- Respondents are asked to make a monetary valuation of the change in question.

All these aspects introduce a number of questionnaire design issues that do not occur in the case of opinion polls or marketing surveys for private goods. In this context, Mitchell and Carson (1989, p. 120) note that 'The principal challenge facing the designer of a CV study is to make the scenario sufficiently understandable, plausible and meaningful to respondents so that they can and will give valid and reliable values despite their lack of experience with one or more of the scenario dimensions.'

The design of a CV questionnaire comprises three interrelated stages. The first and principal stage consists of identifying the good to be valued, con-

```
┌─────────────────────────────────────────────────────────────┐
│    First stage: Formulating the valuation problem           │
│    • What is the policy change being valued? (Section 4.2.1)│
│    • Constructing the valuation scenario (Section 4.2.2)    │
│    • Eliciting monetary values (Section 4.2.3)             │
└─────────────────────────────────────────────────────────────┘
```

```
┌─────────────────────────────────────────────────────────────┐
│    Second stage: Additional questions                       │
│    • Debriefing and follow-up questions (Section 4.2.4)     │
│    • Attitudes, opinions, knowledge and uses (Section 4.2.5)│
│    • Demographics (Section 4.2.6)                           │
│    • Questionnaire structure (Section 4.2.7)               │
└─────────────────────────────────────────────────────────────┘
```

```
┌─────────────────────────────────────────────────────────────┐
│    Third stage: Pre-testing the questionnaire               │
│    • Focus groups (Section 4.3.1)                          │
│    • One-to-one interviews (Section 4.3.2)                 │
│    • Verbal protocols (Section 4.3.3)                      │
│    • Pilot surveys (Section 4.3.4)                         │
└─────────────────────────────────────────────────────────────┘
```

Figure 4.2   Stages of CV questionnaire design

structing the valuation scenario and eliciting the monetary values. In the second stage, questions on attitudes and opinions, knowledge, familiarity and use of the good, demographics and various debriefing questions are added. The third stage consists of pre-testing the draft questionnaire for content, question wording, question format and overall structure and layout and then revising the design based on the pre-test findings. These stages are depicted in Figure 4.2 and discussed in detail in the following sections.

General principles of writing valid questions and of questionnaire form and layout that apply throughout all of the following sections are described in detail in Annex 4.1.

4.2.1   What is the Policy Change Being Valued?

Before starting to design the questionnaire, researchers must have a very clear idea of what policy change they want to value, that is, which quality or quantity change(s) is of interest and of what particular non-market good(s) or service(s). This is in essence the formulation of the valuation research problem. But as fundamental as this is, formulating the problem to be valued may not be straightforward because:

- it may be difficult to get those in charge of a policy or project that will lead to the change to be valued to commit to what the policy or project will actually do;
- there may be scientific uncertainty surrounding the physical effects of particular changes;
- it may be unclear how physical changes affect human wellbeing;
- the effects of some changes may be difficult to translate into terms and sentences that can be readily understood by respondents;
- some changes are very complex and multidimensional and cannot be adequately described within the timeframe and the means available to conduct the questionnaire; and
- textual descriptions of some changes may provide only a limited picture of the reality (for example, changes in noise, odour or visual impacts).

Table 4.2 presents examples of changes that may be difficult to define.

In order to minimise some of these informational issues, CV researchers should thoroughly review relevant existing information and discuss any information gaps and uncertainties with the relevant experts.

One crucial distinction to be made at this stage is whether the policy change to be valued happens in isolation or is part of a more encompassing multidimensional policy that involves other simultaneous or sequential changes as well (Hoehn and Randall, 1989). Failure to take this distinction into account may lead to seriously biased results. Hoehn and Randall show that if a series of changes that happen simultaneously or sequentially as part of a multidimensional policy are evaluated independently, and the values are then summed up to produce a total value for the policy, this total value will overstate the true value of the policy as it will ignore substitution and complementary effects that may occur. Carson et al. (1998) show that this is true of WTP sequences but that the reverse is true of WTA sequences. However, this phenomenon is not specific to surveys but rather is endemic to multi-dimensional changes. Randall et al. (1996) show that the effects of multi-dimensional changes tend to also be pronounced in random utility models.

Given the multidimensional nature of many environmental policies it is important to identify clearly the policy change of interest according to the chart presented in Figure 4.3. It will either be a policy with a single impact or a policy with multiple impacts. In the latter case, the various impacts can happen simultaneously or sequentially. And the researcher might be interested in the value of the total multidimensional policy and/or the value of a specific component/change within the overall policy. These distinctions have important design implications that will be further explored in the next section.

Table 4.2   Possible topics of valuation and the problems that might arise

Change to be valued	Problems
Damages caused in a river from increased water abstractions	Scientific uncertainty surrounding the physical changes caused by increased abstractions. Difficulty in describing a wide range of changes in the fauna, flora, visual amenity, water quality and recreational potential, without causing information overload. Difficulty in isolating abstraction impacts in one river from impacts in other rivers. The damages may be different in different stretches of the river and in different periods of the year.
Reduced risk of contracting a disease or infection	Risk and probability changes are not easily understood. Difficulties in conveying the idea of small risk changes. Difficulties in isolating pain and suffering impacts from the cost of medication or of lost wages.
Damages caused by traffic emissions on a historical building	Difficulties in isolating the impact of traffic related air pollution and other sources of air pollution. Difficulty in explaining the type of damage caused (e.g. soiling of the stone vs. erosion of the stone). Difficulty in conveying the visual impacts of the change if visual aids are not used.
Damages caused by the introduction of a plant protection chemical	Limited scientific information may not permit full identification of the wide range of environmental impacts caused by the chemical. Difficulty in explaining in lay terms the idea of damages to biodiversity and ecosystems. The impacts of a pest may be too complex to explain in the limited time that the questionnaire lasts.

4.2.2   Constructing the Valuation Scenario

Once the policy change of interest has been identified in the light of what was presented in the previous section, the research team can then start to put together a valuation scenario to be shown to respondents.

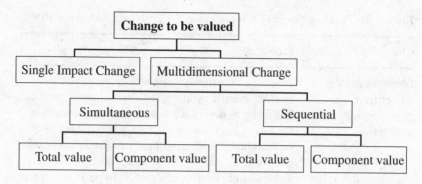

Figure 4.3   Identifying the policy change of interest

As all surveys, CV surveys are context dependent. That is, the values estimated are contingent on various aspects of the scenario presented and the questions asked. While some elements of the survey are expected to be neutral (for example, including a question about family size should not influence an individual's response to the WTP question), others are thought to have a significant influence on respondents' valuation. These include the information provided about the good, the wording and type of the valuation questions, the institutional arrangements and the payment mechanism. Hence, the design of the valuation scenario and the payment mechanism is of crucial importance for the elicitation of accurate and reliable responses.

A valuation scenario has three essential elements:

1.   A description of the policy, project or programme change of interest.
2.   A description of the constructed market.
3.   A description of the method of payment.

1.   Description of the policy change of interest

According to the framework presented in Figure 4.3, researchers might be interested in valuing a policy that implies a single environmental change (for example, low flow alleviation in the River Mimram in the UK) or a multi-dimensional policy that encompasses a number of simultaneous or sequential environmental changes (for example, low flow alleviation in all rivers at risk in the UK). Single impact policies are discussed first followed by the more complex issue of policies with multiple impacts next (multidimensional policies).

For *single impact policies* the description of the policy change to be valued entails a number of steps:

- *Description of the attributes of the good under investigation in a way that is meaningful and understandable to respondents.* This may include a description of the relevant characteristics of the good, the benefits it provides related or not to particular uses, its geographical extent, designated status, existing property rights and so on.

  There are basically three ways of presenting the attributes of interest: (i) describing all relevant attributes in detail; (ii) describing the most important or familiar valuable attributes of the good; or (iii) merely describing the good in general, ignoring its valuable attributes. The level of detail provided matters and there is an obvious need to strike a balance between information overload and vagueness of the scenario description, both of which are undesirable. The pre-testing stages should help inform on the right level of information that allows the change of interest to be well understood, without boring or confusing the respondents. In general, approach (ii) seems to combine the search for short descriptions that capture the respondent's attention with the need to present an accurate scenario.

  Often, complex scientific, engineering, medical and ecological information has to be translated into simple terms that are meaningful in relation to the respondent's quality of life. This is a particularly difficult task but a very useful one as it forces complex and overwhelmingly large amounts of information to be translated into a few meaningful 'headline indicators'.

- *Availability of substitutes.* The description of available substitutes for the good (its degree of local, national or global uniqueness) and of alternative expenditure possibilities may affect respondents' values and should therefore be part of the scenario description.

- *Description of the proposed policy change.* The scenario should include a description of the proposed policy change and of how the attributes of the good of interest will change accordingly. In particular the *reference* (*status quo* or baseline level) and *target levels* (state of the world with the proposed change) of each attribute of interest should be clearly described.

  For example, in a WTP study of improved sanitation in Malacca, Malaysia (Mourato and Day, 1998), sanitation was linked to local river water pollution. First, the currently poor levels of river water quality and its consequences were described. Then the proposed sanitation system was described in terms of its impacts in reducing current local river pollution: better quality of life (recreational possibilities, visual amenities), improved drinking water quality, less public health risks and a generally better environment.

Note that the *status quo* situation need not correspond to a 'no-change' situation; in fact it may be that the policy of interest is aimed at preventing a change in the status of a given good. For example, in a valuation study of the Norfolk Broads flood alleviation scheme (Bateman et al., 1995; Bateman and Langford, 1997a) the baseline/reference situation was to allow saline flood risk to increase progressively with time, whereas the proposed policy was to maintain the area in its present condition, that is, the survey respondents were asked to pay to avoid a loss.

Particular care should be taken in describing the *scope* of the policy change as insensitivity to scope has been one of main arguments used to criticise the validity of the CV method (see Chapter 8 for further discussions of this issue). Insensitivity to scope is normally a product of misspecified scenarios or vague and abstract definitions of the policy change that can lead respondents not to perceive any real difference between impacts of varying scope (Carson and Mitchell, 1995). A clear, detailed and meaningful definition of the scope of the proposed policy change is therefore required.

Nevertheless, there are instances where describing the scope of policy changes is particularly difficult. A typical example is the presentation of small changes in health risks where insensitivity to scope has consistently been found, despite researchers' efforts to convey the information in simple ways.

Describing the good and the policy change of interest may require a combination of textual information, photographs, drawings, maps, charts and graphs. In many circumstances, visual aids are helpful ways of conveying complex information in a simple and concise way, while simultaneously enhancing respondents' attention and interest. For example, a questionnaire that has the objective of valuing different forest management options for a given forest might require a description of the complex landscape impacts of each option. A photograph might be the best way of depicting multiple landscape changes. If the options to be valued are hypothetical and have not actually taken place, researchers might choose to create visual materials especially for the purposes of the study (for example, by using computer-manipulated photographs). Photographs and other visual stimuli need to be pre-tested in the same way as textual descriptions.

Figure 4.4 depicts computer-manipulated photographs that were used to illustrate the visual impacts of constructing a 2,000-metre tunnel for

Source: Maddison and Mourato (1999).

*Figure 4.4   Stonehenge landscape now and with a 2,000 m tunnel for the
A303*

the A303 road that passes near Stonehenge, in England (Maddison and
Mourato, 1999). These photographs were part of a CV survey that
aimed to estimate the impacts of various road options for Stonehenge.

- *Describing an aggregate multidimensional policy.* If all that is required
  is to find out the total or aggregate value of the policy then the scenario
  should provide information about each and all of its relevant components
  and how they change *vis-à-vis* the *status quo*. The benefits of the policy
  will obviously depend on its component parts, so an accurate and complete description is fundamental. In case of a series of sequential changes,
  if the sequence is known in advance, then it is advisable to present the
  series of changes to respondents in that order for increased realism.
  However, the sequence order does not actually affect the total aggregate
  value of the policy since all the relevant relationships between component parts (such as substitution and complementarity effects) will be
  taken into account.

- *Describing a component of a multidimensional policy encompassing a number of simultaneous changes.* If the specific change being valued is part of a more inclusive policy that comprises a number of other changes occurring simultaneously (for example, protecting the white tiger when protection of black rhinos, blue whales, giant pandas and mountain gorillas are also on the agenda), then it is fundamental to present the individual change as part of the broader package. This provides respondents with a chance to consider all the possible substitution, complementarity and income effects between the various policy components, which would have been impossible had the policy component been presented in isolation (which would have led to possible embedding effects and an over-estimation of the value of the policy component).

  There are two ways of doing this. One is simply to describe the overall policy, with all its components, and then to ask respondents to provide a valuation of a specific component (or components) in full knowledge of the fact that other changes are simultaneously occurring and that they will have to pay for all of them. A more accurate approach is to follow a top-down procedure, whereby respondents are first asked to value the more inclusive policy and then to partition that total value across its components. There is an obvious limitation to the number of components that can be valued in such a way: as one tries to value an increasing number of policy changes, the description of each becomes necessarily shorter, reducing the accuracy of the scenario, while respondents may also become fatigued or confused.

  If the exact composition of the policy is unknown at the time of the survey (for example, the policy will encompass protection of five endangered species out of a possible pool of seven species) then the valuation problem becomes much more complex. Even if the composition is known, it can be difficult to describe the components accurately. An all-inclusive approach where all the possible combinations are presented to respondents to be valued is likely to be extremely costly. An alternative procedure is to present a sample of all possible combinations to respondents and then, through econometric techniques, the value of each component can be recovered.

- *Describing a component of a multidimensional policy encompassing a number of sequential changes.* If the change of interest is part of a sequence of changes then its value depends on the point of the sequence in which it appears and can be shown to become progressively smaller as it is placed deeper and deeper in the valuation sequence (Hoehn and Randall, 1989).

In order to obtain valid estimates of a sequenced component of a policy, respondents should be first made aware of all the elements of the sequence so that they can assess the total value of the policy. Then, if the sequence of the policy is predetermined, the various changes should be presented to respondents in the sequence in which they occur and component valuations be obtained at each step of the sequence.

Once more, if the sequence in which the policy occurs is unknown at the time of the survey, the valuation task becomes much more convoluted. An accurate but very costly approach is to try out all possible sequence paths. A simplistic solution is to randomly change the order in which the good appears in the sequence across respondents in order to estimate an 'average' indicative value. Thus, randomly assigning respondents to different sequences 'averages' out the sequence effect but does not get at the basic economic problem. Both approaches have limitations.

Finally, it should be noted that while CV is in theory applicable to value multidimensional changes, as described above, a more efficient way of dealing with such changes might be to adopt a choice modelling approach (see Chapters 6 and 7). However, although a choice modelling approach can be an effective way to estimating the substitution parameters between goods, it cannot eliminate the sequence dependence of the value of the good, which is an economic phenomenon. Using a choice model to look at sequence effects puts a large premium on the strong separability of the choices in the demand system and money as well as on functional form assumptions as one is no longer dealing with marginal changes.

An example of how some of the design principles described so far were applied in an actual CV survey can be found in Box 4.1. The study, sponsored by the Charities Aid Foundation, aimed to elicit the value that homeless people in London placed on the services provided by hostels (EFTEC, 1998b). It is an example of a single impact policy.

This homeless study was a particularly unusual and difficult CV survey. First, there was no previous research indicating how the target population (the London homeless) would be expected to react to a monetary valuation exercise, given their non-traditional lifestyle, severe budget constraints and, in many cases, health and addiction problems. Adverse reactions were minimised by the use of interviewers specialised in working with homeless people and by adopting a WTA mechanism. Second, because the valuation scenario involved closing hostels for one year, it was important to ensure that respondents could think about this policy change without it causing feelings of fear, anxiety or trauma. In the circumstances, respondents were asked to think and

BOX 4.1   VALUING THE BENEFITS OF LONDON HOSTELS TO THE HOMELESS: DESCRIBING THE POLICY CHANGE OF INTEREST

Hostels provide you with accommodation and a number of other support services. We would like to find out how much you *value all of this*. We will use the following question to try and find out how much the accommodation and services are worth to you.

Imagine that, for some reason, *all the hostels in the country* had to shut down for a *whole year* next year and you had to find somewhere to stay. Suppose in order to compensate you for not being able to use the hostels any more, you were given an additional cash payment each week, *over and above* what you said you receive at the moment.

How much money would you have to receive each week during the whole year to give you *the same quality of life* as you have now (not better or worse, but just the same)?

Identification of meaningful attributes	Elsewhere in the survey respondents were asked about the most important attributes of hostel services: sleeping facilities, food services, washing facilities, counselling services, help with finances and job search.
Amount of information to be provided	Limited as respondents were obviously very familiar with the good being changed and were well aware of all the facilities on offer.
Availability of substitutes	Elsewhere in the survey respondents were asked where they would sleep if they could not use hostels for short (a few days), medium (1-year) or long periods (a few years). Preferred alternatives were sleeping rough (for short periods), bed & breakfast (1-year) and council houses (long term).

Sequencing effects	None: all hostels would close down simultaneously.
Scope of the change	All hostels in the country will close down.

Source: EFTEC, 1998b

describe what their life would be like if the policy did happen (which they were well capable of doing) but assured by the interviewers that there were no immediate plans for it to happen.

2. Description of the constructed market

The constructed market refers to the social context in which the CV transaction, that is, the policy change, takes place. A number of elements of the constructed market are important:

- *The institution* that is responsible for providing the good or change of interest. This can be a government, a local council, a NGO, a research institute, industry, a charity and so on. Institutional arrangements will affect WTP as respondents may hold views about a particular institution's level of effectiveness, reliability and trust.

- *The technical and political feasibility of the change* is a fundamental consideration in the design of the questionnaire. Respondents can only provide meaningful valuations if they believe that the scenario described is feasible (see Annex 1.2 for a recent example of using CV in UK policy, in the context of aggregates).

- *Conditions for provision of the good*: this includes *respondents' perceived payment obligation* and *respondents' expectations about provision*. Regarding the former, there are several possibilities: respondents may believe they will have to pay the amounts they state; they may think the amount they have to pay is uncertain (more or less than their stated WTP amount); or they may be told that they will pay a fixed amount, or a proportion of the costs of provision. Regarding the latter, the basic question is whether respondents believe or not that provision of the good is conditional on their WTP amount. Both types of information are important as each different combination evokes a different type of strategic behaviour (Mitchell and Carson, 1989).

It is important to provide respondents with incentives to reveal their true valuations, that is, to design an *incentive-compatible* mechanism. Mitchell and Carson (1989) argue that true preference revelation is induced when respondents believe that provision is contingent on their stated values and that they will have to pay the amount they state. Under these circumstances, it is in a respondent's best interest to reveal their true WTP. Conversely, if respondents believe that provision is guaranteed and that they will have to pay the amount they state, then there will be an incentive to underbid or free-ride. And if they believe that their responses will influence the provision of the good but the amounts actually paid are unrelated to the stated bids, then there will be an incentive to over-estimate true WTP to guarantee provision. Carson et al. (2000) provide a thorough discussion of incentive compatibility issues, which are also addressed in more detail in Chapter 8.

- *Timing of provision*: when and for how long will the good be provided. Given individual time preferences, a good provided now will be more valuable than a good provided in 10 years' time. Also, the amount of time over which the good or service will be provided can be of crucial importance. For example, Mourato and Swierzbinski (1999) show that the value of a programme that saves black rhinos for 50 years is only a fraction of the value of the same programme where protection is awarded indefinitely.

  Using the CV study of the homeless (EFTEC, 1998b) introduced in Box 4.1, Box 4.2 shows how the constructed market was depicted in a real study.

- *Who will have to pay* for the good or change of interest *and who will benefit or lose* from it. Payers can be users, tax payers, donors, industry and so on. For example, in the case of a river clean-up programme, people may be asked to pay increased taxes for the clean-up programme and be told that all tax payers and industries will also be asked to pay. However, it is not always easy to convince respondents that certain third parties (such as industry, in the river example) will also pay their share of the costs of provision.

  Those who pay will not necessarily be those who gain from the change of interest. If a tax payment vehicle is adopted, so that all tax payers pay, and the mean WTP is used as the tax amount, those who stated a zero WTP (or a negative WTP, that is, a need for compensation) would be asked to pay for something they do not value. This can occur when the change in question is of interest to only a minority of

BOX. 4.2 VALUING THE BENEFITS OF LONDON HOSTELS TO THE HOMELESS: THE CONSTRUCTED MARKET

Hostels provide you with accommodation and a number of other support services. We would like to find out how much you *value all of this*. We will use the following question to try and find out how much the accommodation and services are worth to you.

Imagine that, for some reason, *all the hostels in the country* had to shut down for a *whole year* next year and you had to find somewhere to stay. Suppose in order to compensate you for not being able to use the hostels any more, you were given an additional cash payment each week, *over and above* what you said you receive at the moment.

How much money would you have to receive each week during the whole year to give you *the same quality of life* as you have now (not better or worse, but just the same)?

Institution	Implicitly, the government would be responsible for compensating homeless people. This was obvious as most London homeless live on state benefits.
Provision conditions	Provision is certain and independent of stated compensation. The relationship between the stated compensation and the actual compensation is not specified even though other state benefits received are fixed amounts. In terms of strategic bias, if respondents interpret the actual compensation as a fixed amount there is no incentive to act strategically. If they regard the link between actual and stated amounts as uncertain then there is a weak to moderate incentive to overbid.
Timing	Hostels would close next year, for a whole year.
Who receives payment and who loses	Implicitly, all hostel users would receive the cash compensation and all would be potential losers from the change.

Source: EFTEC, 1998b

the population. For example, some changes in cultural heritage goods have been shown to be of interest to selected subgroups of the population only, with the majority being largely indifferent or even opposed to the change (see Maddison and Mourato, 1999 for an example).

3. Description of the method of payment

A number of aspects of the method of payment should be clearly defined in CV questionnaires:

- *Choice of benefit measure*. This is a fundamental step in any CV survey. There are four types of benefit measures that can be elicited: these are described in Table 4.3 (based on Bateman, Langford, Munro, Starmer and Sugden, 2000).

    The discussion between WTA and WTP is conducted elsewhere in this report (see Chapters 1 and 12). Several explanations for the WTP/

Table 4.3   The four welfare change measures

Measure	Example	Proposed change in provision	Does the change in provision actually occur?	Reference level of utility
WTP to secure a gain	*Would you be willing to pay £X for an increase in river water levels due to decreased abstraction?*	Gain	Yes	Initial utility
WTP to avoid a loss	*Would you be willing to pay £X to avoid a decrease in river water levels due to increased abstraction?*	Loss	No	Final utility
WTA to tolerate loss	*Would you be willing to accept £X to accept a decrease in river water levels due to increased abstraction?*	Loss	Yes	Final utility
WTA to forgo a gain	*Would you be willing to accept £X instead of an increase in river water levels due to decreased abstraction?*	Gain	No	Initial utility

Source: adapted from Bateman, Langford, Munro, Starmer and Sugden.

WTA differential based on psychological arguments were put forward (for example, Kahneman and Tversky, 1979) and income limitations on WTP (Randall and Stoll, 1980 and Willig, 1976). But the empirical disparity between both measures was only semi-reconciled with economic theory when Hanemann et al. (1991) showed that, in the case of quantity changes, the difference between WTP and WTA also depends on a substitution effect: the closer the substitutes a commodity has, the smaller should be the disparity between the two measures.

Those chapters and Table 4.3 highlight the importance of choosing the appropriate welfare measure. The choice of benefit measure to adopt is generally case-specific and depends on the characteristics and context of the change valued. In particular, the choice between welfare measures depends on the property rights structure and on the type of change from the *status quo* position (Mitchell and Carson, 1989). For example, if consumers are *entitled* to the utility level implicit in the current situation, then it makes sense to compensate them for any *negative changes* that occur and WTA is the adequate measure.

In a recent study about the value of aggregate externalities in the UK (see Annex 1.2), both WTA and WTP formats were tested. The first part of the research used a WTA measure whereby local residents were asked for the amounts they required as compensation for the noise and inconvenience caused by the proximity of quarries. WTA was chosen as quarry owners were found to have property rights over their quarries, that is, quarry licences. In the second part of the study respondents were told that the current Town and Country Planning Act could be used to force early closure of some quarries and were then asked for their WTP for this to happen. In order to decide which format worked better, two follow-up questions were asked: (i) 'Did you believe that the quarry would close if you did not allow it to remain open?' following the WTA question; and (ii) 'Did you believe that you would have to pay to get the quarry closed?' following the WTP question. The results showed that the respondents did not feel comfortable with the WTA property right concept and did not believe that the quarry would close. Therefore, the WTP format, which was credible, was used effectively changing the perceived property rights.

If WTA is to be used, extra care must be taken to ensure that respondents do not overbid. Below, some suggestions are pointed out while discussing elicitation mechanisms.

- *Payment vehicle*: voluntary or coercive payments. Coercive payment vehicles include taxes, rates, fees, charges or prices. Voluntary payments are donations and gifts. The payment vehicle forms a substantive part of the overall package under evaluation and is generally believed to be a non-neutral element of the survey. Mechanisms such as income taxes and water rates are clearly non-neutral and it is relatively common to find respondents refusing to answer the valuation question on the grounds that they object in principle to paying higher taxes or water rates, in spite of the fact that the proposed change is welfare enhancing. The use of taxes also raises issues of accountability, trust in the government, knowledge that taxes are generally not hypothecated, excludes non-tax payers from the sample and may not be credible when the scenario is one of WTA, that is, corresponding to a tax rebate. Voluntary payments, on the other hand, encourage free-riding, as respondents have an incentive to overstate their WTP to secure provision and to reduce real payments relative to their WTP once provision is secured (free-riding on the donations of others). This implies overbidding in hypothetical markets and underbidding in real markets.[1]

Although there is a strong view that voluntary payments should be avoided as they are not incentive compatible (Carson et al., 1999) as illustrated above, some authors have defended the use of voluntary payments in cases where taxes are unfeasible, together with a certainty scale and adjustment of the responses accordingly (Champ et al., 1997). Credibility and acceptability are important considerations here. A simple guideline is to use the vehicle which is likely to be employed in the real world decision, that is, if water rates are the method by which the change in provision will be affected then there should be a presumption in favour of using water rates in the contingent market. A caveat to this guide arises where this causes conflict with certain of the criteria set out above. For example, Georgiou et al. (1998) found considerable resistance to the use of a water rates vehicle in the immediate aftermath of the privatisation of the public water utilities in the UK. In this case the acceptability criterion seems to have been in conflict with the coercive nature of such a vehicle. In such instances, if other acceptable and credible vehicles cannot be identified then a valuation study may become compromised. Another example comes from Bateman (1996). This 1991 split-sample study investigating elicitation method and payment vehicle effects upon WTP for informal woodland recreation in the UK included a sub-sample which was presented with a community charge ('poll tax') vehicle. This resulted in a highly bimodal distribution of responses reflecting the mixture of support and condemnation of the payment vehicle but revealing little regarding the value of the good in question. This distribution differed very substantially from those obtained using other vehicles such as general taxation.

In general, the use of overtly hypothetical payment mechanisms should be avoided. Nevertheless, in some special cases, for example where the use of taxes is strongly considered not feasible, not credible or very undesirable, it might be worth testing a vaguer definition of the payment vehicle in order to try to increase the accuracy of responses and reduce the number of protests and non-responses. For example, some authors have successfully used generalised price increases as the payment vehicle. And in a recent pan-European study that evaluated the benefits of reduction in morbidity, Day et al. (1999) used the elicitation mechanism described in Box 4.3, where the payment vehicle was left deliberately vague. Extensive focus groups and pilot interviews showed that, in the specific circumstances of this study, this approach worked well and was easily understood and accepted by respondents. But note that vaguer payment schedules will always require extra testing efforts before their use can be validated.

BOX 4.3   EXAMPLE OF A CV SCENARIO WITH NO CLEARLY DEFINED PAYMENT VEHICLE

Imagine the following situation. Imagine you wake up tomorrow to find yourself suffering from an episode of stomach upset, with all the symptoms described before. Imagine also that it was somehow possible to pay an amount of money in order to re-awake that same morning to find yourself in a normal state of health, *completely free of the symptoms described.* Please think for a moment about how much you would be willing to pay to achieve such a change.

Don't worry if the situation seems unrealistic to you! And remember that we are not talking about how much it would cost you in medicines to treat this symptom, but rather how much you would be personally willing to pay in order to avoid experiencing this symptom at all, with all the pain and inconvenience it would entail.

Source: Day et al., 1999

- *Target and reference payment levels.* It is also important to define the reference and target levels of the payment. The reference level is respondent's disposable income (after tax income minus all fixed obligations and all necessary expenditures in food, clothing, interest and so on) and reflects the budget constraint. The target level is respondents' *maximum* WTP or *minimum* WTA (note that it is not just *any* WTP or WTA amounts). When the respondent is already paying for the provision of the good, it should be made clear that any new payments will be over and above what is currently paid. The implications of this for data analysis are discussed in Chapter 5.

- *Individual or household payment.* Individuals may be asked for their individual or household valuations and the reference income elicited in the survey should be consistent with the unit of analysis adopted. Individual payments may be problematic when the person being interviewed has no independent income, while household payments may pose problems when individual respondents are uncertain about the reference household income levels and about other household members' values. Some payment vehicles are more conducive to household valuations than others (for example, water rates are normally paid at the household level while entry fees are normally individually set).

- *Timing of payment.* Payments may be expressed as a one-off lump sum, a yearly, monthly, daily or a per visit amount and so on. Lump sum payment tends to be appropriate for things that are largely provided by a one-time capital expenditure (purchase of a wilderness area, restoration of a cultural site), while annual payments tend to be appropriate for goods like local clean air and water that are provided continually. One advantage of the lump sum payment approach is that it tends to eliminate many of the sequencing problems. Any good that has already been bought and completely paid for does not enter the sequence of possible new goods. The reality is that the number of new goods considered in any particular year is fairly small.

  If repeated payments are used, there is a need to describe the timescale over which repeated payments will take place (for example, yearly payments for the next five years or for the next ten years). It has been shown in the literature that the frequency of payment has an impact on WTP (Hanley, Alvarez-Farigo and Bell, 2000) with respondents showing a form of 'temporal embedding'. This means that when asked for a monthly payment, respondents have a tendency to pay more than the corresponding yearly payment, that is (12 × monthly WTP) > (yearly

BOX 4.4   EXAMPLE OF A PAYMENT CARD USING
MONTHLY AND YEARLY EQUIVALENT
AMOUNTS

£/month	(£/year equivalent)
nothing	(nothing)
10p	(£1.20)
25p	(£3)
50p	(£6)
75p	(£9)
£1.00	(£12)
...	...
£100	£1200
over £100	(over £1200)

Source: Foster and Mourato, 1999.

WTP). An easy way to avoid this issue is to present respondents with monthly and corresponding yearly amounts in the elicitation question. Box 4.4 presents a payment card used in a survey of the value of charitable services in the UK where both monthly and annual payments were specified.

The same study of homeless people in London described in Boxes 4.1 and 4.2 (EFTEC, 1998b) is used to illustrate how these elements were incorporated in an actual CV survey (see Box 4.5).

4.2.3   Eliciting Monetary Values

After the presentation of the valuation scenario, the provision mechanism and the payment mechanism, respondents are asked questions to determine how much they would value the good if confronted with the opportunity to obtain it, under the specified terms and conditions.

The elicitation question can be asked in a number of different ways. Table 4.4 summarises the principal formats of eliciting values as applied to the case of valuing changes in landscape around Stonehenge (Maddison and Mourato, 1999). The examples in the table all relate to the elicitation of WTP but could easily be framed in terms of WTA. How to organise and analyse different types of data produced by different types of elicitation formats is discussed in

BOX. 4.5 VALUING THE BENEFITS OF LONDON HOSTELS TO THE HOMELESS: THE METHOD OF COMPENSATION

Hostels provide you with accommodation and a number of other support services. We would like to find out how much you *value all of this*. We will use the following question to try and find out how much the accommodation and services are worth to you.

Imagine that, for some reason, *all the hostels in the country* had to shut down for a *whole year* next year and you had to find somewhere to stay. Suppose in order to compensate you for not being able to use the hostels any more, you were given an additional cash payment each week, *over and above* what you said you receive at the moment.

How much money would you have to receive each week during the whole year to give you *the same quality of life* as you have now (not better or worse, but just the same)?

Choice of benefit measure	WTA
Compensation vehicle	Coercive: all homeless people would receive an additional cash benefit. Well defined: the payment is an additional state benefit.
Target and reference compensation levels	Reference level: homeless people's current total income (state benefits plus begging proceeds). This was elicited in the survey. Target level: minimum WTA (over and above current state benefits), defined as the compensation needed to afford the homeless the same quality of life as they currently have.
Individual or household compensation	Individual compensations (the target population was single homeless people).
Timing of compensation	Weekly compensation amounts for one year.

Source: EFTEC, 1998b

Table 4.4   Examples of common elicitation formats

Open ended	*What is the maximum amount that you would be prepared to pay every year, through a tax surcharge, to improve the landscape around Stonehenge in the ways I have just described?*
Bidding game	*Would you pay £5 every year, through a tax surcharge, to improve the landscape around Stonehenge in the ways I have just described?* If Yes: Interviewer keeps increasing the bid until the respondent answers No. Then maximum WTP is elicited. If No: Interviewer keeps decreasing the bid until respondent answers Yes. Then maximum WTP is elicited.
Payment card	*Which of the amounts listed below best describes your maximum willingness to pay every year, through a tax surcharge, to improve the landscape around Stonehenge in the ways I have just described?*

0
£0.5
£1
£2
£3
£4
£5
£7.5
£10
£12.5
£15
£20
£30
£40
£50
£75
£100
£150
£200
>£200

Single-bounded dichotomous choice	*Would you pay £5 every year, through a tax surcharge, to improve the landscape around Stonehenge in the ways I have just described?* (The price is varied randomly across the sample.)
Double-bounded dichotomous choice	*Would you pay £5 every year, through a tax surcharge, to improve the landscape around Stonehenge in the ways I have just described?* (The price is varied randomly across the sample.) If Yes: And would you pay £10? If No: And would you pay £1?

Source: Maddison and Mourato, 1999

Chapter 5, while the implications of biases in the answers are presented in Chapter 8. It should be noted that the different elicitation formats have different properties with respect to their incentives for strategic behaviour, how much information they convey to respondents, and how much information they collect from respondents. As a consequence, theoretically one should not expect the elicitation formats to result in the same WTP estimates.

- *The open-ended direct* elicitation format is a straightforward way of uncovering values, does not provide respondents with cues about what the value of the change might be, that is, no *anchoring bias*, is very informative as maximum WTP can be identified for each respondent and requires relatively straightforward statistical techniques. However, it has been progressively abandoned by CV practitioners due to a number of problems. Open-ended questioning leads to large non-response rates, protest answers, zero answers and outliers and generally to unreliable responses (Mitchell and Carson, 1989). This is because it may be very difficult for respondents to come up with their true maximum WTP 'out of the blue' for a change they are unfamiliar with or have never thought about valuing before. Moreover, most daily market transactions involve deciding whether or not to buy goods at fixed prices, rather than stating maximum WTP values.

- *The bidding game* was one of the most widely used formats in the 1970s and 1980s. In this approach, as in an auction, respondents are faced with several rounds of discrete choice questions, with the final question being an open-ended WTP question. This iterative format was thought to facilitate respondents' thought processes and encourage them to consider their preferences carefully. A major disadvantage lies in the possibility of anchoring or *starting bias*, that is, respondents were found to be influenced by the starting values and succeeding bids used. It also leads to a large number of outliers (that is, unrealistically large bids) and to a phenomenon that has been labelled as 'yea-saying' (that is, respondents accepting to pay the specified amounts to avoid the socially embarrassing position of having to say no). Bidding games cannot be used in mail surveys and other self-completed questionnaires.

- *Payment card* or ladder approaches were developed as improved alternatives to the open-ended and bidding game formats. Presenting respondents with a visual aid containing a large number of monetary amounts facilitates the valuation task by providing a context to their bids, while avoiding starting point bias at the same time. The number of outliers is also reduced in comparison to the previous formats. Some versions of the payment card show how the values in the card relate to actual household expenditures or taxes (benchmarks). The payment card is nevertheless vulnerable to biases relating to the range of the numbers used in the card and the location of the benchmarks. It cannot be used in telephone interviews (see Box 4.6 for an example). A variant of the payment card suitable for telephone surveys sequentially names WTP intervals and asks the respondent to stop when their WTP lies in the stated interval. This is a common approach to eliciting income in a telephone survey and practice is to start with the lowest interval first.

- *Single-bounded dichotomous choice* or referendum methods became increasingly popular in the 1990s. This elicitation format is thought to simplify the cognitive task faced by respondents (respondents only have to make a judgement about a given price, in the same way as they decide whether or not to buy a supermarket good at a certain price) while at the same time providing incentives for the truthful revelation of preferences under certain circumstances (that is, it is in the respondent's strategic interest to accept the bid if his WTP is greater than or equal to the price asked and to reject otherwise, see Carson et al. (1999) for a detailed explanation of incentive compatibility). This procedure minimises non-response and avoids outliers. The presumed supremacy of the dichotomous choice approach reached its climax in 1993 when it received the endorsement of the NOAA panel (Arrow et al., 1993). However, enthusiasm for closed-ended formats gradually waned as an increasing number of empirical studies revealed that values obtained from dichotomous choice elicitation were significantly and substantially larger than those resulting from comparable open-ended questions. Such differences between elicitation formats are to be expected. Some degree of yea-saying is also possible, but the problem of nay-saying, typically from protesting an element of the scenario or disbelief that the government can actually provide the good, is likely to characterise a larger fraction of the respondents than is yea-saying. In addition, dichotomous choice formats are relatively inefficient in that less information is available from each respondent (the researcher only knows whether WTP is above or below a certain amount), so that larger samples and stronger statistical assumptions are required. This makes surveys more expensive and their results more sensitive to the statistical assumptions made.

BOX 4.6   EXAMPLE OF A PAYMENT LADDER
USED IN THE ELICITATION OF WTP TO
AVOID INCREASED ABSTRACTIONS
FROM THE RIVER OUSE

On this sheet are written different amounts of money from nothing up to £200. Starting at the top of the list and moving down please ask yourself: 'Am I willing to pay 50p per year to avoid the additional abstraction of water with the consequences just described? Or would I rather not pay this amount and have the water abstracted from the river? And would I pay £1 or £2 or even more?' If you are *almost certain you would pay* the amounts of money in the card to avoid abstraction then place a tick (✔) in the space next to these amounts.

Please don't agree to pay an amount if you think you can't afford it or if you feel that there are more important things for you to spend your money on, or if you are not sure about being prepared to pay or not.

Going down the ladder, when you reach an amount that you are not sure of paying then simply leave it BLANK. When you reach an amount that you are *almost certain that you would not pay*, then place a cross (✘) next to the amount.

£/year	✔ or ✘
nothing	✔
50p	✔
£1	✔
£2	✔
£3	✔
£5	
£7	
£10	✘
£12	✘
£15	✘
£17	✘
£20	✘
£25	✘
£30	✘
£40	✘
£50	✘

£60	✗
£70	✗
£80	✗
£90	✗
£100	✗
£150	✗
Any other amount	✗

Source: EFTEC, 1998c

- *One and a half bound dichotomous choice* procedure was proposed by Hanemann (1999), whereby respondents are initially informed that costs of providing the good in question will be between £X and £Y (X<Y), with the amounts X and Y being varied across the sample. Respondents are then asked whether they are prepared to pay the lower amount £X. If the response is negative no further questions are asked; if the response is positive then respondents are asked if they would pay £Y. Conversely, respondents may be presented with the upper amount £Y initially and asked about amount £X if the former is refused.

- *Double-bounded dichotomous choice* formats are more efficient than their single-bounded counterpart as more information is elicited about each respondent's WTP. For example, we know that a person's true value lies between £5 and £10 if she accepted to pay £5 in the first question but rejected £10 in the second. But all the limitations of the single-bounded procedure still apply in this case. Another problem is the possible loss of incentive compatibility due to the fact that the second question may not be viewed by respondents as exogenous to the choice situation. Finally, anchoring and yea-saying biases can also occur.

   Recently, a number of variants of the standard elicitation formats described above have also been proposed in the literature. One issue of concern in CV studies is respondent's preferences or imprecise preferences regarding the change of interest (Ready et al., 1995; Wang, 1997; Dubourg et al., 1997). Box 4.6 presents an example of a payment ladder designed to identify the range of values over which individual valuations were uncertain taken from a study of WTP to avoid river water abstractions (EFTEC, 1998c). This payment ladder approach has been successfully used in a number of recent studies (Day et al., 1999; Maddison and Mourato, 1999; Mourato and Day, 1998). This approach involves the same statistical formulation of the likelihood function as the double-bounded format (see Chapter 5).

- *Randomised card sorting procedure* is also promising, which is essentially a variant of the payment ladder approach described above. Here respondents are shown a pack of cards each depicting a monetary value. Cards are then shuffled in front of the respondent who is then asked to sort the pack into three piles: amounts which the respondent definitely would pay; amounts the respondent definitely would not pay; and amounts about which the respondent is uncertain.

As mentioned above, the choice of elicitation format is of dramatic importance as different elicitation formats typically produce different estimates. That is, the elicitation format is a non-neutral element of the questionnaire. Carson et al. (2000) summarises a number of stylised facts regarding elicitation formats. These are depicted in Table 4.5.

Table 4.5   Elicitation formats: some stylised facts

Open-ended	Large number of zero responses, few small positive responses.
Bidding game	Final estimate shows dependence on starting point used.
Payment card	Weak dependence of estimate on amounts used in the card.
Single-bounded dichotomous choice	Estimates typically higher than other formats.
Double-bounded dichotomous choice	The two responses do not correspond to the same underlying WTP distribution.

Source: Carson et al., 2000

Overall, considering the pros and cons of each of the formats reviewed above, we would recommend two procedures: payment cards and dichotomous choice formats. Payment cards are more informative and cheaper to implement than dichotomous choice and are superior to both direct open-ended questions and bidding games. Dichotomous choice formats may be incentive compatible and facilitate respondents' valuation task. The new variants described (the one and a half bound approach and the randomised card sorting procedure) also show potential although further research is needed before they become established.

Whatever the elicitation format adopted, respondents are reminded of substitute goods and of their budget constraints and the related need to make compensating adjustments in other types of expenditure to accommodate the additional financial transaction implied by the survey. The former reminds respondents that the good in question may not be unique and that this has implications upon its value. The latter reminds respondents of their limited incomes and of the need to trade-off money for environmental improvements. Box 4.7 contains examples of common statements used as reminders.

Finally, it is worth mentioning some adjustments that have to be made in the arguments presented above when WTA is used rather than WTP:

BOX 4.7   EXAMPLES OF BUDGET AND SUBSTITUTE REMINDERS

Please don't agree to pay an amount if you think you can't afford it or if you feel that there are more important things for you to spend your money on, or if you are not sure about being prepared to pay or not.

Please think carefully about how much you can really afford and where the additional money would come from and try to be as realistic as possible.

Please remember that there are many rivers such as this one in this county, providing similar types of amenities and not affected by pollution.

By agreeing to pay this amount of money to avoid this environmental change less money will be available for your other expenditures. Here is a list of some budget categories that people usually have. Which budget would your money come from?

Food
Clothes
Recreation
Other environmental causes
Savings
Nothing in particular

Source: author's surveys.

BOX 4.8   APPROACHES USED TO INCREASE THE ACCURACY OF WTA ANSWERS

London homeless survey (EFTEC, 1998b): WTA to put up with hostel closure

Hostels provide you with accommodation and a number of other support services. We would like to find out how much you *value all of this*. We will use the following question to try and find out how much the accommodation and services are worth to you.

Imagine that, for some reason, *all the hostels in the country* had to shut down for a *whole year* next year and you had to find somewhere to stay. Suppose in order to compensate you for not being able to use the hostels any more, you were given an additional cash payment each week, *over and above* what you said you receive at the moment.

1.   How much money would you have to receive each week during the whole year to give you *the same quality of life* as you have now (not better or worse, but just the same)?
Compensation amount ....
2.   How would you spend this money?
3.   Taking into account what you have just said about how you would spend the extra money, do you think that your quality of life would be the same, better or worse than what you have at the moment?(If better or worse repeat question 1)

Peruvian slash-and-burn farmers (Smith et al., 1998): WTA to change land use

Some electricity companies in developed countries are interested in investing in forest preservation and agroforestry projects. These firms are willing to compensate farmers who preserve forest and adopt multistrata agroforestry systems. A fixed annual payment will be made for each hectare of preserved forest and agroforestry. Payments will cease if the preserved area was deforested or the agroforestry area was cleared for slash-and-burn.

What is the minimum annual compensation you would require to permanently preserve 1 hectare of primary or secondary forest (or to change from slash-and burn to agroforestry) in your farm?

Please remember that the electricity companies are approaching many farmer communities such as yours in order to choose where to invest. Therefore you are competing with other farmers for this project. As such, there is no guarantee that any bids will be accepted, and it is advisable to minimise your bids in order to stand a chance against competition.

- First, under a WTA format, open-ended elicitation procedures will produce higher average values than dichotomous choice procedures. Open-ended elicitation may also yield very large outliers. In this case, dichotomous choice is the conservative approach.
- Given that WTA measures are not constrained by income, respondents may have a tendency to overbid. Some mechanisms must be found to counteract this tendency. Box 4.8 illustrates two different approaches used that resulted in a successful elicitation of WTA amounts. The first example emphasises that WTA amounts should provide the same quality of life if the change occurs, not a better one. The second example presents the existence of competing uses.

4.2.4   Debriefing and Follow-up Questions

There are two main types of follow-up questions:

1. Questions to explain *why respondents were or were not willing to pay* for the change presented. Box 4.9 presents an example of WTP follow-up questions used in the study valuing reductions in river water abstraction for an English river (EFTEC, 1998c). These questions are important to identify invalid answers, that is, answers that do not reflect people's welfare change from the good considered. These debriefing questions are also important in the pre-testing and design stage of a CV study, as illustrated by the UK aggregates study (see Section 4.2.2(3)).
2. Questions to explain respondents' *views of the scenario presented.* These are important to assess the credibility and meaningfulness of the CV scenario presented in the survey. Box 4.10 contains examples used in the river survey mentioned in Box 4.9 (EFTEC, 1998c) and in a WTP study for a new sanitation system in Malacca, Malaysia (Mourato, 1998).

BOX 4.9   WTP FOLLOW-UP QUESTIONS

Possible reasons why respondents are *not* willing to pay for the proposed change	Valid (✔) Protest (✗)
I/our household cannot afford to pay	✔
The change is too small to be of importance	✔
I/we think this problem is not a priority	✔
I am/we would be satisfied with the future situation	✔
I am/we are not very interested in this matter	✔
I do not live near here	✔
There are many other similar goods around	✔
Spending should be on all rivers, not just this one	✗
I object to paying higher water rates	✗
Everyone should pay for this, not just local people	✗
The government should pay for this	✗
The water company should pay for this	✗
I need more information/time to answer the question	✗

Possible reasons why respondents are willing to pay for the proposed change	Valid (✔) Bias (✗)
I/we think this problem is important	✔
I/we would like to avoid further deterioration of the river water	✔
I am/we are very interested in this river	✔
I/we use this river for recreational purposes	✔
I/we may want to use the river in the future although I/we do not use it now	✔
We should protect the river environment for the animals/plants concerned	✔
We should protect the river environment for future generations	✔
We should protect the river environment for other people to enjoy	✔
My answer reflects my views on the need to preserve all rivers, not just this one	✗
I/we get satisfaction from giving to a good cause	✗
I/we will not really have to pay any extra amount	✗

Source: EFTEC, 1998c

BOX 4.10 SCENARIO FOLLOW-UP QUESTIONS

Valuation of reduction in river water abstractions (EFTEC, 1998a)

Are the proposals regarding this river something that particularly interest you?

Have you previously been interested in river water issues?

Do you feel you are capable of making a decision about the proposals regarding this river?

Do you think the public should be widely consulted about proposed changes to this river?

WTP for a new sanitation system in Malacca, Malaysia (Mourato, 1998)

Do you think the new system will receive strong public support?

Do you think a private company can successfully implement the system?

Do you think the new system will attain the desired results?

Do you believe the new system will actually be put into place?

Do you think that higher sanitation fees/water rates are a good financing method?

Some of the follow-up questions are debriefing questions. These debriefing questions are typically much more extensive in a pilot survey, but the ones that are most useful in explaining differences in the valuation question responses are often retained for the final survey.

4.2.5 Attitudes, Opinions, Knowledge and Uses

Apart from monetary valuations of the policy change in question, CV questionnaires typically collect a wealth of additional qualitative and quantitative information. In particular, CV questionnaires generally contain a number of questions that intend to measure respondents' attitudes, perceptions or feelings about the subject of interest. An *attitude* is a learned predisposition to respond in a consistently favourable or unfavourable manner with respect to a given object (Fishbein and Ajzen, 1975).

According to the 'theory of reasoned action' (Fishbein and Ajzen, 1975), attitudes are learned and are a function of a person's socio-economic characteristics, personality traits and set of beliefs. The theory of reasoned action also tells us that attitudes are a precursor to behavioural intentions such as the expression of a hypothetical WTP (which in turn are good predictors of actual behaviour). Hence, attitudinal questions are an important element of CV surveys, serving mainly four functions:

1. They 'warm-up' respondents and get them involved in the questionnaire.
2. They help respondents to think about all aspects of the change being valued and encourage them to investigate their preferences about it.
3. They provide valuable qualitative and quantitative information that may help to validate the monetary valuations.
4. Often, these variables also turn out to be good predictors of WTP.

If relevant, questions about the use and satisfaction with the good or service of interest are also asked.

4.2.6 Demographics

The survey also includes questions on the socio-economic and demographic characteristics of respondents, such as age, education, job and income. These questions are used to ascertain the representativeness of the survey sample relative to the population of interest, to examine the similarity of the groups receiving different versions of the questionnaire and to study how WTP varies according to respondents' characteristics (see Chapter 5). Sometimes identification information such as name, address and telephone number of respondents is also elicited in order to verify that the interview took place, to conduct a follow-up interview at a later period, or to send the respondent some participation incentive. As an example, Box 4.11 lists the types of information that were collected in a CV survey of willingness to pay for an improvement in the waste management system in Kuala Lumpur (Mourato and Day, 1998). Many of the demographic variables should be defined to match those of major government statistical surveys in order to facilitate benefits transfer.

4.2.7 Questionnaire Structure

The ordering of the questions, that is, the structure of the questionnaire and the sequencing of the questions, is also a crucial stage of questionnaire design. This is mainly for two reasons:

1. Questions asked earlier in a questionnaire can affect the answers supplied at a later stage.

```
┌─────────────────────────────────────────────────────────────────┐
│                                                                   │
│   BOX 4.11    TYPES OF INFORMATION ELICITED IN                    │
│               A WASTE MANAGEMENT CV SURVEY                        │
│                                                                   │
│   Attitudinal variables and      General environmental interests and │
│   lifestyle factors              opinions                         │
│                                  Specific waste-related perceptions │
│                                  and opinions                     │
│                                  Attitude measures                │
│                                                                   │
│   Waste-related variables        Quantity of waste produced       │
│                                  Collection frequency             │
│                                  Container type                   │
│                                  Recycling and re-use habits      │
│                                  Satisfaction with services       │
│                                                                   │
│   Monetary evaluation            WTP information and reasons for   │
│   information                    willingness to pay               │
│                                                                   │
│   Attitudes and opinions         Credibility, feasibility, fairness and │
│   about the proposed             efficiency measures              │
│   scenario                                                        │
│                                                                   │
│   Respondent                     Demographic variables            │
│   characteristics                Socio-economic characteristics   │
│                                  Wealth indicators                │
│                                  Name, address and telephone number │
│                                                                   │
│   Source:   Mourato and Day (1998)                                │
│                                                                   │
└─────────────────────────────────────────────────────────────────┘
```

2. Earlier questions can encourage respondents to answer the rest of the questionnaire by engaging them in the topic and establishing a rapport, or they can deter respondents from continuing to answer the questionnaire by asking difficult, irritating, embarrassing or sensitive questions.

Table 4.6 provides a checklist of general principles that should guide the ordering of questions within a questionnaire. Following these general survey rules, CV questionnaires are usually structured as in Table 4.7.

First, it is customary to ask a set of *attitudinal, behavioural and lifestyle questions* about the good/service to be valued and about the subset of goods/

Table 4.6   Ordering questions: basic principles

Ask the most straightforward questions at the start

Keep the more difficult, contentious and sensitive questions towards the end of the questionnaire

Ask questions in a logical order, keeping questions about related topics grouped together

Ask basic information first, then classification information and only then identification information

---

Table 4.7   Question order in a typical CV questionnaire

Introductory section	Introductory remarks
	Attitudinal and opinion questions
	Use of the good/service of interest
	Use of related goods/services
	Lifestyle questions
Valuation section	Valuation scenario
	Value elicitation questions
	Follow-up questions
Final section	Socio-economic characteristics
(Optional)	Respondent's identification – Interviewer debriefing questions

---

services of which it is a part. If relevant, questions about the use of and satisfaction with the good or service of interest are also asked.

This set of initial questions does not provide an answer to the main aim of the CV questionnaire, that is, valuing the change of interest in monetary terms. However, they are related to that aim as they reveal some of the underlying factors behind respondents' values and are as such basic information. In addition, as mentioned above, these questions serve to warm-up respondents, engage them in the topics of interest and prepare them to answer the more demanding valuation questions. This group of questions is normally easy to answer and non-contentious.

Within this set of questions, the 'funnel approach' can be used whereby general attitudinal and behavioural questions precede more specific questions (a top-down approach). However, in some circumstances it may make sense to follow an inverted-funnel sequencing (a bottom-up approach) whereby questioning begins with specific attributes of the good and then concludes with more general opinions. The choice is context-specific.

The second set of questions provides the main core of basic information, the *monetary valuation*. In this section, the valuation scenario is presented and respondents are asked for their monetary valuations. Follow-up questions are also asked to uncover the reasons behind the values stated. This set of questions is cognitively more demanding than the former and some of the information provided in the scenario description may be considered difficult or dull. Coming up with WTP or WTA values for sometimes unfamiliar and complex changes can also be considered a complex procedure. However, at this point, respondents should be sufficiently engaged in the exercise to be willing to make the effort to continue, that is, it is hoped that the initial questions have a positive effect on the quality of answers to subsequent sections.

Finally, the most *sensitive questions* are asked: these are classification questions about the socio-economic and demographic characteristics of the respondent and, sometimes, identification questions such as names and addresses. The former should precede the latter, according to the rules established above, as the latter are more sensitive and could be construed as illegitimate. Within the classification questions, the rule continues to be to place the more problematic questions at the end, such as income; and within the identification questions, telephone number should be the last question.

Throughout, questions should be presented in a logical order so that related topics are kept together. Both respondents and interviewers should also be able to follow the order of the questions correctly, without difficulty. A questionnaire should be as appealing and as user-friendly as possible. Particularly in self-administered questionnaires, such as mailshots, the appearance, format, spacing, positioning and colour of the questions can have a significant effect on the quality of the results (Dilman, 1978). Table 4.8 provides a checklist of general principles that should guide the ordering of questions within a questionnaire.

4.3   PRE-TESTING

Pre-testing refers to testing out the questionnaire on a small sample of respondents to identify and correct potential problems. All CV questionnaires should be pre-tested and all aspects of the questionnaire discussed above should be pre-tested.

Table 4.8   Basic principles of layout

Use a booklet format	Looks professional Easy to manipulate Prevents pages being lost
Avoid crowding questions too close together	Improves appearance More user friendly Easier to answer
Use large fonts on all the material to be read or visually inspected	Improves appearance More user friendly Accounts for people with short-sightedness
Pre-code all close-ended questions and try to use an answer column	Facilitates coding Minimises mistakes
Consider colour-blindness when preparing colourful charts and graphs	Prevents confusion in colour-blind people
Use coloured paper, visual aids and cue cards when appropriate	Improves appearance More user friendly Less boring
Use good quality printing and visual material	Improves appearance Easier to read and inspect More user-friendly Looks professional
Number the pages and the questions	Improves appearance Looks professional Easy to manipulate Permits skip patterns Easy to identify missing answers
Colour-code various versions of the questionnaire	Easy to manipulate Minimises errors
Fit questions to a page	Minimises mistakes
Place interviewer instructions near the relevant questions in a different letter type	Easy to manipulate Minimises mistakes
Clearly identify skip patterns using distinct letter types and place them straight after the filter question	Minimise mistakes

4.3.1 Focus groups

A *focus group* is an interview conducted by a moderator among a small group of respondents in an unstructured manner. Focus groups are the most important qualitative research procedure (Malhotra, 1996).

In the context of CV surveys, focus groups can be used to gain insights about issues of interest and particular questionnaire design characteristics. More often than not, unexpected findings can be obtained from group discussions and interactions. Focus groups should be used early on in the questionnaire design process to adequately inform it.

Focus groups typically have 6–12 participants plus a moderator and an assistant who takes notes, records the session and provides refreshments. The participants are paid and are normally chosen to be homogeneous on particular characteristics such as sex, age, race or education to facilitate interaction. Focus groups that run longer than one and a half hours are likely to be less productive due to participant and moderator fatigue. In general, more than one focus group should be conducted for each population segment of interest, to make sure that the results of a particular session were not the product of special circumstances specific to the group (such as the presence of a dominant participant).

Note that the CV questionnaire should be revised after each focus group so that the subsequent focus group can deal with new aspects rather than providing the same lessons. On the other hand, the marginal information gains of running additional groups can quickly diminish as the number of groups increases.

It is important to note that focus groups do not substitute for the main survey since the participants are not randomly selected and are too small a sample to yield reliable estimates.

4.3.2 One-to-one Interviews

One-to-one interviews where respondents are asked to complete the questionnaire (or relevant parts of it) and afterwards are debriefed about its contents, structure or wording are useful ways of fine-tuning the survey instrument and detecting early problems.

4.3.3 Verbal Protocols

A *verbal protocol* is an approach where respondents are encouraged to think out loud and verbalise anything they might be thinking, even if trivial and seemingly unimportant, while completing a task such as answering a questionnaire. Verbal protocols are a useful approach to uncovering thought processes. This approach could be helpful at the early stages of questionnaire development.

The sessions are tape-recorded and the verbalised thought processes of respondents are referred to as a protocol (Malhotra, 1996). This approach can be very useful in uncovering how respondents understand the various questions included in the questionnaire, how they think about complex environmental issues presented in the CV scenario, and how they perceive the valuation task.

A problem with this approach is that participants typically have many thoughts that they do not verbalise, so that protocols are generally incomplete. A verbal protocol may also have a tendency not to report obvious factors being considered such as things that were just read to them in the survey.

4.3.4 Pilot Surveys

The final stage of pre-testing the questionnaire involves carrying out a field pilot. A *field pilot* consists in administering a draft questionnaire to a sample of respondents similar to the one that will be used in the final survey and under the conditions to be followed in the final survey.

Field pilot respondents should be *debriefed* extensively. This occurs after the questionnaire is completed and consists of asking the respondents to describe the meaning of each question, to explain their answers, and to state any problems and difficulties they may have had.

The field pilot serves the purpose of fine-tuning the questionnaire and of training the interviewers. The responses should also be coded and analysed to ensure the adequacy of the data collected.

More than one round of field pilots may be required if a significant number of problems is detected in the questionnaire design. Samples typically used in environmental applications range from 25 to 100 respondents per pilot, depending on the total sample size, the complexity of the survey, the elicitation procedure adopted (with dichotomous choice procedures requiring larger samples) and the number of split-samples required for the research (with more split-samples requiring larger sample sizes).

Post-pilot or post-main survey debriefing exercises

Debriefing exercises involve contacting a subset of survey respondents in order to obtain their perceptions of the survey experience, the credibility of the good and payment mechanism and so on, once they have had time for reflection. The exercises can be implemented either after pilot survey so that the questionnaire design can be informed or after the main survey so that data analysis and validity testing can be informed. A number of guidelines, refer-ring to 'survey' covering both pilot and main surveys, are set out below:

- Post-survey debriefing exercises should be principally conducted by a facilitator trained in qualitative techniques.
- Post-survey focus groups can be constituted on a number of criteria depending upon their purpose. Random sub-sampling of survey re-spondents may be useful. However, analysts should be wary of self-selection bias in respect of which respondents agreed to partici-pate in these exercises, in that only those who are already interested in the change in question agree to participate in these groups. This may compound a further self-selection bias in the administration of the main survey. Alternatively, analysis of respondent characteristics can be used to assemble groups that are heterogeneous in terms of vari-ables of particular interest (for example, on the basis of responses to questions concerning environmental or cultural world-views, socio-economic variables and so on). In addition to validity analyses, such groups can be used to test notions of consensus building across groups. Conversely, similar survey response variables can be used to assemble homogeneous groups. Here participants may feel more at ease with expressing particular concerns about the questions used in the survey (for example, they may feel more willing to express viewpoints which do not conform with the prevailing norms of society at large). Such groups can also be used to explore polarisation of opinions regarding the issues under investigation.
- Post-survey one-to-one exercises can sometimes bring out views which may be repressed in focus group settings and provide interesting com-parisons with the latter.
- A combination of one-to-one and focus group work encompassing the same individuals can also be useful. Analysts should be aware of possible sequencing effects in these exercises (for example, a prior focus group experience may condition subsequent one-to-one responses). Such formats can be used to assess whether individual responses tend to converge to consensus if information regarding the responses of others is supplied to all participants (this supply can be controlled through a variety of mechanisms).
- Post-survey debriefing also provides the opportunity to test response reliability (see also subsequent discussion of reliability in Chapter 8). Respondents can again be asked questions they faced in the survey (they can either be reminded of their survey responses or, more usu-ally, not) and responses compared. Such exercises can be used to

examine the impacts of having time to reflect (temporal stability), which may be substantial. Varying reflection times from minutes (within the survey) to days or longer periods can substantially assist assessments both of reliability and content validity.

4.4   THE MAIN SURVEY

The discussions about the choice of sample size and survey method are presented in Chapter 3.

NOTE

1.   The use of prices also poses problems as respondents may agree to pay more but simply adjust the quantities consumed so that total expenditure remains the same.

ANNEX 4.1   Writing survey questions

Translating the information needed to answer the research issues of interest into a set of questions that respondents can understand and are prepared to answer meaningfully is a fundamental stage of questionnaire design. As noted in Box A4.1.1, this is not an easy task for any survey, with CV surveys raising particular design issues related to the hypothetical scenarios and valuation questions. Even seemingly small changes in wording can cause large differences in responses. The example in Box A4.1.1 is illuminating in this respect, and shows how tricky it can be to ask questions and the major implications that question design can have on the answers. Questionnaire design should never be underestimated or taken lightly.

Writing unbiased questions that respondents can understand and answer is not the only challenge. Questionnaires must also be designed so that respondents are motivated to co-operate, to become involved in the interview process and to complete answers to all the questions. If respondents get tired or bored, the number of inconsistent, inaccurate and random answers increases, as do non-response and incomplete answers.

Fortunately, although CV is still relatively young as a technique, questionnaires have been extensively used by researchers in many other fields, such as

---

BOX A4.1.1   FRAMING QUESTIONS

Two priests, a Dominican and a Jesuit, are talking about whether it is a sin to smoke and pray at the same time. After failing to reach a conclusion, each goes off to consult his respective superior. The next week they meet again:

- 'Well, what did your superior say?' asks the Dominican.
- 'He said it was all right', the Jesuit responds.
- 'That's funny', replies the Dominican, 'my superior said it was a sin'.
- 'What did you ask him?' inquires the Jesuit.
- 'I asked him if it was all right to smoke while praying', says the Dominican.
- 'Oh', says the Jesuit, 'I asked my superior if it was all right to pray while smoking!'

Source: Dillon et al., 1994.

psychology, marketing and transport, for many decades. The development of attitude-behaviour models (Fishbein and Ajzen, 1975) and Total Design and Tailored Methods (Dillman, 1978, 2000) are two examples of approaches that can inform CV survey design (see Section 4.1). CV surveys can and should be informed by this wealth of experience that has accumulated in the various disciplines that use survey-based research methods. Obviously, there are aspects of the questionnaire that are specific to CV surveys such as the fact that the changes described are typically hypothetical, the goods or services to be valued are not normally traded in markets (and hence do not have a price), have public good characteristics and may be unfamiliar to respondents, and monetary valuations are the ultimate aim of the study. But, at the same time, there are many similarities with other types of surveys and the potential for cross-fertilisation between disciplines should be explored.

On the basis of the combined experience of marketing practitioners and other researchers using questionnaires, and informed by the lessons learned by CV practitioners in the last two decades, a number of recommendations for successful questionnaires can be made.

GENERAL RULES

Although individual questions and their contents in each questionnaire are context-specific, a number of general rules can be compiled. This section presents such rules for question content, incentives to answer, question type, structured and unstructured questions, and question wording.

Question Content

The first thing that should be considered about each question is the reason why it is being asked. All questions should be relevant, serve a purpose and/ or provide information that can be used to answer the research questions formulated in the first stage. If the information elicited by a particular question is superfluous, then that question should be dropped.

There are some special cases that merit consideration. Some questions may not be directly relevant to the economic valuation exercise but may serve the purpose of 'warming-up' respondents and getting them involved in the questionnaire. Also, certain questions may be included to disguise the purpose or the sponsorship of the research, in cases when full disclosure might prompt protest answers and refusals to participate. This obviously poses ethical and methodological concerns as discussed in Chapter 8. There may also be cases where questions are deliberately repeated in order to test for validity and reliability of responses.

Incentives to Answer

Efforts should be made to minimise the number of respondents that are *unable or unwilling to answer the questions* being posed.

Respondents may be unable to answer a particular question because they are not sufficiently informed about the topic of the question. A typical example is asking a respondent who does not generally do the shopping for his or her household how often the household buys environmentally-friendly products. This problem can be addressed by including an initial *filter question* that screens potential respondents to ensure that they meet the necessary requirements to answer the question.

Respondents may not fully remember events that happened in the past. Inability to remember may lead to errors of *omission* (inability to recall an event that has occurred), *telescoping* (compressing time so that an event is remembered as occurring more recently than it actually did) and *creation* (recalling an event that did not actually occur). A way of minimising these errors consists of presenting cues that may aid the process of recall.

Finally, respondents may be unable to articulate their answer. This happens especially with complex open-ended questions, where no response alternatives are presented. Closed-ended questions, where the response is aided by the fact that respondents only have to select their answer from a number of pre-specified alternatives, greatly reduce this problem. Visual aids and other material may also help respondents to articulate responses. Focus groups and pilot surveys can be used to identify these alternatives.

A different issue regards respondents' unwillingness to answer a question. One reason for refusals to answer lies in questions that are too difficult so that too much effort is required. Table A4.1.1 provides some guidelines on how to word questions so that this kind of problem is avoided. In a nutshell, questions should be kept short, avoiding technical terms, and alternative responses could be provided to facilitate the cognitive task of answering.

Also, respondents may refuse to answer questions that use offensive language, are annoying in any way, and/or are sensitive, indiscreet or embarrassing in nature. For example, sensitive topics include income and religious beliefs where it is not uncommon to find non-response levels of about 30 per cent. Offensive and irritating questions should obviously be avoided; placing sensitive questions at the end of the questionnaire may help to overcome respondents' initial mistrust and increase participation; in addition, adding statements saying that the embarrassing behaviour is common (counter-biasing statement) before requesting the information may also overcome unwillingness to answer (Malhotra, 1996) (see Chapter 5 for how statistical methods can be used to overcome the problem of missing responses).

Question Type

A large variety of question structure types are available to choose from. Using a number of different formats in one questionnaire has the advantage of preventing respondents from becoming bored. It also prevents respondents from falling into a pattern of answers. Conversely, sticking to a consistent style of questions allows respondents to answer more speedily and minimises confusion. Generally, questions fall into two main types: unstructured and structured.

Unstructured questions

Unstructured questions are open-ended questions that respondents answer in their own words. Box A4.1.2 presents examples of open-ended questions. Open-ended questions have some major disadvantages. They are not very suitable for self-administered questionnaires, such as mail surveys, as respondents typically will not write elaborate answers. And when used in personal interviews, they are highly susceptible to interviewer bias, as the interviewers can select what they write down instead of writing the answer verbatim.

BOX A4.1.2   EXAMPLES OF UNSTRUCTURED QUESTIONS

'In your opinion, what are the main environmental problems facing the world today?'
'What is your occupation?'
'What were the highlights of your visit to this site?'

Source: EFTEC, 1999

The coding of open-ended answers is also costly and time-consuming. *Precoding* the answers can overcome some of these problems. Box A4.1.3 illustrates a pre-coded open-ended question. Here, respondents are not shown the pre-coded answers and respond to the question in an open-ended way. Interviewers then select the appropriate response category from the list. This approach is only possible when it is easy to envisage the response categories.

On the other hand, unstructured questions give the respondent the opportunity to freely express his views. The information collected in this way can provide valuable insights into the issue being researched. Hence, such ques-

---

BOX A4.1.3   EXAMPLE OF A PRE-CODED UNSTRUCTURED QUESTION

'In your opinion, what are the main environmental problems facing the world today?'

1. Global warming
2. Biodiversity destruction
3. Water pollution
4. Air pollution
5. Ozone depletion
6. Others, please specify:...

---

tions are normally used at the pre-test stages of a questionnaire. The answers at this stage can be used to set the answer codes in the final design. Open-ended questions can also be used to validate the results obtained in the structured questions.

Structured questions

Structured questions are closed-ended questions that pre-specify the set of response alternatives and the response format. Structured questions constitute the majority of questions that are asked in a typical CV survey. They can take many forms.

In *dichotomous choice questions* respondents are faced with only two response alternatives, such as yes/no, agree/disagree or vote for/vote against. Sometimes a 'don't know' option is also included to avoid forcing respondents into artificially choosing one of the answers. Box A4.1.4 provides an example.

BOX A4.1.4   EXAMPLE OF A DICHOTOMOUS CHOICE QUESTION

'Have you been to Machu Picchu before this time?'

1. Yes
2. No

Source: EFTEC, 1999

BOX A4.1.5   EXAMPLE OF A MULTIPLE-CHOICE QUESTION

'This card lists a series of reasons why people choose to visit the Machu Picchu Citadel only, instead of walking the Inca Trail. Which reason best describes why you decided not to walk the Inca Trail?'

1. Not interested
2. Don't like walking
3. Not enough time
4. Not fit enough/health reasons
5. Too expensive
6. Too crowded
7. Other reason (please specify: ....)

Source: EFTEC, 1999

In *multiple choice questions*, respondents are presented with a number of possible response alternatives and are asked to select one or more of the alternatives according to some criterion. For an example see Box A4.1.5.

The advantages and disadvantages of closed-ended questions are a mirror image of those relating to open-ended questions. They are easy to answer, administer and analyse. Interviewer bias is minimised. On the other hand, these questions allow for less freedom and subtlety in answers. There are also issues of selecting an appropriate number of response alternatives, making sure all the relevant alternatives are included and choosing the order in which

BOX A4.1.6   EXAMPLE OF A SCALE

'Using the scale on this card, how would you classify your knowledge of the role of monasteries in Bulgarian history?

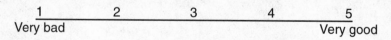

1	2	3	4	5
Very bad				Very good

Source: Mourato et al., 2000

the alternatives are presented. The latter is important as respondents may have a tendency to select an alternative merely because of the place it occupies on the list (order bias). Order bias can be avoided by randomly rotating the items in the list.

Finally, structured questions can take the form of a *scale*. An example can be found in Box A4.1.6. Scales are commonly used in CV surveys.

Question Wording

Question wording is the translation of the desired content and structure of a question into words that respondents can understand and meaningfully answer. It is one of the most critical and difficult stages of questionnaire design and hence one of the most important to get right. Table A4.1.1 provides a checklist of principles that should guide the wording of all questions in general.

In this context it is worth highlighting the importance of conducting a literature review prior to writing the questionnaire. Researchers have been

Table A4.1.1   Basic principles of writing questions

Ask clear and precise questions
Avoid asking irritating questions that might annoy respondents
Avoid ambiguous wording
Response choices should not overlap
Avoid the use of 'leading' or biased questions, that is, questions that suggest
  an answer
Avoid vague questions
Present pre-coded response options
Include sufficient response alternatives in the answer
Avoid generalisations and estimates
Use natural and familiar language
Keep technical jargon to a minimum
Avoid implicit alternatives and assumptions
Keep questions short and straightforward
Avoid making unwarranted presumptions in the questions
Avoid double-barrelled questions, which address two issues at the same time
Avoid relying too much on memory about past behaviour
Avoid words or phrases that might cause offence
Design questions so that they are suited to the target population
Use both positive and negative statements in attitude scales

---

writing and testing question formats and wording for decades. Hence, rather than 're-inventing the wheel' and designing each question from scratch, it is important to review what other people have done, learn from their experience, find out which formats work and which do not, look out for potential problems and work out relevant response categories. In particular, it is useful to try out scales that have already proved to be valid and reliable (for example, when measuring attitudes or risk perceptions). This is why Chapter 10 includes the presentation of the original CV questionnaire as a reporting requirement.

ATTITUDINAL QUESTIONS

As described earlier in this chapter, CV surveys typically include a section containing attitudinal questions about the good or service being valued. Market researchers have developed a large number of scaling techniques to measure people's attitudes towards the object of interest. A *measurement scale* is a scale designed to assign numbers to objects according to certain pre-specified rules.

There are four primary scales of measurement: nominal, ordinal, interval and ratio. Table A4.1.2 summarises their characteristics.

Some of these measurement scales can be very helpful when writing attitudinal questions in CV surveys. The most useful measurement scales for CV surveys are described below:

Comparative Scales

In comparative scales, a respondent is asked to compare one set of objects directly against another. There are several types of comparative scales.

Paired comparisons
In a paired comparison scale respondents are presented with two objects simultaneously and asked to select one according to some criterion. The resulting data are ordinal in nature, that is, all we know is that one object is chosen over another. Box A4.1.7 provides an example.

These scales are most useful when the number of objects to be compared is small. Otherwise, respondent fatigue may occur if faced with a large number of pairs. Known problems include violations of the axiom of transitivity, order bias, no allowance for indifference between objects, and the fact that respondents may dislike both objects. The transitivity axiom is an axiom of rational choice and states that if A is preferred to B and B is preferred to C,

Table A4.1.2   Primary types of measurement scales

Scale	Characteristics	Examples
Nominal	Numbers are used to identify and classify objects into one of a set of mutually exclusive and exhaustive classes, with no implied ordering	Sex classification: male = 1; female = 0.
Ordinal	Numbers indicate the relative positions of the objects but not the magnitude of differences between them	Ranking of environmental priorities: water quality = 1; air quality = 2; waste management = 3; habitat protection = 4.
Interval	Numbers allow us to tell how far apart two or more objects are with respect to a criterion, i.e. differences between objects can be measured	How sure are you about your answer? 100% sure; 75% sure; 50% sure; 25% sure; 0% sure.
Ratio	Has all the characteristics of the above scales plus an absolute zero point, so that ratios of scale values can be computed	Age or income data.

Source: Adapted from Malhotra, 1996.

BOX A4.1.7   EXAMPLE OF A PAIRED COMPARISON

'Please look at the pictures below. Picture A depicts the A303 road as it passes along Stonehenge, as it is today. Picture B illustrates what the landscape would look like if a 2,000 m tunnel were built for the A303. Which landscape do you like the best? Please tick the box below your preferred landscape'

	[PICTURE A]	[PICTURE B]
Preferred landscape:	☐	☐

Source: Adapted from Maddison and Mourato 1999

then A should be preferred to C. Order bias concerns the likelihood of inconsistent or biased answers simply because the questions are in a particular order.

Paired comparisons are often used in choice modelling approaches (see Chapter 6).

Graded paired comparisons

This is a variant of standard paired comparisons in which respondents are asked not only which one of two objects they prefer but they are also asked to indicate by how much it is preferred. A neutral/indifference option may be included. An example is provided in Box A4.1.8.

BOX A4.1.8   EXAMPLE OF A GRADED PAIRED COMPARISON

'Please look at the pictures below. Picture A depicts the A303 as it passes along Stonehenge, as it is today. Picture B illustrates what the landscape would look like if a 2,000 m tunnel were built for the A303. Which landscape do you prefer? Please use the scale below – ranging from 'strongly prefer A' to 'strongly prefer B' – to indicate the strength of your preferences. Please circle the appropriate number on the scale.'

```
                      [PICTURE A]              [PICTURE B]
Preferred landscape:      1   2   3   4   5   6   7
                      Strongly      Neutral      Strongly
                      prefer A                   prefer B
```

Source: Maddison and Mourato, 1999

The scale depicted in Box A4.1.8 identifies the strength of respondents' preferences and allows for indifference between the two items. These scales are also used in choice modelling (see Chapter 6). The difficulty with graded pairs is that it is unlikely that all respondents use the scale in the same way so that the only information that may actually be provided is the same as in a simple paired comparison.

Rank-order scales

In a rank order scale, respondents are presented with several objects simultaneously and asked to order or rank them according to some criterion. The resulting data are also ordinal in nature. Box A4.1.9 presents an example.

BOX A4.1.9   EXAMPLE OF A RANK ORDER SCALE

'Please look at the pictures below. Picture A depicts the A303 as it passes along Stonehenge, as it is today. Picture B illustrates what the landscape would look like if a 2,000 m tunnel were built for the A303. Picture C illustrates what the landscape would look like if a 500 m tunnel were built for the A303. Please rank these alternative landscapes according to your preferences, assigning 1 to your most preferred landscape, 2 to your second most preferred landscape and 3 to your third most preferred landscape (note that no two landscapes should receive the same rank number)'

	[PICTURE A]	[PICTURE B]	[PICTURE C]
RANK:	………	………	………

Source: Maddison and Mourato 1999

This approach is a more efficient way of collecting information than paired comparisons. However, there are limits to how many objects respondents can meaningfully compare. Long ranking lists can be seen to lead to inconsistent and random choices (Foster and Mourato, 2001). Respondents may also have difficulty in ordering lower-ranked objects.

As with paired comparisons, rank-order scaling is frequently used in the context of choice modelling (see Chapter 6).

Constant sum scales

These scales ask respondents to allocate a constant number of units (say points or money) among a set of objects according to some criterion. This approach is most useful when there is a fixed budget for a total project but there are several competing ways within the project for spending the money. An example is provided in Box A4.1.10.

Constant sum scales are normally treated as interval data, within the context of the attributes presented (see Chapter 5 for how to analyse this type of data). The allocation of points in any given situation is, however, influenced

BOX A4.1.10   EXAMPLE OF A CONSTANT SUM
              SCALE

'The table below contains some of the attributes that characterise
the waste management system in Kuala Lumpur. Please allocate
100 points among these attributes so that your allocation reflects
the relative importance you attach to each one. For example, the
more points an attribute receives, the more important you think it
is. And if you think an attribute is twice as important as another,
then please assign it twice as many points. If an attribute is not at
all important to you, then just give it zero points.'

Waste management system characteristics   Total points = 100
Collection frequency
Collection reliability
Container type
Container cleanliness
Waste disposal method
Monthly fee

Source: Adapted from Mourato and Day, 1998

by the specific attributes that are included (Malhotra, 1996). Problems associated with these scales include respondents assigning more or less than the total specified number of points due to the relatively high cognitive burden imposed on respondents.

Non-comparative Scales

In non-comparative scaling respondents are asked to evaluate each object independently, using the scale provided. They typically generate interval data.

Continuous rating scales
In a continuous rating scale respondents are asked to rate an object by placing a mark at the appropriate position on a line that runs from one extreme of the criterion of interest to the other. Box A4.1.11 exemplifies a continuous rating scale.

On the basis of respondents' answers, scores are usually determined by dividing the line into as many categories as desired and assigning scores to

BOX A4.1.11   EXAMPLE OF A CONTINUOUS
             RATING SCALE

'In your opinion, are taxes a fair way of financing Lake Balaton's clean-up programme? Please place a mark at the appropriate location on the scale below'

Very fair ◄─────────────────────────► Very unfair

Source: Adapted from Mourato, 1998

these categories. The scores are then usually analysed as interval data. The disadvantages of this technique lie in the scoring procedure, which is cumbersome and arbitrary.

Itemised rating scales
In an itemised scale, respondents are presented with a scale that has numbers or a brief description associated with each category, and are asked to select one of the categories according to some criterion. The categories are ordered in terms of the scale position. Odd or even numbers of categories may be used. Itemised scales are called *balanced* if an equal number of favourable and unfavourable categories are used and *unbalanced* if unequal numbers are used. Some itemised scales 'force' respondents into taking a position by not including a neutral/no opinion category. A number of scale forms or configurations are possible: scales can be presented vertically or horizontally; categories can be expressed by boxes, lines or units; numbers may or may not be assigned to each category; numbers can be positive, negative or both.

Itemised rating scales are typically used in the context of *multiple item rating scales*. These are complex scales where the respondent is asked to respond not only to one single item, but to a number of items that reflect statements or feelings about the object under investigation. For example, respondents may be asked to complete multiple attitudinal scales that reflect different aspects of the services provided by a museum, such as general atmosphere, entry prices, staff knowledge, queuing time, variety of the collection and convenience of opening hours.

A respondent's overall attitude score is typically obtained by combining the responses to each of the items. In order to construct a multi-item scale it is necessary to have a theory about the object of interest, that is, about which characteristics are important and how they are determined. Then a pool of

BOX A4.1.12   EXAMPLE OF A SIMPLE ITEMISED RATING SCALE

'I am now going to read out a number of features of a visit to the Machu Picchu Citadel. Please use the scale on this card, that ranges from 'very bad' to 'very good', to classify the quality of each of these features, according to the experience you had.'

1	2	3	4	5
Very bad				Very good

Congestion
Information on site
Guided tours
Train transport to/from Aguas Calientes
Quality of the view from site
Toilet facilities on site

Source: EFTEC, 1999

potentially relevant scale items is constructed. Pilot surveys are used to reduce the set of items and refine the scale. In the end, the validity and reliability of the scale should be evaluated. Box A4.1.12 exemplifies a simple rating scale.

One type of rating scale widely used in CV surveys is the *Likert scale*. In this scale, respondents are asked to indicate a degree of agreement or disagreement with statements about the object. Box A4.1.13 presents an example. This is a popular scale as it is easy to construct and administer. It is also readily understood by respondents. But it takes longer to complete than other itemised rating scales as respondents have to read whole statements.

When various statements about the same object are included, an overall evaluative score is calculated for each respondent that reflects his or her attitude towards the object. This is done by summing up the scores obtained for each statement. Care must be taken to use a consistent scoring procedure (for example, high scores consistently reflect a favourable response). This means that scores have to be reversed for the categories assigned to negative statements as agreeing with a negative statement reflects an unfavourable response.

Another type of rating scale is the *semantic differential scale*, a seven-point scale with end points associated with *bipolar labels* (for example, very

---

BOX A4.1.13   EXAMPLE OF A LIKERT SCALE

I am now going to read out a number of statements about Stone-henge and would like you to tell me whether you agree or disagree with each statement. When answering, please use the scale on this card, which ranges from 'strongly agree' to 'strongly disagree'.

1.   Strongly agree
2.   Agree
3.   Neither agree nor disagree
4.   Disagree
5.   Strongly disagree

'I have more important things to think about than a pile of old stones.'
'Stonehenge should be protected for future generations even if that costs us money now.'
'Stonehenge has a value only for those who actually visit it.'

Source: Maddison and Mourato, 1999

BOX A4.1.14   EXAMPLE OF A SEMANTIC DIFFERENTIAL SCALE

'Using the scales below, please insert a cross on the position that best indicates how accurately one or the other adjective in the scale describes the image that you have of yourself.'

Dominating |___|___|___|___|___|___|___| Submissive

Rational |___|___|___|___|___|___|___| Emotional

Orthodox |___|___|___|___|___|___|___| Liberal

Source: Adapted from Malhotra, 1996

---

good, very bad) that have *semantic meaning*. An example can be found in Box A4.1.14.

The response categories are coded afterwards by the researcher and an overall score is computed by summing the responses on each adjacent pair. This approach is generally used to provide a profile or image of the objects being investigated. There is some controversy as to whether the resulting data are interval data.

A modification of the above scale is the *Stapel scale*, which uses a single key word and requires respondents to rate the object of interest on a scale generally from –5 to +5, without a neutral point. An example is presented in Box A4.1.15.

An overall evaluative score can be computed for each respondent by summing the scores given to each scale item. Stapel scales are easy to construct but may be confusing for respondents.

BOX A4.1.15   EXAMPLE OF A STAPEL SCALE

'Using the scales below, please evaluate how accurately each phrase or word describes the waste collection system in Kuala Lumpur. Please select a plus (+) number for the phrases you think describe the collection system accurately. The stronger you feel that a phrase describes the current system, the larger the plus number you should choose. Then select a minus (–) number for phrases that you think do not describe the collection system accurately; the less you feel the sentence describes the system, the larger the minus number you should choose.'

+5	+5	+5
+4	+4	+4
+3	+3	+3
+2	+2	+2
+1	+1	+1
Very frequent	Reliable	Dirty containers
–1	–1	–1
–2	–2	–2
–3	–3	–3
–4	–4	–4
–5	–5	–5

Source: Adapted from Mourato and Day, 1998

---

5.   Analysis of contingent valuation data

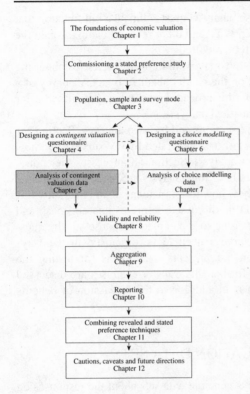

SUMMARY

Broadly speaking the primary objective of a contingent valuation (CV) survey will be to discover the value placed on changes in the provision of a non-market good by the households in a population.[1] Given data on the WTP of every household in the population, the calculation of the total WTP of the population is facile. However, when we only have a sample it is no longer quite so straightforward to calculate the welfare change experienced by the entire population. Indeed, we can only make an *estimate*, employing the tools of statistical analysis.

Moreover, some of the elicitation formats used in stated preference studies do not provide data giving a precise value for each sample household's WTP. Again, statistical techniques must be employed to make use of such data to derive estimates of the sample's WTP.

A second objective of a CV survey may be to determine how WTP is influenced by characteristics of the policy, household or survey design. Such information will be essential in answering a variety of important questions, including:

- How is WTP influenced by the extent of changes in provision of the non-market good or by how the good is to be provided?
- How is WTP distributed amongst different groups in the population? Particular attention is paid to key summary statistics of this distribution, such as mean and median.

- How does the design of the CV questionnaire influence reported values?

To answer questions such as these, analysts must estimate a bid function that describes the relationship between WTP and other relevant factors. Again the tools of econometric analysis will be required.

Finally, in subsequent analysis we may wish to draw inferences about the WTP of other populations based on the results obtained by a CV survey of a particular population. Once again, this procedure, known as benefits transfer (BT), will require the tools of statistical analysis.

This chapter is organised in six sections and has two annexes. Section 5.1 starts with the outline of the types of data generated by CV surveys and how these can be organised for further analysis. Section 5.2 discusses the econometric analysis of WTP. The details of this analysis are presented in Annex 5.1. Section 5.3 and Annex 5.2 show how to estimate mean and median WTP. The econometric analysis of WTP is discussed before estimating mean and median WTP since in most cases (due to incomplete responses to the questionnaire) data collected from surveys need to be organised in the ways suggested in Annex 5.1. Section 5.4 presents the models for testing the validity of WTP values. Models for benefits transfer exercises are discussed in Section 5.5. This information is in addition to the discussion of benefits transfer presented in Annex 1.1.

5.1   CONTINGENT VALUATION DATA SETS

Contingent valuation (CV) surveys generate data sets about the responses on household characteristics, attitudes and opinions and WTP/WTA responses. This section discusses the different forms of data and what to do when some response data are missing.

5.1.1   Data on WTP

Over the years, analysts have developed a myriad of approaches to eliciting WTP values in CV surveys. Broadly speaking, however, the data collected from these different elicitation formats can be classified as falling into one of three basic categories: *continuous data*, *binary data* or *interval data*:

1.   The first category, *continuous data*, results when the survey elicits point estimates of WTP. As an example, open-ended questions of the form 'What is your maximum WTP?' require respondents to reply with one

figure that they believe best represents their WTP for the good being offered.

2. The second category, *binary data*, results when respondents simply state whether their WTP is greater or lower than a value presented to them by the analyst. In CV the amount presented to a respondent in such a survey is termed the *bid level*. Such data are typical of data coming from a single-bounded discrete choice question which requires a 'Yes' or 'No' response to a question such as 'Would you be willing to pay £*x*?'.

3. The final broad category of WTP data is that of *interval data*. Interval data are similar to binary data in that they do not reveal the exact value of the respondent's WTP. Instead, interval data result when respondents are presented with a series of bid levels. Such bid levels may be presented to the respondent all at once (as with a payment card elicitation format) or sequentially (as with the double-bounded discrete choice format). In response to an elicitation format of this type, respondents simply provide details of the interval within which their WTP lies.

BOX 5.1   DATA ON WTP FROM CV SURVEYS

Imagine that we could draw a continuous line that represented all the possible WTP values that a respondent might give in response to a WTP question in a CV survey. Such a line is illustrated below, with low numbers extending to the left and high numbers extending to the right.

Continuous data, as its name implies, result when respondents can reply with any value along this continuous line. By way of illustration, a respondent with a WTP of £12 has been marked in the figure. A survey using an elicitation format that collects continuous data would attempt to elicit this exact value from the respondent.

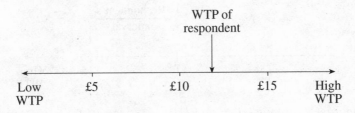

Figure 5.1   Continuous data on WTP

Now imagine that the same respondent had been asked a single-bounded discrete choice WTP question that presented them with a bid level of £8 (see Figure 5.2). Whilst we still assume that the respondent's actual WTP can take any value, data collected from an elicitation format that collects binary data will only reveal whether a respondent's WTP is greater or less than the bid level. Our illustrative respondent with a WTP of £12, for example, will reply 'Yes, I would pay this amount' informing us only that their WTP is greater than £8.

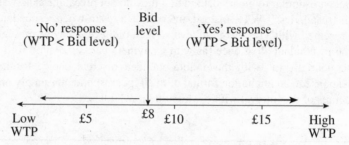

Figure 5.2   Binary data on WTP

Finally, elicitation formats that collect interval data present respondents with a series of bid levels. Continuing our illustration, imagine that our respondent is faced by the series of bid levels £5, £10 and £15. These define a series of intervals, in this case: less than £5, between £5 and £10, between £10 and £15 and greater than £15. As illustrated in Figure 5.3, a respondent with a WTP of £12 would reveal that their WTP was greater than £10 and less than £15.

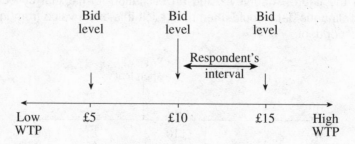

Figure 5.3   Interval data on WTP

Table 5.1   Types of WTP data collected in CV surveys

Data Type	Elicitation Question	Description
Continuous	Open-ended Bidding game	Each respondent states one amount that corresponds to their maximum WTP.
Binary	Single-bounded discrete choice	Each respondent states whether their maximum WTP is above or below a given amount.
Interval	Double-bounded discrete choice Multiple-bounded discrete choice Payment card (and similar approaches)	Each respondent identifies two amounts that bound their maximum WTP (i.e. one amount greater than and one less than their maximum WTP).

The characteristics of these different data types and the elicitation formats they are derived from are illustrated in Box 5.1 and summarised in Table 5.1.

In addition, CV surveys may include a referendum style question along the lines of 'Are you willing to pay anything?'. Data from such a question identify those with zero (or possibly negative) WTP and those with positive WTP. Data may, therefore, contain two separate items of information on a respondent's WTP, details of whether WTP is positive and then details on the level of positive WTP.

5.1.2   Missing Data on WTP

A problem that faces CV analysts is how to deal with respondents who refuse to answer the valuation questions. In survey terminology this is known as the problem of *non-response*. CV analysts tend to recognise three forms of non-response:

1. Households that simply refuse to answer the valuation questions.
2. Households that do not provide their genuine WTP but respond with a zero value instead.
3. Households that do not provide their genuine WTP but respond with an unrealistically high value instead.

The latter two forms of non-response are known as *protest bids*, though this terminology is a little misleading as it is far from clear that all such respondents are actually protesting. Indeed, such responses may have a number of motivations including strategic behaviour intended to ensure the provision of the non-market good or reduce the level of payment that is exacted for the good's actual provision.

Unfortunately, it is not always clear how such responses should be identified from genuine responses. The usual procedure for identifying protest zeros is through follow-up questions in which respondents are asked to list their reasons for being unwilling to pay anything for the non-market good. Analysts use these answers to distinguish between households that place a value of zero on the non-market good because they genuinely do not value it from those that are responding zero for some other reason.[2]

An even larger problem exists in identifying high protest bids. One approach is to compare a household's reported WTP with their reported income. Once allowances have been made for taxation, household size and committed expenditures (on, for example, housing, food, travel and so on), it may be possible to distinguish those who have reported a WTP that is in excess of their ability to pay. Similarly, it may be possible to identify protest bids from follow-up questions that examine a respondent's reasons for answering the valuation questions in the way they did. A further source of information is contained in the interviewer debriefing questions which should allow the interviewer to flag respondents who they believe may have been expressing a protest response.

In all three cases of non-response, it is impossible for the analyst to impute the respondent's true valuation of the non-market good. The only course of action open to the analyst, therefore, is to exclude these responses from the data. The major concern in excluding observations from the data is that this may have some systematic bias on the results of the analysis. We would only expect such a systematic bias to result if non-response were correlated with the true WTP of households. In other words, non-response would bias the analysis if all those who did not answer the valuation questions had, for example, a very low WTP. Unfortunately, since the true WTP of such households is unknown, there is no clear test for this sort of bias.

Instead analysts usually make the assumption that the true WTP of non-responders will be similar to that quoted by households with comparable characteristics. Under this assumption, as long as excluding non-respondents from the data does not bias the representativeness of the sample, it should not bias the analysis of the WTP data.

Following the removal of non-respondents from the sample, therefore, analysts should ensure that the characteristics of the sample have not been systematically biased. Analysts should examine the distribution of key characteristics of households in the sample (for example, household income, age profiles and access to the non-market good) and ensure that it does not differ significantly from the distribution of these characteristics in the population. If the reduced sample is not representative of the population, then the analyst should employ weighting procedures when analysing the data.[3] Annex 5.1 shows how these weighting procedures correct for the lack of representativeness of the sample.

5.1.3   Data on Determinants of WTP

Analysts may frequently be interested in the characteristics of the households included in the sample. Such data are invaluable in ensuring that the sample is representative of the population from which it was drawn. Moreover, analysts may be interested in establishing whether the characteristics of a household explain how much they are willing to pay. We shall return to the issue of how this is achieved in later sections. For now, let us briefly examine the sorts of data that CV analysts might seek to collect in order to explain WTP.

A simple classification of the different types of data that may be collected in a CV survey is presented in Table 5.2. The first category covers a wide variety of data that the analyst could collect on the characteristics of each household. As a minimum requirement every survey should collect a core set of socio-economic characteristics. In addition, analysts will be interested in each household's present knowledge and/or use of the non-market good being valued. Further, many surveys collect details on household's attitudes to the programme being offered in the CV scenario.

As discussed subsequently, analysts should distinguish which of these variables can be considered *exogenous* to the WTP decision and which can be considered *endogenous*. As a broad definition, endogenous variables are those whose values are determined through choices made by the household. For example, a programme to improve the quality of a recreational area might be more highly valued by households that use the recreational area frequently. We might, therefore, wish to explain household WTP through frequency of use. Frequency of use, however, is an endogenous variable since the household chooses its value.

Frequency of use is chosen by the household and will be determined by how greatly the household enjoys the recreational opportunities provided by the recreational area. At the same time the household's WTP for improvements to the recreational area will itself be determined by how greatly the household enjoys the recreational opportunities provided by the area. In this

Table 5.2   Types of data collected in CV surveys

Data Type	Description	Examples
Household characteristics	Variables that describe the characteristics of each household.	• Socio-economic characteristics. • Knowledge of the good being offered. • Attitudes towards the programme being presented.
Programme characteristics	Variables that describe split-sample treatments designed to examine how the characteristics of the programme being valued influence WTP.	Comparison of WTP values between respondents presented with different: • scales of provision of the non-market good; • methods of payment for the non-market good; or • frequency of payment for the non-market good.
Design characteristics	Variables that describe split-sample treatments designed to examine how questionnaire design influences WTP responses.	Comparison of WTP values between respondents answering questionnaires with different: • formats for the WTP elicitation questions; or • quantities of information concerning the qualities of the non-market good.

way we can see that the two choices (that is, frequency of use and WTP) are jointly determined and it is in this sense that we would consider frequency of use an endogenous variable in the determination of WTP. As we shall discuss later, using endogenous variables to explain WTP may generate difficulties in interpreting the analysis of WTP data.

Exogenous variables, on the other hand, are those over which the household has no choice. Examples of exogenous variables include age and sex. To a certain extent most variables involve some element of choice. Household income, for example, is 'chosen' by the household insofar as household members select their employment. However, for our purposes we can consider household income exogenous since the choice of employment is not influenced by their decision on how much they are willing to pay for provision of a non-market good. Thus we can consider a variable to be exogenous so long as it explains WTP but is in no way explained by it.

As well as data describing the characteristics of a household, analysts may undertake surveys in which separate sub-samples are presented with different questionnaires to ascertain whether features of the programme influence reported WTP values. For example, in valuing an improvement in water quality in rivers, analysts may present different sub-samples with different payment vehicles. One sub-sample may be presented with a programme that uses an increase in the household's council tax as a means of paying for the improvements whilst a separate sub-sample may be presented with a programme that suggests an increase in water rates as a payment vehicle.

In a similar vein, analysts may wish to explore the importance of questionnaire design on reported values. In this case one sub-sample may be presented with one questionnaire design and the second with another design. For example, to test the importance of elicitation format, one sub-sample may be faced with an open-ended valuation question whilst a second could be presented with a payment card.

As the following sections and annexes show, one of the analyst's objectives may be to see how significantly these various variables influence the reported values of WTP.

5.1.4 Missing Data on Household Characteristics

A ubiquitous problem in survey data is the refusal of some respondents to provide information on all their household's characteristics. Most commonly, respondents may refuse to answer questions on their income. Again this may cause problems in the analysis if there are systematic differences between those who provide details of their household characteristics and those who refuse to respond.

The most common solution to this problem is to impute values for the missing data. The method works by observing the values for a particular variable reported by other households in the sample. Using regression techniques it is possible to establish how the value taken by this variable are determined by the other observed characteristics of the household. For example, household income will be determined by a number of factors including profession, education, age and sex. A regression of income on these other characteristics will result in an equation that can be used to predict income, given information on the other characteristics of the household. The values for households who refused to reveal their income, therefore, can be imputed from this predictive equation.

5.2 SPECIFICATION OF THE BID FUNCTION

Bid function explains the variation in WTP/WTA response based on the change in and the characteristics of the non-market good, prices of market goods, income and other socio-economic characteristics of the respondents. This section sets out the theoretical model underlying this function and two approaches to estimating this function, namely, utility difference (Section 5.2.2) and bid function (Section 5.2.3) models.

5.2.1 The Theoretical Model

Chapter 1 addresses the relationship between the WTP and WTA values that households state in response to CV questions and the theories of welfare economics. Indeed, it was shown that welfare economics provides the justification for using a household's WTP or WTA as a monetary measure of changes in their welfare.

Many of the issues that have been discussed with regards to the design of CV surveys have revolved around the central concern of ensuring that households are responding to CV questions in a way that is consistent with welfare economic theory. In a similar manner, it is paramount that the analysis of data from CV surveys continues this consistency.

To fix ideas, let us assume that the CV survey presents households with the prospect of securing a change in provision of a non-market good from its present level (Q^0) to a greater level (Q^1). Also we shall assume that the survey is worded so as to elicit a household's maximum WTP to achieve this change.[4]

Following standard economic theory, we can define an *indirect utility function*, $V(\cdot)$, that describes the maximum amount of utility a household can derive from their income, Y, given the prices of goods, P, and the level of provision of the non-market good, Q. It is also assumed that the household's utility will depend on other demographic and economic factors, S. We can write the household's indirect utility function in the general form:

$$V(Y, P, S, Q). \tag{5.1}$$

Under normal circumstances, we would imagine that more income or lower prices would enable the household to purchase more goods and hence realise a higher level of utility. Also, let us assume that increasing the provision of the non-market good represents an improvement. Thus the utility enjoyed by the household will be greater at level Q^1 of provision of the non-market good than at level Q^0, hence:

$$V(Y,P,S,Q^0) < V(Y,P,S,Q^1).$$ (5.2)

When answering a CV question, households are assumed to be comparing their utility or wellbeing at the two levels of provision, Q^0 and Q^1. Since they experience greater wellbeing at the higher level of provision, it seems reasonable to assume that they would be prepared to pay at least something to achieve Q^1. Of course, the more the household pays out to achieve the higher level of provision, the less utility they realise. Indeed their maximum WTP can be formally described as the monetary payment that would ensure that their wellbeing with the higher level of provision is just identical to their wellbeing at the lower level of provision. We can define a quantity C such that:

$$V(Y,P,S,Q^0) = V(Y - C,P,S,Q^1).$$ (5.3)

C is the compensating variation measure of a change in welfare; it is the household's maximum WTP to achieve the increase in provision of the non-market good.

By manipulating equation (5.3), C can be defined as a function of the other parameters in the model. This function, which we denote $C(\cdot)$, is known as the *bid function* and can be written in general form as:

$$C = C(Q^0, Q^1, Y, P, S).$$ (5.4)

Equations (5.3) and (5.4) provide the basic theoretical framework for the analysis of CV data.

A further consideration provided by economic theory is that a household's maximum WTP for any good is bounded by their ability to pay. In other words, their WTP must not be greater than their income, or in mathematical notation:

$$C(Q^0, Q^1, Y, P, S) = WTP \leq Y.$$ (5.5)

The relevant measure of income in this case is discretionary income. Discretionary income is that part of income that is left over once committed expenditures on housing, food, clothing, transportation and other market and non-market goods have been taken into account. Unfortunately, it is notoriously difficult to obtain accurate estimates of discretionary income from survey respondents. Analysts may have to resort to approximations based on reported gross household income (for example, taking a percentage of after-tax household income and dividing by the number of household members), which has the effect of reducing the income coefficient to zero.

Up to this point, we have assumed that the increase in provision of the non-market good from Q^0 to Q^1 represents an improvement to the household. Of course, this is not necessarily the case. More generally, three possible cases exist:

1. A household views the change as an improvement.
2. A household views the change as an improvement or is indifferent to it, that is, places zero value on it.
3. A household views the change as a good thing, or as a bad thing, or is indifferent.

All three cases are equally valid and it will be an empirical issue as to which will be seen in the CV sample.

In general, the CV survey should be designed to identify households that like, dislike or are indifferent to the proposed change in provision of the non-market good. In doing so, the valuation question can be framed appropriately. For example, households experiencing a welfare loss, or those who may have negative WTP, can be asked to reveal the minimum they would be willing to accept in compensation for the change.

For most problems addressed by CV, however, negative WTP is simply wrong. CV typically deals with public goods or public dimensions of private goods. For most public goods, negative WTP is not correct because the good can simply be ignored if it does not provide utility to the respondent. Thus, in the majority of cases, we can impose the restriction that WTP values must be non-negative. The assumption of non-negative WTP will be maintained throughout this section. Our final specification of the theoretical bid function, therefore, can be expressed:

$$0 \leq C(Q^0, Q^1, Y, P, S) = WTP \leq Y. \qquad (5.6)$$

In summary, the WTP values given by respondents to CV questions can be seen as the solution to a constrained utility maximising problem. The solution to this problem is represented by the *bid function* that relates WTP values to household income, characteristics and the characteristics of the non-market good being valued. Furthermore, given certain assumptions, WTP must be greater than zero and less than household discretionary income.

5.2.2   The Analyst's Model: The Utility Difference Approach

Respondents to a CV survey can be assumed to know the exact form of their utility function, that is they know which factors are important in establishing their level of welfare and how these interact in the utility function. The same, however, cannot be said for the analyst. The analyst must make an informed 'guess' as to the structure of the utility function. In other words, the analyst must build a simplifying model of the real utility function that captures the factors that are thought to be of most importance in establishing the welfare change experienced by a household.

In contrast to the true indirect utility function denoted $V(Y, P, S, Q)$ the analyst's model is given by $v(y, p, s, q, \eta)$. Here, we use lower-case y, p, s and q to reflect the fact that the factors included by the analyst in the model of the indirect utility function will not be the exact same set of factors considered by the respondent. Also we use $v(\cdot)$ rather than $V(\cdot)$ to indicate that the functional form of the analyst's indirect utility function (that is, the way in which the factors interact to determine the level of utility enjoyed by a household) is just an approximation of the true form of the household's indirect utility function. To account for these differences, the model of the indirect utility function contains an additional element, η, that represents the part of true indirect utility that the analyst is unable to estimate using the simplifying model. The inclusion of this element allows us to write:

$$V(Y,P,S,Q) = v(y,p,s,q) + \eta. \qquad (5.7)$$

One way of interpreting η is to think of it as unobserved variation in tastes. That is, the analyst can make an estimate of the utility that the household derives from their income given their characteristics, the prices of market goods and the provision of non-market goods, but this will not be precise since each household has different and unobservable tastes.

In general, economic theory gives little guidance as to the form that should be taken by the analyst's model of the indirect utility function. The simplest possible form and one that shall prove quite useful is given by:

$$v_q = \alpha_q + \beta y + \eta_q \quad q = 0 \text{ or } 1. \qquad (5.8)$$

Here, the subscripts q are included to show that the utility function can be evaluated before and after the change in provision of the non-market good, that is when $q = q^0$ and when $q = q^1$. There are a number of points to note about this simple formulation:

- The prices of market goods and the quantities provided of other non-market goods are assumed to be fixed throughout the analysis and are not included in the model of the indirect utility function.
- The parameter β is the coefficient on (discretionary) income. It can be

interpreted as the marginal utility of income. That is, β represents the increase in utility that results from a unit increase in income.

- Utility coming from provision of the non-market good is captured by the expression $\alpha_q + \eta_q$. Here α_q is a parameter that captures the part of this utility that the analyst can observe, whilst η_q is an element representing unobserved variation in tastes for the non-market good.

Notice that in equation (5.8), each extra unit of income is assumed to give the same utility (β). In economic parlance, there are no income effects. Since income enters the indirect utility function linearly this model is referred to as the *linear utility model*.

The assumption of linearity in income seems somewhat unlikely. More usually we would imagine that an extra unit of income would have an increasingly smaller impact on utility at higher and higher levels of income. This declining marginal utility of income is captured in the *log utility model* given by:

$$v_q = \alpha_q + \beta \ln y + \eta_q \quad q = 0 \text{ or } 1. \tag{5.9}$$

A more general form for the indirect utility function which nests both the linear and the log utility models is given by the *Box-Cox utility model*:

$$v_q = \alpha_q + \beta\left(\frac{y^\lambda - 1}{\lambda}\right) + \eta_q \quad q = 0 \text{ or } 1. \tag{5.10}$$

Here, λ is a parameter to be estimated by the analyst. Notice that if λ takes on a value of 1 then the model simply collapses back to a linear utility model as in equation (5.8). If, however, λ takes on a value of zero then the model will result in the log utility model of equation (5.9). The Box–Cox utility model, therefore, is a generalisation of both other models and contains them as special cases.

The choice of an explicit form to model the indirect utility function allows the analyst to derive an explicit form for the bid function that is based on the principles of welfare economics discussed in the last section. Using the linear utility model to illustrate, equation (5.3) tells us that a household's maximum WTP (or C) for a change in provision of the non-market good will be given by the value C that solves:

$$\beta y + \alpha_0 + \eta_0 = \beta(y - C) + \alpha_1 + \eta_1. \tag{5.11}$$

Thus, the bid function that results from the linear utility model is given by:

$$C = \frac{(\alpha + \varepsilon)}{\beta} \quad \text{and } 0 \le C \le y. \tag{5.12}$$

Where $\alpha = \alpha_1 - \alpha_0$ and $\varepsilon = \eta_1 - \eta_0$, and we have included the restriction that maximum WTP must be non-negative but cannot exceed the discretionary income of a household.

The role and interpretation of the expression $\alpha + \varepsilon$ is crucial to the estimation of the bid function. In short, $\alpha + \varepsilon$ represents the difference in utility that results from provision of the non-market good, that is, $[\alpha_1 - \alpha_0] + [\eta_1 - \eta_0]$. Remember that this model assumes no income effects such that a unit of income affords the household the same increase in utility no matter what the income of the household. Indeed, the number of units of utility that are equivalent to a unit of money is given by the parameter β, the marginal utility of income. The linear utility model, therefore, converts the utility change $(\alpha + \varepsilon)$ into a monetary measure of WTP by dividing by the marginal utility of income (β).

Using this same procedure, the bid function for the log utility model is given by:

$$C = y \left[1 - e^{\frac{-(\alpha + \varepsilon)}{1}} \right] \quad \text{and } 0 \le C \le y, \tag{5.13}$$

and that for the Box-Cox utility model by:

$$C = y - \left[y^\lambda - \frac{\lambda}{\beta}(\alpha + \varepsilon) \right]^{\frac{1}{\lambda}} \quad \text{and } 0 \le C \le y. \tag{5.14}$$

The more complex expressions defining the log utility models and Box–Cox utility models result from the fact that the conversion of the utility change into a monetary measure accounts for income effects. That is, these expressions allow for the possibility that money purchases a declining quantity of utility as income rises. Thus, in these models, a relatively rich household would place a higher monetary value on a given change in utility than would a relatively poor household.[5]

In the theoretical model of the bid function given in equation (5.6), a household's WTP was given as a function of that household's characteristics. So far, we have ignored this fact. If an analyst is interested in establishing what factors influence the size of the utility change experienced by the household, these factors must be built into the models. To achieve this, analysts specify α, the observable portion of the utility change, as a function of the household's characteristics (and, where relevant, the CV programme characteristics and survey design characteristics). Most usually this is done assuming a simple linear form:

$$\alpha = \alpha_0 + \alpha_1 X_1 + \alpha_2 X_2 + \ldots + \alpha_k X_k, \qquad (5.15)$$

where the $X_1, X_2 \ldots X_k$ are the values taken by the k factors that the analyst believes may influence the welfare change experienced by the household. The k coefficients $\alpha_0, \alpha_1 \ldots \alpha_k$ measure the impact of each of the factors on the change in utility.

As an example, a CV survey that seeks to assess the welfare change that results from the preservation of a local recreational area may hypothesise that an important factor in determining the resulting utility change will be the household's proximity to the site. The analyst will wish to include distance to the site as one of the X variables in the model. The α coefficient on this variable will measure how a unit increase in distance impacts on the size of the utility change experienced by the household. In this case we would expect the coefficient to have a negative sign since we would envisage households further from the recreational area to experience a smaller utility change than those close to. The exception is the case where locals may oppose preservation whereas those farther away are concerned about preservation. In this case, the distance coefficient would be expected to have a positive sign.

5.2.3   The Analyst's Model: The Bid Function Approach

The utility difference framework presented here is favoured by many analysts (for example, Hanemann, 1984, 1996; Sellar, Chavas and Stoll, 1986; McFadden and Leonard, 1993) because, as has been shown, the bid functions are explicitly derived from the principles of welfare economics. However, it could be argued that such a framework is unnecessarily restrictive. An alternative favoured by other CV analysts (for example, Cameron, 1988) is to model the bid function directly without deriving this from an explicit specification of the underlying utility functions.

In this framework, it is assumed that the true bid function, denoted $C(Q^0, Q^1, Y, P, S)$, is the result of some underlying utility difference problem that is solved by the respondent. However, rather than specifying the exact form of the utility function, the analyst builds a model of the bid function directly. This bid function model can be denoted $c(q^0, q^1, y, p, s, e)$. Again we use lower-case to reflect the fact that the factors included by the analyst in the model of the bid function will not be the exact same set of factors considered by the respondent. The differences between the analyst's model and the true bid function are captured in the element e, which is assumed to be that part of WTP that is determined by the unobservable tastes of the household for the non-market good.

One specification for $c(q^0, q^1, y, p, s, e)$ is given by the *constant only bid function model*:

$$C = a + e \quad \text{and} \quad 0 \leq C \leq y. \tag{5.16}$$

It can be shown that when estimated this model is identical to the linear utility function model of equation (5.12). The constant only bid function model is the simplest possible specification of the bid function and, as we shall see later, is of principal importance in deriving estimates of the mean and median WTP of the survey sample.

Notice that like the linear utility function model, the constant only bid function model does not account for income effects. However, income effects can be incorporated into bid function models through the parameter a. For example, if the analyst wanted to include an income effect it would be possible to specify the simple linear parameterisation of a:

$$a = a_0 + by. \tag{5.17}$$

In this specification the income effect is captured by the term by. As income rises, WTP for a given change of provision in the non-market good also increases at the rate given by the parameter b; b gives the marginal impact of income on WTP. Clearly, the b parameter in the bid function model has a very different interpretation to the β parameter in the linear utility difference model, which gave the marginal impact of income on utility.

Alternatively, we might expect WTP to be increasing in income but at a decreasing rate. In this case a second possible parameterisation of a might be preferable:

$$a = a_0 + b \ln y. \tag{5.18}$$

Further, we could use the Box–Cox transformation to nest both of the specifications in equations (5.17) and (5.18) according to:

$$a = a_0 + b \left(\frac{y^\lambda - 1}{\lambda} \right). \tag{5.19}$$

Again, if λ takes a value of one, the Box–Cox bid function model collapses back to the linear specification of equation (5.17). If, on the other hand, λ

takes a value of zero, then the model will result in the log specification of equation (5.18).

It should be evident that the bid function models incorporate income effects in a very different manner to the utility difference models. In point of fact, rather than rescaling a utility change to take account of the utility purchasing power of money at different levels of income, income effects are incorporated in the bid function models as shifters of WTP.

In a similar way to the utility difference models, a can be further parameterised to account for other factors that the analyst deems may be important in determining WTP. Again the usual specification is a simple linear form. As an example a model incorporating the linear specification of income effects could be written:

$$a = a_0 + by + a_1 X_1 + a_2 X_2 + \ldots + a_k X_k. \tag{5.20}$$

Again the a parameters should not be interpreted in the same way as the α parameters of equation (5.15). Rather than measuring the impact of a variable on the change in utility that the household experiences from the change in provision of the non-market good, they measure the impact of the variable directly on the household's WTP.

5.2.4 Which are Better: Utility Difference Models or Bid Function Models?

There is no clear consensus in the CV literature as to which approach to determining the functional form of the bid function is best. Since the two modelling approaches introduce unobservable elements in different ways, they do not in general result in equivalent specifications (see McConnell (1990) for a detailed account of technical differences between the two models).

If we wish to remain loyal to the neoclassical economic theory of constrained utility maximisation, we would prefer to employ a specification for the bid function derived from an explicit formulation of the indirect utility function. However, as has been shown above, this approach can result in relatively complex specifications for the bid function.

At the same time, the relative simplicity of directly specifying the bid function can be justified on the grounds that such models are merely approximations to functional forms that are derived from a utility difference model. Indeed, we could go one step further and point out that any bid function we care to specify could be derived from some specific formulation of the underlying indirect utility function. Also, the bid function models have the added advantage of allowing relatively straightforward calculation of the marginal impacts of variables on household WTP. This is not always true for utility difference models.

In the final analysis it is the analyst's decision which of the two approaches they adopt. The relative simplicity of the bid function approach must be traded-off against its less explicit connection to neo-classical utility maximisation theory.

5.3   ESTIMATING MEAN AND MEDIAN WTP

Imagine that the distribution of WTP in the sample of respondents to a CV survey is known. There are a number of ways in which this distribution can be illustrated. Annex 5.1 discusses the probability density function (PDF), which gives the probability of observing any particular value of WTP in the sample. This PDF is reproduced in the top left of Figure 5.4. Annex 5.1 also discusses cumulative density function (CDF), which represents the same

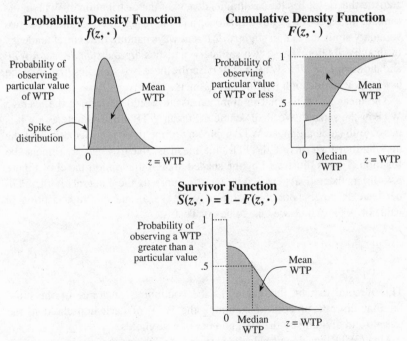

Figure 5.4   Different representations of the distribution of WTP in a hypothetical sample

information but this time as the probability of observing a particular value of WTP or less. The CDF is illustrated in the top right of Figure 5.4. One further representation of the distribution of WTP in the sample to which we will have recourse in the following discussion is given by the *survivor function*. The survivor function gives the probability of observing a particular value of WTP or more and is illustrated at the bottom of Figure 5.4.[6] The survivor function, denoted $S(z, \cdot)$, is simply related to the CDF through the formula:

$$S(z;\cdot) = 1 - F(z;\cdot). \qquad (5.21)$$

The PDF, CDF and survivor function are just three different ways of illustrating the same distribution of WTP. Notice that the random variable z represents WTP and not utility change. Indeed, throughout this section our focus will be the distribution of WTP.

The task at hand is to derive a measure of the average WTP of this distribution. So far we have used the term 'average' rather loosely. A more accurate description would be to say that we wish to derive a summary statistic that describes the 'central tendency' of the distribution of WTP in the sample. In terms of policy decisions, analysts usually concentrate on two summary statistics that in slightly different ways capture the central tendency of this distribution. These two summary statistics are the *sample mean WTP* and the *sample median WTP*. Let us describe these two statistics first and then assess their application in policy assessment.

The mean WTP is what in common usage would be termed the average WTP of the sample. We shall denote the mean WTP in the sample as $\overline{C}$. It is possible to calculate mean WTP using any of the three representations of the distribution. In terms of the PDF, the mean is given by the area under the function. This is illustrated by the shaded area in the top left panel of Figure 5.4. In mathematical terms this area amounts to the integral of the PDF between the lowest possible value of WTP (zero) and the highest possible value of WTP (which we take to be ∞). That is:

$$\overline{C} = \int_0^\infty zf(z;\cdot)dz. \qquad (5.22)$$

This integral can be thought of as the continuous analogue of the more familiar discrete process of summing the WTP of each household in the sample and dividing by the total number of households.

Mean WTP can also be calculated from the CDF and the survivor function. In terms of the CDF, mean WTP is given by the shaded area in the top right hand panel of Figure 5.4. Mathematically this amounts to:

$$\overline{C} = \int_0^\infty 1 - F(z;\cdot)dz = \int_0^\infty S(z;\cdot)dz. \qquad (5.23)$$

Clearly, the simple relationship between the CDF and the survivor function (equation (5.21)) means that we can also express mean WTP in terms of the survivor function. This is shown graphically as the shaded area below the survivor function in Figure 5.4 and mathematically in equation (5.23).

Meanwhile the median WTP, denoted $\tilde{C}$, is the value of WTP that divides the sample exactly in half. That is, it is the value of WTP at which exactly 50 per cent of the sample have a lower WTP and 50 per cent have a higher WTP. Median WTP is most easily calculated with reference to the CDF or the survivor function. It is the value of WTP at which the CDF and survivor function equate to 0.5:

$$F(z;\cdot) = S(z;\cdot) = 0.5,$$

such that:

$$\tilde{C} = F^{-1}(0.5) = S^{-1}(0.5). \qquad (5.24)$$

Where $F^{-1}(\cdot)$ and $S^{-1}(\cdot)$ are the inverses of the CDF and survivor functions respectively. Again these are illustrated in Figure 5.4.

In general, mean WTP ($\overline{C}$) and median WTP ($\tilde{C}$) will take on different values. Frequently, WTP data show a distribution that is skewed to the right. In such a case, the mean will tend to take on a higher value than the median. The intuition behind this result is relatively obvious. Imagine that we had a sample of WTP values that showed a perfectly symmetric distribution as illustrated in the left-hand panel of Figure 5.5. With such a distribution the median and the mean take on identical values; that is, the value that splits the sample into two equally sized subsamples is the same value that splits the probability mass (the area below the PDF) into two equally-sized chunks. Now imagine that we added one more household to the sample who had an extremely high WTP, the one that was in the far right tail of the distribution. The distribution would no longer be symmetric but skewed to the right (see right-hand panel of Figure 5.5). Since there would now be more probability mass in the right-hand tail of the distribution the mean would shift to a higher value. Indeed the higher the WTP of the additional household the greater the shift in the mean. In contrast, adding this extra household has relatively little impact on the median (the value at which 50 per cent of the sample have a lower WTP and 50 per cent have a higher WTP). Further, the impact on the median will be unaffected by the size of the extra household's WTP, and the

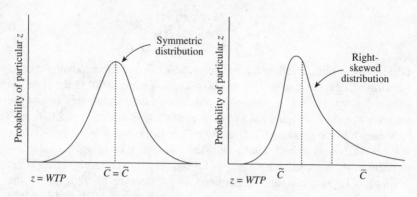

Figure 5.5   Differences between mean WTP ($\overline{C}$) and median WTP ($\tilde{C}$)

impact will be the same so long as their WTP is greater than the current median value.

For this reason, some analysts have argued that median WTP is a more robust measure of central tendency since its value is not so greatly influenced by occasional very high WTP values.

From the point of view of decision-makers the two measures for summarising the distribution of WTP can be seen to have quite different interpretations. If the decision-maker wishes to make a decision based on efficiency criteria, then the mean is the most appropriate measure. So long as mean WTP outweighs costs per head then the decision-maker can appeal to the Hicks–Kaldor compensation principle[7] to pronounce that the project should proceed. Alternatively, the decision-maker may prefer to choose a course of action based on a majority voting rule. In this case the median is the more appropriate measure. If the median WTP is greater than the cost per head, then the decision-maker can conclude that a majority of households would vote in favour of the project.

Since neither measure is innately superior, the analyst should always seek to report both mean and median values of WTP. It should also be noted that a decision-maker may be interested in many aspects of the distribution of WTP, including: how many households receive little or no benefits from the project; whether the benefits are highly concentrated; and, how the benefits vary with different parameters such as geographical area.

5.4 MODELS FOR TESTING THE VALIDITY OF WTP VALUES

A second objective of the analysis of CV data will be to establish the validity of the WTP responses. That is, analysts may wish to test whether the WTP values provided by respondents follow distinguishable patterns and that these patterns conform with prior expectations and economic theory.

In general, analysts will have a number of variables that they conjecture will influence the WTP of a respondent. Typically such variables will include the respondent's income (y) and other socio-economic characteristics, details of their attitudes towards the programme offered in the CV scenario, information on their current knowledge of the good to be provided and, for goods with a spatial dimension, their proximity to the site of provision. To test the validity of CV responses, analysts include these variables as covariates in the model of WTP according to equation (5.15) for the utility difference model or, equation (5.20) for the bid function model.

The analyst should check that estimated parameters (α_0, α_1, ..., α_k in the utility difference models or a_0, a_1, ..., a_k and b in the bid function model) have signs that conform to prior expectation. Thus variables such as income that are expected to increase WTP should be positively signed, whilst variables such as distance to the site of provision which are expected to reduce WTP should be negatively signed.

The statistical significance of these parameters can be tested using a simple *t-test*. A *t-statistic* for each parameter (for example, α_0) is calculated according to:

$$t = \frac{\hat{\alpha}_0}{s.e.(\hat{\alpha}_0)}, \tag{5.25}$$

and this can be compared to the critical value for a two-tailed *t*-test with 95 per cent confidence. If the calculated *t*-statistic is greater than this value, then the analyst can reject the hypothesis that the variable does not influence WTP.

Since our objective is to establish that the respondents' WTP values are not purely random, CV analysts tend to be less interested in the actual parameter values and more interested in the explanatory power of the whole model. Thus the normal procedure is to include all available variables regardless of whether they can be considered endogenous or exogenous to the WTP decision (see discussion in Section 5.2.3) despite the fact that econometric theory predicts that parameter estimates are biased when endogenous variables are included in the model.

A measure of the explanatory power of the entire model is provided by the *pseudo R^2 statistic*. This statistic is calculated as:

$$R^2 = 1 - \frac{\ln L_{max}}{\ln L_0}. \tag{5.26}$$

Where $\ln L_{max}$ is the value of the log likelihood function from the estimated model with covariates and $\ln L_0$ is the value of the log of the likelihood function from the unparameterised model. The pseudo R^2 statistic takes values between 0 and 1 where a value of zero suggests that the included covariates do nothing to explain the distribution of WTP in the sample.

In general, the larger the value of the pseudo R^2 statistic, the greater the explanatory power of the model. Unfortunately, there is no commonly accepted threshold value for the pseudo R^2 statistic that denotes a satisfactory or well-specified model. However, analysts should be concerned if the inclusion of covariates provides very little explanatory power. Certainly one would be concerned if the pseudo R^2 statistic were less than 0.1 and one might draw the conclusion that the WTP values returned from the CV survey show very little in the way of distinguishable patterns.

It should be noted that the best-fitting model when covariates are included does *not* have to make the same distributional assumptions as those used in a parametric model used to evaluate mean and median WTP.

5.5   MODELS FOR BENEFITS TRANSFER EXERCISES

A final objective of the analysis of CV data may be to provide details that can be used in the *transfer of benefit estimates* from the current study to another similar project. In this case it may prove adequate simply to transfer the average WTP value. However, this value is only strictly applicable to the population from which the sample for the study was drawn. To improve the process of BT, analysts may wish to estimate a transfer equation, which measures WTP as a function of households' characteristics. Given that the characteristics of the population to which the estimate will be transferred is likely to differ from those of the study population, it is hoped that benefits estimates can be improved by using the transfer equation to modify the estimate of average WTP to account for these differences.

When BT is the objective, the analysis of CV data demands the estimation of one further model. This model will contain only a limited number of covariates. These covariates will be those that can easily be gathered for the transfer population. Usually this amounts to basic socio-economic details, such as the respondent's income, age and sex, since details of these character-istics in the transfer population can be easily collected from census returns. For goods that have a spatial dimension, however, it is crucial to include a variable that measures the household's distance from the site of provision. The parameter estimated on such a variable is crucial in establishing the rate of distance decay of WTP and hence in defining the boundaries of the popula-tion that may have a positive WTP in a transfer exercise.

It should be standard practice to present the results of such a model in a report on the analysis of data from any CV study.

5.6 CONCLUSIONS

The analysis of CV data can have a number of different objectives. In general these can be narrowed down to:

- estimation of mean and median WTP;
- testing of the validity of WTP responses to a CV survey; and
- provision of a transfer equation to assist in subsequent BT exercises.

To achieve these goals, analysts will need to carry out a number of analyses:

- A non-parametric model should be estimated and used to derive lower bound estimates of mean and median WTP.
- Subsequently, a variety of constant only bid function models should be estimated. The 'best' model should be selected on the grounds of having the highest value for the likelihood function. The value of the likelihood function for the 'best' parametric specification should be compared to that obtained from non-parametric estimation to ensure that the model provides a reasonable fit to the data (see Annex 5.1).
- Mean and median WTP should be calculated from the best-fitting parametric specification and confidence intervals constructed using either the Krinsky–Robb or bootstrapping methods (see Annex 5.2).
- A fully parameterised model should be estimated to establish the de-gree of non-randomness in the data. This model will not necessarily make the same distributional assumptions as that used to evaluate mean and median WTP.
- The parameter estimates should be examined to establish that they are correctly signed and their statistical significance reported.
- Analysts should report the pseudo R^2 statistic for this model so that the degree of non-randomness in the data can be evaluated.

- A final model should be estimated that includes only basic socio-economic variables that can be collected from census returns and, if relevant, a distance to the site of provision variable. The parameter values from this model should be included in the report to aid in subsequent BT exercises.

NOTES

1. The definition of the population of interest is clearly an important consideration. However, for the discussion presented here, it is assumed that this has been previously defined (see Chapter 3).
2. It has been suggested by the critics of CV that these households are unwilling to place a value on the provision of a non-market good because they find it impossible to express their value for such a good in monetary terms. The implication has been that the zero responses of these households actually reflect extremely high values. Amongst CV analysts, the general feeling is that very few zero responses are protests reflecting very high value. Instead it is more likely that they represent the free-riding behaviour of households with low WTP.
3. The Exxon Valdez survey sample, for example, were weighted for region, age, race, household size and marital status so that they more accurately reflected the 1990 census data for the relevant population.
4. As Chapters 1 and 4 show, there are four theoretically valid monetary measures of welfare change; WTP to achieve a gain in provision (i.e. $Q^0 < Q^1$); WTA to forgo a gain in provision; WTP to avoid a loss in provision (i.e. $Q^0 > Q^1$); or WTA compensation for a loss in provision. To fix ideas, the discussion in this section is framed in terms of household WTP to achieve a gain in the provision of a non-market good. The analysis of the data would be no different for surveys using any of the other measures or collecting data for individuals rather than households.
5. This is only strictly true for the Box-Cox utility model if the λ parameter takes a value of less than one.
6. The term 'survivor function' is derived from the biomedical literature. Rather morbidly, the term originates from observations on the portion of a sample of patients that had survived a certain length of time following, for example, diagnosis of an illness or surgery.
7. Even if gainers compensate losers, net profits are still positive.

ANNEX 5.1   Econometric estimation of the bid function

BUILDING A PROBABILISTIC MODEL OF WTP

The econometric estimation of the bid function relies crucially on interpretation of the expression $\alpha + \varepsilon$ in utility difference models and $a + e$ in bid function models:

- $\alpha + \varepsilon$ in the utility difference models is the difference in utility experienced by the household from the change in provision of the non-market good; and
- $a + e$ in the bid function models is the WTP of the household for the change in provision of the non-market good.

Both of these expressions contain two elements: one observable by the analyst and one unobservable.

In the utility difference models the observable part of utility is represented by the parameter α. In the simplest case, we can think of α as the 'average' utility change experienced by households in the sample. Though on average the analyst would expect each household to experience a utility change of α, we know that the actual utility change will differ from this quantity due to unobserved differences in households' tastes. This unobservable element is captured by ε. Since the analyst cannot observe ε it is regarded as a random element. As we shall see, the analyst is unable to *a priori* predict the value taken by ε, but instead can only estimate the likelihood of it taking any specific value.

Similarly, the observable part of a household's WTP is given by a in the bid function models. Again in the simplest case we can think of this as the average WTP expressed by the sample. Unobserved variability in households' tastes for the non-market good are captured by e, which is taken by the analyst to be a random variable. Once more, the analyst is unable to predict the value taken by this random element but can estimate the likelihood of it taking any particular value.

To facilitate further discussion, it is worth noting that any of the models presented in the last section can be solved for the expression $\alpha + \varepsilon$ in utility difference models or $a + e$ in bid function models.

Notice that the general form of the bid function model given in equation (5.16) is already expressed solely in terms of $a + e$. As we saw in the last section, income effects can be incorporated in this specification through a parameterisation of a that involves income (for example, equations (5.17),

(5.18) and 5.19)). For completeness we reproduce the general form for the bid function model here:

$$C = a + e \quad \text{and } 0 \leq C \leq y. \tag{1}$$

On the other hand, some manipulation may be required in order to express the utility difference models in terms of $\alpha + \varepsilon$. Accordingly, the linear utility model can be written:

$$\beta C = \alpha + \varepsilon \quad \text{and } 0 \leq C \leq y. \tag{2}$$

The log utility model as:

$$-\beta \ln\left(1 - \frac{C}{y}\right) = \alpha + \varepsilon \quad \text{and } 0 \leq C \leq y, \tag{3}$$

and the Box-Cox utility model as:

$$\frac{\beta}{\lambda}\left[y^{\lambda} - (y - C)^{\lambda}\right] = \alpha + \varepsilon \quad \text{and } 0 \leq C \leq y. \tag{4}$$

Rearranging the various utility difference models has the effect of isolating the change in utility from the income effects. In effect, the left-hand side of equations (2), (3) and (4) can be interpreted as expressions that reweight household WTP, given by C, so that it is expressed in terms of a pure utility change.

In the rest of this exposition we are not particularly concerned as to whether we are modelling a utility difference model or a bid function model (for details of technical differences between the two models, see McConnell, 1990). Nor will the particular form of the income effect in the utility difference models be of interest. For these reasons it will considerably simplify notation if the left-hand sides of equations (1), (2), (3) and (4) are represented by the symbol z. Since we shall be using z throughout this section it is worth restating exactly how this variable can be interpreted:

- For the *bid function models*, equation (1):

$$z = \text{l.h.s. of (1)} = a + e \quad \text{and } 0 \leq C \leq y. \tag{5}$$

Obviously z is simply C the household's *WTP for the change in provision of the non-market good.*

• For the *utility difference models*, equations (2), (3) and (4):

$$z = \text{l.h.s. of (2),(3) or (4)} = \alpha + \varepsilon \quad \text{and } 0 \leq C \leq y, \qquad (6)$$

and is simply the household's *WTP expressed in terms of the equivalent utility change*. The different forms taken by z in these models reflect the different assumptions that are made about income effects and hence the utility value that can be attributed to each unit of WTP.

To simplify further, the discussion is couched in terms of the bid function model, equation (5). Note that the analysis proceeds identically if we were to use the utility difference model of equation (6), though in this case it is important to remember that the parameters of the model must be interpreted as those coming from a utility difference model rather than a bid function model.

For now then, z represents the WTP of the household for a change in provision of a non-market good. To continue, we have established that since e cannot be observed, the analyst regards it as a random variable. Since z is defined by this random variable through equation (5) it too must be considered a random variable. To account for this randomness, analysts assume that the WTP of any particular household is drawn from some *probability distribution* (see Box A5.1.1).

The majority of distributions used in the analysis of CV data are based on two parameter distributions defined by a *location parameter* and a *scale parameter*. It should be clear from the earlier discussion that the location parameter of the probability distribution (the measure of its central tendency) corresponds to what we have been calling the 'average' WTP of households in the sample. Indeed, the usual assumption is that a is the location parameter of a probability distribution. The spread of WTP values around this point and hence the size of the scale parameter, σ^2, will be determined by the spread of values taken by the random element, e.

As the next section shows, the analyst may need to introduce further parameters to generalise the probability distribution so that it successfully reflects the distribution of WTP. For now, notice that the generalised model presented in equation (5) (or equation (6)) has been transformed from a deterministic form to a probabilistic form.

As an illustration, take the linear utility model of equation (5.12). This is a deterministic model; given knowledge of the parameters α and β, and a value for ε, equation (5.12) will determine that household's WTP for the change in provision of the non-market good. Clearly, ε is not observable so that we could never actually employ equation (5.12) to predict a household's WTP. However,

BOX A5.1.1   PROBABILITY DISTRIBUTIONS

A probability distribution describes the likelihood of observing any particular value of a random variable. In our case this random variable is z (WTP in the bid function models, utility change in the utility difference models).

The range of values over which the probability distribution defines positive probabilities of observing the random variable is known as the distribution's *support*. One can think of the probability distribution as only supporting values of the random variable that fall within this range of values.

A probability distribution is defined by a number of parameters that establish exactly what probability is allotted to observing any particular value of the random variable. The majority of distributions used in the analysis of CV data are based on two parameter distributions defined by:

- a *location parameter* which fixes the value of the central point of the distribution. In our case this central point is defined by the variable a for the bid function models or α for the utility difference models; and
- a *scale parameter* which determines the dispersion of values around the central point. The scale parameter is frequently represented by σ^2.

The shape of a probability distribution is defined by two familiar functions:

1. *Cumulative density function* (CDF) of the probability distribution. This is denoted $F(z; a, \sigma^2)$ and gives the probability that a household's WTP (or utility change) will take a value of z or less given the parameters of the distribution.
2. *Probability density function* (PDF) of the probability distribution. This is denoted $f(z; a, \sigma^2)$ and gives the probability that a household's WTP (or utility change) will take a value of z given the parameters of the distribution.

A plethora of probability distributions have been used to model CV data. Each makes different assumptions about how the random variable z is distributed. Choosing which probability distribution to use to model CV data is one of the major decisions facing the analyst.

by regarding ε as a random element we can derive an estimate of the probability that a household's WTP will take a particular value. Hence we can solve for the random variable $z = \beta C = \alpha + \varepsilon$ according to equation (5.21). Having made an assumption concerning the distribution of this random variable we can form the probabilistic model:

$$\Pr(WTP = C \mid \beta, \alpha, \sigma^2) = f(\beta C; \alpha, \sigma^2) \quad \text{and } 0 \leq C \leq y. \tag{7}$$

Equation (7) defines a model that estimates the probability of a household having a WTP of value C. The estimated probability is dependent on the parameters of the model and of the distribution function (α, β, and σ^2). For now, we shall postpone discussion of how the analyst estimates values for these parameters. Instead, we turn to the issue of selecting a probability distribution.

CHOOSING A PROBABILITY DISTRIBUTION TO MODEL WTP

The final step in formulating an estimable model is to specify the probability distribution of the random variable z. We denote this distribution by the CDF, $F(z)$ and associated PDF, $f(z)$. The choice of distribution for $F(z)$ is a key consideration in the analysis of CV data. The distributional assumption that is to be preferred depends to a large degree on two considerations:

1. Whether the distribution accounts for limits that should be applied to permissible values of WTP.
2. How well the distribution fits the data.

In this section we assess the first of these criteria. We return to the issue of comparing models according to how well they fit the data in the next section.

The literature abounds with possible parametric families of distributions that could be used for this purpose. These include the normal, log-normal, logistic, log-logistic, exponential, Weibull, gamma and beta families of distributions.

One frequently-used assumption concerning the distribution of the random element is that it comes from the *normal family*. Given this assumption the specific form for the probability distribution of z is given by:

$$F(z; a, \sigma^2) = \Phi\left(\frac{z - a}{\sigma}\right) \tag{8}$$

and

$$f(z;a,\sigma^2) = \phi\left(\frac{z-a}{\sigma}\right)\left(\frac{1}{\sigma}\right). \tag{9}$$

Where $\Phi(\cdot)$ and $\phi(\cdot)$ are the CDF and PDF of the standard normal distribution respectively. The normal distribution is symmetric such that the location parameter a defines both the mean and median of the distribution.

A similarly popular distributional choice is the *logistic*, which gives a distribution defined by:

$$F(z;a,\sigma^2) = \left(1 + e^{\frac{z-a}{\sigma}}\right)^{-1} \tag{10}$$

and

$$f(z;a,\sigma^2) = e^{\frac{z-a}{\sigma}}\left(1 + e^{\frac{z-a}{\sigma}}\right)^{-2}. \tag{11}$$

Like the normal distribution, the logistic distribution is symmetric and has a mean and median given by a. The normal and logistic specifications have been particularly popular because of their relative simplicity. However, a potentially disconcerting feature of these distributions is that they do not impose any specific restrictions on the value that may be taken by z. In particular, the normal and logistic distributions are defined across the support $-\infty$ to $+\infty$.

To examine the consequences of this characteristic of the normal and logistic distributions, let us consider the bid function model where, as should be familiar by now, the random variable z defines the WTP of the household for the change in provision of the non-market good. Given values for the parameters of the model (in this case a and σ^2), there is no theoretical reason why the model should not predict positive probabilities for WTP taking a value of less than zero and greater than income. A hypothetical example of just such a case is illustrated in Figure A5.1.1. Clearly, if we believe that these restrictions should hold then the model is misspecified.

One solution to the problem of modelling WTP with distributions that place a positive probability on negative WTP is through *truncation*. In effect this amounts to lopping off the infeasible negative tail of the distribution (the shaded area below zero in Figure A5.1.1) and re-scaling the probabilities of the remainder of the distribution with the mass of the removed tail. Shortly we shall tackle truncated distributions in more detail with reference to the

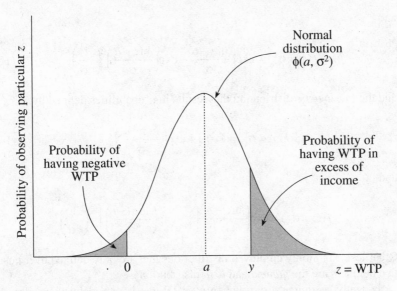

Figure A5.1.1   The normal distribution supporting negative WTP and WTP in excess of income

positive tail of the distribution. For now, however, let us turn to a second, possibly more natural, approach to ruling out the possibility of negative WTP.

The problem with the normal and logistic distributions is that they are supported over the range $-\infty$ to $+\infty$. An alternative, therefore, is to adopt a distribution that is naturally non-negative. Examples of such distributions include the *log-normal distribution* that results in probabilities defined by:

$$F(z;a,\sigma^2) = \Phi\left(\frac{\ln z - a}{\sigma}\right) \tag{12}$$

and

$$f(z;a,\sigma^2) = \phi\left(\frac{\ln z - a}{\sigma}\right)\left(\frac{1}{z\sigma}\right), \tag{13}$$

the *Weibull distribution* that results in probabilities defined by:

$$F(z;a,\sigma^2) = 1 - \exp\left(-\exp\left(\frac{\ln z - a}{\sigma}\right)\right) \tag{14}$$

and

$$f(z;a,\sigma^2) = \exp\left(\frac{\ln z - \alpha}{\sigma} - \exp\left(\frac{\ln z - a}{\sigma}\right)\right)\left(\frac{1}{z\sigma}\right), \qquad (15)$$

and the *log-logistic* distribution that results in probabilities defined by:

$$F(z;a,\sigma^2) = 1 - \left(1 + \exp\left(\frac{\ln z - a}{\sigma}\right)\right)^{-1} \qquad (16)$$

and

$$f(z;a,\sigma^2) = \exp\left(\frac{\ln z - a}{\sigma}\right)\left(1 + \exp\left(\frac{\ln z - a}{\sigma}\right)\right)^{-2}\left(\frac{1}{z\sigma}\right). \qquad (17)$$

Other less commonly employed distributions that are only defined over positive numbers are the *gamma* and *beta* distributions.

Evidently, assuming a distribution of WTP that is only defined for positive values overcomes the problem of the distribution allowing for negative WTP. Unfortunately, such an assumption also rules out the possibility of zero WTP. Consequently, the model must be further revised to account for the possibility that a household drawn from the sample of respondents will have a WTP of zero.[1]

One option open to analysts is to consider the sample as representing two separate groups: one group that does not value the change in provision of the non-market good and has a WTP of zero; a second group that has a positive WTP for the change in provision. Since our model of household WTP is probabilistic, the analyst does not know for certain whether any particular household falls into one group or the other. Instead, the analyst aims to estimate the probability of a household having a zero, as opposed to positive, WTP.

This amounts to introducing a spike to the probability distribution falling at a value of zero. The height of the spike represents the probability of having zero WTP. Simultaneously, those that value the provision of the non-market good are assumed to have a WTP that is drawn from a distribution such as the log normal that only admits positive probabilities to positive values. Since this model involves the interaction of two distributions it is known as a mixture model. Failure to fit a spike to accommodate the zero observations will often lead to over-estimation of mean WTP.

In mathematical notation the spike distribution can be included through the addition of a single parameter, ρ. This parameter estimates the height of the spike; the probability of having a WTP of zero.[2] Using the log normal as an example, the CDF can be written:

$$F(z;a,\sigma^2,\rho) = \begin{cases} \rho & \text{if } C = 0 \\ \rho + (1-\rho)\Phi\left(\dfrac{\ln(z) - a}{\sigma}\right) & \text{if } C > 0 \end{cases} \qquad (18)$$

and the corresponding PDF as:

$$f(z;a,\sigma^2,\rho) = \begin{cases} \rho & \text{if } C = 0 \\ (1-\rho)\phi\left(\dfrac{\ln(z) - a}{\sigma}\right) & \text{if } C > 0. \end{cases} \qquad (19)$$

Notice that this model, as illustrated in Figure A5.1.2, still allows for the possibility of WTP exceeding household income (the shaded area of the distribution above the income level in Figure A5.1.2). Clearly, the model needs further revision so that the distribution does not place positive probabilities on values of WTP that exceed household income.

The favoured approach to imposing this final theoretical restriction is to truncate the distribution of positive WTP values at the level of household income.[3]

Truncating a distribution involves a relatively simple adjustment of the model. For a start we know that WTP will not be greater than income such that we can rule out the possibility of values falling in the infeasible region of the positive tail. In effect we can discard that part of the probability mass that lies above the level of household income. In doing so, however, we introduce a slight problem. The distribution function continues to allot the same prob-

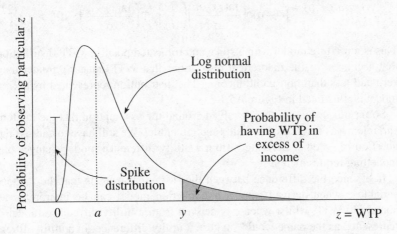

Figure A5.1.2   The mixed spike and log normal distribution supporting WTP in excess of income

abilities to observing values of WTP that are less than income. What we would like to do is rescale these probabilities to account for the fact that we have discarded part of the probability mass.

To do this, observe that the CDF of the probability distribution gives the probability that WTP takes a value of a certain amount or less. Obviously, at a value of WTP equal to the household's income, we would like the CDF to report a probability of one since WTP must be lower than its highest possible value. In the untruncated distribution, however, this is not true. The CDF evaluated at household income will return a probability less than one.

Accounting for truncation amounts to accounting for this fact. In effect, the untruncated probability of observing a value of WTP less than income needs to be scaled up to account for the fact that the total probability of observing a value of WTP less than income is not one.

In mathematical terms this amounts to the simple task of dividing through by the CDF of the distribution evaluated at the truncation point. The model in equations (18) and (19) can be rewritten accordingly. Again illustrating with the log normal distribution we get a CDF given by:

$$F(z;a,\sigma^2,\rho) = \begin{cases} \rho & \text{if } C=0 \\ \rho+(1-\rho)\Phi\left(\dfrac{\ln(z)-a}{\sigma}\right)\bigg/\Phi\left(\dfrac{\ln(y)-a}{\sigma}\right) & \text{if } C>0 \end{cases} \quad (20)$$

And the corresponding PDF as:

$$f(z;a,\sigma^2,\rho) = \begin{cases} \rho & \text{if } C=0 \\ (1-\rho)\phi\left(\dfrac{\ln(z)-a}{\sigma}\right)\left(\dfrac{1}{\sigma z}\right)\bigg/\Phi\left(\dfrac{\ln(y)-a}{\sigma}\right) & \text{if } C>0 \end{cases} \quad (21)$$

This is a mixture model with a spike and truncated positive WTP distribution that accounts for the theoretical restrictions that WTP must be greater than zero and less than household income. The distribution represented by such a model is illustrated in Figure A5.1.3.

So far our discussion has revolved around the assumption that the random variable z was derived from a bid function model. We still have to address the question of whether deriving z from a utility difference model changes our modelling requirements.

In essence the difference between the two approaches is that the random variable z when derived from a bid function model can be interpreted as household WTP, whilst when z is derived from a utility difference model it represents, as the name would suggest, a utility difference. In a utility difference model, therefore, it is the change in utility experienced by the household that is modelled as a random variable and not the household's WTP itself.

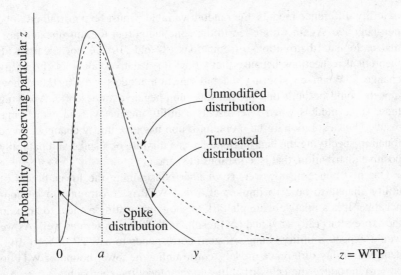

Figure A5.1.3   The mixed spike and truncated log normal distribution

As stated previously, the expressions in equations (2), (3) and (4) define how WTP can be expressed in terms of the equivalent utility change according to the assumptions we have made concerning income effects. By inverting these expressions we can express the utility change, z, as the equivalent WTP. Thus for the linear utility difference model WTP is defined by:

$$C = \frac{z}{\beta}, \tag{22}$$

for the log utility model WTP is given by:

$$C = y\left[1 - e^{-\frac{z}{\beta}}\right], \tag{23}$$

and for the Box-Cox utility model WTP is given by:

$$C = y - \left[y^{\lambda} - \frac{\lambda}{\beta}z\right]^{\frac{1}{\lambda}}. \tag{24}$$

Under the assumption that households regard the change in provision of the non-market good with indifference or as an improvement, we can conclude that households must experience a non-negative utility change. In other words, in utility difference models, the random variable z must be constrained to be non-negative. Again we are led to the conclusion that the untruncated normal or logistic distributions of equations (8) and (10) do not accord with theoretical restrictions because they allow for negative values of the utility change z. When considering the bid function models we illustrated how models could be built that predict only non-negative values of z. Applying these same models when z represents a utility change will have the same result. Thus a solution to the problem of non-negative utility changes can be found in specifying the distribution of z as a mixture of a spike and naturally positive distribution, that is, equations (18) and (19).

Our first concern, however, is whether constraining the lower bound of utility change to be zero implies also that WTP is constrained to be non-negative. It is a relatively simple task to show that setting z equal to zero, in the expressions (22), (23) and (24) results in WTP being zero as well. As we would expect, a utility change of zero corresponds to a WTP of zero. Evidently, in utility difference models, constraining the lower bound of WTP to be zero introduces no new difficulties to the modelling approach.

The question of the upper bound restriction that states WTP must be less than income poses a slightly more difficult problem. Indeed, it will be shown that the imposition of this restriction will depend to a large extent on how the utility difference model incorporates income effects. Let us begin by looking at the linear utility difference model.

Consider Figure A5.1.4. The rearmost graph shows the distribution of the random variable z. This is essentially the same graph as Figure A5.1.2, except here z represents a utility change and not WTP itself. From equation (22) we can derive the relationship between z and WTP. Indeed, using this relationship we can map the distribution of utility change on to another graph that shows the implicit distribution of WTP. The dashed arrows show how points on the utility change graph at the rear of the figure can be mapped to the WTP graph in the foreground. We can see from this graph that the distribution of utility change induces a distribution of WTP that exceeds the household's income, y. The linear utility model, therefore, does not constrain WTP to be less than household income. To overcome this problem, we will need to truncate the distribution of z. Referring again to Figure A5.1.4, it is clear that the relevant truncation point will be where $z = \beta y$.

Thus, a theoretically consistent probability distribution for the linear utility model is given by the CDF:

$$F(z;\beta,\alpha,\sigma^2 = 1,\rho) = \begin{cases} \rho & \text{if } C = 0 \\ \rho + (1-\rho)\Phi\left(\dfrac{\ln(z)-\alpha}{1}\right) \Big/ \Phi\left(\dfrac{\ln(\beta y)-\alpha}{1}\right) & \text{if } C > 0 \end{cases} \quad (25)$$

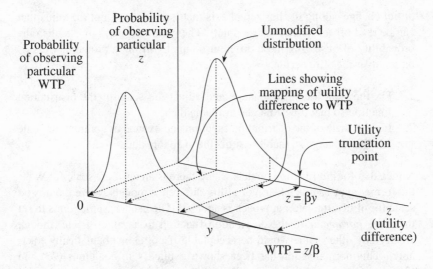

Figure A5.1.4   The linear utility difference model and the mapping into WTP

and the corresponding PDF as:

$$f(z;\beta,\alpha,\sigma^2=1,\rho)=\begin{cases}\rho & \text{if } C=0 \\ (1-\rho)\phi\left(\dfrac{\ln(z)-\alpha}{1}\right)\left(\dfrac{1}{z}\right)\Big/\Phi\left(\dfrac{\ln(\beta y)-\alpha}{1}\right) & \text{if } C>0\end{cases} \quad (26)$$

An issue that might have been troubling readers is how we have been measuring utility change. Whilst WTP has real and measurable units the same cannot be said of utility; there is no such thing as a unit of utility, at least not one for which we have a standard and communal measure. Yet in equations (2), (3) and (4) we presented three expressions for converting units of WTP into units of utility where the parameter β effectively determined the utility value of each unit of WTP.[4] The point is, how is it possible to estimate the value of the conversion factor, β, when we don't have any units in which to measure utility?

The problem is overcome by artificially imposing a scale on utility difference, a process that is known as *normalisation*. First, notice that we have already imposed the implicit assumption that a WTP of zero results in a utility change of zero, effectively fixing one point on the utility scale. Further, since this is a probabilistic model, our concern is in establishing the probability of observing a utility change of a certain magnitude, not in establishing its absolute value. In other words it is only the relative position of different utility changes along the horizontal axis that is of interest, not the value that can be read off the scale at these points. There are two ways to establish the probability of observing these different points by fitting a probability distribution over the utility scale:

1. Fix the scale of utility change and adjust the scale of the distribution function so that it best fits the available data.
2. Fix the scale of the distribution function and expand or contract the scale of utility change so that it best fits the available data.

Notice that for bid function models where there is an absolute scale for WTP, the former approach is taken. For utility difference models where there is no scale for utility, the latter approach is adopted. The usual assumption is to set the *scale parameter* of the distribution function to a value of *one* (though clearly any other value would be acceptable if not as mathematically tractable). This normalisation has been shown explicitly in equations (25) and (26), but for ease of exposition shall be dropped in future presentations of utility difference models.

Next let us consider the *log utility model* where $z = -\beta \ln(1 - C/y)$ (equation (3)). Notice that as the household's WTP (represented by C) approaches the household's discretionary income (represented by y), this expression for the change in utility experienced by the household approaches a value of zero. Further, if the household's WTP were to take a value equal to or greater than the household's income, then the expression for change in utility would become undefined. The log utility model, therefore, naturally confines WTP to be less than or equal to the household's income. This result is illustrated in Figure A5.1.5. Observe that any value of utility difference maps on to the WTP scale at a value of y or less.

In the case of the log utility model, therefore, there is no need to truncate the upper tail of the distribution. A theoretically consistent probability distribution is given by the CDF:

$$F(z; \beta, \alpha, \sigma^2 = 1, \rho) = \begin{cases} \rho & \text{if } C = 0 \\ \rho + (1-\rho)\Phi(\ln(z) - \alpha) & \text{if } C > 0 \end{cases} \qquad (27)$$

and the corresponding PDF as:

$$f(z; \beta, \alpha, \sigma^2 = 1, \rho) = \begin{cases} \rho & \text{if } C = 0 \\ (1-\rho)\dfrac{\phi(\ln(z) - \alpha)}{z} & \text{if } C > 0 \end{cases} \qquad (28)$$

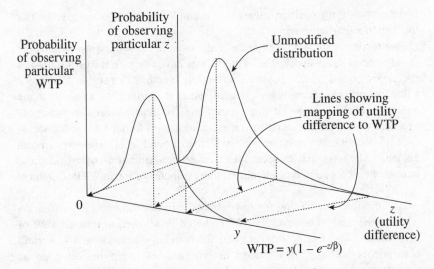

Figure A5.1.5 The log utility difference model and the mapping into WTP

As might be expected, the Box–Cox utility difference model lies between these two extremes. In general, therefore, the Box–Cox model will have to be truncated in the upper tail with the relevant truncation point given by $z = \beta y^\lambda/\lambda$. A theoretically consistent probability distribution for the Box–Cox utility model has the CDF:

$$F(z;\beta,\lambda,\alpha,\sigma^2 = 1,\rho) = \begin{cases} \rho & \text{if } C = 0 \\ \rho + (1-\rho)\Phi(\ln(z) - \alpha) \Big/ \Phi\left(\ln\left(\frac{\beta}{\lambda}y^\lambda\right) - \alpha\right) & \text{if } C > 0 \end{cases} \quad (29)$$

and the corresponding PDF as:

$$f(z;\beta,\lambda,\alpha,\sigma^2 = 1,\rho) = \begin{cases} \rho & \text{if } C = 0 \\ (1-\rho)\dfrac{\phi(\ln(z) - \alpha)}{z} \Big/ \Phi\left(\ln\left(\frac{\beta}{\lambda}y^\lambda\right) - \alpha\right) & \text{if } C > 0 \end{cases} \quad (30)$$

Equations (20) and (21) for the bid function model, equations (25) and (26) for the linear utility model, equations (27) and (28) for the log utility model and equations (29) and (30) for the Box–Cox utility model represent theoretically consistent models for the analysis of CV data. All these models constrain WTP to be non-negative and less than income. Clearly, we could replace the log normal distribution in these equations with any distribution function that is defined only for positive values (for example, the exponential, Weibull or log-logistic distributions).

One further point should be made. The modelling approach developed here is only one of many approaches that analysts have taken. Whilst truncation of the upper bound of the chosen distribution function to restrain WTP to a value lower than income is widely accepted as theoretically consistent, many analysts have not imposed this restriction. The reasons for this are more practical than theoretic; analysts have found it hard to define suitable measures of discretionary income with which to bound WTP. However, recent evidence suggests that even making crude approximations based on gross household income can considerably refine estimates of mean WTP (Carson et al., 2000).

Assumptions concerning the lower bound will depend to a large extent on whether the analyst believes that WTP should be allowed to take negative or zero values. There is no denying that for some applications of CV, certain respondents will regard a change in provision of a non-market good as detrimental. For example, a road building programme that takes traffic away from a busy town centre will be regarded as beneficial to town centre residents but detrimental to those living near the path of the newly built bypass. In such a case there may be grounds for assuming a normal or logistic distribution that allows for negative values of WTP. However, imagine that we were interested in establishing how characteristics of households or the programme were influencing WTP. For example, we might wish to establish how the scale of the project impacted on WTP. We would imagine that the more traffic that was re-routed from the town centre, the greater would be the WTP of town residents. Obviously, completely the opposite would be true of those living near the new bypass. In general, therefore, when we have negative values of WTP we are frequently talking about two populations concerned with very different aspects of the programme being evaluated. In this case it makes sense to model the two groups separately. Again we would be led to the models described above.

Further, the models presented here are not the only possible approaches to modelling the distribution of zero and positive WTP. For example, some analysts have truncated or censored distributions that allow for negative WTP at a value of zero. Though this is theoretically consistent, it rarely attunes with empirical observations on the distribution of WTP. In general, CV surveys return a number of zero values that generate a distinct spike in the empirically observed distribution of WTP. Using a truncated distribution to model such a spike forces the parameters of the truncated distribution to model both the spike and continuous parts of the distribution. In general, this is unlikely to be as efficient as including a separate parameter to model the spike.

ESTIMATING THE ECONOMETRIC MODEL

Armed with a model of household WTP and a distributional assumption, the analyst is in a position to estimate the parameters of the model. Remember that our econometric model is probabilistic; it attributes a probability to observing a particular WTP or a particular utility change.

The model is encapsulated in the CDF of the random variable z, $F(z;\cdot)$, and PDF, $f(z;\cdot)$, and the previous section discussed the various forms that these functions might take. Notice that here a dot is used to represent the various parameters of the model since these will differ according to the modelling approach and distributional assumptions made by the analyst. To reiterate, in the bid function model the parameters consist of:

- a which determines the mid-point of the distribution of the random variable z (which in this case represents WTP); a can be further parameterised according to equations (5.17) to (5.20) to allow the probability distribution to shift up or down the WTP scale according to the characteristics of the household;[5]
- σ^2 which determines the spread of the probability distribution of z, such that higher values of σ^2 would attribute positive probabilities over a larger range of WTP values; and
- ρ which determines the height of the spike representing the probability that a household will have a zero WTP.

In utility difference models, the parameters consist of:

- β and λ which jointly determine how a reported WTP is converted into a utility change;
- α which determines the mid-point of the distribution of the random variable z (which in this case represents utility change); again α can be further parameterised according to equation (5.15) to allow the probability distribution to shift up or down the utility change scale according to the characteristics of the household;
- ρ which again determines the height of the spike representing the probability that a household will have a zero utility change; and
- note that as explained previously, σ^2 is not estimated in utility difference models since to establish the utility scale we impose the normalisation $\sigma^2 = 1$.

The objective in estimating the model will be to choose the values of the parameters that maximise the probability of observing the WTP amounts reported by respondents to the questionnaire.

Data for the estimation of these parameters come from a sample of respondents drawn from a defined population. For now we make the important assumption that this is a representative sample, that is, each household in the population has equal probability of being included in the sample. In our sample we have observations on the WTP of N households indexed $i = 1$ to N.

The first step in model estimation is to select some starting values for the parameters of the model. Given these values for the parameters, we can use the selected model to calculate the probability of observing each of the WTP values reported in the sample. The estimated probability for each household is known as their *likelihood contribution* and is denoted l_i.

Multiplying the likelihood contributions would give us the *total likelihood* of observing these WTP values, given our selected values for the parameters. We can write:

$$L = \prod_i l_i, \tag{31}$$

where L is known as the *likelihood function* and measures the total probability (predicted by the model at the given parameters) that respondents will have provided the WTP responses recorded in the CV survey. It frequently proves more convenient to work with the log of the likelihood function, a function that, not altogether surprisingly, is termed the *log likelihood function*:

$$\ln L = \sum_i \ln l_i. \tag{32}$$

Of course, if we select different values for the parameters we might find that our model predicts a higher total likelihood (and hence log likelihood). We would assume that these values for the parameters are closer to the true values that we are trying to estimate. Indeed, using a technique known as *maximum likelihood estimation* it is possible to establish (with the help of computer software) the set of parameters that best fit the data; that is, to calculate the set of parameters that maximise the total likelihood of observing the reported WTP values.

As Section 5.2 shows, however, not all CV elicitation formats return exact values of WTP. Indeed, the exact form of the likelihood function will depend on the form in which WTP data are returned. Each of the three types of CV survey data is reviewed in turn.

Open-ended Data

Open-ended data provide the most straightforward modelling problem, with the exception that the WTP estimate can be highly influenced by a small number of (very large or very small) outliers. In the bid function models, the probability of observing each household's reported WTP, denoted C_i, is simply the PDF of the probability distribution evaluated at that WTP. Thus:

$$l_i = \Pr(z_i = C_i) = f(z_i; \cdot) \quad i = 1 \text{ to } N, \tag{33}$$

where l_i is household i's *likelihood contribution*.

In the utility difference models we need to make a slight adjustment to account for the fact that we are not modelling the distribution of WTP but of utility change. First, the household's WTP, C_i, must be converted into the equivalent utility change, z_i, using equation (2), (3) or (4) according to the analyst's assumptions concerning income effects. We shall denote this $z_i(C_i)$ which simply stands for the value of z equivalent to a WTP equal to C_i. Then the probability of observing each household's reported WTP is given by:[6]

$$l_i = f(z_i(C_i); \cdot) \frac{dz_i(C_i)}{dC_i} \quad i = 1 \text{ to } N. \tag{34}$$

Here, the derivative dz_i/dC_i adjusts the probabilities of observing a certain utility change into the probabilities of observing a certain WTP.

For example, in the Box–Cox utility difference model we have from equations (4) and (6):

$$z_i(C_i) = \frac{\beta}{\lambda} \left[y_i^\lambda - (y_i - C_i)^\lambda \right]. \tag{35}$$

Replacing $z_i(C_i)$ in equation (34) with the above expression gives the likelihood contribution for each household:

$$l_i = f\left(\frac{\beta}{\lambda} \left[y_i^\lambda - (y_i - C_i)^\lambda \right]; \alpha, \beta, \lambda, \rho \right) \beta(y_i - C_i)^{\lambda-1} \quad i = 1 \text{ to } N. \tag{36}$$

Likelihood contributions can be combined according to (32) to give the log likelihood function and the parameters of the model estimated by maximum likelihood techniques.

Binary Data

The estimation of models from binary data is somewhat complicated by the fact that households do not provide an exact value for their WTP. Instead each household simply states whether they are willing to pay a certain amount or not. In the CV literature this amount is frequently referred to as a bid and henceforth shall be denoted B. If a household's WTP is greater than B it is assumed they will answer 'Yes', whilst they will answer 'No' if their WTP is lower than B. Thus in response to the CV question the respondent will answer:

$$No \text{ if } C_i < B$$
$$and \ \ Yes \text{ if } C_i \geq B. \tag{37}$$

To derive an expression for the likelihood contribution of each household with data of this sort we will need to use the CDF of the probability distribution of z.

Remember that in bid function models z is simply the household's WTP. Thus the CDF of z gives us the probability of a household's WTP being lower than a certain value. Consequently, evaluating the CDF at B will give us the probability of a household answering 'No'. And, by definition, the probability of a household answering 'Yes' must be one minus the CDF evaluated at B. Thus:

$$\Pr(No) = p_i = F(B; \alpha, \sigma^2, \rho)$$
$$\Pr(Yes) = 1 - p_i = 1 - F(B; a, \sigma^2, \rho), \tag{38}$$

where p_i is the probability of a 'Yes' response. The likelihood contribution of each household will depend on whether they answer 'Yes' or 'No' to the particular bid level presented to them. We can write:

$$l_i = p_i^{d_i}(1 - p_i)^{1-d_i}, \tag{39}$$

where d_i is a dummy variable which equals zero if the respondent answered 'Yes', and one if the respondent answered 'No'.

In the utility difference models, the procedure is slightly more complex since z represents a utility change. Rather than evaluating the CDF at B, we first must convert B into the equivalent utility change using equation (2), (3) or (4). We shall denote this utility change as $z_i(B)$, which simply stands for the value of z equivalent to a payment of B. Again, a household will respond 'Yes' if the utility change induced by paying B is lower than the utility change they would derive from provision of the non-market good and 'No' if it is higher. Thus:

$$\Pr(No) = p_i = F(z_i(B); \alpha, \beta, \lambda, \rho)$$
$$\Pr(Yes) = 1 - p_i = 1 - F(z_i(B); \alpha, \beta, \lambda, \rho). \tag{40}$$

As an example, the Box–Cox utility model results in:

$$\Pr(No) = p_i = F\left(\frac{\beta}{\lambda}\left[y_i^\lambda - (y_i - B)^\lambda\right]; \alpha, \beta, \lambda, \rho\right)$$

$$\Pr(Yes) = 1 - p_i = 1 - F_\eta\left(\frac{\beta}{\lambda}\left[y_i^\lambda - (y_i - B)^\lambda\right]; \alpha, \sigma^2\right). \tag{41}$$

The estimated probabilities from (41) can be used in the calculation of likelihood contributions according to (39). Again the likelihoods can be combined according to (32) to give the log likelihood function and the parameters estimated by applying maximum likelihood techniques.

Interval Data

The analysis of interval data follows exactly the same logic as that described for the analysis of binary data. For example, take a payment card approach for eliciting interval data. We can consider the payment card as listing a series of bid levels. When a respondent points out the highest amount on the card that they are willing to pay, we assume that their true WTP must lie between this amount and the next amount listed on the card.

Let us denote the amount the household chooses as B_L (for lower bid level) and the next amount up on the payment card as B_H (for higher bid level). Now in the bid function model, the probability that a household chooses B_L will be the probability that their WTP is greater than B_L and less than B_H. Again we can use the CDF of WTP to establish this probability:

$$\Pr(B_L < C_i \le B_H) = F(B_H; a, \sigma^2, \rho) - F(B_L; a, \sigma^2, \rho). \tag{42}$$

Alternatively, a household might say their WTP is lower than the lowest amount presented on the payment card. Denoting this by B_L^* we can define the probability of this response as:

$$\Pr(C_i \le B_L^*) = F(B_L^*; \alpha, \sigma^2, \rho). \tag{43}$$

Finally, the household may state that their WTP is greater than the highest amount on the payment card. Denoting this B_H^* we can write the probability of this response as:

$$\Pr(C_i > B_H^*) = 1 - F(B_H^*; \alpha, \sigma^2, \rho). \qquad (44)$$

Each household's likelihood contribution can be calculated according to (42), (43) or (44) depending on which case they fall into. Again these can be aggregated into a log likelihood function that can be maximised to find estimates of the parameters of the model.

Applied to a utility difference model, the only change that needs to be made is that the bids must be converted into utility changes. In which case (42) would be evaluated at $z_i(B_H)$ and $z_i(B_L)$, (43) would be evaluated at $z_i(B_L^*)$ and (43) at $z_i(B_H^*)$

DEALING WITH UNREPRESENTATIVE SAMPLES

The data collected in a CV survey contain information on the WTP of a sample of respondents. This sample is merely a subset of a larger target population. Almost always we will want to use the results from the analysis of the sample data to draw inference about the population in general. To do this accurately and reliably it is essential that the sample design selects an unbiased subset of the population (details of sample design can be found in Chapter 3).

Ideally, the data would result from a simple random sample in which each member of the population had an equal probability of being included in the sample. This we would describe as a *representative sample*.

If our sample is skewed such that certain members of the population are more likely to be in the sample than others, then the sample will not be representative. In such a case the analyst must define *analytical weights* that are correct for this sample bias:

- observations that have a low probability of being in the sample are attributed an above-average weight and hence have a greater than average influence on the analysis; and
- observations that have a high probability of being in the sample are attributed a below-average weight and hence have a less than average influence on the analysis.

In fact, the analytical weight attributed to an observation will be the inverse of the probability of that observation being in the sample (known as the sampling weight), normalised such that the weights for all the observation in the sample sum to one. We shall denote the analytical weight attributed to each observation, i, in the sample by w_i, such that $\Sigma_i w_i = 1$. According to the sampling design, three cases present themselves:

1. If a *simple random sample* is used, then each member of the population had an equal probability of being in the sample. Hence each observation should be allotted the same importance in the analysis and, as such, there will be no need to define weights.

2. If the sample has been selected using a *probabilistic process* (for example, by stratified or clustered sampling, see Chapter 3) then weights will be relatively easy to define. Each observation's weight can be deduced from the probability of that household being selected for the sample and this probability should be known from the sampling design.

3. If sampling has been *non-probabilistic* then some members of the population may have a strong chance of being chosen, others may have no chance at all, and there is no way to tell the specific probability in either case. Though such samples are difficult to interpret, the analyst can attempt to define weights so as to improve the representativeness of the sample.

For example, imagine that following the removal of *non-valid responses* (see Section 5.1.2) the analyst examines the characteristics of the sample but finds that the proportion of households in the sample from low income groups is significantly lower than that in the population. Clearly, the sample is not very representative of the population.

To account for this the analyst might want to define two income groups, one group with below-average population income and one group with above-average income. Obviously 50 per cent of households in the population will fall into the lower group and 50 per cent of households will fall into the higher group. At the same time, the analyst can identify the proportion of households in the sample that fall into either group. Now by dividing the population proportion by the sample proportion, the analyst defines an analytical weight. For households from the low income group the weight will be greater than one, since the bias in the sample means that they are under-represented in the sample, whilst for households in the high income group the weight will be less than one.

The analyst may want to use much more complex weighting procedures than the simple example given here. For example, the analyst could define several categories of income and calculate sample and population proportions for each category. Further, the analyst may wish to define categories according to more than one characteristic in which case the same procedure applies; define the strata, find the population proportion in each strata and divide these by the proportion of the sample in the equivalent strata.

In general, given the necessary information the analyst can calculate the proportion of households in the population falling into any particular group. Let us denote the number of households in the population falling into group g as N_g. Similarly, the analyst can calculate the number of households in the sample falling into the same group. Let us denote this number as n_g. The sampling weight for observation i that falls into group g is given by $w_i = n_g/N_g$.

4. If it is *impossible to define sampling weights*, then analysts must proceed without analytical weights and must rely on their own subjective evaluation of the survey results.

Weights are included in the estimation process through adjustment of the likelihood function (equation (32)) according to:

$$L = \prod_i w_i l_i. \tag{45}$$

The inclusion of weights in the likelihood function adjusts the data so that the sample behaves like a representative one. In effect, the weight reduces the importance of observations from households with characteristics that have been oversampled (for example, high-income households) and increases the importance of observations from households that have characteristics that were undersampled (for example, low-income households).

NOTES

1. If there are reasonable grounds for assuming that all households have positive WTP then this will not be necessary.
2. In addition, the analyst may wish to investigate how the characteristics of the household (and possibly characteristics of the programme and survey design) impact upon the probability of a household being in the group with a WTP of zero. In this case the parameter ρ can be parameterised. One possible parameterisation is given by $\rho = e^{\gamma Z} / 1 + e^{\gamma Z}$ where Z is a vector of variables (that may or may not coincide with the X used to parameterise a or α) and γ is a vector of parameters that measure the impact of the Z variables on the probability of having zero WTP. Notice how this functional form restricts ρ to the unit interval, as we would expect for a probability.
3. Another possible solution is to *censor* the positive distribution at the level of household income. This amounts to attributing the probability of having a WTP in excess of income, i.e. the shaded area in Figure A5.1.2, to a spike at the income level. In other words, censoring assumes that no one is willing to pay more than the highest observed income. In some ways this is a simpler solution since the spike can be fitted after the original distribution has been fitted. However, censoring the distribution after estimation is theoretically less appealing than fitting a truncated model. As pointed out by Haab and McConnell (1997), amongst others, censoring the distribution after estimation of the parameters of the model is theoretically inconsistent because it initially assumes that values of WTP in excess of income are acceptable and then arbitrarily rules them out.
4. Notice that for the log and Box–Cox utility difference models these conversion expressions

are more complicated and involve rescaling WTP according to household income and, in the case of the Box–Cox model, the parameter λ. This reflects our assumptions concerning income effects, such that more units of WTP are required to 'purchase' one unit of utility as income rises.

5. For example, in the bid function models we might expect that those with higher income tend to express higher WTP. We would like our model, therefore, to account for the fact that those with higher income have a higher probability of responding with large values of WTP than those on lower incomes. To achieve this, we can include income in the parameterisation of a (as shown in equations (5.17) to (5.20) for example). If the data follow our expectations, then the estimated parameter on income (b in equations (5.17) to (5.20)) will be positive and the probability distribution of WTP will shift up to higher values for those with high income and to lower values for those with low incomes.

6. Equation (34) is derived by using the change of variables technique (see Greene, 1993 for details) to establish the distribution of WTP and C_i, given the assumed distribution of the random variable, z_i.

ANNEX 5.2 Estimating mean and median WTP

In the summary of this chapter, it was suggested that there are a number of possible objectives for the analysis of CV data:

1. Primarily analysts will be interested in establishing a measure of the *average WTP* of individuals in the sample. This value can then be aggregated to estimate the benefits accruing to the whole population.
2. In certain cases analysts may also wish to establish whether aspects of the *CV scenario or survey design influence this average WTP*. For example, analysts may wish to investigate whether respondents are sensitive to the scope of changes in the provision of the non-market good. To achieve this, two CV scenarios will be designed that differ solely in their description of the scope of provision of the non-market good. The two different surveys are administered to different sub-samples and the analyst will seek to establish whether the average WTP of these two sub-samples are significantly different from each other.
3. Analysts may also wish to test the *validity of the WTP values* obtained from the CV survey. That is, they may wish to test whether the WTP values provided by respondents follow distinguishable patterns and that these patterns conform with prior expectations and economic theory. For example, we would be surprised if WTP for improvements to a local amenity, say an urban park, did not decline with distance.
4. A further objective may be to provide details that can be used in the *transfer of benefit estimates* from the current study to another similar project.

The different objectives of the analyst will demand different modelling approaches. This annex focuses on the issue of analysing CV data to address the first two of these objectives. The first two objectives are both concerned with establishing a measure of the average WTP of a sample or sub-sample of respondents. In such situations, we are not interested in determining whether WTP is systematically influenced by the characteristics of households. As a general rule, therefore, we will use the simplest possible models. We seek solely to estimate the distribution of WTP in the sample and from this derive a measure of the sample average WTP.

In the first case listed above, this is our only objective. The value for average WTP can be aggregated to the population to give a measure of the total benefit derived from the change in provision of the non-market good proposed in the CV scenario.

In the second case we wish to compare WTP values across sub-samples facing different CV scenarios or questionnaire designs. In such a case, data from sub-samples responding to different versions of the questionnaire should be analysed separately. The average WTP values calculated from the different sub-samples should then be compared using techniques to be described subsequently.

NON-PARAMETRIC ESTIMATION OF MEAN AND MEDIAN WTP

Section 5.2 and Annex 5.1 focus on how analysts could develop econometric models of WTP that conform with economic theory. Crucial to these models is the assumption that the random variable z (which represented WTP in bid function models and utility change in utility difference models) could be approximated by a parametric probability distribution. It is shown that a number of possible parametric families of distributions could be used for this purpose (for example, the normal, log-normal, logistic, log-logistic, exponential, Weibull, gamma and beta families of distributions). Each of these distributions could be completely described by a mathematical equation. For example, the log-normal distribution is described by the equation:

$$f(z;a,\sigma^2) = \frac{1}{\sqrt{2\pi}} e^{-\frac{1}{2}\left(\frac{\ln z - a}{\sigma}\right)^2} \left(\frac{1}{z\sigma}\right). \tag{1}$$

Given estimates of the parameters of the distribution, a and σ^2, this formula gives the probability of observing a certain value for z. It is also shown that to fit the data better it may be necessary to introduce further parameters. Frequently, for example, a separate parameter, ρ, might be introduced that represents a spike in the distribution at a value of zero WTP. The task of the analyst is to estimate the various parameters of the assumed distribution so that the model's predictions of the probabilities of observing WTP values best reflect their actual frequency in the sample.

Of course, the use of a parametric distribution to approximate the distribution of WTP in a sample represents a fairly large assumption. Indeed, it has been shown that some statistics, the mean in particular, are quite sensitive to the particular distributional assumption made by the analyst. Fortunately, when the objective is to estimate the mean and median values of the WTP distribution, the analyst can turn to an alternative estimation framework. This framework does away with the assumption of a parametric distribution and hence is known as *non-parametric* estimation.

In this section, the methods of non-parametric estimation are outlined. In general, non-parametric techniques provide a purely empirical approach to estimating the *survivor function* of WTP responses. This survivor function, rather than being the continuous curve defined by parametric specifications, is an untidy-looking step function. However, this does not prevent use of the non-parametric survivor function to estimate mean and median WTP values, values that do not depend on an *ad hoc* parametric assumption.

Further, these estimates of mean and median WTP can be taken as lower bounds for these statistics. In other words, they give the minimum value for the mean or median that is consistent with the sample data. As a result, non-parametric estimation is an indispensable step in the analysis of CV data when the objective is to estimate the mean and median WTP of a sample.

Moreover, the non-parametric estimators can also be placed in a maximum likelihood framework. Indeed, the value of the maximised log likelihood function derived from non-parametric estimation is the lowest value that can be derived for the log likelihood function of the available data. As the next section shows, this lower bound value for the log likelihood can guide analysts in their choice of a parametric specification that might be used to obtain 'best' estimates of the mean and median WTP of the sample.

Once again, the exact form of the non-parametric estimator will depend on the type of data that has been collected in the CV survey. In the case of continuous data, non-parametric estimation is extremely simple and intuitive. For binary data the techniques are somewhat more complex but again very intuitive. For certain forms of interval data rather more complex estimation techniques must be used.

Continuous Data

Non-parametric estimation of the distribution of WTP when the CV survey returns continuous data is achieved through a technique known as the *Kaplan–Meier product limit estimator*. As with all the non-parametric techniques discussed here, the Kaplan–Meier estimator is a purely empirical approach to estimating the survivor function for WTP responses. Remember the survivor function gives the probability of observing a WTP greater than a particular value.

For continuous data, estimation of this step function is extremely simple. In short, the technique involves arranging the sample's WTP values in ascending order and tracing out the survivor function by calculating the proportion of the sample that have a WTP greater than each value.

To present the Kaplan–Meier product limit estimator more formally we need to introduce some notation:

1. Imagine a data set reporting the maximum WTP of a sample of households.
2. The total number of households in the sample is represented by N.
3. Now within the data we observe J distinct positive values of WTP; also the data will most likely contain a number of zero values.
4. Ordering these values from lowest to highest we can denote each distinct WTP value by C_j ($j = 0$ to J); C_0 will always equal zero and C_J will be the largest WTP value in the sample.
5. If each household has returned a unique positive WTP value, then J will be equal to N; more usually there will be ties (that is, two or more households reporting the same WTP) such that J will be less than N.
6. Let h_j denote the number of households in the sample with a WTP of C_j.
7. The total number of households in the sample with a WTP that is greater than C_j will be given by

$$n_j = \sum_{k=j+1}^{J} h_k.$$

An empirical estimate of the survivor function at each of the C_j can be calculated as:

$$\hat{S}(C_j) = \frac{n_j}{N} \quad j = 0 \text{ to } J. \tag{2}$$

In words, the estimate of the survivor function evaluated at a WTP of C_j is calculated by computing the number of households with a WTP greater than this amount and expressing this as a portion of the total number of households in the sample. Notice that for C_J, the highest WTP value in the sample, the survivor function will be zero. As we would hope, at the highest WTP value in the sample, the probability of someone returning a value greater than this amount falls to zero.

Thus at each of the J WTP values in the data we have a point estimate of the survivor function. We could plot each of these points onto a graph. The question that remains is how these points should be joined together in order to form a continuous survivor function. With the Kaplan–Meier estimator, the usual assumption is that between successive observed WTP values, C_j and C_{j+1}, the survivor function remains constant at the probability associated with C_j, that is, $\hat{S}(C_j)$.

By way of illustration observe the hypothetical Kaplan–Meier survivor function illustrated in Figure A5.2.1. The survivor function is traced out as a series of vertical steps taken at each successive WTP value where the height of the step is determined by the number of respondents returning this value as their maximum WTP.

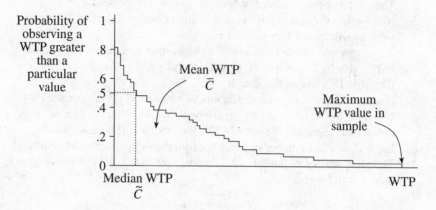

Figure A5.2.1   Hypothetical Kaplan–Meier survivor function for continuous WTP data

As can be seen in Figure A5.2.1, this estimation procedure results in a valid survivor function in which the probability of 'surviving' is always falling (or more technically never increasing) as the WTP amount increases. As we shall see subsequently, the increased complexity of non-parametric estimation with other forms of WTP data is in ensuring that the survivor function is never increasing.

Estimates of mean and median WTP are easily derived from the Kaplan–Meier estimator. As illustrated in Figure A5.2.1, the median value can be read directly from the empirical survivor function by evaluating WTP at the point at which the survivor function reaches a probability of 0.5. This is equivalent to the familiar process of ordering the WTP data in ascending order and taking the middle observation as the median WTP.

The mean value can be calculated as the area bounded by the survivor function in accordance with equation (5.23). With the non-parametric models presented here this formula reduces to:

$$\overline{C} = \sum_{j=0}^{J} \hat{S}(C_j)[C_{j+1} - C_j]. \tag{3}$$

It is relatively simple to show that this estimate of mean WTP is the same as that would be returned from the more familiar calculation of summing the reported WTP values in the sample and dividing by the sample size.

Binary Data

In designing a CV survey using single-bounded WTP questions the analyst decides upon a series of positive bid levels, denoted B_j, $j = 1, 2, ... J$. Each bid level is presented to a number of households who report whether they are willing to pay this amount or not. Also, we assume that there exists a bid level at a value of zero which we denote B_0. It is supposed that if a zero bid level were presented to a sample of respondents they would all be willing to pay this amount.

With binary data the analyst has far less information on the shape of the survivor function than that provided by continuous data. Point estimates of the survivor function can only be calculated at each of the J bid levels, where J is likely to be only a handful of different values. The procedure for estimating these point estimates is very simple. Again, we require some notation:

- If the number of households in the sample is N, then the sub-sample facing bid level B_j can be denoted N_j.
- The number of households replying 'Yes' are willing to pay amount B_j are those that have a higher WTP than this amount. Again we shall denote this amount as n_j.

An empirical estimate of the survivor function at each of the B_j can be calculated as:

$$\hat{S}(B_j) = \frac{n_j}{N_j} \quad j = 0 \text{ to } J. \tag{4}$$

And given our assumption that everyone is willing to pay a non-negative amount for the non-market good, we can set $\hat{S}(B_0) = 1$.

The procedure can be illustrated with reference to the hypothetical data presented in Table A5.2.1. We derive a point estimate of the survivor function at each of the bid levels by dividing the number of respondents answering 'Yes' to that bid level by the number in that sub-sample. These estimates are presented in the last column of the table.

The points corresponding to these estimates have been plotted as crosses in Figure A5.2.2. Notice, however, that with these data the survivor function is not a *non-increasing function*. At a WTP of 25 the survivor function is

Table A5.2.1   Hypothetical discrete choice data

Bid level (B_j)	Respondents in sub-sample (N_j)	Number of respondents answering 'Yes' (n_j)	Estimate of survivor function $\hat{S}(B_j)$
0	–	–	1
5	48	35	.73
10	52	28	.53
25	36	8	.22
50	47	12	.26
100	51	2	.04

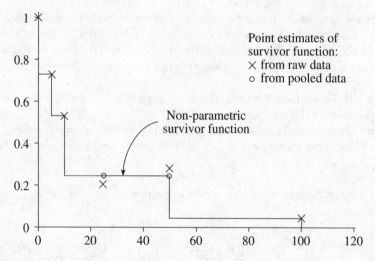

Figure A5.2.2   Hypothetical PAVA survivor function for discrete choice WTP data

estimated to be 0.22, yet at a WTP of 50 the survivor function is estimated to be 0.25. Clearly, the information provided by the sample does not generate a valid survivor function.

To correct this potential problem in discrete choice data, analysts employ a technique known as the *pooled adjacent violators algorithm* (PAVA). Simply put, the technique involves pooling data for two adjacent bid levels if the estimate of the survivor function for the higher bid level is greater than that for the lower bid level. A new estimate for the survivor function over the

range of the two bid levels is calculated by dividing the sum of those responding 'Yes' to the adjacent bid levels by the sum of respondents in the two
sub-samples. More formally, the following steps are taken:

1. Taking each bid level in turn, that is for $j = 0$ to J, calculate $\hat{S}(B_j) = n_j/N_j$
   (equation (4)).
2. Beginning with the first bid level, that is $j = 1$, compare $\hat{S}(B_j)$ with $\hat{S}(B_{j+1})$.
3. If $\hat{S}(B_{j+1})$ is less than or equal to $\hat{S}(B_j)$, then continue.
4. If $\hat{S}(B_{j+1})$ is greater than $\hat{S}(B_j)$, then pool the observations at the two
   bid levels and recalculate the survivor function as:

$$\hat{S}(B_j) = \hat{S}(B_{j+1}) = \frac{n_j + n_{j+1}}{N_j + N_{j+1}}. \tag{5}$$

5. Continue pooling until the sequence of survivor probabilities is mono-
   tonically decreasing.

For the hypothetical data in Table A5.2.1, the PAVA technique would pool the
data for bid levels 25 and 50 and a new estimate of the survivor function
across this combined range would be calculated. These are plotted as circles
in Figure A5.2.2.

Once the sequence of J survivor probabilities has been established, we face
the question of how these points should be joined together in order to form a
continuous function. Different analysts have suggested different approaches
to this problem:

- Some have suggested using linear interpolation, that is, drawing a
  straight line between each of the points.
- Others have suggested that the probability associated with WTP values
  lying between two bid levels B_{j-1} and B_j should be attributed the higher
  survivor probability $\hat{S}(B_{j-1})$.
- Here we suggest taking a conservative approach, that is, the probability
  associated with values of WTP lying between successive observed
  values B_{j-1} and B_j is the lower probability associated with the higher
  WTP value $\hat{S}(B_j)$.

Adopting this last procedure follows the logic that between successive bid
levels, B_{j-1} and B_j, the survivor function must take a value that is at least the
value of the survivor function at B_j. Since this is all that is known for certain,
this lower bound is used to characterise the whole interval. By taking this
conservative approach, the PAVA estimator can be used to construct a

lower-bound approximation to the survivor function. This procedure has been used in Figure A5.2.2 to draw the survivor function for the hypothetical data.

Again median WTP can be read off this graph at the point where the survivor function evaluates to 0.5 and mean WTP can be calculated as the area under the step function according to:

$$\overline{C} = \sum_{j=1}^{J} \hat{S}(B_j)[B_j - B_{j-1}].$$ (6)

Take care to notice that the adoption of the lower-bound approximation to the survivor function means that this formula is slightly different from that suggested for continuous data (equation (3)).

Since the estimation procedure traces out a lower bound for the survivor function, these estimates of mean and median WTP will themselves represent lower bounds.

Interval Data

Interval data are collected when respondents to a CV survey state that their WTP lies within a range defined by a lower value and an upper value. Non-parametric estimation of the survivor function from such data depends on whether the different ranges provided by respondents are overlapping.

Take the sample of data in Table A5.2.2 for example. Here, the intervals for respondents 1, 2 and 3 do not overlap, in the sense that no respondent's range lies partly or wholly within another respondent's range. In effect, non-overlapping interval data define a set of mutually exclusive ranges of WTP values and each respondent declares that their WTP lies in one of these ranges. An example of an elicitation format that results in data of this type is the payment card. Here, the respondent chooses one value from the card and it is assumed that their WTP lies between that amount and the next amount on the card.

Table A5.2.2   Hypothetical binary data

Respondent	Lower bound of WTP range	Upper bound of WTP range
1	12	15
2	5	8
3	0	5
4	12	15
5	8	15

Non-parametric estimation from data of this type presents no new challenges. The usual procedure is to take the lower bound of the range and use the Kaplan–Meier product limit estimator to estimate the survivor function at each of the lower bound values.

Returning to Table A5.2.2, notice that respondent 5's range overlaps with the ranges for respondents 1 and 4. In this case, non-parametric estimation requires the use of a technique known as *Turnbull's self-consistency algorithm* (TSCA).

WTP data containing overlapping intervals may result from double-bounded dichotomous choice WTP questions. Here the respondent is first asked whether they would be willing to pay a specified amount of money (the initial bid level, B) to obtain a change in the level of provision of a public good. Second, the respondent is posed a follow-up question which depends on the response given to the first offered bid. The follow-up question poses a higher amount (B_H) if the respondent answered 'Yes' to the original bid and a lower amount (B_L) if a 'No' answer was elicited. In the double-bounded format, the two answers given by a respondent reveal one of four possible intervals into which their willingness to pay could fall:

1. 'No' to B followed by a 'No' to B_L indicates that their WTP lies in the interval 0 to B_L.
2. 'No' to B followed by a 'Yes' to B_L indicates that their WTP lies in the interval B_L to B.
3. 'Yes' to B followed by a 'No' to B_H indicates that their WTP lies in the interval B to B_H.
4. 'Yes' to B followed by a 'Yes' to B_H indicates that their WTP lies in the interval B_H to ∞.

As with the single-bounded dichotomous choice format, analysts specify a small number of versions of the questionnaire, each version differing in the bid levels presented to the respondent. An example of a simple three-version design for the bid levels in a double-bounded WTP question CV survey is illustrated in Table A5.2.3.

Notice that data from this question format produce overlapping intervals. For example, a respondent answering 'No', 'No' to version 2 of the questionnaire would have a WTP lying in the interval 0 to 10. This interval overlaps with those respondents answering 'No', 'No' or 'No', 'Yes' to version 1 of the questionnaire (whose WTPs lie in the intervals 0 to 5 and 5 to 10 respectively).

Responses to a double-bounded dichotomous choice survey can be classified according to interval. The design illustrated in Table A5.2.3, for example,

Table A5.2.3   Hypothetical bid design for double-bounded dichotomous choice questions

Questionnaire version	Lower bid level (B_L)	Initial bid level (B)	Upper bid level (B_H)
1	5	10	20
2	10	20	40
3	20	40	70

Table A5.2.4   Hypothetical double-bounded dichotomous choice data

Interval code	Interval		Number of respondents in interval
A	0	5	10
B	5	10	9
C	10	20	22
D	0	10	13
E	0	20	25
F	20	40	22
G	40	70	8
H	20	∞	15
I	40	∞	8
J	70	∞	2

defines 10 different WTP intervals. These WTP intervals are listed in Table A5.2.4 where numbers of respondents falling into each interval from a hypothetical survey are also listed.

Notice that with this hypothetical design there are seven distinct boundary values for the various intervals; 0, 5, 10, 20, 40, 70 and ∞. In general, the distinct interval boundaries from any double-bounded dichotomous choice question can be listed in increasing order from 0 to ∞. Once again we shall label these boundary values B_j, such that B_0 is zero and B_{J+1} is ∞. Further we can index the intervening intervals $j = 1, 2, ..., J$, such that interval j denotes the interval between the boundary values B_{j-1} and B_j. We shall refer to these intervals as *basic intervals* to distinguish them from respondents' *WTP intervals*. With the hypothetical data, for example, basic interval 1 is that between 0 and 5, basic interval 2 is that between 5 and 10 and so on.

TSCA seeks to evaluate the survivor function at each of the boundary values, B_j. Under our previous assumptions, we know that the survivor function at 0, $S(B_0)$, must equal 1 (all respondents are at least indifferent to the change in provision of the public good) and the survivor function at ∞, $S(B_{J+1})$, must equal zero (no respondent has an infinite WTP for the change in provision of the public good). Our task is to find a non-parametric estimate of the intervening $S(B_j)$s.

The survivor function is estimated exactly as before. That is, the survivor function at each of the B_js is taken to be n_j, the number of households with a WTP greater than B_j, divided by N the number of households in the sample (equation (2)). The problem with overlapping interval data, however, is in adding up the observations to calculate n_j. The WTP interval reported by each household may span a number of basic intervals such that we cannot say for certain that a household's WTP is contained within any particular basic interval.

The trick then is to split each observation into a number of fractions summing to one. A fraction is allotted to each of the basic intervals spanned by the household's WTP interval. The fractions represent estimates of the probability that a household's WTP lies in each of the basic intervals. In mathematical terminology, they are the conditional probabilities that a household's WTP lies in a basic interval given that their WTP interval spans that basic interval.

For example, WTP interval code E in Table A5.2.4 covers the interval 0 to 20, such that the observed interval spans three basic intervals; $B_0 = 0$ to $B_1 = 5$, $B_1 = 5$ to $B_2 = 10$ and $B_2 = 10$ to $B_3 = 20$. For each household reporting a WTP in interval code E, we would then wish to calculate three fractions, let us say p_1, p_2 and p_3, summing to one. p_3, for example, will be an estimate of the conditional probability that a respondent's WTP lies in the interval B_2 to B_3 given that we have observed that the respondent's WTP is in the interval B_0 to B_3.

By breaking all the overlapping interval observations in this manner and then adding up all the fractions each basic interval receives, we will get a new data set which contains only non-overlapping interval observations. Applying equation (1) to this new data set will give non-parametric estimates of the survivor probabilities at each boundary value.

One problem still remains: how to calculate the fractions? Unfortunately, there is no simple one-step technique to do this. Instead the TSCA adopts an iterative procedure. The survivor function is estimated, these estimates are used to calculate the fractions to be allotted to each basic interval and the survivor function is re-estimated. The process is repeated until the point estimates of the survivor function at each of the B_js become stable; in econometric parlance, until the estimates converge.

The iterations begin by positing a set of starting values for the $S(B_j)$s that conform to the restriction that:

$$1 = \hat{S}(B_0) \geq \hat{S}(B_1) \geq \hat{S}(B_2) \geq \ldots \geq \hat{S}(B_J) \geq \hat{S}(B_{J+1}) = 0. \tag{7}$$

Note that we use a hat to denote the fact that these values are estimates. Then the current estimate of the probability of lying in basic interval j, that is, between B_{j-1} and B_j, is:

$$\hat{S}(B_{j-1}) - \hat{S}(B_j). \tag{8}$$

Now for an observed overlapping interval (say the interval between interval B_i and B_k where $i \leq j - 1$ and $k \geq j$) that spans this basic interval we can calculate p, the conditional probability of a respondent whose WTP is in the interval B_i to B_k having a WTP that lies in the basic interval B_{j-1} to B_j according to:

$$\frac{\hat{S}(B_{j-1}) - \hat{S}(B_j)}{\hat{S}(B_i) - \hat{S}(B_k)} \quad i \leq j-1, k \geq j. \tag{9}$$

Multiplying this probability by the number of respondents that return WTP responses in the interval B_i to B_k, we obtain an estimate of the number of respondents falling in the basic interval B_{j-1} to B_j. Performing the same calculation for each overlapping interval that spans the basic interval B_{j-1} to B_j and summing the results, we obtain an estimate of the number of respondents in the entire sample whose WTP lies in the basic interval B_{j-1} to B_j.

Thus, the first step of the TSCA is to calculate:

$$\text{STEP 1: } \hat{h}_j = \sum_{i=0}^{j-1} \sum_{k=j}^{J+1} h_{ik} \frac{\hat{S}(B_{j-1}) - \hat{S}(B_j)}{\hat{S}(B_i) - \hat{S}(B_k)}, \tag{10}$$

for $j = 1, 2, \ldots, J + 1$, where h_{ik} is the number of respondents in the sample in the observed interval B_i to B_k (for example, column 4 of Table A5.2.4) and $\hat{h}_j$ is our estimate of the number of individuals in the basic interval B_{j-1} to B_j.

Our constructed data set now consists of a series of estimates of the number of respondents lying in each basic, non-overlapping interval. Hence, we can calculate the number of respondents with a WTP greater than the boundary value B_j from:

$$\hat{n}_j = \sum_{k=j+1}^{J} \hat{h}_k \tag{11}$$

and use the Kaplan–Meier estimator to obtain a new set of estimates for the survivor function at these boundary values according to:

$$\text{STEP 2}: \hat{\bar{S}}(B_j) = \frac{\hat{n}_j}{N} \quad j = 1, 2, \ldots, J. \tag{12}$$

The procedure is iterated by using the new estimates of the survivor function, $\hat{S}(B_j) \; j = 1, 2, \ldots, J$, in Step 1 (equation (10)). The procedure is iterated until the point estimates of the survivor function at each of the B_j converge.

To obtain estimates of mean and median WTP we recommend following an identical procedure to that described for binary data. The point estimates of the survivor function at each of the B_j are joined using the conservative approach in which the probability associated with values of WTP lying between B_{j-1} and B_j is the lower probability associated with the higher WTP value $\hat{S}(B_j)$. Again this will result in a lower-bound approximation to the survivor function.

Median WTP can be gleaned from this constructed survivor function as the value at which the survivor function evaluates to 0.5. Also, mean WTP can be calculated as the area under the step function, as in (6), according to:

$$\overline{C} = \sum_{j=1}^{J} \hat{S}(B_j)[B_j - B_{j-1}]. \tag{13}$$

Both the median WTP and mean WTP estimates can be interpreted as lower bound values for these statistics.

Confidence Intervals from Non-parametric Estimation of Mean and Median WTP

Calculating lower-bound mean and median WTP values using non-parametric techniques provides a guide to the central tendency of the sample data. However, we must not lose sight of the fact that these results refer just to our one sample of households. They are simply *estimates* of the mean and median of the entire population based on the information provided by the sample. A separate sample of households would return different WTP values and we would end up with different estimates of the population's mean and median WTP. Thus, analysts should also provide an indication of the accuracy of these estimates and this requires the construction of a 95 per cent confidence interval.[1]

In general, there are two approaches to determining confidence intervals: an *analytical approach* based on statistical theory and a *numerical approach* based on extensive computing. The latter involves a technique known as *bootstrapping*. Bootstrapping is a very robust technique that can be used to construct confidence intervals for mean and median WTP using any type of data (that is, continuous, binary or interval) or results from any estimation method (that is, non-parametric or parametric). Whilst our discussion of confidence interval construction begins with the description of a number of analytical techniques, it is worth bearing in mind that bootstrapping could always be used as an alternative. We shall return to describe bootstrapping in relation to the construction of confidence intervals for median WTP estimated from parametric models.

Continuous data

For continuous data, the variance of the estimate of the mean is calculated using a series of standard results from statistical theory. First we require an estimate of the variance of WTP in the population. Clearly, the only information that we have on the variance of WTP in the population is from our sample of WTP values. Indeed, it turns out that an unbiased estimate of the population variance will be given by:

$$\text{var}(C) = \frac{\sum_{i}^{N} C_i^2 - N\overline{C}^2}{N-1}, \tag{14}$$

where $\text{var}(C)$ is our estimate of the population variance, i indexes the different households, C_i is the WTP of each of those households, $\overline{C}$ is the sample mean WTP and N is the number of households in the sample.

It is possible to use this estimate of the variance of WTP in the population, $\text{var}(C)$, to derive an estimate of the variance of mean WTP values, $\overline{C}$, an amount that we shall denote $\text{var}(\overline{C})$. To be clear, the value $\text{var}(\overline{C})$ is an estimate of the variance of the distribution of values that would result from repeated calculation of $\overline{C}$ from separate and independent samples of size N taken from the population. Again avoiding the theoretical details, it can be shown that the variance of mean WTP is given by:

$$\text{var}(\overline{C}) = \frac{\text{var}(C)}{N}. \tag{15}$$

From equation (15) it is obvious that the larger the sample size, N, the smaller will be the variance in our estimate of the mean, $\text{var}(\overline{C})$. Since $\overline{C}$ is an unbiased estimator of the mean WTP of the population, we can become increasingly confident that our estimate of mean WTP from the sample is a good estimate of the mean WTP of the population as we increase our sample size. Indeed, as we would expect, if our sample grew in size to include the whole population, our estimate of mean WTP would become the true population mean WTP and our estimate of the variance of this mean value would become negligible.

To construct 95 per cent confidence intervals we turn to one further powerful result from statistical theory, the *central limit theorem*. This tells us that no matter how values of WTP are distributed in the population, the distribution of means calculated from random samples of N households from that population will tend towards a normal distribution as N gets larger. The sample sizes used in CV surveys are usually adequate to invoke the central limit theorem (statisticians suggest sample sizes of 30 observations or more will be sufficiently large). If the distribution of mean WTPs calculated from independent samples is taken to follow a normal distribution, then it is a relatively simple task to calculate a 95 per cent confidence interval. In particular, it is known that 95 per cent of the normal distribution lies within ± 1.96 standard errors either side of the mean. The standard error of the sampling distribution can be determined by taking the square root of equation (15):

$$\sqrt{\text{var}(\overline{\overline{C}})} = \frac{\sqrt{\text{var}(C)}}{\sqrt{N}} \qquad (16)$$

and the 95% confidence interval will be defined by:

$$\overline{C} - (1.96)\sqrt{\text{var}(\overline{C})} \text{ and } \overline{C} + (1.96)\sqrt{\text{var}(\overline{C})}. \qquad (17)$$

These two values should be interpreted as stating that, over all possible samples, the probability is about .95 that the range between

$$\overline{C} - (1.96)\sqrt{\text{var}(\overline{C})} \text{ and } \overline{C} + (1.96)\sqrt{\text{var}(\overline{C})}$$

will include the true population mean.

Statistical theory also guides our estimation of confidence intervals for median WTP from continuous data. Consider the distribution of WTP values in the population depicted by the continuous curve in the top graph of Figure A5.2.3. The population median WTP is defined as the WTP of the middle household; that is, the WTP value at which 50 per cent of the population have a lower WTP and 50 per cent of the population have a higher WTP.

When we sample from this population we select at random N households. Figure A5.2.3 depicts the WTP values of two such random samples where $N = 9$. For each of these samples we can define a point estimate of the population median WTP as the middle value in the sample. In this case this

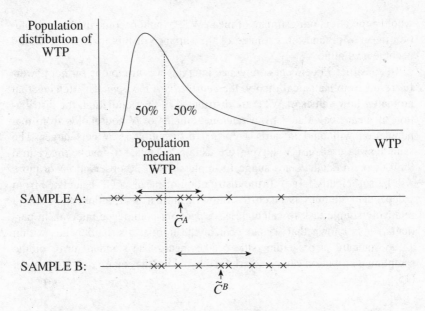

Source: Based on Wonnacott and Wonnacott (1990), Figure 15.3

Figure A5.2.3   Confidence intervals for median WTP from continuous data

will amount to the 5th largest (smallest) observation which is labelled $\tilde{C}^A$ for sample A and $\tilde{C}^B$ for sample B.

Now, to define a confidence interval, we wish to know how far above and below this point estimate we must go before we are 95 per cent certain that we will be including the population median WTP. For example, in Figure A5.2.3 we have constructed a confidence interval based on going two observations either side of the sample median. Equivalently we could define this confidence interval as ranging from the WTP of the 7th largest observation (median plus 2 observations) down to the WTP of the 7th smallest observation (median minus 2 observations).

In Sample A, this confidence interval covers the population median. However, in Sample B the sample is skewed to the right, such that the confidence interval does not cover the population median. Notice that it would also be possible to select a sample that was skewed sufficiently far to the left that the confidence interval would similarly fail to cover the population median.

Our task in defining a confidence interval, therefore, will be to calculate the number of observations we must deviate from the start and end of the sample in order that on average 95 out of 100 random samples will have a confidence interval that covers the population median. Let us call this number of observations x.

To see how we can define such a number, consider the median of the population from which the sample we are studying is drawn. This amount is defined by the fact that 50 per cent of the population have a WTP that is higher than this amount and 50 per cent have a WTP that is lower than this amount. Thus when sampling from the population, each time we draw a household to add to our sample we have half a chance of choosing a household that has a WTP larger than the population median and another half chance that we will select a household that has a WTP that is less than the population median.

The process of selecting a sample therefore can be considered as a Bernoulli process (much like tossing a coin). Each time we select a household with a WTP greater than the population median we can add one to our total of 'successes' and each time we draw a household with a WTP lower than the population median we can add one to our total of 'failures'.

There is a possibility that we will draw a sample with a high proportion of 'successes' or a high proportion of 'failures'. And of course, the greater the proportion of 'successes' in the sample, the more likely it will be that our confidence interval will define a range that is above the true population median. Similarly, the greater the proportion of 'failures', the more likely it will be that our confidence interval will define a range that is below the true population median.

On average we would expect to get 50 'successes' and 50 'failures' out of 100 draws from the population. Of course, we could end up with 60 'successes' out of 100 draws, but this would be less likely to happen. Furthermore, 70 'successes' out of 100 draws would be even less likely. What we need to discover is the number of 'successes' out of 100 draws that only has a 2.5 per cent chance of occurring. Of course, we could end up with a sample that has a large proportion of 'failures' and since we have an equal chance (0.5) of drawing a 'failure' as we do a 'success', we also have a 2.5 per cent chance of drawing this number of 'failures'.

In general if we can identify the number of 'successes' ('failures') out of a population of size N that occur with a probability of 2.5 per cent we have identified our value x. Then if we were to select the xth largest observation in the data set, there would only be 2.5 chances in 100 that the WTP of this household would exceed the population median. In exactly the same way, there would only be 2.5 chances in 100 that the WTP of the xth smallest observation in the data set would be below the population median.

Since the sampling is a Bernoulli process, the probability of getting a certain number of 'successes' ('failures') in a sample of N households will be described by the Binomial distribution. Further, given that N is sufficiently large, the Binomial distribution is well approximated by the normal distribution. Avoiding the statistical details, it turns out that we can use the normal approximation to the binomial distribution in order to devise a simple calculation for x:

$$x = \left(1.96\sqrt{\text{var}(\tilde{C})} - 0.5\right)N. \qquad (18)$$

Where $\sqrt{\text{var}(\tilde{C})}$ is defined as:

$$\sqrt{\text{var}(\tilde{C})} = \sqrt{0.25/N}, \qquad (19)$$

95 per cent confidence intervals for median WTP can be defined as ranging from the WTP of the household returning the xth smallest value up to the WTP of the household returning the xth largest value.

Binary and interval data

A number of procedures have been suggested for determining confidence intervals for mean WTP estimated from binary or interval data. Here we present just one relatively simple approach. In an analogous manner to the development of confidence intervals for mean WTP from continuous data, we will need an estimate of the variance of WTP in the population. For binary and interval data this is given by:

$$\text{var}(C) = \sum_{j=0}^{J}(B_j - \overline{C})^2(\hat{S}(B_j) - \hat{S}(B_{j+1})). \qquad (20)$$

Where $\text{var}(C)$ is our estimate of the population variance, B_j are the $j = 1$ to J bid levels and $B_0 = 0$, $\overline{C}$ is mean WTP calculated from equation (6), $\hat{S}(B_j)$ are the J estimates of points on the survivor curve and we assume that $\hat{S}(B_0) = 1$ and $\hat{S}(B_{J+1}) = 0$.

The variance of mean WTP, $\text{var}(\overline{C})$, can be calculated using equation (15), and once again we appeal to the central limit theorem to devise the 95 per cent confidence intervals according to equations (16) and (17).

Parametric Estimation of Mean and Median WTP

As shown above, non-parametric estimation of mean and median WTP provides lower bound estimates of these statistics. Frequently, analysts will also wish to provide 'best estimates' of mean and median WTP. To achieve this it is necessary to return to the techniques of parametric estimation. Unfortunately, estimates of these statistics (the mean in particular) are quite sensitive to the distributional assumptions made by the analyst. For example, evaluating mean WTP from a log-normal distribution may give a very different value than that obtained from a model using the log-normal distribution truncated above by respondent's income and with a spike at zero. How then should analysts choose between parametric models in order to evaluate 'best' estimates of mean and median WTP? There are three important guidelines for modelling when the estimation of average WTP is the objective:

- A *bid function model* should be used rather than a *utility difference model*. When trying to derive estimates of average WTP from a CV survey we are not interested in the behavioural (structural) model that underlies the WTP values only in the values themselves. The estimation of the β and possibly λ parameters in the utility difference model simply complicates the issue.
- The bid function model should only contain a constant (as in equation (5.16), repeated below), that is, the a parameter should not be made a function of covariates according to equations (5.17) to (5.20):

$$C = a + e \quad \text{and} \quad 0 \leq C \leq y. \tag{5.16}$$

As we have discussed previously, $a + e$ is a random variable and our objective is to use the data coming from the CV survey to estimate the unconditional distribution of this random variable.

- The chosen constant only bid function model should fit the data as best as possible. To evaluate how well the chosen model fits the data, analysts compare the value of the likelihood function at the maximised values of the parameters. Intuitively, one model fits the data better than a second model if the first model returns a higher probability of observing the WTP values returned in the survey. In general, therefore, analysts estimate a number of models using different parametric assumptions and choose the model returning the highest value for the likelihood function.

A useful guide for assessing the quality of fit of the 'best' parametric model is to compare the value of the likelihood function for the parametric model with that derived from a non-parametric model. The likelihood function for non-parametric models is given by:

$$L(S_1, S_2, \ldots, S_J) = \prod_{j=0}^{J-1} \prod_{k=j+1}^{J+1} (S(B_j) - S(B_k))^{h_j}, \tag{21}$$

where h_j denotes the number of households in the sample with a WTP in the interval B_j to B_k. The likelihood function from non-parametric estimation provides the lowest possible value for the likelihood of observing the available data. Thus parametric models whose likelihood function takes a value close to that returned from non-parametric estimation can be considered to have a good fit to the data.

Once a parametric model of WTP has been estimated, mean and median WTP can be calculated. For very simple specifications, mean and median can usually be calculated using straightforward formulae. Table A5.2.5 presents these formulae for a variety of commonly used distributional assumptions.

Table A5.2.5　Mean and median values for some parametric probability distributions

Distribution	CDF: $F(z; a, \sigma^2)$	Mean $\overline{C}$	Median $\tilde{C}$
Normal	$\Phi\left(\dfrac{z-a}{\sigma}\right)$	a	a
Logistic	$1-\left(1+\exp\left(\dfrac{z-a}{\sigma}\right)\right)^{-1}$	a	a
Log-normal	$\Phi\left(\dfrac{\ln z - a}{\sigma}\right)$	$\exp\left(a+\dfrac{\sigma^2}{2}\right)$	$\exp(a)$
Weibull	$1-\exp\left(-\exp\left(\dfrac{\ln z - a}{\sigma}\right)\right)$	$\exp(a)\Gamma(1+\sigma)^{\dagger}$	$a + \ln(-\ln(0.5))\sigma$

Note:　† Γ denotes the gamma function.

　Remembering the discussion in Annex 5.1, the distributions of WTP presented in Table A5.2.5 may well violate restrictions on the range of values for WTP suggested by economic theory. If we were to assume that WTP could not take negative values and introduced a spike parameter to the distribution so as to capture those with zero WTP, then the correction to mean and median WTP calculations is very simple. Of course, in this case we would also have to adopt a distribution that was defined only for positive values (for example, the log-normal or Weibull distributions). The correction involves simply multiplying the mean or median calculated for households with positive WTP by the probability that a household will have a positive WTP.

Thus, denoting ρ as the probability of having zero WTP (the spike parameter), the correction for the log-normal model would give:

$$\overline{C} = (\exp(a) + \exp(\sigma/2))(1-\rho)$$
$$\tilde{C} = \exp(a)(1-\rho). \tag{22}$$

If we were to impose more restrictions on the distribution of WTP, such as limiting it to be less than household disposable income, then the calculations become even more complex. Of course, it is always relatively easy to find the median of the assumed distribution of WTP. Once the distribution, $F(z)$, has been specified then median WTP can be calculated by finding the value of z that solves:

$$F(z) = \frac{1}{2}. \tag{23}$$

However, frequently no convenient formula can be used for the calculation of mean WTP. In these circumstances it may be necessary to resort to methods of numerical integration to compute mean WTP from the estimated PDF or survivor function according to equations (5.22) and (5.23) respectively.

Confidence Intervals from Parametric Estimation of Mean and Median WTP

Once again, estimates of mean and median WTP from parametric models are based solely on one particular sample of the population. Analysts should always provide an indication of the accuracy of these estimates by constructing 95 per cent confidence intervals. Again these intervals are interpreted as stating that, over all possible samples, there is a probability of about .95 that the interval will include the true population mean.

For estimation of confidence intervals for the mean, we can occasionally resort to the techniques of statistical inference described in Annex 5.1. For simple distributions, it is possible to derive formulae that can be used to estimate the variance of WTP, var(C). A selection of such formulae is presented in Table A5.2.6.

The variance of mean WTP, var($\overline{C}$), can be calculated using equation (15), and once again we appeal to the central limit theorem to devise the 95 per cent confidence intervals according to equations (16) and (17).

Though for some simple models there exist analytical formulae for calculating confidence intervals, this is generally not the case. Instead, analysts resort to a number of numerical techniques of which the two that have

Table A5.2.6   *Variance of WTP for some parametric probability distributions*

Distribution	CDF: $F(z; a, \sigma^2)$	var(C)
Normal	$\Phi\left(\dfrac{z-a}{\sigma}\right)$	σ^2
Logistic	$1 - \left(1 + \exp\left(\dfrac{z-a}{\sigma}\right)\right)^{-1}$	$\dfrac{\pi^2}{3}\sigma^2$
Log-normal	$\Phi\left(\dfrac{\ln z - a}{\sigma}\right)$	$\exp(2a + \sigma^2)(\exp(\sigma^2) - 1)$
Weibull	$1 - \exp\left(-\exp\left(\dfrac{\ln z - a}{\sigma}\right)\right)$	$\exp(2a)\{\Gamma(1 + 2\sigma) - \Gamma^2(1 + \sigma)\}$[†]

Note: [†] Γ denotes the gamma function.

enjoyed most widespread application are the *Krinsky–Robb* method and *bootstrapping* which we mentioned earlier.

The *Krinsky–Robb method* bases confidence interval estimation upon the parameter estimates (for example, $\hat{a}, \hat{\sigma}^2$ and $\hat{\rho}$ in a log-normal model with a spike) of the best fitting model. Econometric theory indicates that under a certain set of assumptions these parameter estimates will themselves be distributed as a multivariate normal distribution. The means of this multivariate normal distribution are given by the parameter estimates themselves, and the variances and covariances of this distribution are given by the variance-covariance matrix of the parameters. The Krinsky–Robb method operates by using a random number generator to make repeated draws from this multivariate normal distribution. Each individual draw is treated as a new set of possible values for the parameters from which a mean and median can be calculated. Usually up to a thousand such estimates are made. These estimates can be arranged in order and 95 per cent confidence intervals defined as the values falling on the $2\frac{1}{2}$th and $97\frac{1}{2}$th percentiles.

The drawback of the Krinsky–Robb method is that it relies on the fact that the parameter estimates have a multivariate normal distribution, which may be difficult to justify especially in small samples. As an alternative, therefore, analysts have employed *bootstrapping* to derive confidence intervals. With a data set containing N observations, the analyst creates multiple simulated data sets by sampling N times with replacement from the original set of observations. The model is re-estimated for each simulated data set to obtain a new set of parameter estimates from which estimates of mean and median WTP can be derived. Again these estimates can be arranged in order and 95 per cent confidence intervals defined as the values falling on the $2\frac{1}{2}^{th}$ and $97\frac{1}{2}^{th}$ percentiles.

Of the two methods, bootstrapping is to be preferred. Though computationally burdensome, the confidence intervals constructed make almost no assumptions concerning the nature of the data and the technique is applicable in practically all situations.

NOTE

1. Confidence intervals are also important in testing hypotheses concerning the similarity between means and medians calculated from different samples or CV surveys.

6. Designing a choice modelling questionnaire

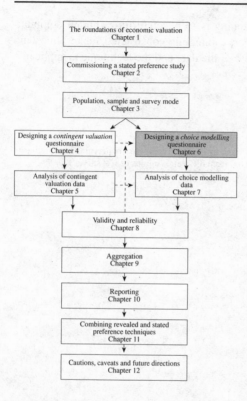

The foundations of economic valuation
Chapter 1

↓

Commissioning a stated preference study
Chapter 2

↓

Population, sample and survey mode
Chapter 3

↓

Designing a *contingent valuation* questionnaire
Chapter 4

Designing a *choice modelling* questionnaire
Chapter 6

Analysis of contingent valuation data
Chapter 5

Analysis of choice modelling data
Chapter 7

↓

Validity and reliability
Chapter 8

↓

Aggregation
Chapter 9

↓

Reporting
Chapter 10

↓

Combining revealed and stated preference techniques
Chapter 11

↓

Cautions, caveats and future directions
Chapter 12

SUMMARY

This chapter introduces an alternative set of stated preference (SP) techniques for the valuation of non-market effects, namely choice modelling. Choice modelling includes the following techniques: choice experiments, contingent ranking, contingent rating and paired comparisons. This set of SP techniques is based around the idea that any good can be described in terms of its attributes, or characteristics, and the levels that these take. However, not all of these techniques are in line with the theory of welfare economics. In fact, only the choice experiment approach definitely fits the theory whilst contingent ranking may do so. For details of why this is so,
see sections 6.3.1 and 7.1.1. Section 6.1 sets out the basic approach, while Section 6.2 presents the individual techniques within the choice modelling approach.

The design and implementation of a choice modelling questionnaire have many aspects in common with a contingent valuation questionnaire. In fact, the only difference between the two is the design of the valuation scenario section. Therefore, Section 6.3 details only those design tasks that are unique to choice modelling techniques. For other sections of the questionnaire, the guidance provided in Chapter 4 should be used. Although some aspects of sampling and survey mode choice are mentioned in Section 6.3, for a complete coverage of these issues see Chapter 3. Finally, Section 6.4 lists the advantages and disadvantages of choice modelling approaches in relation to all other economic valuation techniques and offers some points of discussion as to whether choice modelling solves any of the problems of contingent valuation.

6.1   WHAT IS CHOICE MODELLING?

The term 'choice modelling' (CM) encompasses a range of SP techniques, which take a similar approach to valuing non-market goods. The term includes:

- choice experiments;
- contingent ranking;
- contingent rating; and
- paired comparisons.

These techniques are also sometimes known as 'conjoint analysis', but this is a rather confusing term. As an empirical technique, CM originates in the market research and transport literatures (for example, Henscher, 1994) and has only relatively recently been applied to other areas such as the environment. A summary of environmental applications is given in Hanley, Mourato and Wright (2000).

CM approaches are based around the idea that any good can be described in terms of its attributes, or characteristics, and the levels that these take. For example, a forest can be described in terms of its species diversity, age structure and recreational facilities. A river can be described in terms of its chemical water quality, ecological quality and appearance. Likewise, a bus service can be described in terms of its cost, timing and comfort. Changing attribute levels will essentially result in a different 'good' being produced, and it is on the value of such changes in attributes that CM focuses. CM can tell us four things about non-market values that may be of use in a policy context:

1.   Which attributes are significant determinants of the values people place on non-market goods.
2.   The implied ranking of these attributes amongst the relevant population(s) (for example, in planning national parks, how the provision of waymarked trails is ranked relative to protecting wildlife).
3.   The value of changing more than one of the attributes at once (for example, if a management plan results in a given increase in wildlife protection but reduction in recreation access).

4. As an extension of the above, the total economic value of a resource or
    good.

However, it is important to stress here that not all CM approaches are equal in
this respect (see the discussion later in this chapter and in Chapter 7). In fact,
only two of them (choice experiments and contingent ranking) have demonstrably close links with economic theory which allow the results to be
interpreted as being equal to marginal (or total) values for use in cost–benefit
analysis (CBA) or in other contexts. CM approaches are capable of estimating both use and non-use values.

6.2   MAIN CHOICE MODELLING APPROACHES

This section summarises the main alternative CM approaches concentrating on
two issues: what respondents are asked to do, and what the researcher can get
out of their responses. This is related to the valuation scenario section of the
questionnaire alone. The other sections of a CM questionnaire are the same as a
CV questionnaire (see Chapter 4). Table 6.1 presents the main alternatives in
these terms. As noted above, the methods differ in their ability to produce WTP
estimates that can be shown to be consistent with the usual measures of welfare
change, and which can thus be used as part of a CBA or in other contexts.

Each of these alternatives is summarised below, using the example of an
agri-environmental scheme to protect wildlife and landscape on farmland.

Table 6.1   Main choice modelling alternatives

Approach	Tasks	Welfare consistent estimates?
Choice experiments	Choose between (usually) two alternatives versus the *status quo*	Yes
Contingent ranking	Rank a series of alternatives	Depends*
Contingent rating	Score alternative scenarios on a scale of 1–10	Doubtful
Paired comparisons	Score pairs of scenarios on similar scale	Doubtful

Note: * In order to interpret the results in standard welfare economic terms, one of the options
must always be currently feasible.

In principle, CM values are relative, not absolute. In order to transform relative values into the kind of absolute values that are useful for CA, respondents need one of the choices offered to them to represent the 'do nothing' *status quo*.

6.2.1 Choice Experiments

In a choice experiment (CE) respondents are presented with a series of alternatives and asked to choose their most preferred. A baseline alternative, corresponding to the *status quo*, is usually included in each choice set and must be used for welfare-consistent estimates to be produced. An example is shown in Box 6.1.

BOX 6.1 ILLUSTRATIVE CHOICE EXPERIMENT QUESTION

Here, the 'good' is wildlife habitat on farms, defined in terms of attributes such as habitat areas and cost to the taxpayer.

Which of the following two schemes do you favour? Each would have a cost to your household. Alternatively, you might favour neither scheme: taxes would not rise, but no areas would be protected either.

	Choice A	*Choice B*
Native woodland	500 ha protected	700 ha protected
Heather moorland	1200 ha protected	No protection
Lowland hay meadow	200 ha protected	300 ha protected
Cost per household per year in additional taxes	£25	£15

I would prefer: Choice A .... Choice B .... Neither ....

Choice experiments give welfare-consistent estimates for four reasons. First, they force the respondents to trade-off changes in attribute levels against the costs of making these changes. Second, the respondents can opt for the *status quo*, that is, no increase in environmental quality at no extra cost to them. Third, we can represent the econometric technique used in a way which is exactly parallel to the theory of rational, probabilistic choice. Fourth, we

BOX 6.2   CHOICE EXPERIMENTS FOR FOREST LANDSCAPES

Forest managers are often faced with decisions that impact on the appearance of forests. Given that one objective of forestry management is to maximise the social value of forestry, it is important to know how different elements of the forest landscape contribute to this social value, that is, the marginal benefits of extending or reducing certain landscape features within the forest. CE can address this kind of question. Hanley et al. (1998) report results from a project that employed CE in this way. Focus groups were used to identify features of forest landscapes that were important to the general public. These included species diversity (especially in terms of conifers versus broadleaves), how the forest was felled (large scale versus small-scale areas of felling) and the shape of plantations when seen at a distance (geometric versus 'organic' shapes). A CE design was constructed with these characteristics, incorporating increased taxes as the means of payment for improvements over a 'pure production' forest, which has each landscape element set at the least-desirable level.

The CE questionnaire was then administered, with each respondent getting four choice sets, in which they had to choose between two improved forest designs at additional costs, or the pure production alternative at no additional cost. The sample size was 284 useable responses, which were all collected by face-to-face interview. The main results are given below:

Variable	Coefficient from logit model	Implied ranking	Incremental WTP
Felling regime	0.42434	2	£12.89
Shape	0.45737	1	£13.90
Species diversity	0.37396	3	£11.36
Tax	−0.0329	*	*

Improvements to forest shape were most highly valued, followed by felling regime and species diversity. All coefficients were statistically significant at the 99 per cent level. A CV study was carried out at the same time, using the same characteristics but a different random sample of respondents. This revealed a ranking of landscape features identical to the CE model. The authors also used the CE data to show how values for landscape improvements varied between those who visited forests for recreation and those who did not; and between those living in the countryside and those living in urban areas.

Note: *denotes that tax is not an attribute, but the payment vehicle, and there can be no ranking or WTP.

Source: Hanley et al. (1998).

can derive estimates of compensating and equivalent surplus from the 'output' of the technique.

Each respondent is asked a number (for example, 4 or 6) of these questions. The choice questions typically vary across respondents. Box 6.2 summarises an application of CE in the context of forest management, while Box 6.3 summarises an application of CE in the context of agri-environmental policy.

6.2.2 Contingent Ranking

In a contingent ranking experiment respondents are required to rank a set of alternative options. Each alternative is characterised by a number of attributes, which are offered at different levels across options. Respondents are then asked to rank the options according to their preferences. An example is provided in Box 6.4. Here, respondents are asked to rank three options: in practice, more than three are usually specified.

In order to interpret the results in standard welfare economic terms, one of the options must always be in the agent's currently feasible choice set. This can typically be done by including a 'do nothing' option. This is because, if a *status quo* alternative is not included in the choice set, respondents are effectively being 'forced' to choose one of the alternatives presented, which they may not desire at all. If for some respondents the most preferred option is the current baseline situation, then any model based on a design in which the baseline is not present will yield inaccurate estimates of consumer welfare. There are also some theoretical problems with the way ranking responses need to be transferred to expressions of utility (see Sections 7.1.1 and 7.2).

A contingent ranking exercise can also be framed in terms of a sequential choice process. Following the example in Box 6.4, respondents would be

BOX 6.3   CHOICE EXPERIMENTS AND AGRI-ENVIRONMENTAL POLICY

Agri-environmental policy initiatives stemming from EU regulation 2078/92 have as their objective the encouragement of the production of environmental 'goods' in the countryside (for example, by paying farmers to maintain farm woodlands or to extend wetland areas). Spending on such agri-environmental schemes is becoming an increasingly important component of agricultural policy.

One important question is how agri-environmental schemes can be best designed in order to maximise their economic benefits. Each scheme is aimed at a number of landscape and wildlife features, such as heather moorland, farm woodlands or wetlands. Thinking of these as the attributes of the environmental good, CE could help in policy design by identifying relative values for these attributes. This would tell us, for example, whether spending on farm woodlands should be prioritised over spending on drystone walls, if the marginal value of the former is higher than that of the latter.

Hanley et al. (1998) report results from a CE study on Environmentally Sensitive Areas (ESA) in Scotland, funded by the Scottish Executive. For Breadalbane ESA, the following landscape features were identified as important in terms of being affected by the management agreements paid for by the scheme:

- farm woodlands
- archaeological features
- heather moors
- wet grasslands
- drystone walls.

A CE was designed using these attributes, with each being set at two possible levels: policy on and policy off. Each respondent was asked to answer eight choice questions, which included a pay-nothing, get-nothing alternative, using the payment vehicle of higher taxes. A sample of 256 people was used. Results indicated that the WTP for 'policy on' rather than 'policy off' was highest for farm woodlands (£50.46 household/year) and lowest for archaeological features (£6.65 household/year).

Source: Hanley et al. (1998).

BOX 6.4   ILLUSTRATIVE CONTINGENT RANKING QUESTION

Rank the alternative policy options below according to your preferences, assigning 1 to the most preferred, 2 to the second most preferred and 3 to the least preferred.

	Choice A	*Choice B*	*Choice C*
Native woodland	500 ha protected	100 ha protected	700 ha protected
Heather moorland	1200 ha protected	600 ha protected	No protection
Lowland hay meadow	200 ha protected	No protection	300 ha protected
Cost per household per year in additional taxes	£25	£5	£15

Your ranking: 1 .... 2 .... 3 ....

first asked to choose the most preferred alternative out of A, B and C. That alternative is then removed from the choice set and respondents are asked to choose the most preferred out of the remaining two alternatives. Hence, contingent ranking can be seen to share similarities with choice experiments.

6.2.3   Contingent Rating

In a contingent rating exercise respondents are presented with a number of scenarios one at a time and are asked to rate each one individually on a semantic or numeric scale. This approach does not, therefore, involve a direct comparison of alternative choices. An example is provided in Box 6.5.

Respondents would be asked a series of such questions, in each of which the policy design varies. In this way, data are collected on rating scores for different 'designs' of the environmental good or policy.

BOX 6.5 ILLUSTRATIVE CONTINGENT RATING QUESTION

On the scale below, please show how strongly you would prefer the following policy option.

Characteristics	*Option 1*
Native woodland	500 ha protected
Heather moorland	1200 ha protected
Lowland hay meadow	200 ha protected
Cost per household per year in additional taxes	£25

Please tick one box only

1	2	3	4	5	6	7	8	9	10

Very low preference   *Very high preference*

BOX 6.6 ILLUSTRATIVE PAIRED COMPARISONS QUESTION

Which of the two policy options described below would you be most in favour of? Please indicate your preferences using the scale below.

	Choice A	*Choice B*
Native woodland	500 ha protected	700 ha protected
Heather moorland	1200 ha protected	No protection
Lowland hay meadow	200 ha protected	300 ha protected
Cost per household per year in additional taxes	£25	£15

1	2	3	4	5	6	7	8	9	10

Strongly prefer Choice A   *Strongly prefer Choice B*

6.2.4 Paired Comparisons

In a paired comparison exercise respondents are asked to choose their preferred alternative out of a set of two choices and to indicate the strength of their preference in a numeric or semantic scale. Box 6.6 provides an example.

This approach combines elements of CE (choosing the most preferred alternative) and rating exercises (rating the strength of preference).

Specialised computer software can be used to generate choice sets within each CM approach. Figures 6.1 and 6.2 are examples of computer generated binary choice tasks applied in studies of service and infrastructure improvements for London Underground and London Buses (Steer Davies Gleave, 2000 and 1999). These studies were designed to assess very large numbers of attributes (96 in the London Underground case).

Having outlined the main types of CM approaches available, common design tasks are reviewed below.

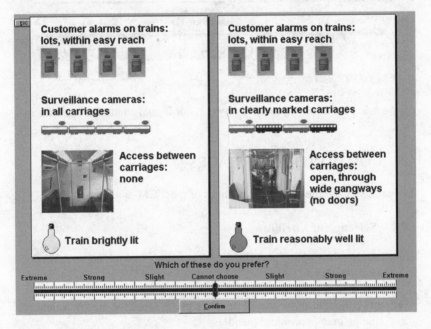

Source: Steer Davies Gleave, 2000

Figure 6.1   Example of pairwise comparison format used for London Underground

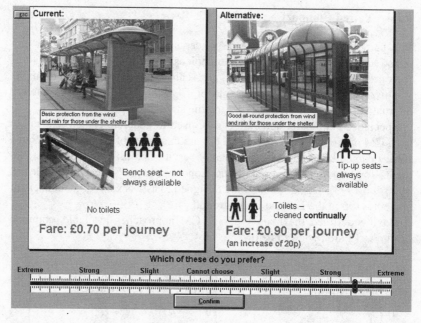

Source: Steer Davies Gleave, 1999

Figure 6.2   Example of pairwise comparison format used for London Buses

6.3   COMMON DESIGN STAGES

Table 6.2 sets out the main design stages of most CM approaches.

6.3.1   Selection of Attributes

This stage involves identifying the relevant attributes of the non-market good in question. These can include:

- those thought to be part of people's preferences for the environmental change being considered; and
- those attributes which can be impacted by policy/project/management option choice.

Focus groups may be useful in identifying attributes relevant on the first of these criteria. For example, in a study of the benefits of cleaner bathing

Table 6.2   Design stages for choice modelling

Stage	Description
1. Selection of attributes	Selection of relevant attributes of the good to be valued. This is usually done through literature reviews, focus group discussions or direct questioning. Sometimes they may be self-evident because of the nature of the problem. A monetary cost should be one of the attributes, to allow the estimation of WTP.
2. Assignment of levels	The attribute levels should be realistic and span the range over which we expect respondents to have preferences, and/or should be practically-achievable.
3. Choice of experimental design	Statistical design theory[1] is used to combine the levels of the attributes into a number of alternative environmental scenarios or profiles to be presented to respondents. *Complete factorial designs* allow the estimation of the full effects of the attributes upon choices: that includes the effects of each of the individual attributes presented ('main effects') and the extent to which behaviour is connected with variations in the combination of different attributes offered ('interactions'). These designs often produce an impracticably large number of combinations to be evaluated. *Fractional factorial designs* are able to reduce the number of scenario combinations presented, with a concomitant loss in estimating power, i.e. some or all of the interactions will not be detected.
4. Construction of choice sets	The profiles identified by the experimental design are then grouped into choice sets to be presented to respondents. Profiles can be presented individually, in pairs or in groups according to the technique being used.
5. Measurement of preferences	Choice of survey procedure, and conduct of survey.

Note: 1.   For more information on statistical design survey, see Louviere et al. (2000).

waters, local residents and beach visitors could be asked what aspects of a day at the beach are important to them. These might include perceived water quality, cleanliness of the sands, and travel distance from home. These attributes may be described and evaluated by respondents in very different terms to those used by regulators. Some attributes may be thought relevant from a decision-making perspective but do not come up strongly in focus groups (for example, measures of the environmental friendliness of transport modes as in Carlsson (1999) or species diversity in a forest, Hanley et al. (1998)). In this case, such attributes can be included in the design, but no great confidence in the statistical significance of these variables will be expected in subsequent statistical analysis (unless, that is, including them in the design forces/encourages respondents to think about variations in these attributes where previously they gave them no such consideration). Unless very large sample sizes are envisaged (see Chapter 3), then the survey designer will wish to restrict the number of attributes chosen for the design to a relatively small number (such as 4, 5 or 6). This is because the minimum required sample size increases exponentially in the number of attributes.

If all that the researcher is interested in is the implied ranking of attributes, or in their part-worths relative to each other, then cost/price does not need to be one of the attributes. If, however, the requirement is for a welfare-theoretic estimate of benefits or costs, say, for use in CBA, then a price term will need to be included in the design. How this price is expressed is a design option and creates very similar problems to the choice of payment vehicle in CV (see Chapter 4). Clearly, the price tag needs to be credible and realistic, and ideally one which also minimises incentives for strategic behaviour.

6.3.2 Assignment of Levels

This stage involves the assignment of levels for the attributes. Here a number of considerations exist:

- some researchers have sought to 'bracket' the existing level of an attribute with higher and lower values; this allows both gain and loss estimates of value to be estimated;
- maximum and minimum levels for the attributes could be identified from scientists and policymakers; target or proposed levels could be incorporated (for example, following implementation of a scheme); and
- the 'do nothing' or *status quo* level should usually be included.

For the price term, relevant ranges could be estimated from pilot CV studies or by studying the literature or through focus groups. However, when setting price changes the crucial thing is to ensure that the prices being offered are commensurate with the levels of the attributes. Prices that are too low will always be accepted, and the result will be a very small or zero price coefficient, which translates into an inflated money value for attributes. Prices which are too high will always be rejected, and this too can mean, paradoxically, that the price coefficient comes out to be small or zero. Pilots are very useful here if the topic is one not previously researched.

6.3.3 Choice of Experimental Design

Each of the methods described above requires the design of a number of alternative scenarios or descriptions to be offered to respondents. As already seen, these alternatives are defined in terms of attributes which may appear at different values or levels, one of which will usually be price. The larger the number of attributes and the larger the number of levels per attribute, the larger the experimental design will be.

We begin with an example: the case of management alternatives for a wetland (adapted from Morrison et al., 1999). The relevant attributes might be:

- the area of wetland protected;
- type of nesting birds;
- local employment; and
- price of the wetland protection measures (expressed as increases or decreases in local taxes).

Suppose there are currently 10,000 ha of protected wetland in the region. If the maximum likely extent by which the wetland could be extended is 10,000 ha, then the highest level is 20,000 ha. If a 'do nothing' policy would see the wetland diminishing to 5,000 ha, then this could be included as a lower level of wetland. Following similar lines of argument for the other attributes, this might give as a basis for the design as presented in Table 6.3.

This is a definition of the attributes being investigated and of the possible levels each attribute can take, but it does not yet define a set of alternatives. In fact, it would be possible to generate $3 \times 3 \times 3 \times 3 = 81$ (the number of levels to the power of the number of alternatives) alternatives from these, simply by considering all the possible combinations, that is *complete factorial design*. Clearly it would not be practical to ask respondents to consider simultaneously 81 possible alternatives. Fortunately it is not necessary to do so. The answer lies in the use of statistical experimental designs, which were originally developed in the field of experimental science and agricultural research. Here

Table 6.3   Attribute levels for a hypothetical wetland management scheme

Area of wetland (ha.)	Types of nesting birds (no. of species)	Local employment (full-time jobs)	Price (additional local taxes per year)
5,000	7	200	−$50
10,000	9	150	$0
20,000	10	125	+$40

similar problems of combinatorial explosion arose in investigating questions such as how crop yields varied in response to different types and quantities of fertiliser, soil type and land management practices. In this case there is a response variable that can be observed – crop yield – and a number of factors to be investigated. In our example the response variable is 'utility', which we cannot observe directly, although we can infer information about it, while the factors or attributes are the area of wetland, numbers of nesting species and so on.

Experimental designs provide the means to select subsets of the total set of possible alternatives for use in an experiment (or questionnaire) in a statistically efficient manner. The underlying design for setting the attributes and their levels can be found in a design catalogue (see US Department of Transportation, 1982, SPSS® software, or other statistical packages). Table 6.4 reproduces such a design suitable for four attributes each at three levels.

Table 6.4   The underlying design suitable for four attributes each at three levels

Case	Variable 1	Variable 2	Variable 3	Variable 4
1	1	1	1	1
2	1	2	2	3
3	1	3	3	2
4	2	1	2	2
5	2	2	3	1
6	2	3	1	3
7	3	1	3	3
8	3	2	1	2
9	3	3	2	1

Table 6.5   A set of alternatives generated for the wetlands example using a fractional design

Case	Area of wetland (ha.)	Types of nesting birds (no. of species)	Local employment (full-time jobs)	Price (additional local taxes per year)
1	5,000	7	200	−$50
2	5,000	9	150	+$40
3	5,000	10	125	$0
4	10,000	7	150	$0
5	10,000	9	125	−$50
6	10,000	10	200	+$40
7	20,000	7	125	+$40
8	20,000	9	200	$0
9	20,000	10	150	−$50

This is a *fractional factorial design*, consisting of just 9 alternatives out of a possible 81. The design merely specifies the level as numbers; it is up to the designer to ascribe meaning to them, which is done in Table 6.5.

The design in Tables 6.4 and 6.5 potentially has the property of *orthogonality*,[1] meaning that each of the variables has zero correlation with any of the others. The practical effect of this is that the influence of changes in any of these four attributes on the respondents' choices can be identified and measured. To understand this, imagine a poor design in which the cost and number of jobs always move up and down together with perfect correlation. Then, while we may measure changes in expressed utility as jobs and cost vary, it would be impossible to say whether jobs or cost were driving the changes, or to say what the trade-off between cost and jobs might be. Orthogonality guarantees that effects like this can be separated. While orthogonality often simplifies both optimising the design and the analysis, care is required because it can result in implausible alternatives.

On the other hand, something must be lost in the reduction from 81 to 9 cases, and that is the ability to measure what are known as *interactions*. Tables 6.4 and 6.5 present a *main effects* design. It assumes that the utility of each case varies with the four attributes, but that the effect of each attribute is not dependent on the value that any other attribute takes (for example, it assumes that the effect of changing the wetlands area from 5,000 to 10,000 ha will always be the same whatever the number of nesting species, jobs or the cost, while the value of the number of nesting species is not dependent on the area of wetland and so on). In reality, it might be that the value of the wetlands area is dependent upon the number of nesting species, so that the value of increasing the wetland area and the number of species is greater than the sum of the values of doing each of these separately. This is an interaction effect, and the design in Tables 6.4 and 6.5 cannot measure *any* of the possible interaction terms.

In fact, there are six possible two-way interactions in this example, that is, six ways of choosing two variables, and four possible three-way interactions, none of which can be measured. Does this matter? If interactions are present but the design cannot detect them, then the estimates of the weights on the other variables will be biased, possibly leading to incorrect valuations. There have been cases where interactions have been found, for instance in work for London Transport Buses (Steer Davies Gleave, 1999) where it was found that improvements in bus service reliability were highly valued and the provision of real-time electronic information about the services was highly valued, but the value of doing both was substantially less than the sum of the two. This is because reliability and information are partial substitutes for each other; real-time information is only needed when the services are not reliable.

If, on the basis of prior knowledge, it is suspected that interactions are important, then designs exist that can detect them. The price usually is that the designs are larger and require a bigger sample. A design capable of detecting any interaction between wetlands area and nesting species would require 27 cases, for example, rather than 9. This increases the size of the questionnaire, which is one practical reason why interactions are often not examined, although strategies do exist to help (see Section 6.3.4).

Elsewhere Louviere (1988) has suggested that in practice more than 80 per cent of respondent behaviour can be explained in terms of main effects. However, he also points out that where interactions are present but the design is incapable of detecting them, they will bias estimates of the main effects. In general, therefore, it is wise to consider each case in terms of what might be expected on the basis of existing knowledge and the additional costs of estimating interactions.

Although orthogonality is a desirable property in a choice task design, there are reasons why, in practice, we may depart from it. The first is that it is good practice to ensure that the alternatives offered to respondents are plausible and realistic. Mechanical use of experimental designs can generate options that may not be credible, and the concern would be that respondents do not treat such cases seriously. An example might be case 9 in Table 6.5, which offers high attribute levels at a reduced cost. There should be no implausible choice cards in the survey design. Researchers need to be clear at the outset about whether they want to study interaction effects, since this has an implication on design. See Bullock et al. (1998) for more details.

The second reason is technical. In WTP research we are not chiefly interested in the magnitude of the main effects coefficients but in their ratios, especially the ratio with the cost coefficient. Orthogonal designs are not necessarily good at generating the best estimates of these ratios. Methods have been developed to produce designs that deliver good estimates of the ratios but they will not usually be orthogonal in the main effects. In general, however, departure from orthogonality is probably best left to the specialist and should always be justified, with supporting analysis of the statistical properties of the design, and perhaps the use of simulation to test it.

6.3.4 Construction of Choice Sets

Once an experimental design has been chosen, the question arises of how to package the alternatives that were identified in order to present them to respondents.

One possibility is simply to present respondents with all the alternatives identified by the experimental design and ask them to rank or rate them. However, the number of alternatives produced by experimental designs can still be too large for respondents to be able to cope with. A judgement must be made about how many choice/ranking or rating tasks the respondent can be asked to perform. This depends partly on the complexity of the issue itself. Is it an issue the respondent is well used to dealing with, such as travel to work modes, or is it something less familiar such as biodiversity conservation programmes? More familiar subjects may allow more choice tasks per respondent. The complexity of the design also has a bearing here: how many attributes and levels are used?

The fewer the number of attributes and levels, the more the number of choice tasks that can be allotted to each person. In general, respondents should not be asked to undertake tasks that are too difficult or complex because they may not perform them reliably and/or may resort to shortcuts or haphazard answers. Nor should they be asked to complete too many choice, ranking or rating tasks because they will become tired and either the quality of responses will fall or they may terminate the interview before completion.

For example, Smith and Desvousges (1987) find that ranking sets of between 4 to 6 elements yield the most consistent answers, with more than 8 becoming too complex for most respondents to handle. However, for paired comparisons, up to 26 profile-pair ratings have been presented to respondents (Johnson and Desvousges, 1997). Johnson and Desvousges argue that individuals engage in a learning process and that later responses may be better indicators of preference than earlier responses.

Another possibility is therefore to construct smaller sets of alternatives to be presented to respondents from the full set of alternatives identified by the experimental design. Respondents can then be asked to choose, rank or rate their most preferred alternative from each reduced subset of alternatives, in sequence. Generating these reduced choice sets involves a second experimental design.

For example, using the design in Table 6.5 to construct a choice or ranking experiment might imply constructing a series of choice/ranking sets using a subset of the nine alternatives. Respondents would be shown each choice set in turn and, for each, asked to rank or choose their most preferred alternative. An example is given in Table 6.6. The first choice set consists of cases 1, 2, 4, 5 and 6 from Table 6.5. The idea is that respondents are shown these and asked to rank the alternatives or to say which one they would choose. Then they move on to the next choice set and so on.

Table 6.6   Possible choice set design for the wetlands example

Choice set	Cases from Table 6.5
1	1, 2, 4, 5, 6
2	2, 3, 5, 6, 7
3	1, 3, 4, 6, 7, 8
4	2, 4, 5, 7, 8, 9
5	3, 5, 6, 8, 9
6	4, 6, 7, 9
7	1, 5, 7, 8
8	1, 2, 6, 8, 9
9	1, 2, 3, 7, 9
10	2, 3, 4, 8
11	1, 3, 4, 5, 9

In practice this method is rarely used because of the effect of dominance. For instance, assuming that more wetlands, species and jobs are desirable, as are reduced taxes, case 9 in Table 6.5 is better on deterministic grounds (that is, dominates) than cases 2, 3, 4, 5 and 7, and would always be expected to be chosen in preference to them. The effect is that choice set 4 in Table 6.6, for instance, only really offers a choice between cases 9 and 8, since all the others are dominated by case 9.

A simpler and more common way of constructing paired choices is to use the experimental designs to define the *differences* between the alternatives. A design such as Table 6.5 might be used, not to define the full profile descriptions of nine alternatives, but to define the differences between pairs. For example, the area of wetland in one choice might be 5,000 ha more than the alternative, the number of species 7 smaller, and so on. This requires specification of the base values too, but typically these might be based on either a reference case of interest to the researchers (such as the world as it is now) or the product as experienced by each respondent now. (The pairs in Figures 6.1 and 6.2 were constructed in this way.)

Frequently there will be too many attributes and/or levels for a single design to deliver a manageable task for each respondent. In such cases the options are to:

- try to reduce the number of attributes and/or the number of levels offered. Judicious use of Occam's razor[2] helps here;
- group the attributes into subsets, possibly with common themes to each set, and to construct a smaller design for each set. Figures 6.1 and 6.2 came from surveys of very large numbers of attributes that were clustered together in this way, to create a number of smaller tasks themed around safety, comfort, information and so on; or
- construct large designs, then to split them into 'blocks' and to offer each respondent only one block. For example, if there is really no way to reduce the design below 27 cases, say, then this might be divided into three blocks of nine, and each respondent randomly assigned one block.

Both of the last two options have implications for the sample size required. If the design is split into several sub-tasks then it will almost certainly not be possible for each respondent to complete all the tasks and they will have to be allocated only some of them, ideally in a random way. This means that more interviews will be needed in order to get enough responses for each attribute. Similarly, if the design is split into blocks, even if each respondent 'sees' each attribute they will only contribute information corresponding to part of the overall design and the sample will have to be increased. For instance, if it is decided that 500 interviews are required, then splitting the design into three blocks with each respondent completing only one block could increase the sample requirement to 1,500.

As already noted, mechanical use of experimental designs can produce either alternatives that are not credible or choices between dominant pairs where one is better than the other on all attributes. Possible solutions include:

- Re-assigning the attribute meanings to the design levels. This simply reallocates the interpretation of the levels while preserving the under-lying design properties and may eliminate the problem.
- Changing the levels themselves, by varying their values.
- Changing individual attribute values in one or more cases to eliminate the problem.

In the latter case the properties of the design will be altered (for example, by loss of orthogonality) and the effects should be carefully tested, for example, by simulation. In fact, simulation is strongly recommended for *any* design, whether or not it departs from the catalogue design. The process, in outline, is:

1. Select some plausible values for the utility weights. These might be assumed to be constant for the whole simulated population or may be sampled from a plausible distribution.
2. For each simulated respondent, calculate the utility for each alternative on offer.
3. Add random error, sampled from an appropriate distribution (for example, Weibull, but Normal is usually sufficient).
4. Calculate the implied choice, rating, ranking and so on for the respondent.
5. Write the attribute levels and implied choices to a data file.
6. Estimate choice models and see how well the initial assumed utility parameters are recovered.

6.3.5 Measurement of Preferences

This last step involves actually administering the survey. Focus groups and piloting are as important in CM as in CV. Both face-to-face and mailshot have proved successful in the UK, whilst both use and non-use values can be estimated. Minimum sample size will depend on the number of attributes, levels and choice tasks per respondent. Recent UK applications to environ-mental issues have involved in the region of 200–500 respondents per survey. See Chapter 3 for more details of the sampling issues and the survey mode.

6.4 ADVANTAGES AND DISADVANTAGES OF CM RELATIVE TO OTHER ECONOMIC VALUATION TECHNIQUES

Box 6.7 summarises a study that combined CV and CM. Sections 6.4.1 and 6.4.2 note some of the advantages and disadvantages of CE in relation to other economic valuation techniques. Section 6.4.3 presents a number of aspects of economic valuation in which CE may or may not perform better than CV.

BOX 6.7 VALUING BIODIVERSITY: CONTINGENT VALUATION AND CONTINGENT RANKING

Environmental Resources Management (ERM, 1996) sought to discover whether people are capable of valuing biological diversity rather than biological resources. The context chosen was remote forests in Britain, the remoteness effectively meaning that few people were likely to visit them. The resulting valuation is therefore a *non-use* value. Two SP techniques were used. The respondents' understanding of 'diversity' is shown in Chapter 2 of their study. Here, our emphasis is on the combination of two SP techniques.

A *CV* questionnaire using a bidding game as the elicitation format was one technique used. The goods in question were varying management standards for the forest, each with different levels of diversity created through the introduction of different tree species, open space and so on. To present these as goods to be valued, three options were presented, each with a different proportion of the forest area subject to higher diversity. Different population samples were asked to express their WTP for one of the resulting options relative to a 'do nothing' option. Note that the cost of achieving the management standards is not included in the questionnaire, but is recorded so that the resulting benefit estimates can be compared with the costs.

A *contingent ranking* exercise in which respondents ranked the different options for managing the forests was the other technique. The options again reflected differing levels of diversity and, in this case, differing costs for achieving the management standards. Thus, respondents in the ranking exercise received cards showing all the options together with their costs. The results of the two exercises are shown below in summary form.

The CV study

Option	Management standards	Weighted truncated mean £/household/year	
		Legitimate bids	All bids
1	70A, 20B, 10C	11.27	10.75
2	10A, 80B, 10C	6.62	6.93
3	70A, 0B, 30C	13.15	12.75

Note: A = some sitka spruce planting, some open spaces, some broadleaves. B = more sitka, larger area devoted to older growth, open spaces, native broad-leaved species. C = management towards semi-natural woodland. A has the lowest biodiversity, and C the highest. 70A means that 70 per cent of the area is under standard A, and so on.

The table shows weighted truncated means (see Chapter 5 of this manual for technical details). The results show that option 3, which has the highest biodiversity, secures the highest WTP. However, WTP bids for options 1 and 2 seem to be counter-intuitive: option 1, which has lower diversity than option 2, secures higher WTP than option 2. The researchers felt that this reflected a belief by respondents that option 2 was not plausible.

Contingent ranking: The contingent ranking exercise produced the results shown below. These results are presented in terms of WTP for a 300,000 ha increase in the area allocated to a particular management option (300,000 ha = 1 per cent of the total forest area). WTP is highest for management option B, but C, with the highest diversity, is ranked below A, the lowest diversity, in terms of WTP. The marked preference for option B was felt by the researchers to reflect the fact that respondents were balancing costs and benefits and thought that B was the 'most sensible' option.

Management standard	All: £/household/year	Income known: £/household/year
A	0.27	0.30
B	0.44	0.52
C	0.11	0.19

Note: A sizeable percentage (30%) of the contingent ranking sample did not provide household income so the results are shown in terms of WTP for those reporting income and for the sample as a whole.

Because the different options are expressed in terms of percentage combinations of management practices (A, B, C), and the contingent ranking produced answers in term of WTP for a one per cent presence of those practices, it is possible to compare the CV and contingent ranking outcomes as WTP for the three options listed in the CV study. This produces:

Option	1	2	3
WTP (CV)	£28.64	£21.41	£27.04
WTP (CR)	£33.40	£46.24	£26.76

Note: The WTP for option 1 under the contingent ranking is wrongly recorded in the original ERM document. Note also that the WTP under the CV is not from the truncated or weighted distribution, so as to make comparison with the contingent ranking technique more direct.

While the WTP estimates are broadly similar, the CV reveals option 1 as the most preferred and the contingent ranking method reveals option 2 as the most preferred. The researchers felt that the contingent ranking method offered respondents most choice since they were presented with all three options and their costs, whereas the CV approach presented only one management option to each subsample of the whole sample population.

This section is written with a focus on CE rather than other CM approaches. The reason for this is that, as mentioned in Section 6.1, CE is the only CM approach that is definitely in line with economic theory.

6.4.1 Advantages

The main advantages of CE in relation to other SP techniques include:

- It is useful to see CE as a natural generalization of a binary discrete choice CV. A binary discrete choice CV study (change or no change) cannot value the attributes of the change (or the attributes of the policy or project leading to the change). The only way that a CV study can estimate these attributes is to design different valuation scenarios for each level of each attribute. This is clearly very costly. Choice experiments, because they look at more than two alternatives, provide a natural way to do this.

- CE do a better job than CV in measuring the marginal value of changes in the characteristics of environmental goods. This is often a more useful focus from a management/policy perspective than focussing on either the gain or loss of the good, or on a discrete change in its attributes. 'Useful' here might mean more generalisable, and therefore more appropriate from a benefits transfer viewpoint (for encouraging evidence on the use of CE in benefits transfer, see Morrison et al., 1999). For example, a forest may be described in terms of the value of its species diversity, recreational facilities, age diversity and shape. Given that forest management decisions are often concerned with potential changes in these attributes, then knowing the marginal value of these attributes is beneficial. Whilst CV can be applied to estimate attribute values, it is clumsier and generates values which are less easily generalised. Since CE models are based on the attribute theory of value, they are much easier to pool with either site choice travel cost models or hedonic price models than is CV (see Chapter 11).

- CE designs can reduce the extreme multi-collinearity problems in models based on variations in *actual* attribute values across sites which troubles revealed preference analysts, where for example water quality, expected fish catch and scenic beauty might all move together. In CE designs, in contrast, attribute levels are usually designed as orthogonal (that is, independent). CE also has advantages over travel cost approaches in that whilst the latter is restricted to modelling choice over existing attribute levels, CE can be used to study preferences for attribute levels beyond the existing. This could include species re-introductions, water quality improvements beyond maximum existing levels, and changes in access prices beyond the range currently observed. It is for this reason that CE has been used in transport research to look at new modes, infrastructure and service levels that may not currently exist.

- CE may avoid some of the response difficulties in CV. For example, dichotomous choice designs in CV may still be subject to yea-saying despite improvements in design standards (Blamey et al., 1999). There are two views on why yea-saying occurs. First, there is the classically defined survey research yea-saying: that is, saying yes because one sees it as the socially desirable response. The second view on yea-saying relates to strategic behaviour, for example, if an individual has a valuation of £20 and is asked if he would pay £100, then he may still say yes, since that is the only way he can register an environmental vote and he knows that the £100 will not be collected from him. (Note that a typical double-bounded design would not avoid this problem). CE do avoid this problem, since respondents get many chances in the interview to express a positive preference for a valued good over a range of payment amounts. Open-ended CV designs avoid the yea-saying problem, but are viewed as facing respondents with a mental task which may be very difficult. This leads to item non-response or random responses. CE face respondents with a much easier problem: do I prefer A, B or neither?

6.4.2 Disadvantages

CM in general, and CE in particular, has been very widely applied in the fields of transport and marketing, but experience in environmental and other related contexts is still fairly limited. Several problem areas seem to be important:

- In order to estimate the value of an environmental good, as distinct from a change in one of its attributes, it is necessary to assume that the value of the whole is equal to the sum of the parts. For example, Hanley et al. (1998) calculate the value of the Environmentally Sensitive Areas programme, with a linear utility function, as the sum of the values of its component parts. This clearly raises two potential problems. First, there may be additional attributes of the good not included in the design which generate utility: in practice, these are captured in the constant terms in the estimated model. Second, the value of the 'whole' is indeed additive in this way. Elsewhere in economics, objections have been raised about the assumption that the value of the whole is indeed equal to the sum of its parts. In order to test whether this is a valid objection in the case of CE, we need to be able to compare 'whole' values from CE with values obtained for the same resource using some other technique (such as CV). In the transport field, research for London Underground and London Buses among others has shown clear evidence that whole bundles of improvements are valued less than the sum of the component values, all measured using CE (Steer Davies Gleave, 2000, 1999). It is now common to include a CE exercise in questionnaires designed to estimate the 'capping' value of such bundles and to use *ad hoc* methods to re-scale individual valuations when valuations are being applied in appraisals. This has become known as the 'packaging problem'.
- As is the case with CV, welfare value estimates obtained with CE are sensitive to study design. For example, the choice of attributes, the levels chosen to represent them, and the way in which choices are relayed to respondents (for example, through the use of photograph

pairs) may all impact on the values of estimates of consumers' surplus and marginal utilities.

- Choice/rank complexity can be a problem for the respondents. Swait and Adamowicz (1996) found an inverted U-shaped relationship between choice complexity and variance of underlying utility amounts; whilst Mazotta and Opaluch (1995) found that increased complexity leads to increased random errors. Bradley and Daly (1994) have found that respondents become fatigued the more choices they are presented with, whilst Hanley, Wright and Koop (2000) found that value estimates for outdoor recreation changed significantly when respondents were given eight rather than four choice pairs. Ben-Akiva et al. (1991) and Foster and Mourato (1998) found evidence of inconsistent responses that increase as the number of rankings increase. This implies that, whilst the researcher might want to include many attributes, and also interactions between these attributes, unless very large samples are collected, respondents will be faced with daunting choice tasks. This may lead them into relying on short-cuts to provide answers, rather than solving the underlying utility-maximisation problem.

- It is more difficult for CE (or any other CM approach) than for CV to derive values for a sequence of elements implemented by policy or project. Hence, valuing the sequential provision of goods in multi-attribute programmes is probably better undertaken by CV.

- CV and CE can both generate results that are consistent with welfare theory. Contingent ranking can also generate welfare theory-consistent results, if 'do-nothing' is included as an option so that the respondents are not forced to rank the other options. On the other hand, contingent rating is not widely used in economic valuation mainly due to the dubious assumptions that need to be made in order to transform ratings into utilities. These assumptions relate either to the cardinality of rating scales or to the implicit assumption of comparability of ratings across individuals.

6.4.3 Do Choice Modelling Approaches Solve any of the 'Big' Problems of CV?

CV has been criticised as a means of eliciting environmental preferences by many authors, whilst practitioners have been very open about areas of sensitivity in applying the technique. The main areas in which difficulties have been encountered are outlined in Chapters 4, 5 and 8. But does CM solve any of these big problems?

- *Hypothetical bias.* The typical result in many comparative studies is that actual WTP is less than (and sometimes much less than) stated WTP. Whilst some would dispute what we take as 'actual' WTP (for example, if the mechanism used to elicit real payments encourages free-riding), this weight of evidence leads to the uneasy feeling that CV estimates are biased upwards due to the hypothetical nature of the payment commitment. Very few calibration tests exist at present for CE in the environmental context (for example, Carlsson, 1999), but there is little reason to suppose, *a priori*, that it does any better than CV in this regard.
- *Insensitivity to scope.* This refers to the situation whereby the value of a good or change is not significantly different from the value of a more inclusive, that is, bigger, good or change. One of the recommendations of the NOAA panel (Arrow et al., 1993) was that CV surveys should include tests of scope, whereby we test whether WTP values are sensitive to the quantity of environmental change being offered. The meta analysis by Carson et al. (1997) has shown that, on the whole, CV studies seem to pass the scope test. But for unfamiliar goods and with between-subject comparisons, scope effects can be less discernible. However, it is rare to find scope tests which allow one to observe WTP values across a wide range of environmental quantities, which would be desirable from the point of view of estimating demand curves. CM might be thought to do better here since scale can be one attribute in the experimental design, whilst the repeated choices used in a CM study mean that more combinations of WTP and quantity can be observed. Nevertheless, Foster and Mourato (1999, 2000a, 2000b) find significant scope insensitivity in separate experiments involving contingent ranking and CE. The main issue with respect to CE is that the scope test is internal rather than external. As the number of attributes in a CE goes up, the likelihood of finding one or more that have insignificant coefficients grows.
- *Sensitivity of estimates to study design.* Another common finding in CV is that bids can be affected by design choices, for example in terms of the choice of payment mechanism, the amount and type of information provided, and the rules of the market. This sensitivity is desirable in some cases, as it mirrors the picture for market goods (for example, we expect WTP to change when respondents' information sets change as shown by Munro and Hanley (1999)). There is not much evidence on whether CM does any better here, although it is quite likely that the way in which information is presented, and the type of information presented, can influence results in CM as much as in CV.

- *Ethical protesting.* A small percentage of respondents in CV studies typically refuse to 'play the game' due to ethical objections to the underlying utilitarian model (Spash and Hanley, 1995; Hanley and Milne, 1996). This implies an unwillingness to pay in principle to prevent environmental degradation or principled unwillingness to accept compensation for environmental losses. Such responses are usually treated as protests and are excluded from the analysis (see Chapters 6 and 8). CM might do better here, as it avoids asking for direct monetary valuations of a good, relying instead in statistical techniques to indirectly infer WTP from choices, ranks or ratings. However, this is still an untested proposition.

NOTES

1. Not all fractional designs are orthogonal.
2. The Aristotelian principle that entities must not be multiplied beyond what is necessary, attributed to William of Occam (1284–1347).

7.   Analysis of choice modelling data

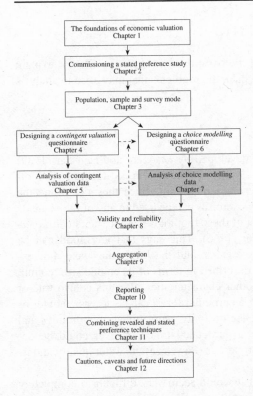

The foundations of economic valuation
Chapter 1

↓

Commissioning a stated preference study
Chapter 2

↓

Population, sample and survey mode
Chapter 3

↓

Designing a *contingent valuation*
questionnaire
Chapter 4

Designing a *choice modelling*
questionnaire
Chapter 6

↓

Analysis of contingent
valuation data
Chapter 5

Analysis of choice modelling
data
Chapter 7

↓

Validity and reliability
Chapter 8

↓

Aggregation
Chapter 9

↓

Reporting
Chapter 10

↓

Combining revealed and stated
preference techniques
Chapter 11

↓

Cautions, caveats and future directions
Chapter 12

SUMMARY

This chapter is concerned with the theory and analysis of choice modelling data and with internal validity checks.

This chapter takes each approach in turn (namely, choice experiments (CE), contingent ranking, contingent rating and paired comparison) and explains how to organise and analyse the data, the problems that arise in analysis and internal tests of validity. Most of the attention in this chapter is given to CE, since as noted in Chapter 6 they are the most attractive from the economic theory point of view.

It is recommended that the sections on data analysis should be read in conjunction with Chapter 5, and also that the discussion on internal validity should be read in conjunction with Chapter 8 (in particular, Sections 8.4, 8.5 and 8.6).

In many cases, the dependent variable of interest in choice modelling (CM) is discrete or limited in nature. For example, in contingent ranking, each respondent ranks a number of alternatives. In CE, people respond 'choice A' or 'choice B' or 'neither' to choice questions. Linear regression models (see Chapter 5) cannot usually be used on such data sets because there is not a suitable dependent variable to regress against the explanatory variables, and limited dependent variable methods such as logit models are typically used instead (see Greene, 1997 and Ben-Akiva and Lerman, 1985 for a detailed description of such methods). In other cases, such as with contingent rating, the dependent variable looks somewhat more like that encountered, say, in open-ended CV, but takes a range of values which is limited by design (since respondents cannot give a score other than those given on the scale). In such cases, censored Tobit models are often used.

7.1 CHOICE EXPERIMENTS

The following sections describe the basic theory supporting CE and explain how to organise and analyse the data, the problems that may arise in analysis and internal tests of validity.

7.1.1 Basics

The CE technique was initially developed by Louviere and Hensher (1982) and Louviere and Woodworth (1983). CE can be seen as having two 'footholds' in economic theory. These are important, since they determine the extent to which the results of CE exercises can be used in any of the contexts mentioned in Chapter 2. The first of these footholds is Lancaster's *characteristics theory of value* (Lancaster, 1966). This says that any good can be described as a bundle of characteristics, and the levels they take. For example, any model of car can be described in terms of its engine size, colour, safety rating, performance and other characteristics. But this is also true of many public goods. For example, a particular forest can be described in terms of its size, species composition, age diversity, recreational opportunities and landscape quality. Equivalently, a particular stretch of river could be described in terms of its physical properties (flow, size), its water quality and its biodiversity.

It might well be objected that it would seem very difficult to completely describe anything in terms of its attributes. For example, in a river management context, the utility received from a river in a given state depends on all sorts of intangible and 'hard-to-measure' things, and not just observables such as pollution levels and flow rate. It is also possible to make errors in measuring attributes and that people's subjective views on how well a river scores on something like landscape quality will vary. This is quite true, and it is here that the other link with economic theory comes in via *random utility theory*. Random utility theory derives from Luce (1959) and McFadden (1973), and is based around an alternative theory of choice to that used to derive conventional demand curves. Suppose that we can represent a citizen's preferences by the following utility function, U:

$$U = U(X_1 \ldots Xm; Z_1 \ldots Zn), \tag{7.1}$$

where utility for this individual depends on the levels of $X = 1 \ldots m$ marketed goods and services consumed, and on $Z = 1 \ldots n$ environmental goods. Now it may well be that many of these elements X and Z are unobservable to the researcher, or are observable only with an error. All the elements of Z and X that should be counted may not be known. One way of representing this situation is to break down the conventional utility function $U(\cdot)$ into two parts: one deterministic and observable, $V(\cdot)$, and an error part, $e(\cdot)$. This means we can re-write equation (7.1) as:

$$U = U(X_1 \ldots Xm; Z_1 \ldots Zn) = V(X) + e(X, Z), \tag{7.2}$$

where the bold letters represent vectors. This is the simplest representation of what lies behind random utility theory. It has one big advantage over conventional utility theory, and one big disadvantage. The advantage is that it may well be a more realistic representation of preferences. The disadvantage is that some assumptions have to be made about the nature of the error component to make any predictions from this theory, since the error is not observable.

Now consider an individual being asked to choose between two alternative goods, which are assumed to be differentiated by their attributes and levels. For example, these could be two alternative transport modes for travelling to work, with different attributes such as time and cost. Equally, they could be different alternative destinations for fishing trips, different designs of forest, or different waste management strategies for a town. Call these alternatives g and h. In choosing between them, the respondent is assumed to compare the utility he or she could get with either choice, and then select the alternative with the highest utility. Respondents make a choice from those offered, since it is assumed that no others are available. An error term is introduced because the respondents may assess the options according to information other than that shown, such as all possible alternatives to the individual: all possible fishing sites they could visit on a day trip, or all available travel-to-work modes (sometimes this may be a small list). This list of 'all available options' is often referred to as the *choice set*.

Given that there is an error component in the utility function used, predictions cannot be made with certainty. Thus, the analysis becomes one of probabilistic choice. The probability that any particular respondent (call them person i) prefers option g in the choice set to any alternative option h, can be expressed as the probability that the utility associated with option g exceeds that associated with all other options, as stated in equation (7.3):

$$P\left[\left(V_{ig} + e_{ig}\right) > \left(V_{ih} + e_{ih}\right)\right] = P[(V_{ig} - V_{ih}) > (e_{ih} - e_{ig})]. \tag{7.3}$$

This says that respondent i will choose option g over option h if the difference in the deterministic parts of their utilities exceeds the difference in the error parts.

In order to derive an explicit expression for this probability, it is necessary to know the distribution of the error terms (e). A typical assumption is that they are independently and identically distributed with an extreme-value (Gumbel) distribution. The Gumbel is similar to the Normal distribution in shape, but the mathematics associated with it is much more tractable. Its distribution is given by:

$$P(e_{ij} \leq t) = F(t) = \exp(-\exp(-t)). \tag{7.4}$$

The above distribution of the error term implies that the probability of any particular alternative g being chosen as the most preferred can be expressed in terms of the logistic distribution (McFadden, 1973). This specification is known as the *conditional logit model*:

$$P(U_{ig} > U_{ih}) = \frac{\exp(\mu V_{ig})}{\sum_j \exp(\mu V_{ij})}. \tag{7.5}$$

If the dependent variable takes only two possible values (for example, A or B), then a *binary logit model* is required. If the dependent variable takes three or more values (for example, A, B, neither), then a *multi-nominal logit* (MNL) model is required. If a normal distribution is assumed, this requires a *multinomial probit model*.

In (7.5), μ is a 'scale parameter', which is inversely proportional to the standard deviation of the error distribution. In a single data set this parameter cannot be separately identified and is therefore implicit in the terms estimated. The value of μ is irrelevant to calculate relative welfare estimates if the utility function is linear in income, since it weights everything the same. However, the scale parameter will influence total absolute measures of value. If one is comparing two CE models from different data sets, then there can be no assumption that the scale parameter is the same in both. This means that, even if the two populations have identical preferences, the parameters in the estimated logit model may vary (Morrison et al., 1999). In this case, the ratio of scale parameters can be measured and used to adjust for differences in error variance to allow models from different data sets to be compared (Swait and Louviere, 1993): this issue is taken up again in Chapter 11.

An important implication of the standard logit model is that selections from the choice set must obey the *independence from irrelevant alternatives*

(IIA) property (or Luce's Choice Axiom; Luce (1959)), which states that the relative probabilities of two options being selected are unaffected by the introduction or removal of other alternatives. This property follows from the independence of the Gumbel error terms across the different options contained in the choice set.

CE are therefore consistent with utility maximisation and demand theory, at least when a *status quo* option is included in the choice set.[1] They therefore permit the correct estimation of monetary welfare measures for use in any context mentioned in Chapter 2. By comparing attributes in terms of their implicit prices, an implied ranking can be uncovered (see, for instance, Box 6.2). Summarising, then, CE can provide:

- estimates of marginal WTP which are welfare-consistent;
- estimates of WTP for a policy or project which changes more than one attribute at once; and
- the implied ranking of attributes.

7.1.2 Organising the Data

Before econometric analysis, CE survey data need to be correctly organised. If computerised interviewing has been used this will usually be handled automatically, but if not it is not a trivial task. Data are collected per individual on attitudes, socio-economic variables and so on and each person gives 'A', 'B' or 'neither' answers to a series of choice pairs (see Chapter 6). These choice pairs are described in terms of their attributes. A code number can be assigned to each choice pair, and then a programme can be written to copy attribute levels specific to that pair to the response. Popular database systems such as Access or SPSS are well provided with routines to do this. A data set must eventually be generated where each person generates n rows, one for each choice made. For each choice task, this will contain the details on the characteristics of both choice alternatives. Quality control procedures would normally be used to screen for incomplete data records, outliers and obviously incorrect entries.

Decisions must be taken over coding of attributes. The three choices are:

1. Some attributes may take continuous values (for example, hay meadows in the example in Chapter 6 were measured in hectares, with 50 ha assumed to be worth less than 100 ha). Such variables can simply be entered in their own units. Marginal utilities can be easily interpreted.
2. Other attributes may only take two values (for example, whether a natural park permits overnight camping or not). This kind of variable is best

set up as a 0–1 dummy. 'Marginal' utilities here are interpreted as the difference in utility from camping not permitted to camping permitted.

3. A third class of attribute exists where there is no continuous scale, but where more than two levels are specified. An example would be noise levels in a city street. These could be described as very quiet, quiet, noisy and very noisy. A trickier example would be different types of fish available for catching in a river (for example, coarse fish only; coarse fish plus trout; coarse fish plus trout and salmon). In both these cases, 'effects coding' is often used. This creates (n-1) dummy variables, where n is the number of levels. In the noise case, three variables would thus be created: very quiet, quiet and noisy. Each one would signify a choice occasion with the requisite value. The marginal utilities now become the extra utility from moving from the excluded case (very noisy) to either of the included cases. The coding would be as follows:

	Dummy 1	Dummy 2	Dummy 3
Very noisy	0	0	0
Noisy	1	0	0
Quiet	0	1	0
Very quiet	0	0	1

7.1.3 Estimation

The logit and conditional logit models can be estimated by conventional maximum likelihood procedures (also see Chapter 5) using a number of software packages such as LIMDEP, STATA®, GAUSS™ and SPSS® with the respective log-likelihood functions stated in equation (7.6), where y_{ij} is an indicator variable which takes a value of one if respondent j chose option i and zero otherwise:

$$\log L = \sum_{i=1}^{N} \sum_{j=1}^{J} y_{ij} \log \left[\frac{\exp(V_{ij})}{\sum_{j=1}^{J} \exp(V_{ij})} \right]. \tag{7.6}$$

The model is usually specified as being linear-in-parameters. If X is a vector of independent variables upon which utility is assumed to depend, and if β is a vector of parameters, this gives:

$$P(choose\ g) = \frac{\exp(\beta'X_{ig})}{\sum_j \exp(\beta'X_{ij})}. \tag{7.7}$$

Socio-economic variables can be included along with choice set attributes in the X terms, but since they are constant across choice occasions for any given individual (for example, their income is the same for each choice they make), then they can only be entered as interaction terms. Some software packages that carry out multi-nominal logit estimation have automatic routines for creating these interactions.

In any multi-nominal logit model run, a series of constant terms will usually be represented; these are known as 'alternative specific constants' (ASCs). There will be one fewer of these than options offered. ASCs reflect the differences in utilities for each alternative relative to the base when all attributes are equal, since they are equal to the means of the differences in the random component of the utility function over choices. ASCs can pick up a mixture of *status quo* bias effects and the impacts of unobserved attributes.

7.1.4   Welfare Measures

Once the parameter estimates have been obtained, a WTP welfare measure for a policy change that impacts on the environmental good which conforms to demand theory can be derived (Hanemann, 1984; Parsons and Kealy, 1992). Let V^0 represent the utility of the initial (for example, pre-project) state and V^1 represent the utility of the alternative (for example, post-project) state. The coefficient b_y gives the marginal utility of income and is the coefficient of the cost attribute:

$$WTP = b_y^{-1} \ln\left\{\frac{\sum_i \exp(V^1 i)}{\sum_i \exp(V^0 i)}\right\}. \tag{7.8}$$

It is straightforward to show that for the linear utility index the above formula can be simplified to the ratio of coefficients given in equation (7.9) where b_C is the coefficient on any of the attributes. These ratios are often known as implicit prices and show WTP for a change in any of the attributes. Thus, if hay meadows are attribute C, the implicit price for this feature is:

$$WTP = \frac{-b_C}{b_y}. \tag{7.9}$$

Notice, however, that specifying t-ratios or standard errors for these ratios is more complex. Each estimate is the ratio of two parameters, each of which is also an estimate surrounded by a range of uncertainty. Even when the t values are statistically significant (see Chapter 5) it does not follow that the ratios are. One approximate solution is to use the following expression for the variance of the ratio of two estimates:

$$\text{var}\left(\frac{\beta_i}{\beta_j}\right) = \left(\frac{\beta_i}{\beta_j}\right)^2 \left(\frac{\text{var}(\beta_i)}{\beta_i^2} + \frac{\text{var}(\beta_j)}{\beta_j^2} - \frac{2\text{cov}(\beta_i, \beta_j)}{\beta_i \beta_j}\right). \tag{7.10}$$

If the covariance is assumed to be zero, which it will be in an orthogonal design, the variance and hence the standard error can be calculated. This formula illustrates why improved estimates can sometimes be obtained when non-orthogonal designs are used, for if the covariance term is positive, the variance can be reduced.

Alternative approaches that are commonly used in environmental economics to calculate standard errors of the welfare measures involve simulation techniques to establish the empirical distribution of WTP. Bootstrapping techniques can be used for this purpose (see Annex 5.2). A popular alternative is the Krinsky–Robb procedure that estimates the empirical distribution of the welfare measure based on N random drawings from the multivariate normal distribution defined by the coefficients and covariance matrix, estimated from the logit model (Krinsky and Robb, 1986; see Foster and Mourato, 1998 for an example and Annex 5.2 for details).

7.1.5 Internal Validity

The choice task used for CE is well suited to tests of internal validity of the type discussed by Green and Srinivasan (1990), particularly in the case of binary choice experiments. The idea here is to ask respondents some additional choice questions, the answers to which are not included in the choice model calibration exercise. The test is then to see how well the models predict the choices actually made in these additional questions.

This is relatively simple to do and requires only that a simulation be set up so that the calibrated choice models can be used to 'predict' what respondents might choose in the additional tasks. This is done relatively easily on a spreadsheet.

While not a true test of expectation-based validity (see Chapter 8), this is a very effective way of testing how well the choice mechanism used by respondents has been captured by the model. If the model scores a high success rate, then this indicates that respondents have been consistent in how they made choices, and the model has captured their preferences. If it does not, this could indicate a poorly-specified model, which it may be possible to improve on, or may simply indicate that respondents have been inconsistent, something that may happen when they have been asked to consider unfamiliar alternatives.

We can also specify other tests of internal validity, including whether dominated options are chosen to be preferred to clearly superior alternatives; whether choices are inconsistent across choice sets; whether parameter estimates have the expected signs; whether the null hypothesis that all parameter values are equal to zero can be rejected; and the overall fit of the model. Testing for IIA is also important (see Section 7.1.6).

Box 7.1 illustrates two examples of choice modelling in the healthcare context.

BOX 7.1 TWO EXAMPLES OF CHOICE MODELLING IN THE HEALTHCARE CONTEXT

Two examples of the successful application of CM techniques in the healthcare context are provided by studies reported in Ryan and Hughes (1995). In the first of these studies the aim was to assess women's preferences over two different forms of miscarriage management *per se* and, within each type of management, their preferences over various attributes whose levels differed significantly between the two types, namely level of pain, time in hospital, time taken to return to normal household activities, cost of treatment to patient and medical complications following treatment. Rather than adopting a ranking or rating approach, respondents were presented with a number of pairwise choices between different 'bundles' of attributes. The bundles were selected using the SPSS® ORTHOPLAN procedure which ensures an orthogonal main effects design, thus avoiding problems of multicollinearity in the data. Following a pilot study carried out on a small convenience sample, the main questionnaire was mailed to a sample of 600 women randomly selected from the Grampian Electoral Register. This produced 196 usable completed questionnaires. Of those respondents who completed questionnaires, 32 indicated a persistent preference for one type of treatment over the other, regardless of the levels of the various attributes, and were therefore omitted from the data analysis. The data were analysed using both a simple probit model and a random effects probit model assuming a simple linear additive underlying random utility model. All estimated coefficients were significant at the 1 per cent level and of expected sign, providing encouraging evidence of theoretical validity. Ratios of attribute coefficients relative to the coefficient of the cost variable were used to estimate marginal willingness to pay for each attribute and this too varied with income in the way predicted by economic theory.

The aim of the second study was to assess both women's and men's preferences over various attributes of *in vitro* fertilisation (IVF) that a previous study had indicated were of significant importance to those undergoing the treatment. These included not only health outcomes, that is, the chances of giving birth to a child, but also non-health outcomes, that is, follow-up support after treatment, and process attributes, including attitudes of medical staff, continuity of contact with same staff, time on the waiting list and cost of treatment to patient. As in the previous study, respondents were presented with a number of pairwise choices, again selected using the SPSS® ORTHOPLAN procedure. However, in this case questionnaires were mailed to 414 women and men who were attending (or had attended) the Assisted Reproductive Unit in Aberdeen and who had responded to a previously administered 'satisfaction' questionnaire. In the event, this produced 331 completed questionnaires. Of these, fewer than 10 displayed clear evidence of inconsistency in responses, that is, selection of a clearly dominated option in a pairwise choice, and these were omitted from the data analysis. In this study the data were analysed using the LIMDEP random effects probit procedure, though once again on the assumption of a simple linear additive underlying random utility model. As in the previous study all coefficients were significant at the 1 per cent level and of the expected sign, providing clear evidence of patients' concern with the non-health outcome and process attributes of IVF treatment, in addition to concern about the health outcome.

7.1.6 Problems

An important implication of using the standard multi-nomial logit (MNL) model is that selections from the choice set must obey the IIA property. As explained above, this states that the relative probabilities of two options being selected are unaffected by the introduction or removal of other alternative. This arises directly from the logit formulation, from which it is can be shown that:

$$p_i/p_j = \exp(U_i - U_j), \qquad (7.11)$$

or, in other words, the odds ratio for alternatives i and j depends only on the utilities of those two options and no others. This property follows from the independence of the Gumbel error terms across the different options contained in the choice set. It arises out of the fact that we cannot perfectly measure utility: each alternative has a deterministic and a random component of utility. IIA means that the sources of the 'errors' contributing to the disturbances must do so in a way such that the total disturbances are independent (Ben-Akiva and Lerman, 1985). In other words, the 'missing' part of utility in alternative i must be uncorrelated with the 'missing' part of utility from alternative j.

What this means practically is that the greater the degree to which utility can be 'pinned down' for each alternative, the less likely the model is to suffer from IIA violations. Including socio-economic variables is often important from this point of view, since including such variables *if they are relevant to choices/preferences* can increase the systematic portion of utility and decrease the random portion.

In practical terms, violation of the IIA assumption may arise in situations where some alternatives are qualitatively similar to others. This commonly arises in mode CE in transport, where people may choose between car and maybe several public transport modes, say, bus and rail. The IIA would imply that the ratio $p(\text{car})/p(\text{bus})$ depends only on the characteristics of bus and car, and *not rail*. If the rail service changed, then the probabilities of choosing car and bus would change, but their ratio would have to be unchanged. Passengers lost or gained from rail as the rail service varied would divert to car and bus in the same proportions as shown by the probability ratio before the change. In many circumstances it is more likely that bus and rail compete between each other for business more intensely than they do with car, so that losses from the rail service would switch predominantly to bus, and the IIA becomes invalid.

Whether IIA is violated in a given model can be tested using a procedure suggested by Hausman and McFadden (1984). This basically involves constructing a likelihood ratio test around different versions of the model where choice alternatives are excluded. If IIA holds, then the model estimated on all choices (the full choice set) should be the same as that estimated for a subset of alternatives.

What can be done if IIA is found to be violated? One possible solution is to re-specify the problem as a *nested logit model*. For example, taking the example above of mode choice, the conventional logit model may fail the IIA test for the reasons discussed. One approach would be to re-formulate the model as a two-stage nested model in which people are assumed to choose between car and public transport at the top level, and between bus and rail at the lower level.

Level 1:   car v. public transport
Level 2:   bus v. rail

In effect, this is done by constructing a binary logit model at the top level and a further one at the second. The lower level model will deal with the service characteristics of each public transport mode, showing how the probability of choosing either one varies with those characteristics. The top level is more complex however, because it describes a choice between car, which can be described in terms of travel time, costs and so on, and a composite public transport measure representing the composite utility of public transport. This is usually handled by what is known as the 'logsum' or inclusive value, defined to be:

$$V_i^* = (1/\lambda) \cdot \log \sum_j \exp(\lambda \cdot V_{i,j}), \qquad (7.12)$$

where λ is a scalar parameter to be estimated. Software packages such as LIMDEP will automatically calculate these values in constructing nested models.

Nested logit models are very commonplace in recreational demand modelling, where, for example, we might nest the decisions over which type of fishing site to choose (river, sea, lake) and then the decision over which site within each type (which river, which sea, which lake). Nested structures can be estimated either by using MNL in two or more steps sequentially, depending on the number of levels in the hierarchy, or by simultaneous estimation using specialised software such as Alogit or LIMDEP. Guidance exists on how to test for the validity of the structure and for comparing the results with a simpler MNL.

An alternative to the nested approach for getting around the IIA problem is to use an econometric model which does not require us to assume it. One of the most popular models in this case is the *Random Parameters Logit* (RPL) approach (Train, 1998). This also allows for preferences to vary across individuals in a deterministic way, since for each attribute the model estimates both a mean effect and a variance effect. However, using RPL also requires assumptions about the underlying distribution of preferences, which may be hard to justify. Multinominal probit models also tend not to be used, since they often have no closed-form solution.

7.2   CONTINGENT RANKING

As with CE, the random utility model provides the economic theory framework for analysing the data from a contingent ranking exercise. Under the assumption of an independently and identically distributed random error with a Gumbell distribution, Beggs et al. (1981) developed a *rank-order logit model* capable of using all the information contained in a survey where alternatives are fully ranked by respondents. Their specification is based on the repeated application of the probability expression given in equation (7.13) until a full ranking of all the alternatives has been obtained. The probability of any particular ranking of alternatives being made by individual *i* can be expressed as:

$$P_i(U_{i1} > U_{i2} > \ldots > U_{iJ}) = \prod_{J=1}^{J} \left[\frac{\exp(V_{ij})}{\sum_{k=j}^{J} \exp(V_{ik})} \right]. \tag{7.13}$$

Clearly, this rank ordered model is more restrictive than the standard conditional logit model in as much as the extreme value (Weibull) distribution governs not only the first choice but all successive choices as well. As with CE, the ranking data model relies critically on the IIA assumption, which in this case is what permits the multiplication of successive conditional logit probabilities to obtain the probability expression for the full ranking.

The parameters of the utility function can be estimated by maximising the log-likelihood function given in equation (7.14):

$$\log L = \sum_{i=1}^{N} \sum_{j=1}^{J} \log \left[\frac{\exp(V_{ij})}{\sum_{k=j}^{J} \exp(V_{ik})} \right]. \tag{7.14}$$

Contingent ranking can also be seen as a series of choices in which respondents face a sequential choice process, whereby they first identify their most preferred choice, then, after removal of that option from the choice set, identify their most preferred choice out of the remaining set and so on. Welfare values can therefore be estimated as described in the CE example (Luce, 1959). Ranking data also provide more statistical information than CE, which leads to tighter confidence intervals around the parameter estimates.

The validity test procedures outlined for CE are also applicable to contingent ranking. In addition, as suggested by Foster and Mourato (1998), contingent ranking experiments lend themselves to a number of additional consistency tests. By including in the ranking sets dominated alternatives and repeated pairs of options, tests of logic, rank consistency and transitivity across choices are possible. It is also possible to detect apparent lexicographic patterns in the choice data, although it is generally not possible to prove that they represent true lexicographic preferences.

One of the limitations of this approach lies in the added cognitive difficulty associated with ranking choices with many attributes and levels. Previous research in the marketing literature by Ben-Akiva et al. (1991), Chapman and Staelin (1982) and Hausman and Ruud (1987) found significant differences in the preference structure implicit across ranks. In other words, choices seem to be unreliable and inconsistent across ranks. A possible explanation is that responses may be governed by different decision protocols according to the level of the rank (Ben-Akiva et al., 1991). Alternatively, the results could indicate increasing noise (random effects) with the depth of the ranking task as, in general, lower ranks seem to be less reliable than higher ranks (Chapman and Staelin, 1982; Hausman and Ruud, 1987). Foster and Mourato (1998) encountered similar problems of ranking inconsistency in an environmental study.

Finally, the fact that a baseline alternative is not necessarily present in all the trade-offs presented to respondents may result in welfare estimates that do not conform with standard consumer theory. However, this point still needs to be demonstrated (Morrison et al., 1999).

7.3   CONTINGENT RATING

Although the contingent rating method does not produce welfare consistent estimates, there are two procedures that can be used to strengthen the link between the contingent rating method and economic theory. First, it is usually possible to analyse contingent rating data by dropping the scale (which people tend to use differently) and only using the information on what choice was preferred. This at least provides a test of whether the 'extra' information in the rating is consistent with the choice data. Alternatively, the rating scores have to be transformed into a utility scale. In this context, the utility function is assumed to be related to individual's ratings via a *transformation function*:

$$R_{ij}(X_{ij}) = \phi[V_{ij}(X_{ij})], \tag{7.15}$$

where R represents the rating of individual i for choice j and ϕ is the transformation function. In marketing applications, these data are typically analysed using ordinary least squares (OLS) regression techniques which imply a strong assumption about the cardinality of the ratings scale.

An example of this approach may be given in the context of the value of leisure time (Alvarez-Farizo and Hanley, 1999) presented in Box 7.2. Respondents were shown different combinations of travel to site time, on-site time and cost, for visits to a popular national park site near Zaragoza. In terms of levels, they chose *time on-site* (1 day, 1 weekend or 1 week), the *journey time* (2 hours, 6 hours or 8 hours) and the *monetary cost of the trip.* This last attribute was allocated possible values of 3,000, 4,000 or 6,000 pesetas. Here, it is very important to notice that there is no status quo situation. All of these possibilities (levels in attributes) were possible taking different routes (roads, train, bus, etc.) to reach the National Park.

For each alternative, respondents were asked to give a score based on their preferences on a scale of 1 to 10. The contingent rating model may then be formulated as shown below in equation (7.16), assuming an additive

---

BOX 7.2   CHOICE ALTERNATIVES USED IN A SURVEY OF LEISURE TIME

Visit	Time stayed	Journey time	Journey cost (in pesetas)
1	1 Day	6 hours	4000 pts
2	1 Day	8 hours	3000 pts
3	1 Day	2 hours	6000 pts
4	1 Weekend	6 hours	6000 pts
5	1 Weekend	8 hours	4000 pts
6	1 Weekend	2 hours	3000 pts
7	1 Week	6 hours	3000 pts
8	1 Week	8 hours	6000 pts
9	1 Week	2 hours	4000 pts

Source: Alvarez-Farizo and Hanley (1999)

specification of the utility function, and the presence of the relevant attributes (Steenkamp, 1987):

$$\text{Evaluation} = \beta_0 + \sum_{i=1}^{n} \beta_{1i}^* D_{1i} + \sum_{j=1}^{m} \beta_{2j}^* D_{2j} + \sum_{k=1}^{p} \beta_{3k}^* D_{3k} + \varepsilon, \qquad (7.16)$$

where β_{1i}, β_{2j} and β_{3k} are the part-worths associated with levels i ($i = 1, 2, ..., n$); j ($j = 1, 2, ..., m$) and k ($k = 1, 2, ..., p$), of attributes 1, 2 and 3 respectively. The dummy variables D_{1i}, D_{2j} and D_{3k} have a value of 1 if the corresponding level of attribute is present and 0 in all other cases, and *evaluation* denotes the individual's overall evaluation (that is, rating) of the alternative proposed. This additive model is the most used in applications where the respondent is assumed to add up the part-worths or values for each attribute to get the total value of an alternative.

The model defined in this study has to incorporate, as well as the above attributes and levels, additional dummy variables which measure differences in evaluations depending on each respondent's employment situation. Interest in this breakdown is centred on the clear differences which we expect to observe among respondents with regard to their assessment of the value of leisure time depending on their employment situation (Bockstael et al., 1987). This employment situation has been divided into three groups. The first group includes salaried people and wage-earners. The second group comprises self-employed people (freelances and businessmen/employers). Finally, the third group comprises other people with a fixed leisure time/income structure (housewives, students, the unemployed and pensioners).

In accordance with the attributes and levels defined for the service to be evaluated and in line with the distinction made on evaluations carried out by different labour groups, the formulation of the model is shown in equation (7.17):

$$\begin{aligned} \text{Evaluation} = &\beta_T + \beta_1^* Est1 + \beta_2^* Est2 + \beta_3^* time + \beta_4^* \text{cost} + \beta_5^* Tra1 + \\ &\beta_6^* Tra2 + \beta_7^* Tra1\_Est1 + \beta_8^* Tra1\_Est2 + \beta_9^* Tra1\_time + \\ &\beta_{10}^* Tra1\_\text{cost} + \beta_{11}^* Tra2\_Est1 + \beta_{12}^* Tra2\_Est2 + \\ &\beta_{13}^* Tra2\_time + \beta_{14}^* Tra2\_\text{cost} + \varepsilon, \end{aligned} \qquad (7.17)$$

where 'evaluation' denotes evaluation assigned by each respondent to each of the hypothetical visits; *Est*1 is a dummy variable for a stay of 1 weekend; *Est*2 is a dummy variable for a stay of 1 week; *time* is journey time; *cost* is monetary cost of journey; *Tra*1 is a dummy variable for group 1 workers; *Tra*2 is a dummy variable for group 2 workers; '_' indicates interaction between the variables and ε is the error term.

This model was estimated using the *doubled-censored Tobit method* (Lin et al., 1996 and Sánchez et al., 1997) due to the censored nature of the data. The value assigned by the individual has a continuous character and follows the form as shown below:

$$Evaluation = \begin{cases} 0 \; if \; evaluation^* \leq 0 \\ evaluation^* \; if \; 0 < evaluation < 10, \\ 10 \; if \; evaluation^* \geq 10 \end{cases}$$

where '*Evaluation*' is the same variable defined in (7.17) and '*evaluation**' a hidden slack variable which is related to the explanatory variables of preferences. In this case, we assume that random perturbations, for each observation, are normally distributed with a zero mean and a constant variance (σ^2), coinciding with the variance of the hidden slack variable, which in turn is scattered according to a normal distribution. In fact, this hidden variable is a mixture of two components, one continuous and the other discrete associated with the two levels. It might seem that the Tobit model is a linear regression model and therefore we could estimate it by OLS. However, Maddala (1983) has shown that OLS estimators are biased and inconsistent in this case, and so we have to resort to a maximum-likelihood estimate. A fundamental assumption in the estimation is that of homoscedasticity, since if the random perturbation is heteroscedastic, the estimates of the β_1 parameters are nowhere near consistent. With the estimates for the βs obtained from the Tobit model, we can calculate implicit prices for each attribute (Mackenzie, 1992). For example, we can obtain the implicit price of travel time from $\beta_{travel\,time}$ *divided by* β_{cost}.

An alternative approach to OLS and Tobit models to analyse the data, which relaxes the cardinality hypothesis and effectively allows them to be treated in a random utility framework, is to use *ordered probit and logit models* that only imply an ordinal significance of the ratings.

Roe et al. (1996) have shown how to estimate compensating variation measures from ratings data based on ratings differences. The approach consists in subtracting a monetary cost from income until the ratings difference is made equal to zero:

$$R_{ij}^1(X_{ij}^1, M - \text{WTP}) - R_{ij}^0(X_{ij}^0, M) = 0, \tag{7.18}$$

where R^0 is the rating of the baseline choice, R^1 the rating attributed to the alternative choice, and M is income. Other procedures to derive welfare estimates from rating exercises are reviewed by Morrison et al. (1999).

Despite its popularity amongst marketing practitioners, rating exercises are much less used in environmental economics. The main reason for this lack of popularity lies in the dubious assumptions that need to be made in order to transform ratings into utilities. These assumptions relate either to the cardinality of rating scales or to the implicit assumption of comparability of ratings across individuals. In a nutshell, there is no clear-cut consistency with economic theory. However, the methodology can be improved, for example, by including money as an attribute: the rating scale can be converted into money trade-offs, that is, 10 pence equals 12 points, for each respondent separately. This provides a common unit of measurement across respondents, and it is not necessary to assume the scales mean the same for everyone.

7.4 PAIRED COMPARISON

This approach combines elements of CE (choosing the most preferred alternative) and rating exercises (rating the strength of preference). If the ratings are re-interpreted as providing an indication about choices only, then this approach collapses into a CE. If instead it is assumed that a change in rating is related to a change in utilities, then the resulting data can be analysed using ordered probit or logit techniques, similarly to the contingent rating procedure. Hence the comments and procedures described above for CE and contingent rating also apply in this case.

In particular, if the data can be analysed as per a CE, then welfare consistent estimates may be obtained. But if this is the decision, then why not specify a CE in the first place? One reason is that respondents like to be able to express a strength of preference as it allows them to be more discriminating. If the data are analysed as rating information, then the same problems occur as noted in Section 7.3. With a sequence of paired comparisons one needs to be able to test for consistency of choices.

Pairwise comparisons are extremely popular amongst marketing practitioners, especially after the introduction of computerised interviewing techniques and the development of specialised computer software such as Adaptive Conjoint Analysis (Green et al., 1991 or Sawtooth Software) which determines attributes, levels and pairwise comparisons, tailor-made for each respondent.

NOTE

1. It is necessary to include a *status quo* option in the choice set in order to achieve welfare measures that are consistent with demand theory. This is because, if a *status quo* alternative is not included in the choice set, respondents are effectively being 'forced' to choose one of the alternatives presented, which they may not desire at all. If for some respondents the

most preferred option is the current baseline situation, then any model based on a design in which the baseline is not present will yield inaccurate estimates of consumer welfare. The issues about the lack of information about *status quo* or the subjective interpretation of this information by the respondents mentioned in Section 7.1.1 are valid here.

8.   Validity and reliability

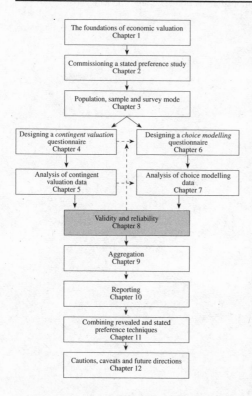

The foundations of economic valuation
Chapter 1

Commissioning a stated preference study
Chapter 2

Population, sample and survey mode
Chapter 3

Designing a *contingent valuation*
questionnaire
Chapter 4

Designing a *choice modelling*
questionnaire
Chapter 6

Analysis of contingent
valuation data
Chapter 5

Analysis of choice modelling
data
Chapter 7

Validity and reliability
Chapter 8

Aggregation
Chapter 9

Reporting
Chapter 10

Combining revealed and stated
preference techniques
Chapter 11

Cautions, caveats and future directions
Chapter 12

SUMMARY

This chapter addresses the twin issues of the *reliability* and *validity* of estimates from contingent valuation (CV) studies. *Reliability* refers to the degree of replicability of a measurement. Validity refers to the degree to which a study measured the intended quantity. It is clearly possible to have a highly reliable study result that does not represent a valid measurement.

Reliability can be conceptualised in three forms: (i) the classic psychology test-retest notion cast in terms of obtaining willingness to pay (WTP) estimates for the same individuals at two different points in time. The difficulty with this approach is that the act of surveying an individual may legitimately influence subsequent views; (ii) compare the WTP distributions from two independent but statistically equivalent samples from the same population, typically interviewed at two different points in time; and (iii) compare the stability of the estimated bid function in repeated samples.

Validity can also be conceptualised in different ways. Ideally, the results of a CV study are valid when the value stated by a survey respondent for a given good is equal to the actual value which the respondent would express for that good if given the opportunity in a real market. However, it is the basic rationale for using the contingent valuation (CV) method that such real market transactions cannot be observed. At the simplest level, one can look at the *face/content validity* of a CV survey instrument. Does the survey instrument present the 'correct' good in a manner that is likely to be understandable to respondents from a wide range of different backgrounds and education levels? Is the method of providing the good and collecting payment for its provision plausible?

The other major type of validity is *construct validity*, which is an assessment of whether the measurement is related in particular ways to other indicators of what should be measured. Some of these indicators are predictors from economic theory and some are empirical regularities in the form of associations with other variables, which seem intuitively correct and which hold across a large number of studies. Another form of construct validity occurs when there are multiple ways to measure the same underlying quantity. In such cases, the different measurements can be compared in a test of *convergent validity*, that is, a process of using different valuation techniques to see if they produce similar answers or answers that vary in a predicted manner. This chapter makes three distinctions:

1. The difference between assessing the *general* reliability and validity of CV versus the reliability and validity of the results from a *particular* CV study. The general evidence is presented first. This is useful for those considering commissioning a CV study and for considering the results of a particular CV survey that has already been conducted.
2. The difference between the predictions of the standard neoclassical economic theory and empirical CV results that support these predictions. In fact, as the chapter shows, most predictions rely upon empirical regularities, rather than economic theory, reflecting the paucity of economic expectations.
3. Philosophical objections to the use of cost–benefit analysis (CBA) as an input to public decision-making. Discussion of this critique was touched on briefly in Chapter 1 (and further in Chapter 12).

This chapter should be read in conjunction with Chapters 4–7, which cover issues relevant to choice modelling as well as contingent valuation.

8.1 PREFERENCES, VALUES AND VALIDITY

CV practitioners typically make two, often implicit, assumptions: (i) that respondents have preferences and use these to determine valuation responses; and (ii) that these preferences are consistent with standard economic theory. Under such conditions the task of the CV exercise is simply to elicit these preferences in an unbiased manner. Such values are then readily compatible with economic assessments such as CBA.

Considering assumption (i), there seems to be little evidence that responses to well-designed CV studies are entirely random or without some consistency from the internal perspective of the respondent. Even cases where respondents appear to be giving values which are invariant to the characteristics of the good under investigation can still be rationalised (sometimes by the respondent themselves) in terms of valuations for some other good. In fact, more often than not such results are found in studies which fail to apply the precepts of good CV survey design. However, regarding assumption (ii), there is some evidence which suggests that preferences may not always be consistent with standard economic theory (Sugden, 1999a, b).

It is important to recognise what economic theory does and does not say about preferences. Contrary to common criticism, economic theory does not dictate that individuals have prior-formulated values for all possible options that might be offered to them.[1] Indeed, individuals have no incentive to work out values for such options prior to them being offered a relevant choice. Contingent values are defined in response to the choices, information and alternatives presented in the survey context. However, the neoclassical economic view is that such survey responses will be driven by preferences which are consistent with economic theory (Mitchell and Carson, 1989). A contrary view is that such survey responses will be 'constructed' largely as a function of how the questions are asked rather than as a function of stable underlying preferences (Payne et al., 1992). This is the issue of *constructed preferences*. A spectrum of intermediate views exists between these extremes.

8.2   RESPONSES TO SURVEY QUESTIONS: SOME BASIC ISSUES

As far as responses to a CV questionnaire are concerned, 'the basic issue is whether the necessarily hypothetical character of CV studies automatically renders their findings meaningless' (Mitchell and Carson, 1989, p. 171). A more useful critique is to examine what type of questions are likely to deliver useful information even when they are asked in respect of some survey scenario (see Chapter 4). Carson et al. (1999) examine this issue by considering whether survey respondents will consider questions of some wider consequence or not. A question will be considered *consequential* if, and only if:

- the respondent feels that their response may influence the actions of relevant agencies; and
- the respondent cares about the outcome.

Only if both conditions hold will the question be consequential. For such questions respondents can be expected to answer on the basis of whatever underlying preferences they hold. Some assessment of validity is, in principle, feasible. However, if either or both conditions do not hold, then the respondent will consider the question to be of no consequence and any response has the same influence on his or her utility. For consequential questions we can consider two response possibilities:

1. respondents will answer so as to maximise their expected wellbeing, therefore they will respond to the incentives as set out in the survey design; or
2. respondents will answer truthfully irrespective of 1.

If respondents always answer truthfully then the analyst's problem is to verify whether respondents' concepts of the truth in a survey situation correspond with actual payments or compensation amounts demanded. This is no simple task, given the absence of markets for public goods. However, the task becomes considerably more complex where (1) is in conflict with (2), that is, the respondent feels that the survey market provides some incentive to do other than truthfully reveal their preferences. There are a considerable number of possible situations in which truth-telling might not seem the best way in which to maximise expected utility (wellbeing) and these are reviewed in the remainder of this chapter. However, the objective of the CV practitioner is to design a valuation mechanism in which truth-telling and utility maximisation coincide. This is the issue of *incentive compatibility* and determining whether a given CV study design is incentive compatible is one of the major foci of validity analysis (see also Chapter 4).

This drive for incentive compatibility can be complicated by what is known as the *face-value dilemma* (Carson et al., 1999). Taking answers at face value implies both that respondents always answer truthfully and that they also answer the specific question asked. Both assumptions may be suspect (Sudman et al., 1996). Survey respondents are not automata and interpret questions in the light of their own prior knowledge and beliefs. For example, if respondents feel that the specified government agencies are incompetent or wasteful, that the specified scenario is implausible, or the good described is unlikely to be as specified or will cost some amount other than that stated, then their response is likely to be conditioned by these opinions. This should not be surprising as it has long been recognised in marketing that beliefs about the reliability of the seller of a good have a strong influence on durable goods purchases. In effect, the respondent will be answering a different question to that understood by the analyst and stated values are not commensurate with the face-value question.

In summary, whether CV questions are consequential, incentive compatible and can be taken at face value are all key issues for validity analysis.

8.3 VALUE TYPES AND THEIR CONSISTENCY WITH ECONOMIC THEORY

The attitude-behaviour model developed in Chapter 4 refers to three value types as pertinent to the CV experiment as presented in Table 8.1. So, for example, in a survey concerning possible flood alleviation strategies, a respondent will only consider a valuation question consequential if they feel that their response may influence, say, the decisions made by the Environment Agency *and* they gain use value from the improved flood protection of their property and/or non (passive) use value from the improved risk protection enjoyed by others. If they either do not care about the outcome or feel that their response will have no impact upon that outcome, then they will consider the question inconsequential. With a coercive payment mechanism, the agent may have an incentive to say 'no' to avoid the loss of having to pay for something they do not care anything about.

Table 8.1 Value types

Formulated value	This is the WTP or WTA amount that a respondent *genuinely* believes they would be prepared to pay or accept in respect of the provision change scenario presented in a CV survey.
Stated value	This is the WTP or WTA amount that the respondent tells the interviewer that they would be prepared to pay or accept in respect of the provision change scenario presented in a CV survey.
Actual value	This is the WTP or WTA amount that the respondent actually does pay or accept in respect of the provision change when it occurs.

These definitions are necessary to allow for the possibility that the corresponding amounts are not all identical. Note first that formulated values are those which respondents hold as being true. However, as discussed above, in certain circumstances respondents may perceive some strategic advantage in misreporting their values within a CV study such that stated value may either exceed or be less than formulated value. Economists argue that this may occur if respondents feel that they can increase their utility through such a strategy. This explains the emphasis upon making CV questions compatible with truth-telling such that it is in the respondent's interest to ensure that stated value equals formulated value (see also Chapter 4).

If incentives are such that stated values differ from formulated values, we would expect the former also to differ from the actual values which respondents would express if given the opportunity to conduct a real exchange. However, it may also be the case that formulated values differ from their actual counterparts. This can happen if time and information change between elicitation of these values. Another reason why this might occur is that respondents may expend greater cognitive effort upon determining actual as opposed to formulated values. Such a problem could, in theory, be overcome through improved study design. However, a more fundamental problem may be that, while CV studies provide respondents with information regarding the good under evaluation, they can rarely offer respondents the *experience* of paying or receiving compensation for the good in question. If experience is a fundamental part of determining actual values, then a difference between formulated and actual values cannot be ruled out. In many cases, a CV respondent spends more time considering information and the relevant decision than that spent for many on voting decisions or market goods decisions with similar monetary expenditures. As such the divergence may come from the agent spending less time in actual markets. The task of the CV instrument is to provide an unbiased and transparent vehicle which gives respondents the best possible chance to deliberate about their preferences and approach as closely as possible to the values that they would affirm in the light of experience. The instrument must also incorporate whatever validity tests may be useful for examining how far responses are the product of constructed or 'true' preferences and how confident we may be of the relationship between stated and actual values.

The principal biases that occur in CV WTP estimates are outlined in Table 8.2.

Some of the differences between stated WTP/WTA and formulated or actual WTP are termed as 'bias' since their existence constitutes a validity problem. Table 8.2 adapts the typology of biases from Mitchell and Carson (1989). Note that differences between value types do not always constitute a validity problem. Information bias (WTP/WTA sensitive to the amount and quality of information provided), for example, is a reliability problem. The rest of this chapter discusses validity tests to see if such biases exist.

Table 8.2   Typology of potential biases in CV studies

---

1.   Incentives to misrepresent responses

Biases in this class occur when a respondent misrepresents his or her true willingness to pay (WTP).

A.   *Strategic bias*: where a respondent gives a WTP amount that differs from his or her true WTP amount (conditional on the perceived information) in an attempt to influence the provision of the good and/or the respondent's level of payment for the good. This type of bias is explained further in 12.2.1.
B.   *Compliance bias*

    1.   *Sponsor bias:* where a respondent gives a WTP amount that differs from his or her true WTP amount in an attempt to comply with the presumed expectations of the sponsor (or assumed sponsor).
    2.   *Interviewer bias:* where a respondent gives a WTP amount that differs from his or her true WTP amount in an attempt to either please or gain status in the eyes of a particular interviewer.

2.   Implied value cues

These biases occur when elements of the contingent market are treated by respondents as providing information about the 'correct' value for the good.

A.   *Starting point bias*: where the elicitation format or payment vehicle directly or indirectly introduces a potential WTP amount that influences the WTP amount given by a respondent. This bias may be accentuated by a tendency to yea-saying.
B.   *Range bias*: where the elicitation method presents a range of potential WTP amounts that influences a respondent's WTP amount.
C.   *Relational bias*: where the description of the good presents information about its relationship to other public or private commodities that influences a respondent's WTP amount.
D.   *Importance bias*: where the act of being interviewed or some feature of the instrument suggests to the respondent that one or more levels of the amenity has value.
E.   *Position bias*: where the position or order or sequence in which valuation questions for different levels of a good (or different goods) suggests to respondents how those levels should be valued.

3.   Scenario Misspecification

Biases in this category occur when a respondent does not respond to the correct valuation scenario. Except in A in the outline that follows, it is presumed that the intended scenario is correct and that the errors occur because the respondent does not understand the scenario as the researcher intends it to be understood.

Table 8.2   continued

A.   *Theoretical misspecification bias*: where the scenario specified by the researcher is incorrect in terms of economic theory or the major policy elements.

B.   *Amenity misspecification bias*: where the perceived good being valued differs from the intended good.

1.   *Symbolic:* where a respondent values a symbolic entity instead of the researcher's intended good.

2.   *Part-whole*: where a respondent values a larger or a smaller entity than the researcher's intended good.

    a.   *Geographical part-whole*: where a respondent values a good whose spatial attributes are larger or smaller than the spatial attributes of the researcher's intended good.

    b.   *Benefit part-whole:* where a respondent includes a broader or a narrower range of benefits in valuing a good than intended by the researcher.

    c.   *Policy-package part-whole*: where a respondent values a broader or a narrower policy package than the one intended by the researcher.

3.   *Metric*: where a respondent values the amenity on a different (and usually less precise) metric or scale than the one intended by the researcher.

4.   *Probability of provision:* where a respondent values a good whose probability of provision differs from that intended by the researcher.

C.   *Context misspecification bias:* where the perceived context of the market differs from the intended context.

1.   *Payment vehicle*: where the payment vehicle is either misperceived or is itself valued in a way not intended by the researcher.

2.   *Property right*: where the property right perceived for the good differs from that intended by the researcher.

3.   *Method of provision*: where the intended method of provision is either misperceived or is itself valued in a way not intended by the researcher.

4.   *Budget constraint*: where the perceived budget constraint differs from the budget constraint the researcher intended to invoke.

5.   *Elicitation question*: where the perceived elicitation question fails to convey a request for a firm commitment to pay the highest amount the respondent will realistically pay before preferring to do without the amenity. (In the discrete-choice framework, the commitment is to pay the specified amount.)

6.   *Instrument content*: where the intended context or reference frame conveyed by the preliminary nonscenario material differs from that perceived by the respondent.

7.   *Question order*: where a sequence of questions, which should not have an effect, does have an effect on a respondent's WTP amount.

8.4   OVERVIEW OF THE VALIDITY PROBLEM AND TYPES OF VALIDITY TESTING

The central problem in assessing the validity of value measures obtained from any SP technique is the absence of an unambiguously clear and definitive criterion against which to compare those measures. This is not a generic problem of all survey research (for example, election opinion polls can be compared against the results from the subsequent elections they set out to predict). However, it is generally a problem for public goods in that, with very few exceptions, actual values are unobservable. The issue with all Hicksian consumers surplus measures, be they for marketed or non-marketed goods, is

Table 8.3   Types of validity testing

Content/face validity	This assesses whether the CV study asked the right questions in a clear, understandable, sensible and appropriate manner with which to obtain a valid estimate of the construct (say maximum WTP for a specific good) under investigation.
Construct validity	This examines whether the relationships between measures produced by a CV study and other measures are in accordance with expectations.
Convergent validity	Measures obtained from a given CV study are compared with some combination of: • results obtained from other valuation approaches such as the travel cost and hedonic pricing methods; • the findings of cross-study analyses (e.g. meta-analyses or benefits transfer exercises); and • simulated markets such as those used in experimental tests.
Expectation-based validity	CV measures are related to other constructs in a manner which is consistent with prior expectations. Two sources of these expectations can be identified: • theoretical expectations derived from economic theory; and • intuition and empirically driven expectations derived from prior intuition and regularities across prior studies.

that they are inherently 'unobservable' measures with respect to actual trans-actions because they represent the difference between what an agent is willing to pay or willing to accept and what they actually pay (or receive). It is possible with respect to market transactions to identify some (but not all) behaviour related to the consumer surplus measure. This implies that, at least, part of the Hicksian consumer surplus estimate must always be driven by assumption. Analogous problems arise generally in psychological attitude-behaviour research (American Psychological Association, 1974) where validity is treated as a multidimensional issue. Table 8.3 shows the two basic strands of validity testing, each of which is discussed in turn.

8.5   CONTENT VALIDITY

Studies with high content validity may be characterised as those in which 'the survey descriptions and questions are clear, reasonable and unbiased, ... [such] that respondents are put in a frame of mind that motivates them to answer seriously and thoughtfully' (Schumann, 1996, p. 77). Assessing the content validity of a CV survey is essentially a subjective expert appraisal task. The objective of this section is to highlight those issues which should be appraised in assessing content validity and in so doing provide guidelines for satisfactory design and implementation.

Content validity judgements encompass the entirety of the study from considering how reasonable the aims of the study are, to the clarity, interpret-ability and plausibility of the questions posed, and to the way in which the survey was conducted. The guiding principle should be whether the diversity of components which constitute a CV study (administration of the survey, the information and materials provided to respondents, the description of the good and associated provision change scenario and so on) are conducive and sufficient to induce respondents to reveal valid stated values. This task, and that of ensuring content validity, is most demanding where respondents are confronted with what are, at least in the context of valuation, unfamiliar goods or scenarios. The rest of this section provides a checklist of general components which should be present to contribute to the content validity of the study. This should be taken in conjunction with the subsequent discussion of specific causes of measurement bias and effect in later sections.

There are three broad areas for inspection in undertaking content validity assessments:

1.   Basic study design and implementation issues.
2.   The good and its attributes.

3.   The payment/compensation scenario.

Post-survey debriefing exercises which help to gather information for validity testing are covered in Chapter 4 as these are largely implementation issues.

8.5.1   Basic Study Design and Implementation Issues

Design-related validity testing can be presented in three parts in terms of actions to be taken to ensure high validity:

1.   Prior to commencement of the survey (also see Chapters 2–4).
2.   During the survey (also see Chapter 4).
3.   After the survey (also see Chapter 5).

Prior to commencement of the survey

- The purpose and rationale of the study and how the study findings are going to be used should be clear to both the commissioning agency and the analysts.
- Peer review of questionnaires is strongly encouraged. This should be seen as a core element of an iterative process of questionnaire development.
- Access to a reference library of questionnaires is expected to be highly conducive to high-quality survey design. However, to date no such library exists. Even well-known sources, such as Carson et al. (1995) and the EVRI database (http://www.evri.ec.gc.ca) provide only lists of CV surveys, the latter of which also provides some summary information. The establishment of such a resource, together with accompanying reports and critiques, is to be strongly encouraged.
- A variety of techniques such as focus groups, one-to-one pretests and piloting are effective in assessing the adequacy of the informational, descriptive and other elements of the valuation scenario. For the purposes of validity assessment, a study should be able to demonstrate the iterative and considered incorporation of such information so as to avoid misinterpretation and enhance the clarity, comprehension and credibility of the survey scenario.
- Question design should in general be guided by basic attitude/behaviour principles. It is well known that as the gap between question focus and construct focus widens, so responses to the former become less reliable predictors of the latter. For example, questions aimed at

estimating payment behaviour should ask about intention to pay rather than about more general attitudes towards payment.

- The researcher should be able to demonstrate identification of the extent of the relevant market for sampling purposes and how the survey has addressed that population (see Chapter 9).

- The choice of survey method(s) should be adequately justified and related to the extent of the market and the intended use for, and required accuracy of, results. Survey administration and execution should also be of a high and consistent standard with high quality and with specifically trained interviewers being employed. Note that mail surveys do not require interviewers; the main issue here is multiple mailings to ensure a high response rate.

- The sample size collected should be chosen with respect to: (i) the relevant population for the good in question (different goods will generate value for different populations, for example, while small-scale assets of only local importance may require only local population sampling, goods of national importance may require both a large and more spatially diverse sample); (ii) response variability (accurate measures of response variability may not be available until the survey is completed and therefore expert statistical judgement complemented by pilot data are likely to be required here); and (iii) the survey design employed (different designs have inherently different efficiency characteristics, for example, dichotomous choice/referendum approaches are relatively inefficient and have greater data requirements for a given level of estimation accuracy. Such efficiency concerns have to be balanced against the incentive compatibility properties of different designs; a design which requires relatively little data to produce an estimate with a tight confidence interval is of little use if it is known to encourage respondents to misreport their values).

- The design should permit the gathering of sufficient data of a quality and type to permit high-quality construct validity testing to be carried out. This should include the collection of potential explanatory variables for statistical analysis of theoretical validity such as respondent and household characteristics, attitudes to both the good, the survey market scenario and wider attitudes both within the general domain of the good and much more broadly regarding general attitudes to life and underlying world views. Questions should be multipurpose in that they should support the analysis of survey responses and facilitate post-survey qualitative assessments of scenario credibility, appropriateness and acceptability (see subsequent discussion). Respondents should also be asked if they are prepared to participate in post-survey debriefing exercises and reliability testing (for example, resurveying of the same respondents at a later date) and contact details should be gathered to facilitate this.

During the survey

- Within the confines of incentive compatibility and informational limits, the objectives of the study should be made clear to survey respondents. Frankness concerning the purpose of the study is very likely to be conducive to the credibility and clear understanding of the questions asked. Allied to this, design transparency is also highly desirable.
- Respondents should be clearly informed about who the relevant institutional actors are, including the authorities responsible for the asset in question and those (if different) responsible for affecting the change in provision. The body carrying out the study and their relation to the above should also be made clear with demonstrable impartiality being a clear premium here.

After the survey

- Adequate data handling and accurate data encoding procedures should be demonstrated.
- High quality and appropriate use of data analysis techniques should be demonstrated.

8.5.2   The Good and its Attributes

With respect to the good under valuation, the scenario presented to respondents should comprise clear and unambiguous descriptions as discussed in Chapters 4 and 5 and summarised below:

- The relevant attributes of the good under investigation (for example, its geographical extent, the various value streams associated with the good, its degree of uniqueness, designated status and so on). This may require a combination of textual information, photographs, maps, charts and graphs.
- The proposed change in provision (in terms of quantity, quality and the timing of such changes) including details of the *status quo* or 'do nothing' situation (note that a 'do nothing' situation need not correspond to a 'no change' situation, in fact it may be that the scenario is intended to estimate the value of preventing a change in the status of a given good).

- The combination of information on the attributes of the good and its provision should be such that respondents have a clear and unambiguous understanding of precisely what it is they are being asked to pay or accept compensation for. This in turn should clearly define what they are not being asked to value.
- Respondents should be given enough information in a clear-enough fashion so that they should be comfortable making a decision. Further, they need to be made comfortable giving either a 'Yes' or 'No' response. This can be done in a number of different ways, such as telling them reasons why they might be opposed to the programme (for example, Carson, Mitchell, Hannemann, Kopp, Presser and Ruud, 1992). Giving respondents the option to 'opt' out before the valuation question is asked provides an easy way to not have to think about the issue and leaves the researcher with the issue of how to treat their responses. Failure to include such an option may make the respondent feel that such an option is not open to them and increases the pressure to provide 'good' responses, that is, those which are perceived to be what the interviewer wants – so called '*yea-saying*'.[2] The interviewer should gracefully accept all volunteered 'don't know' responses, which along with other indifferent responses should be treated as 'No'.
- How the proposed change in provision will be achieved and the extent to which changes in both the proposed good and in the 'do nothing' state are due to human or natural processes.
- The degree of certainty regarding both the 'do nothing' and provision change scenarios should be made as clear as possible and in readily comprehensible quantitative terms if at all feasible. This may be more difficult to achieve successfully where relatively small probabilities are concerned.
- Details of who is likely to gain from the provision of the good should be made clear. Unlikely or controversial specifications regarding who is excluded from use of the good may undermine the credibility of the scenario.

These descriptions should be comprehensive to the extent that salient facts are presented to respondents but they should not be overly long or complex, or induce uncertainty or boredom amongst respondents. These are potentially conflicting demands and as Bishop et al. (1995, p. 633) state: 'There is a delicate balance to be struck between providing too little and too much information.'

In addition to the informational requirements spelt out above, examinations of the perceived clarity and credibility of the good and the provision change scenario are vital to the assessments of the construct validity of a study (see also Section 8.6). The most direct approach is to ask respondents questions regarding the various issues raised above (for example, trust in and perceptions of the relevant delivering authorities, credibility of the proposed provision change, divergence of expectations from the proposed scenario, perceived probability of provision and so on). Both closed- and open-ended questions should be used to gain a rich diversity of quantitative and qualitative assessments. This can be a very fruitful exercise which can also contribute to subsequent theoretical validity analysis as such responses can provide useful explanatory variables in a bid function. Some sensitivity analysis of scenario credibility can be conducted through varying the description of the project (for example, by changing the scale of the good on offer – see subsequent discussion of scope) and seeing how this is reflected in credibility measures and consequent stated values.

8.5.3 The Payment/Compensation Scenario

The validity of the specified payment or compensation mechanism should be established via a clear line of argument running through and supported by the pre-survey qualitative analysis, explicit survey responses and post-survey debriefing. The content validity exercise should assess the *credibility*, *appropriateness* and *acceptability* of the following aspects of the payment/compensation scenario to respondents:

- The welfare measure (WTP or WTA for gain or loss). This should be both technically and subjectively appropriate (from the respondent's perspective) with details of relevant property rights provided as necessary. Particular attention should be paid to the acceptability of measures which may contravene respondents' innate feelings regarding appropriate property rights.
- Who will pay for the good and what is the specified payment unit (for example, is the requested payment in respect of the individual, the household or some wider unit?). The objective here is to adopt a unit which is both useful in terms of the wider objectives of the study (for example, readily amenable for aggregation) and is considered by the respondent to be a natural and thereby credible, unit of account.[3]
- The temporal incidence of the payment (for example, lump sum, monthly, yearly and so on). This should be seen by the respondent as relating in a credible fashion to the characteristics of the good in question and the way its provision can be credibly financed.
- The mode of payment. The use of controversial vehicles should be

avoided unless they are intended to be used in the real world case[4] as should those which only apply to a subset of the sample. Uncertainties regarding payment should be avoided if possible. If this is not possible, such uncertainties should be clearly quantified.

- The elicitation format chosen and wording of the valuation question should be demonstrably incentive compatible, that is, it should be clearly established that it is in the best interests of the respondent to state the actual amount that they would be prepared to pay, or to accept in compensation, for the good.

The issues of substitute availability (local, national or global uniqueness) and alternative expenditure possibilities should also be considered. Defining the extent of these issues is a complex problem as full definition is probably infeasible and undesirable. The uniformed preference argument suggests that the prior level of knowledge and awareness which individuals bring to CV studies of complex public goods may be insufficient to provide a basis for stable values. However, it will typically be infeasible to provide the individual with perfect information. Furthermore, even if it were possible, this would be different to the market situation where information availability is rarely perfect. Therefore, a trade-off exists between what is desirable and what is feasible, the solution of which will typically be the product of expert judgement, trial and error. On the basis that there are effective constraints in terms of survey time and the ability of respondents to process new information, one should attempt to inform the respondent of the most obvious public good substitutes and to remind them that they can spend their money on available private goods.

In the same way that content validity of the description of the good is supplemented by explicit questions to respondents regarding the credibility and understanding of the good, similar questions can be asked regarding the payment scenario as follows:

- All respondents should be asked why they gave the valuation responses that they did. This includes both those who paid/agreed compensation for the good and those who did not. Reasons should not be strictly limited to some pre-prepared list, and to facilitate this it may be advisable to allow an open-ended response to be subsequently coded by an analyst with expertise in relevant qualitative techniques.
- Specific measures should be put in place to clearly identify 'protest' responses, that is, respondents who in some way reject the valuation scenario presented to them. Protest bids might be of a variety of forms. For example, respondents who clearly value the asset in question may

respond with a zero bid, not as a result of free-riding but because they object to some feature of the survey or valuation scenario (for example, they may object to a particular payment vehicle and thus register a zero WTP even though they have a non-zero value for the good). Efforts should be made to distinguish protests from both valid bids and those prompted by strategic bias.[5] In particular, in WTP formats, the distinction should be made between those respondents who state that they refuse to pay on some moral, ethical or other 'protest' grounds and those who have either a valid zero WTP or have a positive WTP but are free-riding. Similarly, in WTA formats a line should be clearly drawn between those who have negligible compensation needs, those who genuinely have a very high WTA and those who object to the principle of monetary compensation. Clearly ascertaining through non-valuation questions whether respondents' utility is a function of the resource in question would be a useful piece of information in each instance. No pressure should be exerted upon such respondents to make them 'conform' to the valuation exercise. However, their reasons for protesting should be clearly determined and noted as these are important to the assessment of content validity. The method in which refusal reasons (including protests) are elicited may have some impact upon the reasons stated. We favour using an open-ended question approach rather than offering respondents an analyst-defined list of refusal reasons.

- Examinations of the perceived understanding and credibility of the payment mechanism are fundamental elements of content validity assessments. In a manner similar to assessment of perceptions regarding the good, the most direct approach is to ask respondents some combination of closed- and open-ended questions regarding the various aspects of the payment mechanism. Normally these will be asked after the valuation response has been elicited. Overt questions regarding possible strategic behaviour can be highly revealing here (although incentives to also misreport answers should obviously be considered). This provides both direct checks on credibility and allows the definition of explanatory variables for bid function analysis. Dichotomous choice/referenda elicitation formats readily lend themselves to sensitivity analyses of payment mechanism credibility as the analyst can examine how the variation of bid amounts impinges upon respondents' perceived credibility of whether the specified payment/compensation amount will in fact be implemented and whether it is credible to believe that the good will in fact be provided as specified at that amount.

8.6   CONSTRUCT VALIDITY

The two types of construct validity, namely convergent validity and expectations-based validity, are discussed in Sections 8.6.1 and 8.6.2.

8.6.1   Convergent Validity

Convergent validity assessments typically compare measures obtained from CV studies with:

- those obtained from other methods;
- multiple CV studies (for example, of the same or similar resources) in a process known as *meta analysis*, or transferred across applications using *benefits transfer* (BT) techniques (see Annex 1.1); and
- those obtained via experimental simulated markets, which is commonly (although mistakenly) referred to as a criterion validity test.

In convergent validity testing no measure can automatically claim superiority in terms of being a naturally closer approximation of the value of the underlying construct. This could be thought of as being 'validity by association'. However, strictly speaking even this would be overstating the case. Just because two approaches deliver similar or logically related measures does not mean that those measures are valid; instead they may be equally invalid. Nevertheless, it is clear that a large and unexpected difference between estimates would show that at least one measure is invalid or two different questions are being addressed.

Comparisons across methods
Soon after the first applications of the CV, and perhaps motivated by an underlying (although possibly misplaced) trust in revealed preference (RP) techniques (by both decision makers and many economists alike), analysts began comparing hypothetical market estimates with those of other nonmarket valuation methods, most commonly RP approaches such as the hedonic pricing (HP) or travel cost (TC) method.[6] CV measures are the product of hypothetical markets, whereas HP and TC measures are based upon observations of actual behaviour. However, this does not mean that HP or TC measures should be treated as criterion values against which CV measures should be assessed. This arises because:

- Apart from the fact that TC studies themselves can be subject to bias, the measures produced are essentially based upon economic interpretations of behaviour and therefore cannot unambiguously claim to be precise reflections of true values. Randall (1994) notes that in TC studies it is the analyst who calculates the travel expenditure and travel time cost against which observed visitation behaviour is modelled. While such an approach may be reasonable for calculating relative value comparisons between recreation sites, that is, where any errors between analyst-calculated costs and those perceived by visitors will be reasonably consistent, this method may be suspect when estimating the absolute value of visits to any given site for use within CBA. As Randall points out, at least in CV studies respondents are fully aware of the cost amount they are supposed to be reacting to.

- The hypothetical market underpinning CV estimates allows the possibility of disparities between formulated, stated and actual values, whereas TC (and HP) studies concern only actual values.
- The TC and CV techniques typically address overlapping but not identical value sets. While TC measures are ex-post and exclude non-use values, CV measures are ex-ante, may or may not be based upon direct experience of the level of provision described in the scenario and often embrace both use and non-use values.

High quality CV and TC comparisons seem to have consistently found a satisfactory similarity between value estimates (for example, Hoehn and Randall, 1985). Such single, within-study, comparisons of, typically, just two measures are relatively weak tests where these estimates have wide confidence intervals. An interesting variant on this approach is presented by Carson, Flores, Martin and Wright (1996) in a meta-analysis of 84 separate studies of quasi-public goods yielding 616 comparisons of CV with RP techniques. This analysis found a high correlation between CV and other measures, with the former slightly, although significantly, lower on average than the latter. This result contrasts with the widely held prior belief that CV estimates would exceed RP measures. Although, as indicated above, the relationship between such measures is complex, the fact that these measures were (in most cases) not wildly different does indicate that specific CV estimates cannot be dismissed by such cross-method convergent validity tests.

One development which may assist in the conduct of cross-method convergent validity comparisons is the increasing accessibility of previous valuation studies through specific study cataloguing resources such as the EVRI database referred to above. Box 8.1 illustrates construct validity in the context of safety.

BOX 8.1   CONSTRUCT VALIDITY IN A SAFETY
CONTEXT

A simple and direct example of a test of internal consistency/
construct (theoretical) validity in the safety field is provided in
Jones-Lee et al. (1993), which reports the findings of a nationally
representative sample survey commissioned by the then UK
Department of Transport and aimed at estimating WTP-based
values for the prevention of non-fatal road injuries in Great Britain. In this study all respondents had first ranked and 'scored'
various severities of road injury in terms of badness on a visual
analogue scale. Half of the sample then answered CV questions
concerning annual WTP for specified reductions in the annual
risk of each injury, while the other half answered standard gamble
questions.

In the CV questions, the annual risk reduction for the more
severe injuries was specified as 4 in 100,000, while the reduction
for the lesser severities was specified as 12 in 100,000 (for one
intermediate severity of injury, two successive questions asked
about *both* risk reductions). Clearly, in the case of the CV questions, in the absence of binding budget constraints (and setting
aside protest responses), standard economic theory (and, indeed, common sense) indicates that if one injury is regarded by
a respondent as being strictly worse than another, then that
respondent should be willing to pay more for a given reduction in
the worse of the two injuries than for the same reduction in the
risk of the injury judged by the respondent to be 'less bad'. In the
event, over all pairs of comparable severities of injury, that is,
those involving the same reductions in annual risk, between
approximately 10 per cent and 20 per cent of respondents gave
CV responses that were strictly *inconsistent* with their ranking
responses.

Within method meta analysis and benefits transfer

The valuation literature contains a number of *meta-analyses*, the majority
of which focus upon revealed preference studies. However, the number of
CV based meta-analyses is growing. A recent study by Brouwer, Langford,
Bateman and Turner (1999) quality screened an initial list of 60 wetland
CV studies to obtain a final set of 30 studies yielding 103 value estimates

(see Annex 1.1 for details).[7] The fitted meta-analysis model explained a large proportion of the variation in CV estimates across the studies. Furthermore, this variation was shown to be significantly related to the characteristics and functions of the various wetlands with relative values being in strong agreement with prior expectations. Interesting and theoretically plausible cross-cultural/socioeconomic effects were also noted (for example, even when adjusted for purchasing power parity, US values were consistently higher than those obtained from European studies). However, CV measures were also shown to be explained by a number of design differences between studies. Nevertheless, inspection of these variations showed that they were consistently related to differences in the incentive compatibility characteristics of the various studies analysed, for example, those studies which used designs which provided respondents with a strategic incentive to understate WTP yielded lower value estimates than other studies which were more incentive compatible. An interesting further finding was that, *ceteris paribus*, value estimates were clustered within studies. This might suggest either design effects or that the clustering of location and population effects within studies is reflected in resultant values. The impact of this effect upon value estimates was not, in absolute terms, particularly large, but it was statistically significant.

Benefits function transfer tests are inherently more demanding than meta-analyses. While the latter typically just looks for consistency of value estimates, the former can comprise an array of intricate statistical tests from comparisons of explained variance to more rigorous examinations of coefficient equality (for example, testing if the relationship between income and WTP in one study is consistent with that in another – see Brouwer and Spaninks, 1999). To date such tests have achieved mixed results, although CV studies have fared at least no worse and possibly better than benefits transfers of revealed preference studies (see Downing and Ozuna, 1996; Bateman, Nishikawa and Brouwer, 1999; Brouwer and Bateman, 2000). However, the reasons for this may be as much to do with the need to rethink questionnaire design and sampling strategies explicitly for benefits transfer purposes as anything to do with validity, and this remains a very active area of research.

In summary, while meta-analyses seem to provide some support for convergent validity within CV studies, to date BT exercises have produced mixed results. It is unrealistic to expect anything but the most major individual valuation studies to undertake convergent validation of this kind as such exercises may be as demanding as the valuation study itself. However, research into the transfer of results has the potential eventually to yield very substantial rewards, as the promise of such techniques is to provide estimates of resources without the need to undertake new surveys thus saving both time and money. In order to attain this goal a more substantial catalogue of studies needs to be developed, each designed to a consistently high quality and with BT in mind.

Comparisons with simulated markets

Simulated markets are frequently used by *experimental economists* to test hypotheses and a variety of techniques have been devised for designing such markets to be incentive compatible with truth-telling. CV researchers have appealed to simulated markets as a method of validating their research findings. However, the major limitation to such attempts (indeed, the major problem of all attempts to validate CV results) is that, in all but a few exceptional cases (discussed below), there exist no criterion values for public goods against which either simulated market or CV value estimates may be measured. Many environmental public goods are non-rival and non-exclusive and as such are not paid for in any direct manner. Even for those which are funded through central taxation, the level of payment is not individually determined and therefore a valid criterion measure is unobservable.

Given this difficulty, the majority of CV/simulated market testing has concerned quasi-public goods (such as permits for hunting) or private goods with the implicit assumption being that results obtained in such circumstances may say something of relevance regarding the public goods case. There have been a number of surveys of this literature (see, for example, Mitchell and Carson, 1989; Carson, Flores and Mead, 1996, 1999; Fisher, 1996; Hanemann, 1996; Schulze et al., 1996; Cummings, 1996). There is also some considerable divergence in interpretation of this literature. Balistreri et al. (2001) argue that while survey dichotomous choice WTP responses typically exceed survey open-ended WTP amounts, the latter prove to be reasonable predictors of actual payments in simulated markets. In contrast Mitchell and Carson (1989), Carson, Flores and Meade (1996) and Hanemann (1996) argue that the available literature on simulated markets provides a strong endorsement of the validity of CV estimates of quasi-public good values in general and dichotomous methods in particular.

However, it is in relation to public goods that the CV debate is fiercest, since in the vast majority of cases criterion values are not observable for such goods. In the US the use of real referenda to determine the provision of certain public goods at stated costs provides such a criterion. Furthermore, because the results of referenda are binding, that is, the provision is made and posted prices are coercively enforced, surveys which emulate the referendum decision can be made incentive compatible. Two such assessments have been carried out to date. Carson et al. (1987) used a survey referendum duplicating an actual referendum on water quality which was implemented several months after the CV survey. Findings indicated that survey results quite closely predicted the subsequent actual vote. A similar result is reported by Polasky et al. (1996) concerning a referendum to purchase open space in Oregon. Although this is only a very small empirical literature, the incentive compatibility of such studies and their public goods nature make their findings of considerable importance.

A larger set of studies has attempted convergent validity assessment of public goods under conditions which are not fully incentive compatible (for example, Navrud, 1992). A typical example is provided by Foster et al. (1997), who compare survey open-ended WTP for wildlife habitat with actual donations to wildlife conservation bodies in respect of such goods. The problem here is that the latter donations are voluntary rather than coercive and are therefore not incentive compatible. In such situations a reasonably consistent pattern can be identified wherein, compared to actual markets, survey markets tend to overstate the willingness of respondents to participate in paying for public goods but provide reasonable predictors of the amounts that those who do participate actually pay. However, given the imperfect incentive properties of such comparisons, the implications for the validity of CV estimates are somewhat speculative (Randall, 1996).

8.6.2 Expectations-based Validity

The valuation estimate produced by a CV study has *expectations-based validity* if 'the measure performs in a variety of theoretically sensible ways in relation to other variables, and ... any non-obvious associations can be explained so as not to cast doubt on the assumed meaning of the measure itself' (Schumann, 1996, p. 78). More generally, the objective is simply to see whether survey findings conform to prior expectations. Some of those expectations will be derived from theory and those from economic theory are particularly important if value estimates are to be used in cost–benefit or similar analyses. However, there is considerable debate regarding the extent to which economic theory can provide firm and positive expectations regarding CV outcomes (Hanemann, 1996). Indeed, it is frequently the case that economic theory can often only indicate the direction of a given effect *if* it occurs, but not whether or not that effect *will* occur to any significant degree and, if it does, the extent of that effect. This means that such theory is perhaps useful as a source of negative expectations (for example, stated values should not fall as the scope of a good increases). This paucity of theory-driven expectations makes it difficult to establish clearly that CV measures are compatible with those considered in routine economic assessments. It also means that other sources must be relied upon if expectations-based validity testing is to have some wider consequence. Here the psychological and sociological sciences together with expectations drawn from introspection and reasoned thought can be helpful.

Expectations-based validity testing is typically approached on two fronts; bid function analysis and simple cross tabulations and related testing of data. The estimation of a bid function relating WTP or WTA response to a variety of covariates collected in the survey allows the inspection of whether variables for which there are prior expectations prove to be both significant in determining valuation responses and affect those responses in the manner expected. If crucial variables are found to be either insignificant or, even more importantly, affect stated values in an unexpected and inexplicable way, this mitigates against the theoretical validity of results. If values are being determined by unexpected factors, then this may raise further questions regarding validity or indicate that the processes determining stated values are more complex than realised and/or these unexpected predictors are proxies for significant omitted variables. The overall explanatory power of estimated bid functions is a further indicator of theoretical validity, although interpretation of fit statistics is somewhat of an art. Rough guidelines regarding threshold levels of fit can be found in the literature; however, many researchers prefer instead to emphasise the need for logical and significant relationships between the response variable and expected predictors. Nevertheless, very low levels of explanation should usually be treated as a negative reflection on the theoretical validity of a study (see Chapter 5).

The use of cross tabulations and other simple analyses[8] to examine expected or possible relationships between variables is useful both as a precursor to estimating a comprehensive bid function and as a direct contribution to the analysis of theoretical validity (Arrow et al., 1993). While the controlled assessment of any one single factor upon another can only strictly be achieved through specific techniques such as multiple regression, cross tabulations often provide a readily comprehended insight into data relations.

To illustrate, consider the case of a CV study of the open-access recreation benefits provided by a seaside beach. Here a reasonable cross tabulation investigation might examine the WTP distributions of locals and holiday-makers. If the study was specifically focussed upon bathing water quality at the beach, a further division of both groups of respondents according to whether they ever swam in the water off the beach would again provide a useful insight into valuation responses. This example can also be used to illustrate just how difficult it might be to formulate prior expectations regarding valuation results. It might be that, prior to the study, WTP is expected to be positively linked to use of the good and consequently that local residents will have the highest WTP as they enjoy the benefits of the beach year round.

However, the study may find that the opposite is true, because the values of local residents are primarily driven not by use but by equity concerns that holidaymakers are the cause of low bathing water quality and therefore that they should pay more for the benefits under assessment. Indeed, further examination might show that those who bathe in the sea most often have the very lowest WTP, not because they do not value the resource but because they are of the firm belief that the sea is already clean enough. Simple cross tabulation may be confounded by a variety of conflicting factors and therefore should always be used in an intelligent and discriminating fashion in conjunction with the findings of bid function analysis.

The remainder of this section is divided into those expectations which may be derived from economic theory and those which may be derived from prior intuition and observed empirical regularities.

Theoretical expectations
In this section we review those expectations which can be derived from economic theory and consider the extent to which these can provide a basis for validity testing (also see Chapter 5).

Price of the good   Perhaps the most fundamental of all the expectations afforded by economic theory is that as the price of a good increases then, *ceteris paribus*, consumption of that good should fall. Dichotomous choice elicitation format in effect provides highly powerful, split-sample tests of this expectation. In a WTP experiment, as bid levels rise between randomly selected sub-samples of respondents the expectation will be that the proportion of respondents agreeing to pay that bid amount will fall. Conversely, in a WTA study acceptance rates should rise with increasing compensation amounts. All WTP studies of a reasonable quality have managed to achieve this result.[9] Indeed, the price variable is typically the most highly significant predictor of WTP response in a CV study.

It should be made clear that responsiveness to price does not equate to some criterion test of validity. Indeed, no theoretical test can provide such evidence, as all that can be concluded is that such results are consistent with expectations. It could still be that stated values are biased indicators of actual values. Nevertheless, the fact that WTP responses pass this particularly important theoretical test so completely is important.

Respondent's income   Positive associations between stated values and the respondent's disposable income are to be expected. However, the size and significance of these relationships is unclear. McFadden and Leonard (1993) assert that the income elasticity of consumption should be high and usually exceed unity. However, Hanemann (1996) shows that this is not the case for other public goods and argues that there is no obvious reason why this should be the case for environmental goods.

Inappropriate expectations frequently arise from the common confusion of the *income elasticity of demand*; a measure based on varying quantity, and the *income elasticity of WTP*, a measure based upon holding the quantity fixed. Flores and Carson (1997) show that these two types of income elasticity are fundamentally different. The income elasticity of demand shows how the quantity demanded increases as income increases, while the income elasticity of WTP looks at how WTP for a fixed quantity of the good changes as income increases. Flores and Carson show that for any fixed value of the income elasticity of demand, the income elasticity of WTP can differ significantly in magnitude and will in many cases be substantially less than one, a result which conforms to empirical findings (Kriström and Reira, 1996).

Scope and embedding   The terms 'scope' and 'embedding' (or nesting) are often used interchangeably, although there is an important distinction to be drawn between them (Carson and Mitchell, 1995):

- *Scope* concerns a change in just one argument of a multivariate utility function. For example, a change in the scope of a good occurs when the quantity of that good increases or decreases, say, when we move from considering a project which will preserve 100 hectares of a given wetland to another project which will preserve 150 hectares of that same wetland.
- *Embedding* concerns changes to two or more arguments within a multivariate utility function. For example, when we move from considering a project to preserve 100 hectares of a given wetland to another which will preserve the same 100 hectares of wetland plus 50 hectares of woodland we can state that the former project is perfectly embedded within the latter.

Concerns regarding embedding arise from 'the frequent finding that WTP for a good is approximately the same for a more inclusive good' (Fisher, 1996, p. 19). Although Carson (1997) argues that there is not general insensitivity to scope in CV, there is certainly a general problem with respect to scope insensitivity to small risk changes and this is as expected given the similar lack of responsiveness to small risk changes in market transactions.

An allied concept to scope and embedding is that of *part-whole effects*. Here, when a set of goods (the 'parts') are valued individually, the sum may exceed that for the same set of goods valued together (the 'whole'). If the part goods have differing attributes, then this can be thought of as an embedding phenomenon. However, if all parts were the same good (possibly of differing sizes), then this could be classed as a scope effect.

The key issue is whether or not to incorporate tests into a survey design in order to see how far responses are sensitive to the scope of the good being valued. While it might seem generally desirable to conduct such tests, there is also a need to avoid overloading the study design. Thus scope tests should not be considered a compulsory part of all CV studies irrespective of the study context.[10] Rather, the following issues should be borne in mind when reaching a judgement:

- the nature of the good under consideration, that is, whether scope problems (the issue of scope is discussed in Section 4.2.2) are thought likely to arise (for example, in studies estimating the value of preventing fatalities through inspection of valuation responses to changes in low probability risks); whether scope tests are relevant and feasible (for example, for unique goods which cannot credibly be divided such tests may not be applicable);
- the scale of the issue (modest studies of relatively low value and/or local resources probably do not warrant scope tests);
- the scale of the study, that is, small, medium or large-scale study; and
- the relevant policy context and objective (if a study is required in a short timescale or for a decision for which a scale effect has little relevance).

Consideration of these factors should indicate whether a scope test may be useful (also see Chapter 4 on how to integrate these concerns in questionnaire design). Studies that are deemed to require but then fail a scope test should be treated with caution. Box 8.2 illustrates insensitivity to scope in the context of risk reduction.

Sequencing   An alternative to undertaking a series of independent valuation studies of a variety of goods is to value all of them together within one study. One way of doing this is to present the respondent with a series or *sequence of goods* in which the policy package is built up incrementally, with valuations being sought at each stage. To the extent that the goods under valuation at any given stage are either more or less inclusive sets of previously presented goods, there can be either '*bottom-up*' or '*top-down*' sequences. In the former a 'small' package of goods is progressively added to, while in the latter a 'large' package of goods is progressively reduced in size. Economic theory suggests that the particular values obtained should vary with the

BOX 8.2   SCOPE AND RISK REDUCTION

Evidence of insensitivity to scope comes from several SP studies in the safety field. For example, in a CV study involving a nationally representative sample survey commissioned by the then UK Department of Transport and carried out in Great Britain in 1982, 34 per cent of respondents gave the same non-zero willingness to pay response to two questions, one of which involved a 5 in 100,000 reduction in the annual risk of a fatal car accident and the other a 2 in 100,000 reduction. A further 13 per cent of respondents gave the same zero willingness to pay response to these two questions – see Jones-Lee (1989) Ch. 4. Similar findings are reported in Smith and Desvousges (1987); Jones-Lee et al. (1995); Desaigues and Rabl (1995).

Beattie et al. (1998) conducted a regression analysis of 26 contingent valuation studies to see if WTP varies directly with the size of risk. Their equation was:

$$\text{Log}_{10}\text{VOSL} = 4.57 - 0.52 \cdot \text{log}_{10}\text{RISK REDUCTION.}$$

Both coefficients were found to be statistically significant. The relevant statistic is the coefficient –0.52. If the value of risk reduction (VOSL) was very sensitive to the size of risk, one would expect this coefficient to be close to zero, whilst complete insensitivity would produce a coefficient of minus unity. The coefficient of –0.52 therefore suggests that risk values are only partially affected by the size of risk.

In a separate review, Hammitt and Graham (1999) bear out the Beattie et al. results. Of 14 CV studies, they found that 6 revealed WTP to be related to the size of risks of fatality, and 2 showed no significant relationship. In all cases, WTP varied less than proportionally with risk. A similar lack of sensitivity was found with a smaller sample of studies that dealt with non-fatal risks.

Part of the problem may arise from difficulties that individuals have in comprehending small-scale risks. Many of the contexts for SP studies concern small changes in already small probabilities. This suggests that risk communication is crucial, that is, the ways in which risk change is conveyed to respondents matter a great deal. Hammitt and Graham suggest that visual aids may help, whereas verbal protocols such as '2 in 10,000 is like 105 minutes in a year' are not helpful. Jones-Lee and Loomes (1999) report on an experiment in which probabilities were translated into frequencies of occurrence, for example, number of road fatalities in a given area. They still found insensitivity to scope. They also found that people were insensitive to scope where scope is defined in terms of the inclusive range of risk reduction strategies. One would expect WTP to be higher for the wider-ranging measures, but a significant proportion of respondents gave exactly the same response to varying combinations of measures.

The results of SP studies showing insensitivity to scope in various forms could reflect poor questionnaire design, but Jones-Lee and Loomes (1999) raise the possibility that the underlying model of well-formed preferences waiting to be elicited by carefully-worded preferences may not be sound. Responses to SP questions may therefore be 'constructed' by the respondent in the questionnaire context, rather than simply being elicited by the process. But not all research reveals insensitivity of WTP to the scope of risk. Romer et al. (1998) report on a CV study for hazardous waste risks in Berlin. They find that WTP varied with the scale of risk and that the relationship between WTP and risk was improved once risk was 'endogenised' by allowing for avertive behaviour on the part of respondents, that is, actions they might take themselves to reduce a public risk (for example, by relocating some of their activities). They used the frequency of occurrence approach to convey the risks, the procedure that Jones-Lee and Loomes report did not work in their case.

sequence. Empirical results are consistent with the theoretical predictions. For example, a common result in such studies is that a good presented at the top of such a sequence is accorded higher stated WTP values than the same good presented lower down in the sequence (Brookshire et al., 1981).

The economic explanation for such results relies upon the income and substitution effects which may occur when a list of purchase possibilities is extended (Randall and Hoehn, 1992; Carson and Mitchell, 1995; Carson, 1997; Carson, Flores and Hanemann, 1992, 1998). If the sequence is composed of normal goods which are in some way substitutes for each other, then the presentation of a given good lower down in the order must result in its value being assessed once respondent income has been reduced and substitutes have been purchased in the course of prior valuations. However, there are other explanations of sequencing effects that may fit less easily into a standard economic framework. Since this is a potentially controversial area, a few simple guidelines can be spelt out to address the specific issues raised by sequencing (see also Chapter 4):

- The use of a sequencing approach should be carefully justified; cost saving alone is unlikely to be an adequate reason for adopting a sequential design.
- Sequencing should be coherent in both questionnaire design and policy terms. Unlikely conjunctions of goods and provision sequences may undermine scenario credibility (the realism of top-down versus bottom-up sequences should be considered). Conversely, if decision-makers have a specific provision sequence in mind, this should be adopted.
- The 'surprise' element of an unexpected sequence should be avoided by informing the respondent in advance of the structure of the valuation experiment.

Economic theory indicates that sequencing effects are to be expected in mutually inclusive lists where each successive good is provided in addition to those appearing earlier in the list. Such effects are not predicted by such theory for a mutually exclusive list wherein each successive good is offered as an alternative to preceding goods. We can refer to any list bias effects in such cases as 'ordering effects'. Simple rules regarding the magnitude of such effects are likely to prove elusive for the time being. See Box 8.3 for embedding and sequencing effects in the context of safety.

Intuition and empirically driven expectations

Intuition and empirically driven expectations are based on the regularities across prior studies and concern the effects of the following on the responses: characteristics of the good, whether WTP or WTA question is asked, elicitation format, payment vehicle, socio-economic, use and attitudinal factors, credibility of the scenario, survey and interviewer, information, budget, estimation and distance.

The characteristics of the good   One of the most basic tests of theoretical validity is to examine whether stated values vary in accordance with the characteristics of the good under consideration. A CV survey values not only the simple physical definition of a good but the wider package which describes the mode of its provision including institutional arrangements, payment vehicle, paying and non-paying populations, who will use the good and who

---

BOX 8.3   EMBEDDING AND SEQUENCING IN THE SAFETY CONTEXT

Evidence of significant embedding and sequencing effects in responses to CV questions concerning safety improvement is provided in Beattie et al. (1998). Thus, as part of a developmental pilot study, one half of a convenience sample of 83 respondents drawn from the York and Newcastle areas were asked about their WTP for a sequence of increasingly comprehensive bundles of road safety improvements, ranging from a given reduction in the risk of death at one end up to a bundle comprising the same reduction in the risk of death, as well as reductions in the risk of three severities of non-fatal injury at the other (the 'bottom-up' sequence). In turn, the other half of the sample was presented with the same sequence, but in reverse order (the 'top-down' sequence). In the event, in the bottom-up sequence 24.4 per cent of respondents gave the same WTP response for the most comprehensive bundle as for the reduction in the risk of death on its own, while in the top-down sequence the corresponding percentage was 15.0 per cent.

As far as the order of the sequence itself was concerned, the difference between the bottom-up and top-down mean WTP for the most comprehensive bundle was statistically significantly at $p = 0.05$, with the mean for the top-down sequence being some 40 per cent larger than its bottom-up counterpart.

---

will be excluded and so on. Despite common, often implicit, presumptions by critics to the contrary, there are no prior expectations about the invariance of results with respect to the wider delivery package surrounding a good. If, for example, the property rights surrounding a good are changed, then this is a material difference in the package under evaluation and is expected to be reflected in stated values.

Simple expectations here include that goods of demonstrably national or global importance (for example, the preservation of National Parks, preventing deterioration of the ozone layer and so on) should, *ceteris paribus*, be accorded higher aggregate values than minor assets of local interest.

Two caveats are important in the assessment of CV values for different goods, the first of which applies to all of the expectations discussed in this section:

1. It is only sensible to compare estimates obtained from studies of consistent and high quality. The finding that a result obtained from a below-par study is inconsistent with expectations proves nothing. This is a very substantial issue which should be kept at the forefront of all validity analyses. Similarly, studies which evoke different concerns regarding the non-physical attributes of the good in question (for example, different distributional aspects of the scenario, different payment vehicles, elicitation methods and so on) should be expected to yield differing values. In essence this may restrict such comparison to studies with virtually identical designs.

2. Aggregate differences may not be immediately apparent through inspection of simple univariate statistics regarding sample WTP. It may be that a certain local asset is of very great value to those that live nearby and this will be reflected in high mean or median values, possibly higher than those given by a relatively wider sample asked questions regarding a national asset.

Aside from the embedding and scope literature, there have been relatively few cross-study comparisons of whether CV values are logically related to the characteristics of different goods. One exception is provided by Carson (1997) who makes a strong argument in favour of sensitivity across goods. Rosenberger and Loomis (2000) examine different types of outdoor recreation. Bateman and Langford (1997a) compare values obtained from a small set of CV studies conducted using a common design format. They found that values were logically related to substitute availability, the degree of provision change and whether use plus passive use or just passive use alone had been elicited. However, as with almost all theoretical expectations, there is no clear guide as to the scale of difference which should be expected. Generally we can only rely upon thoughtful introspection regarding relative values.

Willingness to pay and willingness to accept Chapter 1 noted that one of the most common results found in the CV literature is that the amount respondents are willing to pay for gaining an increment of a good is exceeded by the amount they are willing to accept in compensation for giving up that same unit of the good (see also Chapter 12). There are five main issues concerning the WTP/WTA disparity. First, there is a debate in the literature over how large the divergence should be from a theoretical perspective. It is clear that the famous Willig (1976) paper was only talking about price changes whereas most environmental amenities involve imposed quantity changes. Hanemann (1991) has shown that for well-behaved utility functions the divergence between the two can be arbitrarily large. Sugden (1999b) has argued that under conditions that he considers 'plausible' the differences between the two should still be small. This does not in anyway invalidate either Hanemann's (or for that matter Hicks') original analysis but rather focuses attention on what plausible means in an economic sense. Other neo-classical rationales for divergence have been put forth by Kolstad and Guzman (1999) who look at bargaining behaviour, risk aversion and uncertainty. Second, there are sizeable divergences between the two in surveys. Third, these differences also appear to be present in market transactions. Fourth, following the recent Horowitz and McConnell (1999) review paper, the ratio between WTP and WTA does not seem particularly related to whether one looks at SP versus RP data. Finally, if the divergence is large, then there are substantial implications to using a WTP estimate as proxy when the appropriate measure is WTA. Opinion is divided concerning the extent to which such results can be reconciled with standard economic theory. In the context of validity, WTP/WTA disparities are likely to be inflated by poor design, low scenario credibility, rejection of the assumed WTA property right and unfamiliarity with the good in question. In effect WTP/WTA disparity should be viewed as both a theoretical problem and a content validity issue (see Chapter 4 regarding the design choices based on this issue). Box 8.4 illustrates the WTP–WTA disparity in a safety context.

BOX 8.4   WTA AND WTP IN A SAFETY CONTEXT

The starkest evidence of the disparity between WTA and WTP responses in the safety field comes from a CV study involving a nationally representative sample survey commissioned by the New Zealand Land Transport Safety Authority and carried out in New Zealand during 1997/98.

In this study, half the sample of over 1,000 respondents were presented with WTP and WTA questions relating to a 20 per cent reduction and a 20 per cent increase respectively in the risk of being killed or injured in a car accident. The resultant median WTA response exceeded its WTP counterpart by a factor of more than 8, while in the case of means, even after fairly severe trimming of upper-tail outliers, the WTA/WTP ratio exceeded 3.75 – see Guria et al. (1999). Similar findings are reported in Gerking et al. (1988), McDaniels (1992) and Lanoie et al. (1995).

Elicitation format   Chapter 4 presents an in-depth discussion of the various formats available for eliciting WTP and WTA responses in CV studies. In principle, if it is assumed that respondents have well-defined preferences and that they try to answer as truthfully and accurately as possible, any of these formats should be capable of eliciting responses which reflect those preferences. To the extent that those assumptions break down, different formats may be more or less vulnerable to various 'effects', as discussed more fully in Chapter 12. In any study it is necessary to consider the balance between vulnerability to undesirable effects, the extent to which any desired internal consistency checks can be incorporated, the ease with which questions can be administered and understood, and the sample size requirements and other variable costs associated with different elicitation procedures.

Payment vehicle   The payment vehicle describes the route through which payments or compensation will be effected. An appropriate payment vehicle must be: (i) credible; (ii) relevant; (iii) acceptable, and (iv) coercive.

The payment vehicle forms a substantive part of the overall package under evaluation. A simple guideline is to use the vehicle which is likely to be employed in the real world decision, that is, if water rates are the method by which the change in provision will be effected, then there should be a presumption in favour of using water rates in the contingent market unless this is in conflict with the acceptability criterion. A caveat to this guide arises where this causes conflict with certain of the criteria set out above. In general one needs a plausible payment mechanism that cannot be avoided if the good is provided. For a public good this requires some type of coercive (in the sense that all must pay but in proportion to their circumstances) payment mechanism such as a tax or an increase in a utility bill. However, there are clearly instances where a satisfactory payment vehicle cannot be found. The situation is usually easier the more ways there are for the government to be able to coercively extract payments. Note that a charitable contribution payment vehicle is not coercive, so is far from ideal.

A frequently-adopted approach is to use a taxation-based vehicle as this is often seen as an acceptably just and desirably coercive approach. A problem with this approach is that many respondents may be aware that UK taxes are non-hypothecated. Furthermore, the political sensitivity of tax-raising measures means that respondents may be concerned that contingent tax increases will in reality transpire to be the reallocation of existing tax funds between ends. Here respondents may be more concerned with trade-offs than tax increases. In such circumstances the common finding that tax vehicles appear to work well may say more about respondents' willingness to overlook certain logical inconsistencies of many valuation studies and answer honestly rather than an obsession with perfect incentive compatibility and credibility.

Socio-economic, use and attitudinal factors   In any CV study there are usually several expectations regarding the relationship between stated values and factors such as use of the good, the socio-economic characteristics of the respondents and the positive and normative attitudes that they hold. Indeed, the assertion that such relationships hold forms the basis of the CV technique.

The relationship between the use of a good and stated values is also expected to be positive and vary directly with the particular degree of use. For example, in valuing the benefits of a coastal defence project one would expect the positive association between values and having a property which is at risk of flooding to be stronger in absolute terms than the (also positive) relation between recreational use of the coast and stated values. This in turn can be compared to the values of respondents who neither have properties at risk nor use the area for recreation.

Associations between stated values and reported attitudes, membership of interest groups and other indicators of concern regarding a good can also be reasonably hypothesised. Both CV protagonists and critics support the testing of such hypotheses as a basic element of theoretical validity analyses (Arrow et al., 1993; Desvousges et al., 1996; Schumann, 1996). Arrow et al. (1993), for example, recommend the use of cross-tabulation as a way of examining whether values differ across groups in a manner which conforms to expectations.

As indicated above, the formulation of testable expectations cannot be driven solely by economic theory and common sense, and previous studies are a rich source of such hypotheses. As per the basic attitude-behaviour model, the nearer the attitude in question relates to the good under investigation, the more impact we would expect that attitude to exert upon stated values. So, in a study of a bird sanctuary, we would expect that membership of a bird protection group might be a stronger (positive) predictor of stated values than some general agreement with a statement concerning the preservation of wildlife.

Recent research has examined the potential for identifying cultural groups sharing common attitudes and beliefs as a way of formulating testable hypothesised associations with stated WTP (Langford et al., 1999 and 2000). This has shown that attitudes, as opposed to socio-economic or demographic indicators, can in many cases be the primary driver of stated values. Despite this, the emphasis in many CV studies has been upon the latter at the expense of the former, an approach which seems unbalanced given the paucity of clear and definite expectations afforded by economic theory.

Finally, attitudes will range across the full remit of the perceived package of attributes under evaluation and will not be confined to the simple physical boundaries of the good in question. Therefore, attitudes regarding the equity, fairness, justice and trust dimensions of the valuation scenario will impact upon stated values. Again prior expectations can be formulated and tested, although to the extent that these concerns constitute bias in value estimates these attitudinal tests will simply confirm the presence of such bias.

Credibility of the scenario   The credibility and realism of the good and provision change scenario presented to respondents are crucial to the validity of any CV study. Tests should be undertaken to assess such credibility and examine impacts upon stated values. Because scenario credibility is a cornerstone of the incentive compatibility of any contingent market, any significant problems are liable to induce strategic behaviour and any major problems will undermine the valuation exercise. However, more minor variations may provide useful expectations. For example, if some respondents feel that the good described is in some way smaller or of lower quality than that which will be delivered, then this should depress stated values for those individuals. Similarly variations in, say, the degree to which the relevant providing authorities are trusted, or the efficiency or equity of payment collection, may provide useful predictors of variations in stated values. However, a tension exists between expanding study objectives and the cognitive demands upon respondents, and expert design input and pretesting are irreplaceable in this respect.

Survey and interviewer effects   Theoretical expectations are that there should not be substantial survey mode or interviewer effects. Survey effects will arise where the choice of mode implies a choice of underlying population but if the population is identical then differences can be viewed as biases (see Chapter 3).

Interviewer effects have been detected in a considerable number of studies. Effects may arise as a result of the interviewers' gender, race, education, perceived orientation to the issue and dress of interviewers. The magnitude of effects is variable but is generally considered to be relatively minor. Interviewer impacts can be reduced through the use of high-quality, that is, consistent and neutral, interviewers and screening out interviewer types thought likely to induce effects.[11] A test for such effects is readily implemented and should be considered as a standard feature of all studies.

Information effects   There is a strong body of evidence showing that the provision of information can have an effect upon the values stated in CV surveys (Munro and Hanley, 1999). This is as expected and empirical tests indicate that the direction and even magnitude of these effects are typically in accordance with prior expectations; namely that additional valid and accurate information tends to increase stated values and that this increase is generally more significant for non-use value of goods (where prior information levels are often relatively low) than for use values (where prior information is typically more substantial). In the absence of prior consideration of the good, the provision of information can be justified. However, such provision raises three questions: (i) what is the optimal amount of information to provide? (ii) how is true, accurate and unbiased information defined? and (iii) to what extent is information accepted at face value?

Questions (i) and (ii) are important to the extent that excessive and biased information can produce invalid estimates of value.[12] Given this, the major thrust of assessment of information effects should come under content validity. However, theoretical validity testing (via bid functions and split-sample tests) can be affected through variation of the degree of information and inspection of impacts upon stated values.[13] Similarly, question (iii) can be examined through the addition of survey questions and via debriefing focus groups.

Budget effects   The NOAA report (Arrow et al., 1993) makes specific recommendations for the inclusion of measures to ensure respondents consider budget constraints when answering CV questions. A variety of empirical approaches have been tested (see, for example, Burness et al., 1983, Schulze et al., 1983 and Willis and Garrod, 1993), including simple requests for respondents to consider their available budget prior to stating valuations, to asking respondents to name which current consumption items they would forgo in order to pay for the good under evaluation, or helping respondents calculate the size of the relevant sub-budget from which payments would be made (see Chapter 4). Relatively mild requests for respondents to consider their budgets appear to have little impact upon stated values. For example, prior to a question eliciting WTP for wilderness fire prevention, Loomis et al. (1994) remind roughly half the sample that any money they spend on this good 'would reduce the amount of money your household will have available to spend on the other environmental problems (mentioned) as well as on the everyday products you buy' (p. 502). Comparison with respondents who did not face this prior statement indicated no significant difference in WTP between the two groups. However, Bateman and Langford (1997b) use a more trenchant reminder of budget constraints by asking respondents to calculate the amount of disposable income they have available for the general class of goods encompassing the specific good under consideration (for example, the 'mental account' for recreation goods). Here a split-sample test revealed significant budget effects with those who calculated their budget giving higher WTP amounts. However, it is unclear whether this arises because of a deeper consideration of the importance and amount of money devoted to this type of activity or as a result of anchoring on the size of the calculated budget.

Use of a budget constraint reminder can be justified on similar grounds to that of the introduction of new information, namely that the respondent is facing a novel and previously unconsidered decision. However, some uncertainty exists regarding the optimum design of such a reminder and this remains a somewhat open question (see Chapter 4).

Estimation effects The issue of estimation is considered in Chapter 5. However, from the perspective of theoretical validity different functional forms which have neither theoretical nor statistical superiority should not significantly affect derived valuation estimates. The common result that different functional forms yield differing value estimates means that the assessment of statistical performance is a task which is both highly important and requires expert statistical guidance.

Distance effects For spatially confined goods there are good theoretical reasons to expect certain categories of value to decline with increasing distance. In particular mean use values, calculated across the entire population, that is, users plus non-users, should decay with increased distance. Such expectations have been borne out by a number of empirical studies (Sutherland and Walsh, 1985; Bateman and Langford, 1997a; Bateman, Langford, Nishikawa and Lake, 2000). The collection of spatially diverse data will often be a fundamental element of aggregation procedures and hence the testing of an expected *distance decay effect*, that is, how WTP varies as the respondent's distance from the object in question increases, can form a useful addition to theoretical validity assessments (see Chapter 9). The exception to the distance decay relationship comes when the issue is one of development versus preservation. In this case, the local people may benefit from development as well as want preservation, while the people outside the area experience no effect from development and only potentially gain from preservation. Carson, Wilks and Imber (1994) find this situation with respect to Kakadu National Park, Australia.

8.7   RELIABILITY

The time dimension raises a number of issues for CV studies. Perhaps the most studied issue concerns the stability of stated values for the same good over time, that is, the reliability of estimates. Reliability has been assessed both within and across samples. Comparisons across different samples collected using the same survey instrument administered at two points in time indicate that estimates are reasonably reliable. For example, Carson and Mitchell (1993) find that two surveys of national water quality improvement benefits conducted three years apart gave inflation adjusted values which were very similar to each other. Similarly, the Exxon Valdez study (Carson, Mitchell, Hanemann, Kopp, Presser and Ruud, 1992 and 1994) was repeated two years after the initial survey yielding both per household values and regression equation coefficients which were almost identical to those originally estimated (Carson et al., 1997).[14] Whitehead and Hoban (1999) administered the same WTP survey involving air and water quality improvements to two separate samples of the same population five years apart and found the estimated valuation function unchanged, even though WTP estimates were different because values of some of the main predictor variables had changed. However, while this suggests that in many cases attitudes towards a good may be reasonably stable, intervening events may shift these attitudes. In some cases these shifts may be merely transitory (for example, attitudes to transport safety in the wake of an accident), while in other cases these changes may be more permanent (for example, attitudes towards the gender/employment issue). Therefore, analysts should consider whether consistency or change is to be expected prior to conducting replicability exercises.

Comparisons taken within samples, that is, classic test-retest experiments using the same sample of respondents, across different points in time have exhibited reasonable if variable degrees of reliability with correlations in the 0.5 to 0.9 range (see, for example, Loomis, 1989; Reiling et al., 1990; Teisl et al., 1995 and Box 8.5). A number of valid reasons may explain differences in a given individual's answers at different times. As Carson, Flores and Meade (1996, p. 34) state: 'Respondents may not give the same answer for many reasons, such as changes in the respondent's financial situation, changes in expenditure opportunities, and perhaps most importantly, a retesting effect.' In a more ambitious variant of this type of test, McConnell et al. (1998) interviewed respondents at two different points in the fishing season and found that the valuation function obtained was similar in both instances. After accounting for the differences in the nature of the fishing opportunities in the second time period, they were able to predict the results of the second interview based upon the first interview.

BOX 8.5 CV RELIABILITY IN THE SAFETY CONTEXT

Examples of follow-up surveys intended to examine test-retest reliability in the safety field are provided by two CV studies involving nationally representative sample surveys commissioned by the UK Department of Transport and carried out in Great Britain in 1982 and 1991. The findings of these studies are reported in Jones-Lee (1989) Ch. 4 and Jones-Lee et al. (1993).

The follow-up survey associated with the 1982 study involved 210 of the 1,103 respondents who had given complete interviews in the main study and involved a subset of the questions asked in the main study, including one CV question about WTP to prevent 100 premature deaths by one of three causes selected by the respondent from car accidents, heart disease and cancer. The follow-up survey was carried out about one month after the main survey. While the differences between the follow-up and original WTP responses were fairly widely distributed, the distribution itself was essentially symmetrical with mean, median and mode in the interval (−£5, +£5), the original mean and median WTP responses having been £68.80 and £9.53 respectively. In addition, 71 per cent of these differences were located in the interval (−£15, +£15).

The follow-up survey carried out as part of the second study involved 101 of the 823 respondents who had participated in the main study and again included a subset of the questions asked in the main study, including two CV questions for approximately half of the sample and two standard gamble questions for the other half. As in the 1982 study follow-up survey, differences between follow-up and original responses were fairly widely spread, though again the distributions for the CV and standard gamble questions were both broadly symmetrical with central tendency measures at or close to zero.

Another issue concerns the responsiveness of stated values to the specified payment period, that is, the period over which payments might be made. Empirical studies suggest that significant sensitivity can be observed. However, simple relationships should not be expected. For example, budget constraints and time preference should mean that a lump-sum payment covering

10 years of benefits should be significantly lower than 10 times the annual WTP stated for the same benefits. Again empirical evidence supports such an expectation (see, for example, Bateman et al., 1992).

A further issue concerns the stability of stated values with respect to the amount of time respondents are given to consider their response. Empirical studies from the developing world have shown that increasing the amount of time which respondents have can substantially change stated values, typically by reducing them (Whittington et al., 1992 and Lauria et al., 1999). Such results do not appear to be inconsistent with theory as the extra time can presumably be used to gather extra information or consider other existing expenditure commitments further. If the difference in values is primarily due to such additional information, then neither the immediate nor delayed response can be considered invalid. Two caveats should be noted. First, from a relative perspective the decisions that these studies consider are quite large and to be incurred over a long time frame relative to the CV surveys and goods in developed countries. Second, much of what appears to be taking place is an internal household discussion on household priorities for a very large purchase. Disagreement in such a case tends to move the numbers downward. In a developing country, if the commitment to a good offered in a CV survey is smaller, there is likely to be less disagreement over its desirability and there is typically random selection of respondents within the household with the notion that each responsible member can 'vote' independently. However, given that economic theory emphasises the importance of information in decision-making it would seem that the delayed, considered values are preferable for policy use. Where feasible, allowing respondents sufficient time to think seems a desirable feature in any CV study.

There are a number of open issues regarding reliability. Kahneman and Knetsch (1992) question the responsiveness of stated values to the temporal distribution of contingent benefits and costs.[15] Similarly, there is a relative lack of studies examining how stated values may respond to scenarios concerning different goods distributed over time (for example, trade-offs of current road risks against future acute air pollution mortality effects). Further research into such issues is needed. An example of follow-up surveys in a developed country context is provided in Box 8.5.

8.8   SUMMARY OF FACTORS RELEVANT TO DETERMINING VALIDITY AND RELIABILITY

The recent debate surrounding the use of CV is, to some degree, simply a reflection of the large sums at stake in major environmental decisions involving non-use values and the distrust that some critics have for information collected from surveys. In an academic context, that debate has often been healthy. CV research has matured as a result of the spotlight that has been placed upon it. The theoretical foundation underlying CV has been elaborated and many problems of empirical measurement usually ignored or avoided by economists have been highlighted by its use forcing such economists to think much more deeply about what the underlying theory says about the provision of environmental amenities. As Smith (2000) recently pointed out, 'Contingent valuation has prompted the most serious investigation of individual preferences ever undertaken in economics.'

A long-standing issue with CV is that it seems to many like an easy, even trivial, task to ask people what they are willing to pay for a good. Many CV critics fail to appreciate the difficulty of asking such a question. If preferences can be measured by asking people survey questions, then the CV critics effectively argue that it should not matter how implausible the questions are to respondents or how many counterfactuals the respondent is told to 'suppose'. Given that premise, if the responses to such questions are deemed implausible, or violate economic theory in some fashion, CV, as an approach, is deemed to be flawed. However, the results of a survey question should not be given a direct economic interpretation unless the good to be valued is clearly explained, its delivery to the public made plausible, and a realistic expectation of payment created. A valid and reliable CV survey is neither simple nor inexpensive to implement. Indeed, the key objective in terms of methodological development should shift to trying to determine how to reduce the cost of conducting CV studies while still maintaining most of the quality of the very best studies now being conducted. Development and research along these lines will be crucial in effectively incorporating the public's preferences into the environmental decision-making arena.

The factors that should be considered in assessing the validity and reliability of any given CV study are summarised below.

8.8.1 Consequential and Inconsequential Questions

Studies should establish whether respondents feel that the valuation question is of some consequence in that they care about the outcome of the study and believe their response may influence the actions of relevant agencies. A brief typology of inconsequential questions includes:

- questions that, from the respondents' perspective, are being asked of a population/location which is clearly unlikely to be of interest for the relevant agency seeking input;

- questions that provide an unreasonably brief description of the good concerned or the conditions of its provision;
- scenarios in which the hypothesised change in provision is implausible; and
- scenarios where the change in provision is hypothesised to incur implausible costs (either too high or too low).

8.8.2   Content/Face Validity

Face validity assessments provide the crucial first hurdle for any CV study. This assesses whether the CV study asked the right questions in a clear, understandable, sensible and appropriate manner with which to obtain a valid value estimate. Studies should be assessed against the full list of pertinent considerations set out above. In summary, the key questions to be asked here include:

- Is the good offered clearly specified to and understood by respondents?
- Is the information provided adequate and reasonable to describe the provision change and payment scenario?
- Are substitutes and the consequences of non-payment adequately described?
- Is the chosen welfare measure appropriate?
- Is the chosen elicitation format appropriate?
- Is the method of provision (and allied institutional arrangements) plausible?
- Are respondents likely to have an expectation of having to pay for the good if it is provided?
- Are respondents likely to feel that they are providing an input to the decision-making process?
- Has the correct population been identified and adequately sampled?
- Is the choice of survey mode appropriate?
- Has the survey administration and data preparation been conducted to a sufficiently high standard?
- Does the questionnaire design collect adequate data concerning predictor variables to permit construct validity testing (including the elicitation of attitude and response reason data)?

More general assessments of the questionnaire design process should also be undertaken, including considerations of the pre- and post-survey analyses undertaken to assist design of the instrument and understanding of responses.

8.8.3 Indicators of Low Content Validity

A number of indicators of low content validity may be examined within which the following should be included:

- inadequate sample size or poor coverage of the relevant population;
- non-stratified or biased sampling methods (where the representativeness of the sample is an issue, for example, for predictive or aggregation purposes);
- high survey or item non-response rates;
- large numbers of 'protest' bids;
- prevalence of free-riding behaviour;
- high numbers of infeasibly large bids;
- inadequate responsiveness to the scope of the good in question;
- the valuation scenario and corresponding valuation task is poorly understood and/or has low credibility;
- the provision change description is poorly understood and/or has low credibility;
- the relevant authorities are not trusted or considered to be of low competence/efficiency;
- low explanation of responses in terms of theoretical or other expectations; and
- survey or post-survey respondents provide answers which indicate that strategic behaviour may have affected responses.

8.8.4 Construct Validity: Convergent Validity

Convergent validity assessments compare the findings of a given CV study with other measures obtained from previous studies or from other methods. This chapter has highlighted three approaches:

1. Comparison with results from other methods (for example, travel cost or hedonic pricing).
2. Comparison with results from other CV studies (for example, via meta-analysis and BT assessments).
3. Comparisons with simulated markets.

It seems reasonable to expect that even modest CV studies should conduct some degree of convergent validity testing.

8.8.5   Construct Validity: Expectations-based Validity

Expectations-based testing will frequently be the major form of validity testing conducted upon any given study. High quality and appropriate use of data analysis techniques should be demonstrated in the conduct of these tests.

In order to enhance clarity of exposition our discussion has separated out those expectations, which are derived from economic theory from those which are driven by intuition and empirical regularities. From the former we would expect a high-quality study to undertake analyses of the impact upon stated values of:

- the price of the good;
- respondent income; and
- the scope (optional) and embedding of the good.

A somewhat richer set of expectations can be derived from intuition and consideration of observed empirical regularities. Full consideration of these factors is given above. However, studies should at minimum consider the impact of the following upon stated values:

- the characteristics of the good;
- the chosen elicitation method, payment vehicle and payment unit;
- use and attitudinal factors;
- survey and interviewer effects;
- information effects,
- budget and substitution effects; and
- estimation effects.

8.8.6   Reliability

Reliability exercises typically entail the repetition of studies at different points in time and so are not considered to be a reasonable requirement for each individual study. The literature to date is on the whole supportive of the temporal reliability of CV results; however, there is an ongoing debate and the reliability issue should not be overlooked as a vital part of any future programme of research.

NOTES

1. In the case of new goods such values are inherently *a priori* unknown (e.g. prior to the introduction of the video recorder individuals could not have values for such a good. This did not prevent them determining such values when such a choice became available).

2. For a subset of respondents the opposite reaction might occur, i.e. indignation at the lack of an explicit payment principle question resulting in a refusal to pay/accept compensation irrespective of whether this reflects underlying preferences.

3. Bateman, Brower, Cubitt, Langford, Munro, Starmer and Sugden (2000) show that respondent perceptions of a natural unit of account vary with both the composition and age structure of the household.

4. In a 1991 split-sample study investigating elicitation format and payment vehicle effects upon WTP for informal woodland recreation in the UK, Bateman (1996) includes a subsample which was presented with a community charge ('poll tax') vehicle. This resulted in a highly bimodal distribution of responses reflecting the mixture of support and condemnation of the payment vehicle but revealing little regarding the value of the good in question. This distribution differed very substantially from those obtained using other vehicles such as general taxation.

5. Incentives for strategic behaviour arise when respondents feel that their valuation response will not directly translate into an exactly equivalent payment amount (the expected cost) and that the latter will be determined via some population statistic such as the sample mean. If respondents feel that their personal WTP exceeds the expected cost, then they have an incentive towards strategic overstatement of WTP. Conversely, where expected cost exceeds personal WTP they have an incentive to understate their WTP to the point where a zero WTP response may become optimal.

6. Early comparisons include Knetsch and Davis (1966), Thayer (1981) and Brookshire et al. (1981). Note that for open-access recreation studies the CV and TC techniques require a heavily overlapping set of predictor variables and the design of a common questionnaire to facilitate the execution of both methods is relatively straightforward.

7. There are CV meta-analyses on other topics such as outdoor recreation (see Rosenberger and Loomis, 2000) and 'scope' tests for CV estimates (see Smith et al., 1996).

8. Other simple tests include correlations and restricted variable models. For example, in a dichotomous choice experiment one might wish to estimate a series of two variable models in which valuation responses are related to bid level (as the likely dominant predictor) and one further predictor, the choice of the latter variable being iterated through the data set.

9. Note that the evidence from WTA studies is more equivocal. Bateman, Langford, Munro, Starmer and Sugden (2000) test all four Hicksian welfare measures (see Table 4.3) for which the bid amount variable was highly significant in both payment scenarios ($p<0.001$) but only significant (at $p<0.05$) for one of the compensation scenarios and insignificant for the other. However, this is an imperfect test for the point under debate here in that the compensation bid vector had to be constrained within the confines of payment vehicle employed (rebates of local council taxes) and even within these limits there is liable to be some credibility problems with the upper range of compensation amounts offered to survey respondents.

10. Note that this is a departure from the Arrow et al. (1993) recommendations.

11. Schumann (1996) suggests interviewer effects in face-to-face surveys might be reduced through the use of ballot boxes or postal responses to elicit potentially controversial responses (e.g. to the valuation question). Carson, Hanemann, Kopp, Krosnick, Mitchell, Presser, Ruud and Smith (1994) adopt the ballot box approach in a split-sample design which finds no significant difference to responses gathered via conventional face-to-face methods.

12. Arrow et al. (1993) are particularly concerned about the potential bias that may be induced by the use of misleading photographs and suggest that all such visual information should be subjected to particular scrutiny and pilot testing.

13. Note that to ensure an unbiased test control group sub-samples (which have lower levels of relevant information than other sub-samples) should also be presented with irrelevant but neutral information to ensure that the overall amount of information provided is constant across all sub-samples. For an example see Samples et al. (1986).
14. The two studies by Carson et al. (1987) and Polasky et al. (1996) discussed previously with respect to convergent validity comparisons with simulated markets also provide strong support for the reliability of CV estimates.
15. Kahneman and Knetsch (1992) found that respondents' WTP answers were unresponsive to significant changes in the length of time to which valuation questions related. However, Carson, Mitchell, Hanemann, Kopp, Presser and Ruud (1992) do find significant responsiveness in this respect.

9. Aggregation

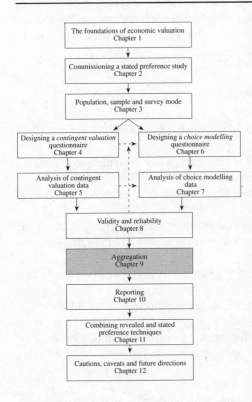

The foundations of economic valuation
Chapter 1

↓

Commissioning a stated preference study
Chapter 2

↓

Population, sample and survey mode
Chapter 3

Designing a *contingent valuation* questionnaire
Chapter 4

Designing a *choice modelling* questionnaire
Chapter 6

Analysis of contingent valuation data
Chapter 5

Analysis of choice modelling data
Chapter 7

Validity and reliability
Chapter 8

↓

Aggregation
Chapter 9

↓

Reporting
Chapter 10

↓

Combining revealed and stated preference techniques
Chapter 11

↓

Cautions, caveats and future directions
Chapter 12

SUMMARY

The first section of this Chapter gives the conditions necessary for valid aggregation and states corresponding formulae. However, most aggregation problems arise because of inadequate sampling design and/or execution bias and these are discussed in detail. Consideration is then given to how these problems may be addressed or avoided. The chapter concludes with illustrations from a recent UK case study showing the aggregation approaches, namely administrative area approach, *ad hoc* user-defined zonal approach and aggregation by nonresponse and bid functions.

Stated preference (SP) techniques secure estimates of willingness to pay (WTP) (or willingness to accept compensation (WTA)) for a given good for each of the individuals or households sampled. The issue arises of how best to aggregate these individual valuations. A debate surrounds this issue. Such debate is justified within its own terms for, as many studies have shown, different 'recipes' for obtaining such estimates can have a substantial effect upon the size of aggregate measures. Problems to do with the definition of the relevant aggregation population, or variability in the methods used to generate aggregate WTP estimates, can result in very much greater uncertainties regarding total values than does the estimation of univariate WTP or WTA values. Fortunately, best practice guidelines can be identified for addressing both the univariate statistics and aggregation problems. The former is considered in Chapter 5, while the latter is addressed here. This chapter considers the issues arising when we wish to move from univariate welfare measures such as the mean WTP of a given sample, to aggregate measures such as the total WTP of the respective population. This task is typically undertaken at the very end of an SP exercise; however, as the chapter shows, survey instruments must be designed and sampling procedures executed in specific ways in order that successful and valid aggregation measures can be calculated.

9.1   CONDITIONS FOR VALID AGGREGATION

The aggregation of economic values is a relatively straightforward task if:

- the population of interest has been chosen (for example, the population of users at a given recreation site) (see Chapter 3);
- the unit of observation has been chosen (for example, the visiting household) (see Chapter 3);
- a random sample of those units has been drawn with each unit in the population having a known and positive probability of inclusion in the sample (see Chapter 3);
- all units chosen for the sample agree to be interviewed (see Chapters 3 and 4);
- all the units interviewed provide complete responses to all questions (see Chapters 3, 4 and 5); and
- the statistic(s) of interest has been chosen (for example, mean WTP has been chosen and an unbiased estimate has been obtained) (see Chapter 5).

If these conditions are met, the aggregation process is simple. If we denote the statistic of interest (often the sample mean or median WTP) as $W\hat{T}P$ and the total number of units in the population as N, then:

$$Aggregate \text{ WTP} = N.W\hat{T}P. \qquad (9.1)$$

That is, aggregate WTP can be calculated simply by multiplying $W\hat{T}P$ by the number of economic units in the population, N.

However, the above conditions are strong requirements and much of the art of aggregation concerns strategies for dealing with failures to meet all the above. A relatively simple digression occurs where the sample is probabilistic but not perfectly random. That is, a random sample of units has been drawn from the population with each unit in the population having a known and positive, though not equal, probability of inclusion in the sample.

The analyst can use the probability of inclusion in the sample to define an analytical weight for each observation i, that is denoted w_i, which sum up to one (see Chapter 5). If these weights are used in the estimation of $\widehat{WTP}$, then the above formula applies. Alternatively, the analyst can define $\widehat{WTP}_i$, for each observation in the sample of n observations. If the data are collected using an open-ended question format, then $\widehat{WTP}_i = WTP_i$, the stated WTP of each respondent. If the data are collected using a different elicitation format, then $\widehat{WTP}_i$ can be estimated from the bid function. The aggregation formula is then modified to:

$$Aggregate\ WTP = N.\sum_{i=1}^{n} w_i \widehat{WTP}_i. \qquad (9.2)$$

Estimates of N multiplied by a quantile of the WTP distribution (such as the median) can be derived in a similar manner using weighted individual predictors to first obtain an estimate of the WTP distribution.

Two common problems afflict the aggregation of survey data:

1. The extent and nature of the relevant 'aggregation population' (those that hold values for the good in question) may not be identified. Here, *who* benefits from the total value of the good is not known (for example, in a use value study of some open-access area, if the analyst does not know how many people visit the area in any given period, total values cannot be estimated).
2. The sample obtained is neither completely representative nor entirely random. Here, how those individuals contribute to total value is not known (for example, in a non-use study of some remote area it is possible that values may, *ceteris paribus*, fall with increasing distance from that area. In fact, such an effect is reported by Sutherland and Walsh, 1985; Bateman and Langford, 1997; and Bateman, Langford, Nishikawa and Lake, 2000). If no information is available regarding such 'distance decay' relationships, then aggregation can only proceed via a series of strong assumptions.

From the conditions set out above it is clear that the underlying determinate of whether a valid aggregation exercise can be conducted is the adequacy of the sampling strategy employed. Guidelines for sampling are set out in detail in Chapter 3.

Unbiased sampling design and questionnaire implementation is a necessary, though not sufficient, condition for valid aggregation. For this the techniques applied to convert marginal WTP responses into a total WTP measure must also be valid and unbiased; an issue which is addressed through illustrative examples at the end of this chapter. Most of the problems (or biases) with ensuring high-quality sampling design and questionnaire implementation and how these can be addressed are discussed in earlier chapters. Here a short overview and references to the relevant chapters are presented for completeness:

- *Population choice bias:* The population sampled is not that which receives the benefits/costs of the good (for example, when in a survey of wetland conservation values, the survey interviews only those walking along riverbanks and ignores all those in boats or in other areas) (see Chapter 3).
- *Sampling frame bias:* The chosen list of potential interviewees is incomplete in some biased manner (for example, when a telephone directory is used, those who are ex-directory will be ignored) (see Chapter 3).
- *Unit non-response bias:* When a chosen respondent is not included in the sample (for example, because they are always out when visited) (see Chapters 3 and 4 for how to avoid it and Chapter 5 for how to deal with it if it occurs).
- *Item non-response bias:* When a survey participant fails to answer some key question (for example, controversial questions such as income are not answered) (see Chapter 4 for how to avoid it and Annex 5.1 for how to deal with it if it occurs).
- *Sample selection bias:* Where the probability of an individual agreeing to be interviewed is related to the construct under investigation (for example, when an individual with a relatively high WTP is more likely to participate in a survey) (see Chapter 3 for how to avoid it and Annex 5.1 for how to deal with it if it occurs).

Neither unit nor item non-response would be a problem for aggregation if these were random occurrences. Unfortunately this is unlikely to be the case. For example, those who have no interest in nor value for the good in question are relatively more likely to refuse to participate in an associated CV survey. This in turn means that the remaining sample respondents hold higher values than the overall population. Unit and item non-response rates will typically be higher for studies where: (i) the sample is random rather than focussed upon a population which is already known to value the good (for example, users); (ii) the scenario is incomplete; and (iii) respondents are not familiar with assessing the good in question in monetary terms (Carson, 1991).

Sample selection bias can be seen as the corollary of non-response problems. Note that a survey which interviews a certain sub-population (say, the users of a particular resource as opposed to the general population) is not, *a priori*, guilty of inducing sample selection bias provided that the limits of the selected population are respected in the aggregation process; for example, sample mean WTP is not applied to the general population and so on. The implementation of such a survey may still incur sample selection bias within the chosen sub-population, for example, if only those users of the resource who value it highly agree to be interviewed.

9.2 AGGREGATION APPROACHES

Once the sampling and implementation problems set out above have been addressed, the task of aggregation is a reasonably mechanical, two-step process:

1. Defining the aggregation population.
2. Defining the marginal WTP function.

By addressing issues such as population choice the desired aggregation population should ideally have been identified prior to the survey. However, the survey findings may in themselves identify certain design mis-specifications. In such cases the survey data themselves become a useful and sometimes optimal source of information regarding the true aggregation population. For example, sections of the wider population which were originally thought to hold relatively insignificant values and were perhaps only surveyed to test this belief, may be discovered to hold quite substantial values for the good in question.

The following sections illustrate the mechanics of aggregation via two examples, the first looking at the aggregation of user values and the second examining non-user values. For clarity of exposition and to facilitate meaningful comparison of the total WTP values obtained, both examples are drawn from a large-scale UK CV study examining values for the preventing of saline flooding in the Norfolk Broads (a unique, national park status wetland in the East of England).

9.2.1 Aggregation in Practice 1: Users' WTP to Prevent Saline Flooding in the Norfolk Broads

This illustration is taken from Bateman et al. (1992) which reports on the results of a CV study to estimate the recreation and environmental preservation value of the Norfolk Broads. At the time of the aggregation exercise there were no direct counts of the visits or visitors to the Broads, which is also the case for a large proportion of other recreation sites. The only estimates regarding the site were the British Tourist Board random household surveys across the country, the expert knowledge of the East Anglia Tourist Board and Broads Authority officials, the Countryside Commission and estimates from other pertinent recreational suppliers, in particular the Broads Hire Boat Federation. The estimate from the Countryside Commission was 3 million visitor days per year spent in the Broads. The Broads Authority in turn estimated that this represents some 1 million visitors (the implication being that each visitor spends three days in the Broads).

A number of adjustments to the visitor numbers needs to be performed before aggregation can proceed. As the WTP estimate was a per-household sum, the number of annual visits figure must be adjusted to an estimate of annual household visits.

A simple approach would be to calculate an average household size (individuals per household) for the whole sample and divide total annual visits by this number. However, this approach is vulnerable to extreme outliers (for example, households containing high numbers of individuals) upwardly biasing the mean household sample.

Another approach is to categorise households by the activity named as their main reason for visiting the Broads, arguing that different activities might defensibly be thought to have differing WTP for the Broads. However, whilst household WTP per main activity category was calculated to examine differences across categories, this approach was not adopted for aggregation because of the extreme variability of sample size between categories (smallest activity category sample size was 3, largest 625) and small absolute size of certain activity categories, with 5 of the activity categories containing less than 30 respondents, that is, less than 1 per cent of total sample size.

The preferred aggregation procedure was to categorise visitors according to whether they visited the Broads for holidays, day trips or for both. This route can be justified both on theoretical and practical grounds. Differences in mean WTP between these categories can be defended as reflecting preferences rather than being mere statistical artefacts. Furthermore, each category has a statistically significant number of respondents (55.7 per cent of the total sample are holiday visits only, 30.2 per cent day trips only and 14.1 per cent both holidays and day trips). Total visits were therefore allocated to these categories according to observed proportions.

The two aggregation processes that are reported depend on the two estimates of visit/visitor numbers.

The first aggregation is based on the Countryside Commission's estimate of 3 million visitor days to the Broads per year. The following steps were implemented:

1. Calculate the weighted average number of days spent in the Broads per individual based on responses to the survey of 3,206 visitors to the question of whether they were on holiday or day trip. This figure was about 14 days per annum.
2. Calculate total WTP: the number of separate individuals visiting the Broads per year is found by dividing the total number of visitor days per year by the average number of days spent in the Broads per individual (3 million/14 = 214,421). This total visitor number is split into holiday, day trip and mixed trip visits based on the proportions of the same in the Countryside Commission sample of visitors.
3. Convert these individual visit figures to household visit figures by assuming the average household size for each type of visitor, again as presented in the Countryside Commission. Total individual visit figures divided by the average household size for each trip category gives the number of visiting households per trip category.
4. Multiply the WTP per household estimates with the number of visiting households. The results show that, using the open-ended WTP estimate gives an annual aggregate value of just under £6 million, while the dichotomous choice estimate gives an annual aggregate value of about £19 million.

The second aggregation is based on the Broads Authority estimate of one million visits annually. As before, these visits were first categorised according to sample results as either holiday, day trip or mixed visitors. These visit numbers then had to be adjusted to household numbers to permit aggregation by household WTP. The first stage of this adjustment involved converting from visitors per category to the number of annual party visits. The number of party visits then had to be converted to the number of annual household visits.

Allowance then had to be made for repeat visits by the same household in order to obtain the number of separate visiting households per year per category. The results show that aggregation using the open-ended WTP estimate gave an annual total WTP estimate of £7.7 million, while using the dichotomous choice format gave an annual total WTP estimate of about £25 million. For further information on what may give rise to such a disparity, see Section 4.2.3.

9.2.2   Aggregation in Practice 2: Non-users' WTP to Prevent Saline Flooding in the Norfolk Broads

This illustration is taken from Bateman, Langford, Nishikawa and Lake (2000) and Bateman and Langford (1997a) which provide further details of the calculation summarised here. The objective of this exercise is to compare different approaches to the aggregation of data and indicate the sensitivity of total value estimates to these different aggregation methods.

The data used for this exercise were taken from a national mail survey sent to addresses across Great Britain, asking respondents questions about their WTP to fund flood defence works in the Norfolk Broads and so prevent saline flooding in the area, that is, the WTP to avoid loss or equivalent loss measure of welfare change (see Chapters 1 and 4 for definitions). All respondents were, at the time of surveying, present non-users. However, a clear division was established between those who had previously visited the area and those who had not. Therefore a simple classification of all respondents as expressing pure non-use value would be erroneous. Such a classification might (or might not) describe those who had never visited the Broads but the remainder were expressing a mixture of use and passive use values.

The Dillman (1978) 'total design method' for mail surveys was followed with the original mailing being supplemented by two follow-up mailings to non-respondents. Each mailing included a questionnaire, maps, personally signed covering letter and freepost return envelope. The intended sample was stratified on both distance and socio-economic grounds, the latter factor being determined through Census data so as to be nationally representative.

Of 1,002 questionnaires sent out, 310 useable responses were received. This response rate is not unusual for such a diverse and stratified sample; indeed, high response rates from distant and socioeconomically deprived areas are not expected. There was very little item non-response amongst the questionnaires received but, as expected, the obtained sample was not nationally representative, being biased towards higher socio-economic areas and locations closer to the Norfolk Broads. This sample self-selection was addressed in a conservative manner by assuming that non-respondents had zero WTP for the good in question (as per Bishop and Boyle, 1985). Of those which did return a completed questionnaire, 166 (53.5 per cent) responded positively to an explicit question asking if they were or were not willing to pay extra taxes to fund the flood prevention measures (this 'payment principle' question was included primarily to justify a zero WTP and thereby reduce warm-glow giving). As with the decision to respond to the questionnaire, the decision to pay for the good in question was positively related to higher socio-economic status and proximity to the Broads. Other positive predictors were related to participation in outdoor activities of the type offered in the Broads. Finally, those who responded positively to the payment principle were asked to state their maximum WTP for the good.

Three approaches to aggregation are considered, each of which is illustrated graphically.

Administrative area based approach
Many early valuation studies defined the relevant aggregation population through reference to some administrative boundary. One of the most common reasons for using an administrative boundary is that the decision-making authorities put no weight on the utility gained by those outside the administrative boundaries. This can be for one of two reasons. First, a politician may only care about the preferences of voters within the political jurisdiction. Second, there may be no way to tax those receiving utility outside the political jurisdiction. Although this approach frequently led to over-simplifications and aggregation errors, it is used here for comparative purposes. The method can be broken down into two constituent parts as follows:

1. Defining the aggregation population: the relevant non-use population is chosen using the administrative boundaries that are felt to be most appropriate. This assumes that *all* those within the administrative boundary potentially value the resource, that is, no account is made of non-response, while those outside do not.
2. Defining the marginal WTP function: the unadjusted, sample mean marginal WTP value is applied to the chosen population. This assumes that the value held by the defined aggregation population is constant at the mean marginal WTP of the obtained sample, that is, those who responded to the survey. In other words, non-respondents have the same marginal WTP as respondents. Sample self-selection means that this is unlikely to be the case in reality and so resultant total WTP is likely to be an overestimate.

Figure 9.1 illustrates the two steps of the administrative area approach as two functions with respect to distance from the asset. In Step 1 the distribution of population is taken (left-hand graph) and everyone living within a certain distance of the asset (described by the chosen administrative boundary, illustrated in the central graph as distance D) is included in the aggregation population, whereas everyone residing beyond this distance is excluded. Step 2 shows the constant mean marginal WTP, estimated from the sample

Step 1: Defining the aggregation population   **Step 2: Defining marginal WTP**

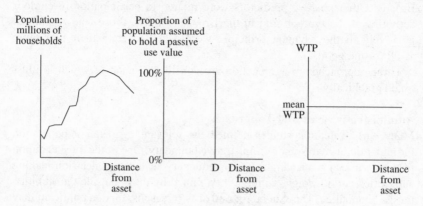

Figure 9.1   The administrative area approach

(right-hand graph). The method calculates total WTP by effectively multiplying these functions together.

With respect to the case study, the Norfolk Broads is a unique asset with National Park status, that attracts visitors from all areas of the country. Those holding non-use values typically come from an even wider area than do users, which suggests that the appropriate administrative boundary for defining the relevant aggregation population for the passive-use value of the Norfolk Broads should be the whole of Great Britain. In contrast, most administrative area aggregations concern assets of comparatively local interest and as such use relatively small boundaries such as counties.

Ad hoc zonal approach

Here the approach is as the administrative area method except that some account is taken of the decline in marginal WTP values with increasing distance from the asset. To do this, *ad hoc* distance zones are defined and sample mean WTP calculated for each of these zones. Figure 9.2 illustrates this approach and comparison with Figure 9.1 shows that the only difference from the previous approach is in the final (right-hand side) graph. Here marginal WTP is allowed to decline with increasing distance. This allows for the fact that closer zones have higher than average individual WTP, while distant zones have lower than average values. Both approaches should give the same mean marginal WTP, because Step 1 in Figure 9.2 is simply a disaggregated version of Step 2 in Figure 9.1. However, this approach does not explicitly account for non-response and is therefore liable to yield

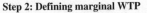

Step 1: Defining the aggregation population   **Step 2: Defining marginal WTP**

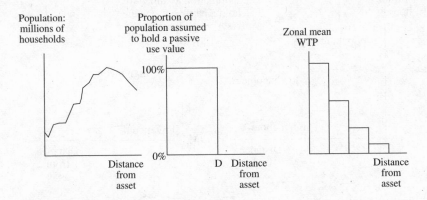

Figure 9.2   The ad hoc *zonal approach*

upwardly-biased estimates of aggregate WTP as it is again implicitly assumed that non-respondents have the same marginal WTP as respondents; a state of affairs which is unlikely to hold in practice.

Aggregation by non-response and bid functions
The fundamental difference between this and preceding methods is that the relevant aggregation population is now determined by the data rather than by the analyst (see the identification of the relevant aggregation population problem, discussed in Section 9.1). This is a particularly desirable feature in cases where non-use values are concerned, as no simple rules can be written down to define in advance who will or will not hold such values. Aggregation by functions also permits the characteristics of the population to play a part in determining both the aggregation population and marginal WTP levels.

The approach is illustrated in Figures 9.3(a) and 9.3(b). The left-hand graph of Figure 9.3(a) shows the distribution of population disaggregated by the two factors which were found to significantly determine response rate; distance from the asset and the income level of the area to which a given questionnaire was sent. The distribution of population and relevant socio-economic circumstances can be assumed to be random with respect to the asset in question. This may not be strictly true. First, most environmental assets are not typically located in the centre of high population areas, there-fore population will usually rise at some points away from the site, as illustrated here. Second, the travel cost literature gives some indication that, for some assets and locations, the proportion of higher-income households may be

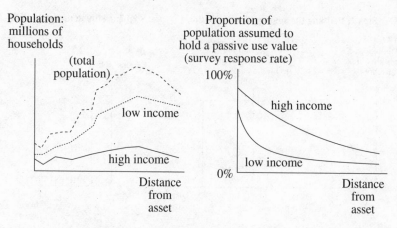

Source: Bateman and Langford (1997a).

Figure 9.3(a) Aggregation by non-response and bid functions – Step 1:
Defining the aggregation population

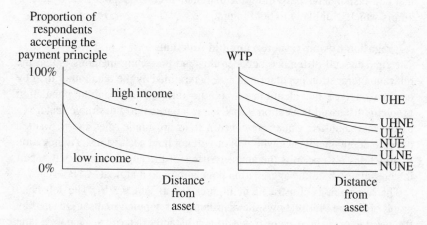

Notes:
UHE = user/high income/environmental
UHNE = user/high income/non-environmental
ULE = user/low income/environmental
ULNE = user/low income/non-environmental
NUE = non-user/environmental
NUNE = non-user/non-environmental.

Figure 9.3(b) Aggregation by non-response and bid functions – Step 2
Defining marginal WTP

relatively high in nearby locations (Parsons, 1991). However, there are limits on this relationship imposed by the constraint of being able also to get to places of employment for those of employable age. Given this, the random-ness assumption seems reasonable.

The right-hand graph illustrates the survey response rate for both high- and low-income groups against distance from the site as predicted by the esti-mated response function. As expected, as distance increases so response rate falls; however, high-income areas consistently yield higher response rates than low-income areas. As the graph shows, both the slope and intercept of these functions may differ across income groups, that is, there is an inter-action between the income and distance effects. As noted, both the distance and income effects are statistically significant in predicting response rates (Bateman and Langford, 1997a). Note that other factors, such as whether respondents had ever visited the site, might determine response rates in other studies. However, this was not the case in this instance. This graph incorpo-rates non-response into the aggregation process. In this case this is achieved through the very conservative assumption that non-respondents have zero WTP for the asset. Ideally, an intermediate approach in which non-respond-ents have a non-zero WTP should also be investigated.

Figure 9.3(b) illustrates the derivation of WTP sums for the aggregation population defined above. The left-hand graph shows the proportion of sur-vey respondents who answered positively to the payment principle question. So, taken together with Step 1, roughly 31 per cent of those sent question-naires replied and of those 53.5 per cent responded positively to the payment principle. This gives an overall rate of about 16.5 per cent of the total sample holding a positive WTP. However, as Figure 9.3(a) and 9.3(b) show, this is primarily motivated by those who live closer to the assets and/or have higher incomes. Therefore, it would be incorrect to assume a blanket rate of 16.5 per cent for the whole country. Such an approach would result in an overestimate of aggregate WTP.

Analysis showed that, in line with expectations, the proportion of respon-dents citing positive responses fell with increasing distance from the asset and rose with higher income levels (Bateman and Langford, 1997a). The right-hand graphs show the relationship of marginal WTP with four factors: distance, income, whether respondents had previously used the area and whether respondents were members of environmental groups. For those who were previous users of the site, as distance increased marginal WTP declined. *Ceteris paribus*, the marginal WTP of higher-income groups exceeds that of lower-income groups; however, a positive if relatively weaker relationship was also detected with membership of environmental groups. For non-users factors such as income and distance from the site proved not significantly to affect WTP; however, environmental group membership was a significant predictor for this group. For both users and non-users Bateman, Langford, Nishikawa and Lake (2000) incorporate this effect into their aggregation by using the mean rates of environmental group membership recorded in the sample.

With these functions estimated, aggregation may proceed as follows for users:

1.   A degree of analysis resolution is decided upon to produce the base area for analysis (for example, Census ward, County and so on).
2.   For each area, information on population and income distribution (or other socio-economic indicators) is extracted from national statistics and the distance from the area to the asset is calculated, that is, the left-hand graph in Figure 9.3(a) is constructed.
3.   The data gathered at (2) above are fed into the survey response probability function (right-hand graph in Figure 9.3(a)) to calculate the predicted respondent population in each area (by each income category chosen).
4.   The payment principle function (left-hand graph in Figure 9.3(b)) is used to calculate the proportion and number of respondents in each area and income category who would pay for the good in question.
5.   The valuation function (right-hand side of Figure 9.3(b)) is used to calculate the marginal WTP of payees in each income category and each area.
6.   By multiplying the number of payees in a given income category within an area by the predicted marginal WTP for that group and summing across income categories we obtain our estimate of total WTP for that area.
7.   Summing across all areas provides our estimate of total WTP for the good in question.

For non-users the procedure is similar except that distance and income are no longer significant determinants of WTP amounts.

Using non-response and bid functions allows the data to define the aggregation population and preserves variation in marginal WTP amounts across that population. As such it should provide substantially more valid estimates of total WTP than either of the other methods discussed.

Box 9.1 presents total WTP estimates for the non-use (or, more accurately, present non-user) value of preserving the Norfolk Broads from saline flooding. As can be seen, both the administrative area and *ad hoc* zonal approaches yield estimates which are very much larger than that provided by the non-response and bid function aggregation method (two variants of the latter

BOX 9.1 THE PRESENT NON-USER'S BENEFITS
OF PRESERVING THE PRESENT
CONDITION OF THE NORFOLK BROADS
AGGREGATED ACROSS GREAT BRITAIN
USING VARIOUS PROCEDURES
(£ MILLION/ANNUM)

Aggregation approach	*Untruncated*	*Truncated*[1]
Administrative area approach: aggregation using administrative boundary to define payee population (no allowance for non-payers) and sample mean to define WTP.	159.7	98.4
Ad-hoc user defined zones: used to define payee population (no allowance for non-payers); WTP level set to mean sample WTP for each zone.	19.1	98.0
Aggregation using non-response rates: to define payee population and bid functions to define WTP:		
(i) using *ad hoc* zones[2] to define distance variable and national income level to define income variable for bid functions; and	27.3	25.3
(ii) using county centroids[3] to define distance variable and regional income level to define income variable for bid functions.	25.4	24.0

Notes:
1. Truncated results remove the upper and lower 2.5% of WTP responses so as to adjust for possible outlier/strategic response effects (see Chapter 5 for why and how to do truncation).
2. These are the same zones as used in *ad hoc* user defined zones approach.
3. Centroids and distances were calculated using a geographical information system (GIS), although any route-mapping software package should provide reasonable measures for large-scale assets (the advantages of a GIS may be more apparent where small-scale local resources with small aggregation populations are considered).

approach are shown, differing only in the accuracy of the distance and income measures used to operationalise the method – details are given in notes). Given the strong assumptions underpinning the first two methods, the results obtained from the latter method provide a superior estimate of total value.

10. Reporting

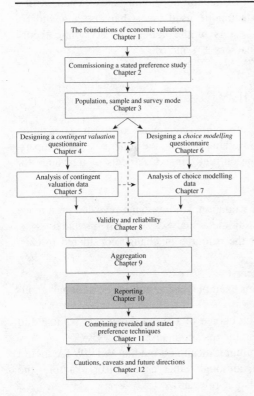

The foundations of economic valuation
Chapter 1

Commissioning a stated preference study
Chapter 2

Population, sample and survey mode
Chapter 3

Designing a *contingent valuation* questionnaire
Chapter 4

Designing a *choice modelling* questionnaire
Chapter 6

Analysis of contingent valuation data
Chapter 5

Analysis of choice modelling data
Chapter 7

Validity and reliability
Chapter 8

Aggregation
Chapter 9

Reporting
Chapter 10

Combining revealed and stated preference techniques
Chapter 11

Cautions, caveats and future directions
Chapter 12

SUMMARY

This chapter suggests an outline for the presentation of the results of a stated preference (SP) study, with a broad checklist of the relevant steps.

Reporting the results of an SP study should be as thorough as possible, covering all aspects and stages of the work completed as outlined in Chapters 3 to 9 of this manual.

For further work, results given in the final report should cover all potential future uses of the results, as well as those relevant to the immediate objectives of the study. In particular, results should be thorough enough and presented in such a way to enable their use in future benefits transfer (BT) exercises and meta-analyses. This guidance is provided in the interest of building up the present literature in a uniform way to inform such future exercises. Transparency of the results also allows easier comparison of the results with other similar studies, to inform on the likely range of possible values which might be expected for a given resource or change.

10.1 OBJECTIVES

The description of the objectives of the study should include a detailed account of the non-market effect being valued; descriptions of attributes of the non-market effect that might vary in a final programme or policy and other relevant information concerning the attitudes or opinions of the population that might usefully be collected as part of a survey.

10.2   METHODOLOGY

The methodology of the relevant SP technique should be explained, with a justification for the choice of technique used (see Chapters 2, 4 and 6). Interpretation of the expected results in the context of economic theory should also be addressed (see Chapters 2, 4 and 6).

10.3   LITERATURE REVIEW

This section should provide a comprehensive review of existing valuation studies similar to the current study. This should give some basis of comparison for the results derived in the current context. Aspects of relevance for comparison include:

- the methodology used for valuation; studies using revealed preference techniques as well as existing meta-analyses should be included;
- relevant characteristics of the resource or change considered in each case;
- the country and site of interest;
- the population sampled (for example, users, non-users, nationals, non-nationals);
- relevant information on the choice of scenario, payment vehicle and institutional context used in the questionnaire;
- valuation results: at a minimum, mean and median WTP/WTA should be given for each group, although other aspects (for example, the valuation function) may also be relevant;
- evidence of the population affected, and an estimate of the total value of the change; and
- the difficulties and lessons to be taken on in the current study should be highlighted.

10.4   POPULATION AND SAMPLING STRATEGY

Details on sampling are given in Chapter 3. At a minimum, the following should be covered in the report:

- choice of sample frame population (for example, visitors) and the reason for this choice;

- choice of sample (for example, quota or probability sample) and the reason for this choice;
- choice of survey mode (for example, in-person interviews, mail survey) and the reason for this choice; and
- the sample size.

10.5   QUESTIONNAIRE DESIGN AND IMPLEMENTATION

This should provide a brief overview of the questionnaire or questionnaires, outlining the relevant sections (for example, attitudes, uses, valuation scenario, socio-economic characteristics) and the objectives of each. Details are given in Chapters 4 and 6. For each section of the questionnaire, the following should be discussed:

- the type of data collected, and why it is of interest;
- the structure of the questions and the techniques used (for example, paired comparisons, Likert scales – see Annex 4.1);
- the relevance of the questions (for example, to help explain WTP answers, to encourage the respondent to think about the relevant issues); for CM studies, descriptions of choices, attributes and attribute levels should also be presented; and
- the structure of the valuation question, including the hypothetical scenario, the payment mechanism and the elicitation technique.

Regarding implementation of the survey, brief summaries of the pre-survey findings should be summarised. These include findings from the focus groups, pre-pilot and pilot surveys and the main survey. For each of these, the summary should cover:

- who conducted the focus group or survey;
- timing and location of the focus groups or survey;
- field dates and locations for the main survey and major pilots;
- brief characteristics of respondents and sample size; and
- main findings and how they affected the final questionnaire design.

10.6   RESULTS

The main results from the survey fall into two parts: summary statistics from the sections on attitudes, uses and socio-economic characteristics (or similar, depending on the survey design) and the full econometric analysis of the valuation results. The former are addressed in Chapters 4 and 6, while the latter are discussed in Chapters 5 and 7.

Summary Statistics

This section should present summary statistics for all sections of the questionnaire. Suggestions of items to include in each section are given below:

Socio-economic characteristics:

- main summary statistics: number or percentage of respondents with each characteristic of interest; and
- an assessment of the representativeness of the sample compared to the population of interest where relevant (for example, national or regional households) or profile of the relevant group (for example, users).

Uses and attitudes:

- main summary statistics: number or percentage of respondents indicating each possible response for each question;
- disaggregation according to readily-identifiable groups of interest (for example, users, non-users) and
- exploration of relationships between variables of interest (for example, correlation between attitudinal and use variables).

Analysis of WTP/WTA Data

Detailed technical discussion of the econometric results may be presented in the annexes. However, the main findings should be presented in the body of the report, including:

- type of data (for example, WTA/WTP, continuous, binary, interval);
- treatment of refusals and protest bids, and checks for any systematic bias in the characteristics of the sample if these bids are excluded;
- weighting procedures to correct for lack of representativeness, if relevant;

- treatment of missing data (for example, for income);
- specification of the model (for example, bid function, utility difference model);
- model estimation and results including goodness-of-fit estimates, including standard errors, t-statistics, (pseudo) R^2 and tests for IIA in conditional logit models; and
- estimation of mean/median.

10.7 VALIDITY TESTING

The different types of validity testing are outlined in Chapter 8. The study report should consider the implications of the following validity tests:

- *Content/face validity testing*: whether the study asked the right questions in a clear, understandable, sensible and appropriate manner should be discussed in reporting the questionnaire design and implementation. Findings from focus groups, pilot and main surveys are useful here. Whether there are indications of the existence of scope, embedding and other biases, the likely reasons for these and how they are tackled (if possible) should also be reported.
- *Convergent validity assessing*: whether the results of the SP study are comparable to other market and non-market valuation studies should be presented by comparisons of the study results and the results of the literature review section. It is possible that either or both relevant market and non-market valuation studies may not exist.
- *Expectation based validity testing*: whether the SP study results are in line with theoretical and intuitive expectations should be addressed in the section on the analysis of the data. If there are departures from such expectations, these should be explained.

Note that crucial reliability testing is not considered to be a reasonable requirement for each individual study given that it typically entails repetition of studies at different points in time.

10.8 AGGREGATION AND IMPLICATIONS

Details of three different types of aggregation strategies are given in Chapter 9. This section of the report should include:

- which aggregation strategy was used and why;
- a discussion of forms of bias (see Chapter 9), whether they occurred (see Chapters 3 and 4) and if so, the strategy used to deal with them (see Chapter 5 and Annex 5.1);
- assumptions used in the analysis, with a discussion of their possible implications (see Chapter 9); and
- an estimate of the total value(s) of interest, with sensitivity analysis to test the effect of the main assumptions upon the results.

The sources of supplementary data required for aggregation (for example, estimates of relevant populations) should also be included.

10.9   ANNEXES

The technical material suitable for inclusion in the annexes will differ depending on the nature of the project such as site-specific issues or technical discussions. However, at a minimum, the annexes should contain:

- the full version of the questionnaire(s) used;
- any screening instrument used to select respondents; and
- detailed econometric analysis of the results (see Chapters 5 and 7).

Part III

Further issues

11. Combining revealed and stated preference techniques

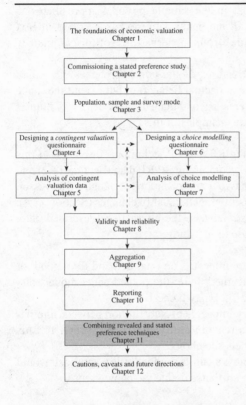

The foundations of economic valuation
Chapter 1

Commissioning a stated preference study
Chapter 2

Population, sample and survey mode
Chapter 3

Designing a *contingent valuation* questionnaire
Chapter 4

Designing a *choice modelling* questionnaire
Chapter 6

Analysis of contingent valuation data
Chapter 5

Analysis of choice modelling data
Chapter 7

Validity and reliability
Chapter 8

Aggregation
Chapter 9

Reporting
Chapter 10

Combining revealed and stated preference techniques
Chapter 11

Cautions, caveats and future directions
Chapter 12

SUMMARY

This chapter describes a number of different approaches to combining stated preference (SP) and revealed preference (RP) information about the demand for environmental quality and how to choose between them. There are three main approaches. In each case, the basic approach is set down and then an example from the literature is provided. Examples of combining RP and SP are Huang et al. (1997), Hensher et al. (1999) and Kling (1997). Examples also exist in the transport literature (for example, Ben Akiva and Morikawa, 1990) and in marketing (Swait and Louviere, 1993).

The reasons for wanting to combine RP and SP data can be summarised as providing a check on convergent validity, a means of more efficient sampling and combining the best features of the two approaches.

However, there are problems with combining SP and RP, not least the level of complexity involved. The advantages and disadvantages of this approach are discussed.

11.1 WHY COMBINE REVEALED AND STATED PREFERENCE TECHNIQUES

There are several possible reasons for combining revealed and stated preference techniques:

367

- As a check on convergent validity: SP and RP data from the same sample can be compared to see whether, for instance, they reveal the same underlying model of preferences.
- As a means of more efficient sampling: in most (but not all) combined approaches, each individual in the sample provides more than one observation. For instance, in the panel data model described in Box 11.2, each person provides four observations of price/quantity combinations.
- To combine the desirable features of the two approaches: we might want to ground SP estimates in actual behaviour, but extend the range of goods and services of interest beyond that currently observed. Studies described in Section 11.2 are examples of this.

The three approaches to combining RP and SP techniques discussed in this chapter are Random Utility Models combining SP/RP data (Section 11.2) and two versions of the contingent behaviour approach: price changes in a Poisson panel model (Section 11.3) and environmental quality changes (Section 11.4).

The key issue is how to choose between the alternatives described here. This choice depends on the purpose of the study:

- Cases where the main policy impact is on total demand for a good, or where only one site is concerned: here, the pooled/panel models discussed in Sections 11.3 and 11.4 may be best.
- Cases where the main policy impact is on substitution between alternative recreation sites: here, a random utility approach (Section 11.2) is best, since it explicitly models site choice.
- Changes in multiple attributes: again, a random utility approach would be best here, since multiple attributes define the choice sets.

11.2   RANDOM UTILITY MODELS COMBINING SP AND RP DATA

Joint estimation of choice models using stated and revealed preference data is widely used in transport applications, although there remain technical difficulties. The basis for the approach is that while people make hypothetical responses to choice tasks in an SP interview, and their answers may not correspond to what they would actually do, RP data are based on real choices actually made and may therefore be more reliable. Recall from Chapter 6 that we assume that the 'utility' of each alternative offered comprises a deterministic component, based on the weightings attached to each alternative's attributes, and a random component, reflecting influences that are unknown to the researcher. The key assumption made in joint estimation is that the difference between hypothetical responses to the SP tasks and the observed real choices in the RP data can be explained entirely by differences in this random term (see Annex 11.1).

Cameron (1992) made one of the first efforts in environmental economics to combine RP and SP data, while Adamowicz et al. (1994 and 1997) pioneered an approach to environmental valuation that pooled SP and RP recreational site choice data in a random utility framework. The advantages of their approach are:

- attribute levels can be specified outside of the range of observed values (for example, higher water quality, better fish catches);
- stated and revealed preference answers can be compared;
- stated preference responses can be calibrated on revealed preference behaviour; and
- econometrically, we can estimate the ratio of scale parameters in the two logit models.

Box 11.1 presents an example of their work for moose hunting in Alberta.

11.3 CONTINGENT BEHAVIOUR PANEL DATA MODELS OF PRICE CHANGES

This method has been applied to the study of the demand for recreation by Englin and Cameron (1996). Their insight was to recognise that some of the weaknesses of traditional travel cost models could be addressed by using a *panel data* approach. Panel data are data where each individual in the sample provides a number of observations. It is widely employed in labour economics, where data on hours worked by n workers over m months may exist giving a $(n \times m)$ data set, with each worker generating m observations.

In travel cost models, data are collected by interviewing recreationalists on site or by mailshot. However, it would be very expensive to repeat the survey for the same group of individuals many times to collect panel data similar to the workers' example. In a travel cost study, each person gives two vital pieces of information: how many trips they made to a site or group of sites and the cost to them of visiting the site. If each respondent was asked how they would change their behaviour if these costs rose or fell by some precise amount, then this would generate extra observations for each individual (for example, we could ask 'how many fewer trips would you make next year if

BOX 11.1 MOOSE HUNTING IN ALBERTA, CANADA

Moose hunting experiences in different wildlife management units were described by a series of attributes including distance from home, quality of roads, access within hunting area, encounters with other hunters and moose population. Some 312 hunters were interviewed in local meetings. Each person gave RP data relating to actual trips, from which a random utility travel cost model could be estimated relating choice of hunting sites to site characteristics. The SP data were collected as a choice experiment: the smallest orthogonal main effects design gave 32 choice pairs, and these were split into 2 groups of 16 pairs. Each hunter thus made choices over 16 pairs of 'hunting experience', defined in terms of the same attributes as the travel cost model.

In the SP experiment, a multinomial logit (MNL) model was estimated. This showed that almost all attributes were significant determinants of choice, with the expected signs. Two RP models were estimated, one based on observed levels of attributes and the other based on hunters' subjective perceptions of these levels. In general, the objective-based model performed poorly, due to problems with the data (for example, collinearity between attributes, lack of variation within attributes). The RP model based on perceptions of attributes did rather better. However, Adamowicz et al. (1994 and 1997) then combined the SP and RP data together and estimated a joint model. They could do this because both were defined in terms of similar choices as a function of a given set of attributes. Differences in scale (variance) between the data sets were allowed for. The result was that the joint model was found to out-perform either of the RP or SP models (based on the sum of squared errors relating to predicted versus actual trips). The authors also found that once differences in scale were allowed for, the models of preferences underlying both SP and RP were statistically similar.

your costs were 30 per cent higher than they are at present?'). This process thus provides a data set where for each person there is one observation on existing trips as a function of actual costs (RP data) and a series of observations on predicted trips for a range of hypothetical prices (SP data). This is a type of panel data.

But what are the advantages in having a panel data set in this context?

- There are more observations from each person in the sample. Sampling thus becomes cheaper.
- The range over which welfare change estimates can be produced can be extended beyond the range of existing environmental or cost variables by including higher or lower than observed levels in the contingent behaviour parts of the exercise.
- Differences in observed and hypothetical behaviour can be tested.
- Individual heterogeneity can be controlled. In panel models using a 'fixed effects' specification, individual variations in, for example, tastes or what is expected to happen to environmental quality in the future, get picked up in individual-specific intercepts.
- Omitted variable bias in the travel cost parameter estimates (from which consumers' surplus estimates are obtained) can be reduced. The standard travel cost model plots the relationship between the number of visits and the cost using cross-sectional variation in the cost. However, if omitted variables cause variations in the number of visits as well as the cost, and are correlated with the cost, then we will get biased estimates of consumers' surplus. The panel data approach solves this to an extent by having exogenously-determined variations in the cost to plot against changes in the number of visits for each person.

One major problem is that if a research objective is to study the effects of changes in socio-economic variables on demand, then the fixed-effects panel model is problematic as it hides all these socio-economic terms in the intercept. The approach is best explained using an example such as that in Box 11.2.

11.4   CONTINGENT BEHAVIOUR MODELS OF ENVIRONMENTAL QUALITY CHANGES

This approach is very similar to that outlined in Section 11.3, except that instead of asking respondents how their demand for the environmental good would change if its price changed, the interest is in how their demand would change if environmental quality alters. Both pooled and panel models can be used, and the advantages are similar to those set out in the preceding section. Principally, scenarios that lie outside of the range of currently (or historically) observed levels for environmental quality can be used, and the differences in revealed and stated behaviour tested for. Examples of this approach are given in Box 11.3 and Box 11.4.

BOX 11.2 FISHING IN NEVADA

Englin and Cameron (1996) studied the economic benefits of fishing in Nevada using the panel data approach. Some 2,002 anglers were sent questionnaires asking them how many fishing trips they had taken during the past year, and how these trips were allocated across different sites in the state. They were then asked how their total trips would change if their travel costs increased by 25 per cent, 50 per cent and 100 per cent. This gave four observations per person: one actual and three hypothetical. They were not asked how these new total trips were made up, that is, which sites the respondents would visit less. The useable sample was 1,395 people giving 5,580 rows of data.

Two kinds of model were estimated, relating total trips to travel cost. The first kind is referred to as a *pooled Poisson* model, which pools all actual and hypothetical trips together but does not use a panel estimator. Poisson models are very common in recreational demand analysis, since they allow for the fact that the dependent variable is an integer and censored at zero. The second kind of model was a panel model, using fixed effects.

The main empirical conclusions that emerged were that the observed data gave lower welfare estimates per angler than the hypothetical data ($752 versus $1152 per season in their panel model), and that differentiating the pooled model and the panel model between real and hypothetical data improved precision.

BOX 11.3 WALKER LAKE, NEVADA

Eiswerth et al. (1999) studied the economic benefits of protecting water levels at a large and important water body in Nevada. Walker Lake is a somewhat unique recreational fishing lake in the state, which is threatened by declining water levels. These declines are due to up-stream extraction of irrigation water for agriculture and are causing actual and potential future problems for fish. Since the range of predicted fluctuations in the lake lies outside those historically observed, a contingent behaviour approach was used. A sample of fishermen was asked how many trips they made to the lake in the last year. Travel costs were calculated for each respondent. People were then asked how many trips they would make if water levels changed according to some scenario. Three such scenarios were used, each with a different implied water quality; each person, though, received just one of these 'what if?' scenarios.

A pooled model was then estimated (panel data approaches were not used). Total trips were regressed against costs (Cost), respondent-specific attributes, water level (water: this could be the actual level or either of the two 'what if' scenario levels) and dummy variables according to whether the observation was real (D = 0) or intended behaviour (D = 1). Results are given below.

Variable	Parameter estimate
Constant	−92.55***
Water	0.024***
Gender	0.529**
Age	0.036***
Household	0.102
Education	−0.151
Income	−6 x
Cost	10^{-6}
Retired	−0.011***
D	−0.498*
D*Cost	−0.239
log likelihood	0.005*
	−2725

Note: ***, **, * significant at 99, 95, 90 per cent levels.

These results allowed the authors to estimate the benefits of a policy to safeguard/improve water levels in the lake. This showed that the mean consumer surplus per trip was $88, but that this would fall if water levels fell, by $11.60 annually per person for each one foot fall in water level. This implied that a policy to raise water levels 20 ft would produce annual benefits to visitors of around $6–$13 million in total.

BOX 11.4 BATHING WATER QUALITY IN
                SCOTLAND

A somewhat different approach is taken in Hanley, Alvarez-Farizo
and Bell (2000). Here, the policy issue is the benefits of improving bathing water quality to EU standards at seven popular
beaches on the SW Coast of Scotland. These beaches have a
long history of failing to meet EU standards on faecal and total
coliform bacteria levels. An intercept survey of visitors to the
beaches in summer 1999 yielded around 400 observations. Visitors were asked how many trips they had taken to the beach
where questioned in the last 12 months, and how they rated
water quality at that site (on a scale of 1 to 5). They were also
asked what activities they or their children currently enjoyed on
their visits. Information was then given on a plan to improve
water quality to EU standards, and respondents asked whether
they would increase their visits and if so whether this would be
an increase in total trips or a re-allocation of trips from other
beaches. They were also asked if they would change their behaviour on a typical beach visit, for example, by swimming where
they would not before due to worries over water quality. Most
respondents indicated they would increase total trips.

A random effects panel model was then estimated on total
existing trips and expected future trips as a function of travel
costs, water quality improvement and intended changes in behaviour in terms of swimming. This was compared to a pooled
Poisson model using the same variables. From this we can
estimate the benefits to beach visitors of an increase in water
quality to EU minimum standards at all beaches, both in terms of
the predicted increase in visits and in terms of the change in
consumers' surplus per visit.

11.5   CONCLUSIONS

This chapter reviewed several different ways in which SP information can be
combined with RP information. The main advantages of these combined
methods were argued to be:

- a combined approach means that the researcher can get away with smaller samples can be sufficient, since each person in the sample generates more than one observation;
- as Cameron has shown, in some cases a combined approach results in an improvement in statistical efficiency;
- unlike pure RP techniques, a combined approach allows for observations outside the observed range of policy variables; and
- it allows for a test of the equality of SP and RP representations of people's preferences.

The main disadvantages of the combined approach are:

- it is harder to implement;
- the models can get very complex statistically;
- contingent behaviour may be inconsistent with real behaviour;
- it does not work in all contexts, as there must be a RP technique that fits the problem;
- there is still limited experience of using combined approaches (at least for environmental issues); and
- a longer questionnaire must be used: this could mean lower item response rates, more protesting and lower quality responses.

When is a combined approach best used? The answer lies in looking at the advantages and disadvantages outlined above. For example, if the policy issue concerned resource availability or physical circumstances of surveying mean that it is hard to acquire large samples, the combined approach allows for more observations from a given sample size. Another example would be where the environmental change being studied lies outside of the existing range, yet where there is a wish to 'bed' the welfare estimates in actual behaviour. However, if a survey is mainly concerned with non-use values, for instance, then there will be no RP approach to combine with the SP data. If acquiring a large sample size is reasonably easy, then one of the advantages of a combined approach is lost.

ANNEX 11.1   Random utility models combining SP and RP data

Suppose the utility of a transport mode j as presented in a SP exercise is:

$$U_{j,SP} = V_j + \varepsilon_{SP}, \tag{1}$$

where V_j is the deterministic component of utility. This will typically be defined to be a linear function of the attribute levels, as in:

$$V_j = \sum_i a_i \cdot x_{i,j}, \tag{2}$$

where the $x_{i,j}$ are the attribute levels and the a_i are parameters to be estimated. As shown earlier, if $x_{1,j}$, say, is cost, then a_k/a_1 is a measure of the willingness to pay for a unit change in attribute $x_{k,j}$.

Assume that 'real' observed choices can be explained in terms of utility in the same way, but that the only difference lies in the random error term, then we have:

$$U_{RP,j} = V_j + \varepsilon_{RP}. \tag{3}$$

If the error terms are assumed to be Gumbel distributed, then, as also explained earlier, the logit model can be derived in which the probability of choosing alternative j is found to be:

$$P_j = \frac{\exp(U_j^*)}{\sum_i \exp(U_i^*)}, \tag{4}$$

where:

$$U_j^* = \alpha + \beta \cdot V_j, \tag{5}$$

and α and β are parameters depending on the mean and variance of the error term. It follows that since this applies to both the RP and SP data, while the V_j term is common to both, the U^* expressions for RP and SP data are simply linear transformations of each other, with a scalar and shift term depending on the differences in the two error distributions. These new terms can, given satisfactory RP data, be estimated in turn. The process is either two-stage, in which a SP logit model is developed and the parameters used in a second estimation based on the RP choices, or simultaneous estimation based on the use of a hierarchical logit structure.

In transport this idea has been applied in the following way. Estimates of the deterministic component of utility, V, are obtained using SP research. This gives a set of weights, a_i, for the attributes. These weights are then used to calculate utilities for each alternative available in the observed RP data set, and the observed choices are used to calculate re-scaling parameters so that the observed choices are 'explained' by the re-scaled utility expression.

An early example of this was in air traffic forecasting (Swanson, 1986). In this case SP was used to derive weights for attributes thought to govern choice of UK airport for travellers in and out of the country. These attributes included surface access time, air fares and service frequency. RP data providing information about the actual choices of airport were then used to re-scale the utility expression to produce a choice model that could predict market shares for competing airports and its sensitivity to changes in surface access, air fares and frequencies.

Unfortunately this method has two drawbacks. First is the obvious one that RP data may not exist; the reason for using SP may well be to investigate circumstances which do not yet exist. The second is that the re-scaling has no effect on the willingness to pay estimate. This is because while we have:

$$U^*_{RP,j} = a + b \cdot U^*_{SP,j} = a' + b' \cdot V_{SP,j}, \tag{6}$$

the re-scaled willingness to pay for attribute k is:

$$(b' \cdot a_k)/(b' \cdot a_1) = a_k/a_1, \tag{7}$$

which is the same as the estimate derived from the SP alone. For this reason, joint use of RP and SP in transport applications has been used mostly to develop mode or market share models, which are affected by the re-scaling, but less so for WTP. An exception is a study by Wardman and Whelan (1998) into WTP for railway rolling stock improvements. Here SP and RP choices were pooled and a choice model was estimated based on the pooled data, in effect assuming that the error term for the RP and SP situation is the same.

12. Cautions, caveats and future directions

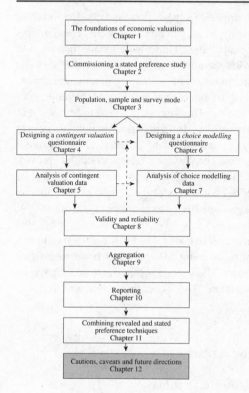

The foundations of economic valuation
Chapter 1

↓

Commissioning a stated preference study
Chapter 2

↓

Population, sample and survey mode
Chapter 3

Designing a *contingent valuation* questionnaire
Chapter 4

Designing a *choice modelling* questionnaire
Chapter 6

Analysis of contingent valuation data
Chapter 5

Analysis of choice modelling data
Chapter 7

Validity and reliability
Chapter 8

↓

Aggregation
Chapter 9

↓

Reporting
Chapter 10

↓

Combining revealed and stated preference techniques
Chapter 11

↓

Cautions, caveats and future directions
Chapter 12

SUMMARY

Although the principal objective of this manual is to provide guidance about how to make the best possible use of stated preference (SP) techniques to generate data which will be useful to decision-makers, it is important to remember that there is a continuing debate about the suitability of SP techniques for decision-making. This chapter sets out some of the salient issues germane to that debate. But first, to put them in context, it may be helpful to summarise briefly the conceptual framework within which this debate takes place.

The chapter starts with a discussion of the standard neo-classical model of preferences then goes on to assess the different results generated by elicitation formats and WTP and WTA questions. Scope, embedding and sequencing effects discussed in Chapters 4 and 8 are revisited and the issues of altruism and reciprocity are also discussed.

12.1 THE STANDARD NEO-CLASSICAL MODEL OF PREFERENCES

The standard economic model underpinning cost–benefit analysis (CBA) assumes that: (i) individuals have underlying preferences, which are clear, comprehensive, well-behaved and reasonably stable; and (ii) their expressed choices reflect those underlying preferences. Thus, when presented with any two options, A and B, it is supposed that the individual will either prefer A to B, or will prefer B to A, or will be indifferent between them in the sense of regarding them as equally (un)desirable. It is further supposed that individuals will be able to express their preference over *any and all* sets of options; and that, if presented with an array of goods and information about their prices, they will be able to spend whatever budget they may have in a way that maximises the wellbeing they can derive from that expenditure.

An important implication of this model is that if some new good is added to the available array, individuals will be able to judge how consumption of various quantities of that good would contribute to their wellbeing. However, since individuals are operating under a budget constraint, they must forgo some of their current bundle of purchases in order to release money to obtain some quantity of the new good. The individual is assumed to be able to judge how she can alter her pattern of expenditure, and how much money she can thereby release in order to pay for the new good, without making herself worse off. Analogously, if presented with some 'bad', the individual is assumed to be able to judge what additional acquisition of other goods she would require in order to exactly offset the reduction in her wellbeing entailed by that bad, and thereby to be able to identify how much money she would need to receive in order to be no worse off than before.

This model is supposed to apply not only when the options A and B are reasonably familiar private goods such as a glass of wine or a loaf of bread but also when they are more complex prospects involving a substantial public goods component.[1] But of course this *is* only a model, necessarily involving a degree of abstraction and simplification, as with all social science. Moreover, in the interests of analytical tractability, a number of supplementary assumptions about the nature and shape of people's preference 'map' have come to be incorporated into the standard model. It would be unrealistic to imagine that such a model – or any other model – will ever be a fully adequate description of actual behaviour: at best, it can probably only be expected to capture the core characteristics and central tendencies of people's preferences.

So when SP studies produce data which depart to some extent from the model, one possibility is that the model is essentially sound and the departures are attributable to random errors and unsystematic inconsistencies. These may arise in any reasonably demanding social survey administered to a cross-section of the population. If so, the central tendencies of the data may be taken to be an adequate basis for guiding policy. A second possibility is that a substantial proportion of the 'deviant' observations may be attributable to flaws in the study design, in which case the solution would be to ensure that freshly commissioned studies adhere to principles of best practice of the kind set out in this manual.

However, a third possibility is that it is the model, rather than the evidence, which is defective, either in terms of some of the supplementary assumptions or else in terms of the fundamental premises. In this case, we may need to consider the implications of modifying the assumptions underpinning the standard model. Indeed, it may even be necessary to confront the possibility that for some less-familiar goods respondents have, at best, only partially formed, relatively imprecise and potentially unstable preferences which do not conform well with *any* formal model.

The sections below focus on certain patterns of response in previous CV studies which have given rise to concern and/or controversy. Within each section there is some discussion of different explanations that have been advanced and the possible implications of those different explanations for practice and policy.

12.2   ELICITATION AND RESPONSE MODE EFFECTS

Assuming that respondents know their preferences and try to answer truthfully, different elicitation formats might all be expected to yield much the same estimates of whichever values are being sought. However, problems may arise if either (or both) of those assumptions break down.

12.2.1   Incentives to Give Truthful Responses

Much attention has been paid by academic economists to the question of how far people can be expected to answer truthfully and how far they are liable to tailor their answers in order to try to manipulate the outcome of a survey. Often this debate involves assuming a population of individuals with highly articulated preferences who can more or less instantly comprehend the nature and purpose of the questions being presented to them; who can generate an answer which is intended to influence the survey in whatever way would maximise their own wellbeing; but which may not itself be a truthful revelation of their preferences. The proposed solution to this perceived problem is to use an 'incentive compatible' elicitation procedure: that is, one where the questions are formulated in such a way that it is in each respondent's interest to give a truthful answer.

A number of responses to this debate about incentive compatible survey design are possible. First, many surveys necessarily involve hypothetical scenarios such that there is no way in which those being surveyed could figure out the relationship between what they say they are willing to pay, the consequent likelihood of provision and the amount they would then actually have to pay.[2] Under such circumstances none of the elicitation procedures will be incentive compatible in the sense usually intended.

Second, some might argue that if only it were the case that the majority of respondents had such a clear idea of their own preferences and understood so readily the full implications of the questions being put to them, then many of the survey design issues addressed in earlier chapters and many of the 'anomalies' discussed in this chapter would be a great deal less problematic. Unfortunately, the majority of the response patterns which appear to depart from standard models of preferences cannot be explained simply in terms of strategic responses, while the kinds of patterns that would be consistent with strategic responses are rarely observed in practice. Nevertheless, some studies, such as Hoehn and Randall (1987) and Carson et al. (1999), do find that the pattern of responses to different elicitation formats is as one would expect to see from strategic and informational effects.

Third, psychological or cultural motivations, such as the desire to reduce the cognitive load involved in answering questions, may make 'telling the truth' the least demanding thing to do. Individuals may also have a willingness to contribute to the common good by providing public bodies with information which is as accurate as the respondent can easily manage. Presented with questions which are fairly straightforward and to the point (even if this requires some suspension of disbelief and a preparedness to 'play the game'), most respondents appear willing to try to answer thoughtfully and honestly. Arguably, such responses may be a better basis for policy than data generated by questions overloaded with information which is intended to give credibility to a scenario and further complicated by instructions intended to meet the formal demands of the standard notion of incentive compatibility.

Finally, much of the debate about what constitutes incentive compatibility rests on standard assumptions about the nature of people's preferences. If those assumptions are not satisfied, formal 'proofs' of incentive compatibility may simply break down. For many practical purposes, then, the question of the supposed incentive compatibility of any particular elicitation procedure may be very much a second-order issue. Much more to the point is the question of how far and in what ways different procedures are liable to distort the data collected even from those respondents who are trying to give the survey their 'best shot'.

12.2.2 Response Mode Effects

A basic assumption in standard economic theory – so basic that it is rarely explicitly stated – is that individuals' preferences exist in a more or less stable form and that (strategic responses aside) the expression of those preferences will not be greatly affected by the procedure used to reveal them. Moreover, this assumption of *procedure invariance* generally applies not only to the standard model but also to many of the alternative formal models.

One implication of this assumption is that the contingent valuation (CV) method discussed in Chapters 4 and 5 is essentially a special case of the choice experiment (CE) described in Chapters 6 and 7. CE presents respondents with a series of alternatives involving various quantities of different characteristics and infer the rates of trade-off between those different characteristics from the choices respondents make. CV studies tend to focus just on the trade-off between goods and money and seek to elicit valuation responses which directly reflect that particular trade-off.

However, psychologists have suggested that the assumption of procedure invariance frequently fails. Some particularly striking examples come from experiments reported by Tversky et al. (1988) which compare choice and 'matching' tasks. To illustrate the basic point, consider the following pair of options concerning the risk of premature death from a road accident:

	% Reduction in risk of death	*Annual cost*
Option A	a	£x
Option B	b	£y

A matching task involves setting three of the parameters and then asking the respondent to adjust the fourth so that both options appear equally preferable. To put flesh on the example, suppose the respondent is told that option A would reduce the annual risk for each member of the household by 10 per cent, and would cost the household £50 per year, while option B would reduce the annual risk by a total of b per cent but would cost £100 per year. The respondent is then asked to say what b would have to be in order to make both options equally desirable. Alternatively, the investigator could set the risk reduction offered by option B at, say, 15 per cent and then ask the respondent to say what y would have to be to make both options equally desirable.

What experimental evidence shows is that the preferences implied by such responses are often not consistent with each other, nor with simple pairwise choices made by the same respondent. Suppose, for example, that in answer to the second matching task posed above, the respondent states that options A and B would be equally desirable if B cost £60 per year. This implies that if B were to cost any more than that, option A would be preferred. Yet if the investigator constructs a choice which tests this implication (for example, by setting the parameters so that option B offers a 15 per cent risk reduction for £80) it will quite often be the case that option B is chosen.

What Tversky et al. (1988) and others have shown in one form or another is that differences between choice and matching are not only numerous but also systematic and predictable. Since a standard CV question could be thought of as a case where option A is the *status quo*, that is, both a and x are set at zero, where b is a quantity determined by the investigator and where the respondent is asked to state the value of y which will make B exactly as good as, the susceptibility of matching tasks to systematic influences and their frequent departure from the preferences revealed by choice tasks may be a cause for serious concern.

Broadly speaking, the reason suggested by psychologists for the disparities between choice and matching, and between one kind of matching task and another, is that different tasks give different degrees of prominence to different characteristics of the options, and thereby encourage respondents to weight certain characteristics more heavily in some tasks than in others. This violates the assumption of procedural invariance. The concern for CV is, first, that the valuation responses obtained may not tally with the choices people would make if asked to do so and, second, that even within the realm of valuation tasks, different elicitation procedures might systematically influence the patterns of valuations they elicit, either because they encourage respondents to place different weights on the various characteristics of the scenario or else because they offer different 'cues' or 'anchors' to respondents.

This concern appears to be borne out by the evidence. For example, comparisons between open-ended (OE) and dichotomous choice (DC) designs suggest that OE systematically elicits lower values than DC. One possible reason is that because it asks people to give a money value response, OE focuses more attention on the money dimension and in particular on the *outgoing* of money involved, which respondents may wish to rein in. The DC question gives relatively more even weight to both the good and the money, and may therefore strike a balance which implies higher money values. Another possibility is that in the absence of any guidance from the OE question itself, respondents trying to provide a reasonable answer may think about the likely *cost* of the good rather than the *value of the benefit*. To the extent that the costs of projects being evaluated may well be lower than the value of the benefits, anchoring on costs may pull the response downwards. At the same time, since DC questions *do* present respondents with some money amount, and since respondents might suppose that this is a reasonable amount (otherwise the designers of the question would surely not have presented it), they might feel encouraged to say 'Yes', thereby causing the implied demand for (and hence estimated value of) the good to appear higher than in cases where no such explicit cues are provided.

Further evidence of the potential influence of whatever amounts are presented to respondents comes from the experience of starting point effects in modified DC and iterative bidding procedures. Strong evidence exists to show that the initial DC-type amount used at the start of a typical iterative bidding exercise can exert a strong starting point effect upon not only the final response (Roberts et al., 1985; Boyle et al., 1985; Bateman et al., 1995) but also upon intermediate discrete responses (Bateman, Langford and Kerr, 1999). Moreover, when some attempt is made to allow for people's imprecision or haziness about their values by eliciting an interval around their point estimate – that is, the interval between the largest amount they said they were sure they would pay and the smallest amount they felt sure they would not pay – Dubourg et al. (1997) found that the starting point did not merely influence the position of the point estimate within the interval, but shifted whole intervals so that the lower bound from the sub-sample presented with the higher starting point was generally strictly greater than the upper bound elicited from the sub-sample who started with a lower initial value. If starting point effects can be observed to exert such strong influences upon responses within the iterative bidding tree, there are serious grounds for concern that similar anchoring effects may occur (but possibly go undetected) in single-response DC designs.

One possible strategy for trying to counteract such starting point effects may be to tell respondents in advance about the full range of possible values they might encounter. But this may itself not be without difficulties, as some experience of using payment cards has shown. For example, Dubourg et al. (1997) showed that payment cards with higher top values tended to elicit higher mean and median values, the latter indicating that this was not simply the result of higher top values allowing bigger outliers, but that the whole distribution of responses was influenced in an upward direction.

One possible way of reducing the impact of cues such as starting points or payment ranges may be to explicitly randomise the first and subsequent values presented to respondents. Using portable computers to aid the administration of questionnaires may be one way of doing this; but an even more transparent method may be to use a randomised card sorting (RCS) procedure where respondents see the cards shuffled before being asked to sort them. It may be that this not only reduces the significance respondents may attach to the first value they see, but also encourages them to treat the exercise as a series of dichotomous choices. To date, however, the use of RCS in CV studies has been rather limited.

To sum up, then, while OE may be the most direct route of all, it involves a task with which many respondents may be unfamiliar (most people's daily lives do not involve the generation of values) and which many appear to find quite difficult, so that they are tempted to resort to other considerations – what the good might cost or what they could afford – which do not reveal what the investigator really wants to know, namely the value of the change in the good to the respondent. On the other hand, the DC procedure which is supposed to mimic best the situation respondents encounter with most private goods – a 'posted' price which they either pay or decline – may itself suffer from anchoring effects and certainly requires much larger samples in order to allow the inference of the desired estimates of value.

Extending the DC process to include follow-up questions may provide more information per respondent, but this process, like iterative bidding, may also be vulnerable to starting point effects and reactions to being presented with further values conditioned on earlier responses. Payment card methods are likely to be quicker and simpler, but they too appear to affect the patterns of response. Alternatively, the set of values listed on a payment card could be printed on different cards and administered via an RCS procedure, thereby arguably reducing starting point and range effects. But this procedure does give more room for respondents to make 'errors' when sorting the cards into different categories and it may require more time and effort to record the data. Moreover, although there would seem to be grounds for optimism about RCS, its use in CV studies has not been tested as extensively as some of the other elicitation procedures, so that its properties (and possible limitations) in this context are not yet so well understood.

In conclusion, the choice of elicitation format requires some balance to be struck between any difficulties for respondents, any difficulties of administration, vulnerability to cues and biases, the amount of information yielded per respondent, the amenability of the data to analysis and the sample size required to conduct any necessary internal consistency checks and obtain final estimates. At present, there is no single method which clearly outperforms all others and a degree of judgement must be exercised to determine which elicitation format seems most suitable (or least problematic) for any particular study.

12.3   THE DISPARITY BETWEEN WTP AND WTA

The various 'effects' discussed in Section 12.2.2 suggest that the assumptions made by the standard model may not be met in their entirety. On the other hand, at least some of the response patterns discussed there could be explained in terms of the basic model being essentially correct, but with people's preferences being rather more imprecise than formally supposed and therefore vulnerable to external influences. Thus a story could be told along the lines of differences between formats and the need to choose one out of the various imperfect instruments for eliciting underlying preferences which are nevertheless broadly as the standard model supposes.

In the following discussion, it should be noticed that the WTP/WTA disparity is not specific to SP techniques. The recent Horowitz and McConnell (1999) review of this issue in both CV and experimental markets suggests that, at least to a first order approximation, the WTA/WTP ratio is not a function of whether the source is stated versus revealed preference.

The various formulations of WTP and WTA and the relationships between them were analysed in Chapters 1 and 4. On the basis of the assumptions generally made about the configuration of people's preferences, together with the condition that the goods under consideration account for only a small fraction of each respondent's total expenditure, traditional approaches generally suppose that WTA will be bigger than the corresponding WTP, but that the difference will be relatively small.

It is possible, as Hanemann (1991, 1999) has done, to produce a theoretical account of how larger than expected differences between WTP and WTA might occur within the framework of standard theory. Essentially, one would expect such disparities for goods with few substitutes. But others have argued (for example, Milgrom, 1993 and Sugden, 1999b) that under plausible values of the relevant parameters it is extremely difficult to generate the magnitude of disparity so often observed. The idea that few substitutes are available for the good in question, which in many cases is *prima facie* implausible, is also at odds with the argument advanced to accommodate the kinds of effects discussed below in Section 12.4 which requires that there are close substitutes available.

An alternative explanation of the disparity is that it is due to some kind of strategic bias. One version of this bias is that when people are asked to state the maximum they would be willing to pay for some good, they may (subconsciously, perhaps) react as if making an opening bid in a bargaining procedure, where the customary gambit for a buyer is to start with an offer lower than their true maximum value and then raise the offer only as far as necessary to make the purchase, in the hope of getting the good at a price below the maximum they would really be prepared to pay. By the same token, when presented with a question about the minimum they would be willing to accept to forgo some good, some individuals may react as if they were sellers at the beginning of a bargaining process, initially asking rather more than their true reservation value in the hope of getting a better deal.

It is often argued that open-ended questions are particularly vulnerable to this source of bias, since that form of question seems more likely to encourage people to adopt a bargaining stance which is not appropriate to the objectives of the study. It is suggested that a closed-ended format where people are asked 'If it costs x, would you pay?' or 'If offered y, would you accept?' would be less vulnerable to this kind of bias. While this may well be the case, it is not necessarily so: after all, if someone is reacting as if they are at the early stage of a bargaining process, it would not be at all surprising to observe them rejecting the first proposal put to them – which would translate into a WTA–WTP disparity in the direction often found. However, to the extent that the closed-ended form of question provides fewer cues to adopt an inappropriate bargaining frame of mind, it may help to reduce any component of the disparity which may be due to that cause. See Section 4.2.3 for further information on this.

Another possible contributor to the disparity which might be viewed as a type of strategic bias are 'protest' responses. If a respondent objects to the proposed payment vehicle (for example, if it is proposed that the good be paid for by some additional tax and the respondent holds the view that taxes are already too high, or are used inefficiently or are liable to get hijacked before they reach their intended destination) he may say that he wouldn't pay anything at all (or, in closed-ended format, say 'No' to any value of x presented to him), thereby exerting a downward influence on aggregate WTP. On the other side, if a respondent believes that the authorities have some duty to undertake a policy, or that the reduction/removal of some existing good is objectionable, he or she may go as far as saying that there is no amount of money that would be acceptable in compensation (a response which would show up in a closed-ended format as saying 'No' to any WTA value of y, or which, in an open-ended format, might be converted to some large finite cut-off amount in order to be included in the quantitative analysis).[3]

One way in which some studies attempt to deal with 'protest' responses is to try to identify them by asking for reasons for the given response and/or inserting preliminary screening questions such as 'Would you be prepared to pay something for this good?' before eliciting a specific valuation response. However, it is still quite possible that there may be elements of protest which are not identified – perhaps taking a less extreme form than a zero WTP or an infinite WTA – and which enter into the data, contributing to some extent to the disparity between the two measures.

A further possible factor may be respondents' uncertainty about their true values for goods which are complex and unfamiliar, whose characteristics and implications they have had only a very limited opportunity to reflect upon. Under these circumstances, it may be that at the stage of the interview/questionnaire when they have to give their response, people may only have been able to go part of the way towards 'homing in' on the precise value of the good to them and they may only be able to say that the value lies within some interval. Natural caution might suggest that when asked a WTP question, they may be inclined towards values at the lower end of the interval, while WTA questions may draw more responses from the higher end.

Since the types of goods which are the subject of SP studies can be those for which most people are unlikely to have formed refined preferences through repeated purchase and consumption, the problem of uncertainty about values is not easy to resolve entirely. While good study design may make every effort to use the time and resources available to give respondents as clear an impression as possible of the nature of the good(s) under consideration, in practice that time and those resources are often quite severely constrained, and a degree of uncertainty about the value of the good might be expected to persist and may contribute something to a disparity between WTP and WTA.

If factors described in Chapters 4 and 8 were the principal causes of the WTP–WTA disparity, the implication is that refining features of the study design could go a significant way towards reducing the disparity. However, if it is believed that the true WTP and WTA amounts should not be very different, what should be done in the event that a disparity attributed to one or more biases persists? The fact that WTA responses are unbounded above, together with some experimental evidence (see Coursey et al., 1986) that the main effect of experience is to cause WTA to be revised downwards, might incline decision-makers to use a single value very much closer to the WTP figure. Indeed, WTP is often recommended over WTA precisely because it is 'conservative'. However, this is clearly a matter of judgement and presupposes that the expectation based upon the conventional model, that is, that there really should be no great difference between WTP and WTA, is correct. Such a view is not uncontested, however.

For example, a number of other experiments, often involving relatively straightforward private goods, have reported much smaller tendencies for WTP and WTA to converge than found by Coursey et al. (1986); for a review, see Sugden (1999a). Nor does the 'caution in the face of uncertainty' explanation seem to provide more than a partial explanation. Dubourg et al. (1994) not only elicited specific WTP and WTA responses but also tried to identify whole intervals between the values that respondents were sure they would pay (alternatively, accept) and those which they were sure they would not pay (alternatively, accept). The picture that emerged was not that the specific responses were drawn from different ends of essentially the same interval, but that for many respondents there was little or no overlap between their WTP and WTA intervals. More recently, a transport safety study conducted on a one-to-one in-home basis, with considerable efforts being made to familiarise respondents with the subject matter and with value responses elicited via a computerised iterative closed-ended procedure, found that the great majority of respondents gave WTA responses substantially higher than their WTP amounts (Guria et al., 1999).

One interpretation of this body of evidence is that the disparities reflect limitations in the standard theory. In this context, the most prominent alternative theory is that proposed by Tversky and Kahneman (1991), in which preferences are *reference-dependent*.[4] The idea is that an individual's preferences are defined in relation to that individual's *reference point*, normally the *status quo*. Losses, measured relative to the reference point, in any dimension have greater subjective significance than gains. This asymmetry is *loss aversion*. One interpretation is that the experience of losing something is painful or aversive over and above its consequences in terms of reduced consumption. The implication of this theory is that each reference point has its own family of indifference curves and that these indifference curves are kinked at their respective reference points.

Figure 12.1 shows *reference-dependent indifference curves* for the same case as was represented in Figure 1.2 in Chapter 1. The solid curves I_A and I_A' are indifference curves for preferences as viewed from the reference point A. Note that I_A is kinked at A, and I_A' is kinked at D and B. The dotted curve I_B is an indifference curve for preferences as viewed from B. I_B is kinked at B.

Again, consider the valuation of the change in the public good from x_0 to x_1. If the individual starts at A, his WTP for an increase in the public good to x_1 is BC. That this amount is relatively small reflects the fact that the

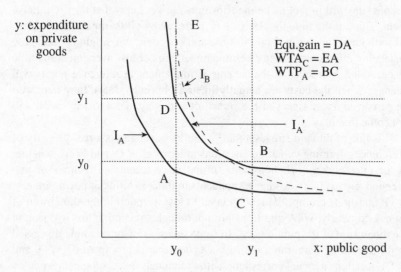

Figure 12.1   Welfare measures when there is reference-dependence

individual is reporting the *loss* of private consumption that would just offset a *gain* of the public good. If instead the individual starts at B, his WTA for a decrease in the public good to x_0 is EA (the relevant indifference curve is I_B). That this amount is relatively large reflects the fact that he is reporting the *gain* of private consumption that would just offset a *loss* of the public good.[5]

In reference-dependent theory, WTA and equivalent gain are not necessarily equal. In Figure 12.1, equivalent gain is DA. This is the gain of private consumption which is just as preferable as a given gain of the public good. If losses have greater subjective significance than gains, we should expect equivalent gain to lie between WTA and WTP.

According to reference-dependent theory, the WTA–WTP disparity reflects a real and robust characteristic of people's actual preferences. If one accepts this view, one possible conclusion is that policy-makers should use quite different WTA and WTP values, choosing between them according to whether the change under consideration is generally regarded as a gain or a loss *vis-à-vis* the *status quo*. However, there are some further considerations.

First, it is not always clear that what CBA treats as 'gains' and 'losses' are necessarily gains and losses in the sense that is relevant for loss aversion. For example, consider a CBA of a traffic management scheme. Relative to the 'do nothing' scenario, this scheme reduces the time taken to make certain trips and increases the time taken to make others. If we classify benefits and costs by trips, we identify gains to some groups of road-users and losses to others. But, typically, little is known about who these people are; indeed, even the people who will in fact make the trips may not yet know that they will make them. Thus, at the time the decision is made, many of its impacts on particular individuals are both distant in time and uncertain. We might expect these distancing effects to weaken or eliminate feelings of loss aversion at the time of decision.[6] Moreover, if the scheme is implemented, reference points will change. When the costs are actually incurred by individuals, they may well be perceived as an aspect of the *status quo*, in which case loss aversion will not come into play.

This line of thought suggests that, while loss aversion is a real property of preferences, framing valuation questions in terms of WTP and WTA, whether in the open-ended or dichotomous format, may accentuate feelings of loss aversion. By explicitly asking respondents to think in terms of paying money, WTP questions prompt thoughts related to loss aversion in the dimension of money. Similarly, WTA questions prompt thoughts related to loss aversion in the dimension of the public good. In some cases, as in the example discussed in the preceding paragraph, the loss aversion that is prompted by WTP and WTA questions may not correspond with individuals' psychological responses to the project itself.

In such cases, there may be an argument for eliciting valuations in ways which do not prompt attitudes of loss aversion. One way of doing this is to elicit equivalent gain valuations. Since these valuations are derived from choices among different kinds of gain, they do not require respondents to think about losses in any dimension. Of course, respondents are required to consider opportunity costs, but in a way that is symmetrical as between money and the public good rather than in terms of losses in one dimension and gains in another. Notice, however, that such an approach does not strictly satisfy the standard compensation test as described in Chapter 1.

A second concern about using a WTA figure that is considerably larger than its WTP counterpart relates to a possible asymmetry between the introduction and abolition of policy measures. Suppose that a policy, for example, a new regulation of some kind, is evaluated. WTP-based estimates of the value of some benefits are incorporated into the evaluation, the benefit–cost ratio exceeds the required level and the regulation is introduced. However, suppose that some time later changed circumstances mean that the benefits, as valued on the original WTP basis, no longer justify the costs. If the current costs and benefits had been obtained at the time of the original decision, the regulation would not have been introduced. Still, it has been introduced and now constitutes part of the current *status quo*; so the question now is whether or not to remove it. Removing it would deprive people of certain benefits, for which the appropriate measure would be the WTA value. But suppose that the WTA value is, say, three times the WTP figure so that the use of the WTA value outweighs the cost savings that would result from abolishing the regulation. Thus a regulation which would not now be introduced nevertheless remains in place.

A further issue relates to cases where a policy would benefit many members of the population but worsen things for a minority. Suppose, for example, that 55 per cent of the population would be expected to receive some benefit, while 25 per cent would lose a benefit of equivalent magnitude. Overall, when measured in 'real' terms, there would be a net benefit equivalent to 30 per cent of the population being made better off. Moreover, if the 'gainers' were people currently at some disadvantage, while the 'losers' were in the upper regions of the income/wealth distribution, the policy might appeal to equity as well as efficiency. And yet, with WTA, say, three times higher per unit than WTP, the WTA-based measure of loss for the 25 per cent would outweigh the WTP-based aggregate value of the gain for the 55 per cent. The implications of these outcomes may not be satisfactory from a policy standpoint. At present, there does not appear to be any evidence which directly addresses this issue. But clearly, if reference-dependence and loss aversion are part of a more descriptively valid model of people's preferences, the prescriptive implications need to be carefully considered.

12.4   SCOPE, EMBEDDING AND SEQUENCING EFFECTS

Chapter 8 considered in some detail the issue of scope and embedding effects and how to deal with them by improving the questionnaire design. These occur when respondents state that they are willing to pay just the same, or only a little more, for a benefit that appears to be much larger and which might be expected to register as a good deal more valuable. Sequencing effects, which are arguably related to scope/embedding effects, are manifested when the value placed on a good when it is presented later in a series of goods is different from the value placed on that same good when it is positioned earlier.

Many studies have produced one or more of the 'effects' listed in the heading to this section. Early examples are the studies by Kahneman (1986) and Kahneman and Knetsch (1992), the former of which observed a lack of sensitivity to values for deacidifying either a few or all lakes in Ontario, while the latter noted a similar insensitivity regarding stated values for rescue services or a wider environmental services good within which rescue services were perfectly embedded. Similarly, in a pure scope test Desvousges et al. (1993)[7] found no significant difference between the values people expressed for schemes to avoid quite different numbers of bird deaths.

From the perspective of the standard model of preferences, there are two lines of defence in the face of this evidence. The first is to argue that the designs of many of these studies have been inadequate in some way (see Hanemann, 1996), while other better-designed studies have exhibited significant responsiveness in the direction predicted by standard theory. In addition, in a major review of the scope and embedding issue, Carson (1997) surveys a large number of split-sample studies and argues that, in the overwhelming majority of cases, statistically significant responses to scope can be detected, with only a handful failing such tests. In his analysis, Carson draws attention to the relationship between apparent lack of sensitivity to scope and the perceived credibility of studies which vary the scale of a proposed provision change in ways which respondents perceive as lacking in realism. In particular, Carson notes that when stated values for, say, a modest change in provision (which respondents see as having high realism) are compared with values for a major change in provision (when the latter change is seen as having lower credibility), then an apparent lack of responsiveness to scope may say more about the change in perceived realism than it does about the scope of the change in provision concerned.

However, the fact that there may be statistically significant differences between mean WTP for different magnitudes of benefits does not in itself answer the question of whether the size of the differences between means is commensurate with the differences between the quantities or qualities of the goods. So the second line of defence involves arguing that even though the WTP responses are far from being proportional to the quantity of the good being valued, this result is not necessarily incompatible with the basic principles underlying the standard model so long as that model is appropriately specified. This second line of defence is the principal focus of this section.

Under what circumstances might the conventional model allow that when each of two goods, A and B, are valued on their own they are each found to have substantial positive value, but that when they are taken together the value for the pair of them is little (or not at all) different from the higher of the two solo values?

It is not enough that they are close substitutes for one another. A bag of ten £1 coins is a close substitute for a £10-pound note, but for most people the value of both together (expressed, perhaps, by the time they would be willing to spend to earn both) would generally not fall far short of twice the value of either one. For the value of A and B together to be little or no greater than the value of either one on its own, we require that either of the two can, by itself, more or less satiate the individual's demand for that type of good during the time period concerned. So if we observe cases where the total WTP is substantial for some initial quantity or subset of goods, but grows very much less rapidly than the quantity of the good or the size of the set of goods, the first question to ask is whether it is plausible that satiation levels are being approached. If so, we should then ask: what is it that is being satiated? And if satiation does not seem plausible, we should ask what else might be explaining the observed pattern of responses.

Consider the much-debated study by Desvousges et al. (1993) where three separate versions of a questionnaire were presented to different sub-samples asking respondents for their WTP for measures to clean up ponds and thereby prevent the deaths of, respectively, 2,000, 20,000 and 200,000 migratory waterfowl. The study is much debated since the WTP question, in fact, does not feature the numbers of birds but a percentage of bird population (much less than 1 per cent, less than 1 per cent and about 2 per cent, respectively). Given this, the results are reflective more of the difficulty in expressing quantities as percentages rather than a clear embedding or warm glow. Despite this, the remainder of this discussion looks at the implications of warm glow. Some (although not all) ways of analysing the data do find statistically significant differences between the sub-samples' responses in the direction expected, but the increases in WTP fall far short of being proportional to the numbers of birds saved. Should we draw the conclusion that preventing the deaths of 2,000 of these birds goes much of the way towards satiating people's desires? And if so, just what desires are being satiated? Are they desires related to the lives of the birds *per se* or to something else?

For example, could it be that what is being elicited here is a willingness to make a contribution to a 'good cause', sometimes referred to as a desire to achieve 'moral satisfaction' or obtain a 'warm glow' or register a 'virtuous response', where this desire may be to a considerable extent satiated by the very gesture of stating a willingness to contribute some moderate amount, irrespective of the particular numbers of birds in question?

If such a 'warm glow' effect is behind embedding and scope effects – although, as discussed below, it is not the only way of explaining the data – what should be done? Should the value of such a warm glow be incorporated into the value of the change in the good in question? Or should some attempt be made to separate out the warm glow component and identify the good-welfare-specific element in people's responses?

To expand upon the point, suppose that a representative sample of people are asked about their WTP to protect some habitat for a class of migratory birds. If a number of these respondents generally favour the idea of looking after wildlife habitats, and wish to express this via their stated values, the average WTP might contain, say, a £5 element reflecting this warm glow effect. Meanwhile, a different but equally representative sample is asked about protecting habitats for owls. Yet another study considers the protection of red squirrels. Another focuses on deer. And so on. In each case, since it is the only issue being presented to them, respondents' favourable general disposition towards good wildlife causes manifests itself to the tune of a £5 component. But would it be safe to conclude from the four studies on migratory birds, owls, red squirrels and deer that if all four projects were implemented, the average citizen would derive £20-worth of warm glow? Or does a single £5 donation more or less satiate the average person's warm glow response for the general cause of wildlife habitats? In which case, as far as this element is concerned, the four projects are close substitutes for each other, so that a total of £20 would be a gross overestimate of the total warm glow value to be derived from undertaking all four. In principle, it would seem that a more appropriate total figure might comprise a single warm glow element plus the four (possibly very modest) elements specific to the four sets of creatures being protected.[8]

What has been said in the previous paragraph supposes that the warm glow explanation is the correct one, and that if it is, it is appropriate to include the value of at least some measure of warm glow somewhere in the calculus. But other explanations have also been explored.

One explanation suggests that particular kinds of budget constraint might account for at least part of the effects. In terms of the standard model, this seems implausible: the WTP amounts stated by most respondents in most surveys constitute only a relatively small fraction of their income. So it seems unlikely that they are coming sufficiently close to their overall budget constraint to cause them on those grounds to be unwilling to pay much more for a greater quantity of the good or a larger set of goods. However, the idea proposed by Thaler was that people may mentally subdivide their income into sub-budgets, or *mental accounts*, for different classes of goods such as accommodation, food, clothing, transport, holidays and so on, and that although expenditure on a particular good might constitute only a small fraction of *total* income, it might amount to quite a large proportion of the relevant mental account so that 'local' income effects become quite pronounced. However, no such constraints would be expected to operate upon WTA questions. Yet when Dubourg et al. (1994) and Baron and Greene (1996) compared WTP responses with the corresponding WTA responses, they found very similar patterns of insensitivity in both sets of data, leading them to reject the mental accounting explanation. Rather, it was as if people were simply somewhat – or in a substantial minority of cases, very – insensitive to information about the magnitude of the benefit.

Baron and Greene (1996) reported an extensive set of experiments where such quantity insensitivity was repeatedly manifested. In parallel, a series of studies considering safety benefits of various kinds produced similar findings (see Jones-Lee and Loomes (1997), Beattie et al. (1998) and Carthy et al. (1999) for details). Consider, for example, two questions, presented consecutively, which asked for WTP for reductions in the risk of sustaining a road injury involving some slight permanent disability. One question involved a reduction of 4 in 100,000 in the risk of suffering this injury, while the adjacent question asked about a reduction of 12 in 100,000 (both from the same baseline of 24 in 100,000). Although it is implausible that people's desire for safety improvements would be satiated by the 4 in 100,000, nearly half of the sample – 178 out of 395 – gave exactly the same WTP answers to both questions, and overall the mean WTP for the larger risk reduction was only a little more than 20 per cent higher, despite the fact that it conferred three times as much benefit. However, this difficulty with low-level risk is also seen in actual market transactions. Thus, it would be surprising to see 'different' behaviour in SP studies with respect to low-level risk.

One reaction to insensitivity to the scope of a benefit might be to suggest that more effort needs to be made to encourage respondents to attend to the quantitative information. Having encountered the problem in earlier developmental phases, Beattie et al. (1998) decided that prior to asking them to state their values, respondents would be asked to discuss the various benefit scenarios in small groups and undertake a ranking exercise. This clearly indicated

that people distinguished between the two scenarios involving different reductions in the expected numbers of road accident deaths and ordered them
in the expected way. Yet more than 40 per cent of those providing usable
responses gave the same non-zero WTP response for both scenarios, with the
result that the mean WTP for the three-times-larger risk reduction was only
33 per cent higher.

Such insensitivity to the quantity of a good means that the estimated value
of a unit of that good (for example, the value of cleaning up a kilometre
stretch of river or the value of preventing a road accident fatality) may be
greatly affected by the study designers' choice of the magnitude of the good
presented to respondents, making benefits transfer more hazardous. In the
example given at the end of the previous paragraph, the value of preventing a
road fatality derived from the lower-quantity scenario was two-and-a-quarter
times the value derived from the higher-quantity scenario. Clearly, this is
worrying, since it suggests that the unit value is highly vulnerable to inad-
vertent manipulation of the study design.

If the problem is thought to lie principally in respondents' difficulties with
processing all dimensions of a good appropriately, and if this is particularly
problematic when the goods in question are both complex and unfamiliar,
one strategy suggested in different forms by both Baron (1996) and Carthy et
al. (1999) is to try to simplify the task by breaking it down into more
manageable component parts. Baron advocates drawing on the techniques of
standard decision analysis. He acknowledges that in its full-blown form,
decision analysis of this kind is very labour-intensive and makes considerable
demands upon respondents' time and goodwill, as well as on the funds of the
commissioning agency. Thus, it may often not be feasible with anything more
than very modest sample sizes and some judgement would need to be made
about whether the higher quality of those responses gathered is sufficient to
offset the smaller numbers of individual observations that can be afforded.

Carthy et al. (1999) broke the task of trading money off against a reduction
in the risk of being killed in a road accident into two parts: WTP and WTA
questions to elicit monetary values for avoiding/compensating for the effects
of less serious road injuries; and standard gamble questions[9] to establish risk
trade-offs between less serious and more serious injuries and death. Answers
to the different types of question were then 'chained' together to derive
monetary values for reducing the risk of death. However, while decomposing
the overall task in this way has the advantage that each component is easier
for respondents to deal with – it is easier to make trade-offs between money
and the certainty of less serious and more readily imaginable injuries and
then to handle the risk trade-offs within the health dimension, evaluating one
health state relative to another – it has the disadvantage that if errors or biases

creep into any component question, they are liable to be compounded when the components are chained together.

A more general concern about using decision analysis of the kind advocated by Baron, or breaking down tasks in the way described by Carthy et al., or using any other form of decomposition and reintegration, is that in choosing the method and implementing it, the study designers may be distorting the results. If people's preferences for the complex and unfamiliar goods in question *are* only partially formed, imprecise and vulnerable to bias, they may also be vulnerable to cues suggested by the structures and constraints imposed by the study design. The need for thorough piloting, the incorporation of internal consistency checks and the careful and dispassionate debriefing of at least a sub-sample of respondents is no less important when employing more intensive and deliberative methods than when using more standard questionnaire approaches.

Finally, possible difficulties may arise from the fact that, for practical reasons, most surveys have a very narrow focus and consider just one or two environmental issues among many that may have some claim upon scarce public resources. The danger is that if the values elicited from each of, say, 20 separate studies considering 20 different (but not mutually exclusive) environmental projects were taken together, they would add up to an implausibly large proportion of average income. Although this issue has received little direct empirical attention,[10] the mass of within-study evidence of scope and embedding effects suggests that if people were asked their WTP for a programme of 20 different environmental projects and were then asked to allocate this total sum between the component projects, the value placed on any one component would be very much lower than is the case when each project is evaluated in a separate survey.

If it turned out that the relativities between values elicited in separate studies were more or less in line with those that would be elicited in the context of a broader programme, decision-makers may be reassured about using those estimates, at least for the purposes of ranking projects within the confines of some predetermined departmental budget (although the absolute values may still be suspect as reflections of the trade-offs people would really be prepared to make between particular projects and all other goods which they might wish to consume). However, even if the current manual produces greater consistency in the way that different studies are designed and conducted, there is no guarantee that the relativities between the values generated by those studies will give decision-makers a reliable indication of the way respondents would prioritise the various projects, were they invited to do so. Until there is a body of good-quality empirical evidence which directly addresses this issue, this worrisome question is likely to remain open.

12.5 'OTHER-REGARDING' ISSUES: ALTRUISM AND RECIPROCITY

By their very nature, public goods are likely to entail benefits for a large number of people. As a result, when individuals are asked about their (or their household's) WTP for the provision of such goods, it would not be at all surprising to find that respondents are inclined to take some account of the benefits enjoyed by other people (or people other than just those in their own households) and/or the degree to which others are willing to contribute to the provision of the good under consideration.

This raises several questions. First, how far is it legitimate, within the terms of CBA, to take such concerns into account? What dangers are there of neglecting considerations that *should* be valued, or alternatively, of over-weighting (through double or multiple counting) considerations that should only be valued once? Indeed, to what extent might attitudes to others' benefits or contributions undermine the CBA enterprise at a fundamental level?

12.5.1 Altruism

Consider a situation in which individual i displays altruistic concern for individual j. Under these circumstances, it might be supposed that i's WTP for a proposed increase in the level of provision of some public good would reflect not only her concern for 'own' consumption of the good but also her concern for j's consumption. However, if i realises that in order to finance the increased level of provision of the public good it will be necessary either to increase taxation or (more probably) to curtail the level of provision of some other public good(s), then i's WTP for j's increased consumption of the public good will, to some degree, be offset by i's requirement of compensation, that is, WTA, for j's share of the increased taxation or the opportunity cost to j of the curtailment in provision of other public goods. Indeed, under quite plausible circumstances this latter WTA sum will exactly offset the altruistic WTP, so that i's net WTP for the proposed increase in the level of provision of the public good will be precisely equal to her purely selfish WTP for the increase in 'own' consumption of the good. In this case, any attempt to include an allowance for altruistic WTP in the overall benefit measure would unequivocally entail unwarranted 'double counting'(for example, Bergstrom, 1982 or Jones-Lee, 1992).

To illustrate the point, consider an example adapted from Milgrom (1993). Assuming a two-person world, suppose individual i's selfish WTP for a particular public good is £60, while j's selfish WTP is £100. Suppose also that i displays pure altruism towards j[11] and that i is therefore willing to pay a further sum equal to half of j's *net* benefit (defined as £100 minus whatever j is required to pay towards the provision of the public good). To keep things simple, suppose that j has no altruistic concern for i. It can then be shown that if the provision of the public good is to pass the compensation test, it must cost less than the sum of i and j's selfish WTP, that is, £160. However, if i neglects the fact that j will be contributing something to the provision of the public good and focuses exclusively on j's benefit, there is a danger that i will state a WTP of £60 + 0.5(£100), that is, £110 which, added to j's own WTP of £100, would give a total of £210, £50 of which arises from i's neglect of the fact that if j were actually to pay £100, her net benefit would be zero. In short, in the case of pure altruism, and on the assumption that the level of provision of the public good is close to a social optimum, the appropriate way to value the provision of the public good is to count only the selfish WTP of those being surveyed.[12]

All of this having been said, it is important to appreciate that there *are* forms of altruistic concern under which it *would* be appropriate to include altruistic WTP in addition to the 'own' WTP figure. In particular, if a person's altruistic concern is focused on other people's consumption of some particular good (for example, their safety) and takes no account of their consumption of other goods, then that person's stated WTP for an increase in the level of provision of the particular good concerned will quite properly include an altruistic component as well as the 'own' WTP component and under these circumstances it would be quite inappropriate to exclude the altruistic component; see Jones-Lee (1992) or Hanemann (1996).

In summary, therefore, the question of whether and how people's altruistic concern for others should be incorporated in WTP-based values for the provision of public goods hinges crucially on the *nature* of that concern (for example, whether it is 'pure', 'paternalistic', 'focused' and so on). In view of this, whenever it is felt that altruistic concern may be a potential influence on responses in a SP study, it is desirable that some attempt should be made to establish the nature of respondents' altruistic predispositions.

But how might one establish where a particular person is, in fact, located on this spectrum of altruistic concern? Clearly, one possibility would be simply to ask the person concerned, though given the potential sensitivity of the question it would be necessary to proceed with some caution. Thus, for example, suppose that one wished to determine the nature of person i's altruistic concern for person j's safety. If he could be persuaded to answer it, then the following question would at least give a broad indication of the nature of i's altruistic concern for j.

Suppose that, for whatever reason, you had to make a decision on j's behalf about whether or not it would be worthwhile for j to spend £50 on a car safety feature that would halve j's risk of being killed or seriously injured in a car accident during the coming year. Which of the following most closely reflects the way you would make such a decision on j's behalf?

1. I would try to find out what j would want and then respect her preferences.
2. I would make the same decision as I would if it were a question of whether or not I should spend £50 of my own money to halve my own risk.
3. I regard j's safety as so important in relation to other things she might want to spend her money on that, regardless of whether or not either of us thinks that the safety improvement is good value for money, I'm going to decide she should go ahead and buy it. The fact that she would be out of pocket by £50 is neither here nor there to me: all that matters is that her safety would be improved.
4. While I wouldn't go quite so far as to adopt the position outlined in (3), I would tend to err in the direction of favouring j's safety over the other things she might want to spend her money on.

Clearly, if i were to indicate that (1) or (2) best represented his attitude to j's wellbeing, then he would reveal that his altruistic concern (however weakly or strongly felt) was of the pure or paternalistic form and, as already indicated, no account need be taken of this concern in estimating aggregate WTP for safety improvement. If, on the other hand, i selected (3) or (4) as best describing his attitude to j's safety, then this would reveal at least a degree of safety-focused altruism and it would be necessary to take steps to elicit the extent of such concern on i's part in the form of some indication of the broad order of the amount that he would be willing to contribute to the provision of the safety improvement for j.

Finally, McConnell (1997) points out that the double-counting problem goes away if altruism is defined over the good itself (which seems to be the typical case for things like wilderness areas) and in cases where the respondent is aware that the other respondents will also pay a specified cost if the programme is implemented (a condition often explicitly or implicitly stated in binary discrete choice CV questions). This suggests that the most troublesome area is likely to be risk reductions where respondents are not informed about how others will be charged for the risk reduction.

It must be noted, however, that although it is a potentially important factor in people's responses, little progress has so far been made to devise techniques which identify the nature of any altruistic concerns and which measure the fraction of any stated value that is attributable to some altruistic component.

12.5.2 Reciprocity

Another respect in which an individual's responses to WTP surveys may be 'other-regarding' concerns the way in which her contribution to provision compares with other people's. Many people's moral attitudes to public goods seem to involve principles of reciprocity: they recognise an obligation to make a 'fair' contribution to a collective enterprise that works to everyone's benefit but are willing to make this contribution only if they are assured that other people also contribute fairly.[13] For someone who thinks in these terms, WTP for a public good cannot be defined independently of what other people will be called on to pay. Much recent experimental evidence suggests that people are particularly concerned with negative reciprocity. That is, the motivation to respond positively when others' contributions are unexpectedly large is weaker than the motivation to respond negatively when they are unexpectedly small. Another way of putting this is to say that people are strongly averse to paying for other people's free rides – as they see it, to being suckered.

Motivations of reciprocity may help to explain some cases of embedding effects. A person who recognises an obligation to make a fair contribution to some broadly-defined public good may feel that this obligation can be discharged by contributing to some particular instance of that good, on the implicit expectation that other people will contribute to other instances. For example, consider someone who would be willing to pay up to £20 in additional taxes for a programme of tree-planting across the UK, provided that other British taxpayers pay corresponding amounts. Suppose this person is asked about her willingness to contribute towards tree-planting programmes. If she is asked about her willingness to contribute towards a national programme, she might construe the question as having an implicit matching clause, to the effect that other British people will make similar contributions to hers; accordingly, she might report a WTP of £20. Now suppose instead that she is asked about her willingness to contribute towards that component of the national scheme which takes place in her local area. Suppose that in this case she imagines the implicit matching clause to be that other people in her locality will contribute to the local programme and that people in other localities will contribute to theirs. On this understanding, she would again report a WTP of £20. At first sight, these two responses seem to indicate that she cannot distinguish between the benefits of a small programme and the benefits of a large one. But in terms of a reciprocity model, these responses are different ways of expressing exactly the same conditional preference.

If people are liable to be motivated by reciprocity, it is important that preference-elicitation questions make clear to the respondent what is to be assumed about other people's payments. As far as possible, those assumptions should be realistic. In most practical cases in which projects to supply public goods are appraised by CBA, the financial costs of those projects fall on national or local taxpayers. The distribution of cost shares between individuals is determined by the structure of marginal tax rates, and is independent of individuals' WTP for the particular public goods. Thus, in reality, each person's contributions will be matched by corresponding contributions from others: no one can take a free ride at anyone else's expense. This should be spelt out to respondents so as to avoid a downward bias in reported valuations due to negative reciprocity. Some forms of CV question (for example, those which use voluntary contributions as the hypothetical payment vehicle) can invoke feelings of negative reciprocity by giving the impression that people who report relatively high values of WTP may actually have to pay more than other people.

To date, the issue of how to adapt the efficiency criterion to cope with reciprocity-influenced preferences does not seem to have been tackled. For example, consider a three-person society. Suppose that each person is willing to pay towards a certain public good, but only if everyone pays equally. Subject to this proviso, A is willing to pay up to £300, B is willing to pay up to £200 and C is willing to pay up to £100. Applying the normal methods of CBA, we can conclude that total WTP for the public good is £600. However, the maximum amount of money that the three people will willingly pay is only £300. (C is willing to pay no more than £100, and A and B are willing to pay more than £100 only if C does so too.) The figure of £600 might be defended as a summary statistic about people's WTP, but it does not have the strict relationship to the compensation test that total WTP has when preferences are not influenced by reciprocity.

12.6   CONCLUSIONS

As with all social science, debates about the validity and usefulness of particular procedures continue. There would be no advances without this debate. Understandably, policy-makers want some stability in research findings. Their task is to decide whether to apply a body of guidance or not. If guidance were to be adopted only when there is 100 per cent certainty that it is sound guidance, then all decision-making would effectively be placed in limbo. That degree of certainty does not and will not exist. The issue then reduces to one of considering one body of guidance against the alternative body of guidance. While this chapter has focused on some of the serious debates surrounding SP techniques and the use of economic valuation, there are just as many debates about alternative procedures. Indeed, the 'irrationalities' that some find in SP techniques are the same as those found in so-called 'normal' markets, for example, auctions and stock markets. No-one suggests abandoning normal markets because of these irrationalities, but it is quite legitimate to ask whether market functioning could be improved by addressing them. One object of this manual has been to place the debates about SP before potential users of economic valuation approaches. Ultimately, a judgement has to be made about how useful they are, with the decision about whether or not to use these techniques being taken after due consideration of what else could be done instead.

NOTES

1. Supposing, of course, that the nature of each prospect is sufficiently well specified to enable its impact upon the individual's wellbeing to be assessed by her.
2. This may be particularly true for studies intended to produce generic values, such as the value of preventing a 'statistical' road accident fatality or the value of reducing the risks to health attributed to air or water pollution, since these values are intended for use in evaluating projects which may not even have been thought of yet. For specific, well-defined environmental projects, or for particular cases where a referendum associated with a hypothecated tax is feasible, respondents *may* find it more plausible that they could have to pay according to their response. However, UK respondents are not familiar with the kinds of referenda held in some states in the US, and such a format may be more likely to excite expressive rather than instrumental values (see Sugden 1999a, pp. 145–8).
3. Someone holding such views who is presented with a WTP question may also wish to give as large an amount as possible, but in the WTP case may be inhibited by income/wealth constraints from stating an excessively large number, whereas no such constraints operate on WTA responses.
4. The implications of this theory for valuation measures are discussed by Bateman, Munro, Rhodes, Starmer and Sugden (1997), who also report an experimental test of these implications.
5. In reference-dependent theory, there can be significant differences between WTA and WTP, even if the responsiveness of WTP to income is quite weak. To see why, notice that if the individual starts from E, his WTP for an increase in the public good may be much less than EA.
6. There is some experimental evidence that loss aversion is weakened when individuals report preferences that will take effect later in time or take effect only subject to some uncertain event and when individuals express judgements in the form of advice to other people. See, for example, Knetsch and Sinden (1984) and Loewenstein and Adler (1995).
7. Schkade and Payne (1994) present results from a verbal protocol analysis of the Desvousges et al. (1993) scenario. They conclude that this test fails to yield significant scope sensitivity, a conclusion which is disputed by Carson (1997) on the basis of it being driven by outliers within a series of small sample tests.
8. Not everyone would agree that the warm glow element should be included even once. For some discussion of the issue, see Diamond and Hausman (1993) and Willis (1995).
9. In this context, the nub of the standard gamble format was to ask respondents to balance the (virtual) certainty of an injury of lesser severity against a riskier treatment which, if successful, would improve the prognosis but which would result in a worse health state – and in some cases, death – if it failed.
10. A study by Kemp and Maxwell (1993) compared the results of a questionnaire which focused just on reducing the risks of oil spills off the coast of Alaska with a parallel questionnaire that elicited WTP for a much broader range of policies, then asked respondents to distribute the total sum between progressively disaggregated subsets of goods, one of which was the reduction of oil spills off Alaska. The 'stand-alone' study produced a

mean WTP of $85, while the 'disaggregation' study generated an average figure of 29 cents: that is, the stand-alone study resulted in a figure almost three hundred times bigger than the study where oil spills off Alaska were considered in the context of a wide range of other public programmes. However, many reservations about the Kemp and Maxwell study have been expressed – and its small scale undoubtedly *does* limit its power.

11. That is, i respects j's preferences and hence values any increase in j's wellbeing, whatever the source of that increase may be.

12. Moreover, it turns out that there is another quite plausible form of altruism that produces approximately the same result, namely 'paternalistic' altruism in which i imposes her own preferences on j's consumption pattern; see Jones-Lee (1992).

13. This issue is discussed in more detail in Sugden (1999a).

Bibliography

Adamowicz, W., Louviere, J. and Williams, M. (1994) 'Combining revealed and stated preference methods for valuing environmental amenities', *Journal of Environmental Economics and Management*, **26**(3), 271–92.

Adamowicz, W., Swait, J., Boxall, P., Louviere, J., and Williams, M. (1997) 'Perceptions versus objective measures of environmental quality in combined revealed and stated preference models of environmental valuation', *Journal of Environmental Economics and Management*, **32**(1), 52–64.

Adger, N. and Whitby, M. (1993) 'Natural resource accounting in the land-use sector: theory and practice', *European Review of Agricultural Economics*, **20**(1), 77–97.

Alberini, A. (1996) 'Efficiency vs. bias of willingness-to-pay estimates: bivariate and interval-data models', *Journal of Environmental Economics and Management*, **29**(2), 169–80.

Alberini, A., Cropper, M., Fu, T-T., Krupnick, A., Liu, J-T., Shaw, D. and Harrington, W. (1996) 'What is the value of reduced morbidity in Taiwan?', in R. Mendelsohn and D. Shaw (eds), *The Economics of Pollution Control in the Asia Pacific*, Cheltenham: Edward Elgar, 78–107.

Alfsen, K. (1993) *Natural Resource Accounting and Analysis in Norway*, Oslo: Central Bureau of Statistics.

Alvarez-Farizo, B. and Hanley, N. (1999) 'The value of leisure time: a contingent rating approach', *mimeo*, University of Edinburgh: IERM.

American Psychological Association (1974) *Standards for Educational and Psychological Tests*, Washington, DC: APA.

Andreoni, J. (1990) 'Impure altruism and donations to public goods: a theory of warm-glow giving', *Economic Journal*, **100**(401), 464–77.

Arrow, K., Solow, R., Portney, P.R., Leamer, E.E., Radner, R. and Schuman, H. (1993) *Report of the NOAA Panel on Contingent Valuation*, Washington, DC: Resources for the Future.

Atkinson, G., Hett, T. and Newcombe, J. (1999) *Measuring Corporate Sustainability*, CSERGE Working Paper GEC 99–01, University College London: CSERGE.

Atkinson, G., Marchado, F. and Mourato, S. (1999) *Balancing Competing Principles of Environmental Equity*, London: Department of Geography and Environment, London School of Economics.

Balistreri, E., McClelland, G., Poe, G.L. and Schulze, W. (2001) 'Can hypothetical questions reveal true values?: a laboratory comparison of dichotomous choice and open-ended contingent values with auction values', *Environmental and Resource Economics*, **18**, 275–92.

Banford, N., Knetsch, J. and Mauser, G. (1977) *Compensating and Equivalent Measures of Consumers Surplus: further survey results*, Vancouver: Department of Economics, Simon Fraser University.

Baron, J. (1996) 'Rationality and invariance: response to Schuman', in D.J. Bjørnstad and J.R. Kahn (eds), *The Contingent Valuation of Environmental Resources*, Cheltenham, U.K. and Brookfield, U.S.: Edward Elgar.

Baron, J. and Greene, J. (1996) 'Determinants of insensitivity to quantity in valuations of public goods: contribution, warm glow, budget constraints, availability and prominence', *Journal of Experimental Psychology: Applied*, **2**, 107–25.

Bateman, I.J. (1996) 'An economic comparison of forest recreation, timber and carbon fixing values with agriculture in Wales: a geographical information systems approach', *Ph.D. Thesis*, Department of Economics, University of Nottingham.

Bateman, I.J., Brouwer, R., Cubitt, R., Langford, I.H., Munro, A., Starmer, C. and Sugden, R. (2000) 'Perception and valuation of UV risk reduction as a public and private good', *ESRC Risk and Human Behaviour Newsletter*, **6**, 2–5.

Bateman, I.J., Diamand, E., Langford, I.H. and Jones, A.P. (1996) 'Household willingness to pay and farmers' willingness to accept compensation for establishing a recreational woodland', *Journal of Environmental Planning and Management*, **39**(1), 21–43.

Bateman, I.J. and Langford, I.H. (1997a) 'Non-users willingness to pay for a National Park: an application and critique of the contingent valuation method', *Regional Studies*, **31**(6), 571–82.

Bateman, I.J. and Langford, I.H. (1997b) 'Budget constraint, temporal and ordering effects in contingent valuation studies', *Environment and Planning A*, **29**(7), 1215–28.

Bateman, I.J., Langford, I.H. and Kerr, G.N. (1999) 'Bound and path effects in multiple-bound dichotomous choice contingent valuation', *CSERGE Global Environmental Change Working Paper GEC99–12*, Centre for Social and Economic Research on the Global Environment, University of East Anglia and University College London.

Bateman, I.J., Langford, I.H., Munro, A., Starmer, C. and Sugden, R. (2000) 'Estimating the four Hicksian measures for a public good: a contingent valuation investigation', *Land Economics*, **76**(3), 355–73.

Bateman, I.J., Langford, I.H., Nishikawa, N. and Lake, I. (2000) 'The Axford debate revisited: a case study illustrating different approaches to the aggregation of benefits data', *Journal of Environmental Planning and Management*, **43**(2), 291–302.

Bateman, I.J., Langford, I.H. and Rasbash, J. (1999) 'Elicitation effects in contingent valuation studies', in I.J. Bateman and K.G. Willis (eds), *Valuing Environmental Preferences: Theory and Practice of the Contingent Valuation Method in the US, EU, and Developing Countries*, Oxford: Oxford University Press.

Bateman, I.J., Langford, I.H., Turner, R.K., Willis, K.G. and Garrod, G.D. (1995) 'Elicitation and truncation effects in contingent valuation studies', *Ecological Economics*, **12**(2), 161–79.

Bateman, I.J., Langford, I.H., Willis, K.G., Turner, R.K. and Garrod, G.D. (1993) 'The impacts of changing willingness to pay question format in contingent valuation studies: an analysis of open-ended, iterative bidding and dichotomous choice formats', *Global Environmental Change Working Paper 93–05*, Centre for Social and Economic Research on the Global Environment, University of East Anglia and University College London.

Bateman, I.J., Munro, A., Rhodes, B., Starmer, C. and Sugden, R. (1997a) 'Does part-whole bias exist? An experimental investigation', *Economic Journal*, **107**(441), 322–32.

Bateman, I.J., Munro, A., Rhodes, B., Starmer, C. and Sugden, R. (1997b) 'A test of the theory of reference-dependent preferences', *Quarterly Journal of Economics*, **112**(2), 479–505.

Bateman, I.J., Nishikawa, N. and R. Brouwer (1999) 'Benefits transfer in theory and practice: a review', presented at *Recent Developments in Environmental Valuation*, Forestry Commission/Civil Service, Barony Castle, Peebles, Scotland, 9–13 May 1999.

Bateman, I.J. and Willis, K.G. (eds) (1999) *Valuing Environmental Preferences: Theory and Practice of the Contingent Valuation Method in the US, EU and Developing Countries*, Oxford: Oxford University Press.

Bateman, I.J., Willis, K.G. and Garrod, G.D. (1994) 'Consistency between contingent valuation estimates: a comparison of two studies of UK National Parks', *Regional Studies*, **28**(5), 457–74.

Bateman, I.J., Willis, K.G., Garrod, G.D., Doktor, P., Langford, I. and Turner, R.K. (1992) 'Recreation and environmental preservation value of the Norfolk Broads: a contingent valuation study', Report to the National Rivers Authority, Environmental Appraisal Group, University of East Anglia.

Beattie, J., Covey, J., Dolan, P., Hopkins, L., Jones-Lee, M., Loomes, G., Pidgeon, N., Robinson, A and Spencer, A. (1998) 'On the contingent valuation of safety and the safety of contingent valuation: part 1', *Caveat Investigator, Journal of Risk and Uncertainty*, **17**(2), 5–25.

Becker, G.M. DeGroot, M.H. and Marschak, J. (1964) 'Measuring utility by a single-reponse sequential method', *Behavioural Science*, **9**, 226–32.

Beggs, S., Cardelland, S. and Hausman, J. (1981) 'Assessing the potential demand for electric cars', *Journal of Econometrics*, **16**, 1–19.

Ben-Akiva, M. and Lerman, S. (1985) *Discrete Choice Analysis: Theory and Application to Travel Demand,* Cambridge, MA: MIT Press.

Ben-Akiva, M. and Morikawa, T. (1990) 'Estimating switching models from revealed preferences and stated intentions', *Transportation Research A,* **24**(6), 485–95.

Ben-Akiva, M., Morikawa, T. and Shiroishi, F. (1991) 'Analysis of the reliability of preference ranking data', *Journal of Business Research,* **23**, 253–68.

Bergh, van den, J.C.J.M., Button, K.J., Nijkamp, P. and Pepping, G.C. (1997) *Meta-Analysis in Environmental Economics*, Dordrecht: Kluwer Academic Publishers.

Bergland, O. (1999) 'Valuation of landscape elements using a contingent choice method', *International Journal of Agricultural Economics.*

Bergstrom, T. (1982) 'When is a man's life worth more than his human capital?', in M. Jones-Lee (ed.), *The Value of Life and Safety*, Amsterdam, New York and Oxford: North-Holland, 3–26.

Bishop, R.C. and Boyle, K.J. (1985) 'The economic value of Illinois Beach State Nature Preserve', *Final Report to the Illinois Department of Conservation*, Madison, WI: HBRS Inc.

Bishop, R.C., Champ, P.A. and Mullarkey, D.J. (1995) 'Contingent valuation', in D.W. Bromley (ed.), *The Handbook of Environmental Economics*, Blackwell: Oxford.

Bishop, R. and Heberlein, T. (1979) 'Measuring values of extra market goods: are indirect measures biased?', *American Journal of Agricultural Economics,* **61**(5), 926–30.

Bishop, R.C., Heberlein, T.A. and Kealy, M.J. (1983) 'Hypothetical bias in Contingent Valuation: results from a simulated market', *Natural Resources Journal,* **23**(3), 619–33.

Blamey, R., Bennett, J.W. and Morrison, M.D. (1999) 'Yea-saying in contingent valuation surveys', *Land Economics,* **75**(1), 126–41.

Bleichrodt, H. and Quiggin, J. (1999) 'Life-cycle preferences over consumption and health: when is cost-effectiveness analysis equivalent to cost-benefit analysis?', *Journal of Health Economics,* **18**, 681–708.

Boardman, A., Greenberg, D., Vining, A. and Weimar, D. (1996) *Cost-Benefit Analysis: Concepts and Practice*, New Jersey: Prentice Hall.

Bockstael, N.E., Strand, I.E. and Hanemann, W.M. (1987) 'Time and the Recreational Demand Model', *American Journal of Agricultural Economics,* **62**(2), 293–302.

Boxall, P.C., Adamowicz, W.L., Swait, P., Williams, M. and Louviere, J. (1993) 'A comparison of stated preference methods for environmental valuation', *Ecological Economics,* **18**(3), 243–53.

Boyle, K.J., Bishop, R.C. and Welsh, M.P. (1985) 'Starting point bias in contingent valuation bidding games', *Land Economics*, **61**(2), 188–94.

Boyle, K., Desvouges, W., Johnson, F.R., Dunford, R. and Hudson, S. (1994) 'An investigation of part-whole bias in contingent valuation studies', *Journal of Environmental Economics and Management*, **27**(1), 64–83.

Bradley and Daly, (1994) 'Use of logit scaling approach to test for rank-order and fatigue effects in stated preference data', *Transportation*, **21**(2), 167–84.

Brennan, G. and Lomasky, L. (1985) 'The impartial spectator goes to Washington: toward a Smithian theory of electoral politics', *Economics and Philosophy*, **1**(2), 189–211.

Brookshire, D.S. et al. (1982) 'Valuing public goods: a comparison of survey and hedonic approaches', *American Economic Review*, **72**(1), 165–77.

Brookshire, D.S., d'Arge, R.C., Schulze, W.D. and Thayer, M.A. (1981) 'Experiments in valuing public goods', in V.K. Smith (ed.), *Advances in Applied Economics: Volume 1*, Greenwich, CT: JAI Press.

Brookshire, D.S., Randall, A. and Stoll, J.R. (1980) 'Valuing increments and decrements in natural resource service flows', *American Journal of Agricultural Economics*, **62**(3), 478–88.

Brouwer, R. (1998) 'Future Research Priorities for Valid and Reliable Environmental Value Transfer', *Working Paper 98–28*, Centre for Social and Economic Research on the Global Environment, University of East Anglia and University College London.

Brouwer, R. and Bateman, I.J. (2000) 'Public perception and valuation of UV health risks: a comparison across low and high-risk countries', presentation at *Transitions Towards a Sustainable Europe: Ecology – Economy – Policy, 3rd Biennial Conference of the European Society for Ecological Economics*, Vienna, 3–6 May.

Brouwer, R., Langford, I.H., Bateman, I.J. and Turner, R.K. (1999) 'A meta-analysis of wetland contingent valuation studies', *Regional Environmental Change*, **1**(1), 47–57.

Brouwer, R., Powe, N., Langford, I.H., Bateman, I.J. and Turner, R.K. (1999) 'Public attitudes to contingent valuation and public consultation', *Environmental Values*, **8**(3), 325–47.

Brouwer, R. and Spanninks, F. (1999) 'The validity of environmental benefits transfer: further empirical testing', *Environmental and Resource Economics*, **14**(2), 95–117.

Bullock, C., Elston, D. and Chalmers, N. (1998) 'An application of economic choice experiments to a traditional land use – deer hunting in the Scottish Highlands', *Journal of Environmental Management*, **52**(4), 335–51.

Burness, H.S., Cummings, R.G., Mehr, A.F. and Walbert, M.S. (1983) 'Valuing policies which reduce environmental risk', *Natural Resources Journal*, **23**(3), 675–82.

Cairns, J. (1994) 'Valuing future benefits', *Health Economics*, **3**, 221–9.

Cairns, J. and van der Pol, M. (1997) 'Saving future lives: a comparison of three discounting models', *Health Economics*, **6**(4), 341–50.

Cairns, J. and van der Pol, M. (2000) 'The estimation of marginal time preference in a UK-wide sample', (TEMPUS) project, *Health Technology Assessment*, **4**(1), 1–73.

Cambridge Econometrics, EFTEC and WRc (1999) *Estimating the Fixed External Effects of Landfill*, Cambridge: Cambridge Econometrics, report to DETR, London.

Cameron, T.A. (1988) 'A new paradigm for valuing non-market goods using referendum data: maximum likelihood estimation by censored logistic regression', *Journal of Environmental Economics and Management*, **15**(3), 355–79.

Cameron, T.A. (1992) 'Combining contingent valuation and travel cost data for the valuation of non-market goods', *Land Economics*, **68**(3), 302–17.

Cameron, T.A. and James, M.D. (1987) 'Efficient estimation methods for "closed-ended" contingent valuation surveys', *Review of Economics and Statistics*, **69**(2), 269–76.

Cameron, T.A. and Quiggin, J. (1994) 'Estimation using contingent valuation data from a "dichotomous choice with follow-up" questionnaire', *Journal of Environmental Economics and Management*, **27**(3), 218–34.

Cameron, T.A., Shaw, W.D., Ragland, S., Callaway, J. and Keefe, S. (1996) 'Using actual and contingent behaviour data with differing levels of time aggregation', *Journal of Agricultural and Resource Economics*, **21**(1), 130–49.

Carlsson, F. (1999) *Essays on Externalities and Transport*, PhD thesis, University of Gothenburg.

Carson, R.T. (1991) 'Constructed markets', in J.B. Braden and C.D. Kolstad (eds), *Measuring the Demand for Environmental Quality*, Amsterdam: North-Holland, pp. 121–62.

Carson, R.T. (1997) 'Contingent valuation surveys and tests of insensitivity to scope', in R.J. Kopp, W.W. Pommerehne and N. Schwarz (eds), *Determining the Value of Non-Marketed Goods: Economic, Psychological, and Policy Relevant Aspects of Contingent Valuation Methods*, Boston, MA: Kluwer Academic Publishers.

Carson, R.T. (1999) 'Contingent valuation: a user's guide', *mimeo*, Department of Economics, University of California, San Diego.

Carson, R.T., Carson, N., Alberini, A., Flores, N. and Wright, J. (1995) *A*

Bibliography of Contingent Valuation Studies and Papers, La Jolla, CA: Natural Resource Damage Assessment Inc.

Carson, R.T. and Flores, N.E. (1996) 'Another Look at "Does Contingent Valuation Measure Preferences?: Experimental Evidence" How Compelling is the Evidence', *Discussion Paper 96-31*, Department of Economics, University of California, San Diego.

Carson, R.T., Flores, N.E. and Hanemann, W.M. (1992) 'On the creation and destruction of public goods: the matter of sequencing', paper presented at *The Annual Conference of The European Association of Environmental and Resource Economists*, Cracow, Poland.

Carson, R.T., Flores, N.E. and Hanemann, W.M. (1998) 'Sequencing and valuing public goods', *Journal of Environmental Economics and Management*, **36**(3), 314–23.

Carson, R.T., Flores, N.E., Martin, K.M. and Wright, J.L. (1996) 'Contingent valuation and revealed preference methodologies: comparing the estimates for quasi-public goods', *Land Economics*, **72**(1): 80–99.

Carson, R.T., Flores, N.E. and Meade, N.F. (1996) 'Contingent valuation: Controversies and evidence', *Discussion Paper 96-36*, Department of Economics, University of California, San Diego.

Carson, R.T., Flores, N.E. and Meade, N.F. (2000) 'Contingent valuation: controversies and evidence', *mimeo*, Department of Economics, University of California, San Diego.

Carson, R.T., Groves, T. and Machina, M.J. (1999) 'Incentive and informational properties of preference questions', Plenary Address, *9th Annual Conference of the European Association of Environmental and Resource Economists (EAERE)*, Oslo, Norway, June.

Carson, R.T., Hanemann, W.M., Kopp, R.J., Krosnick, J.A., Mitchell, R.C., Presser, S., Ruud, P.A. and Smith, V.K. (1994) *'Prospective interim lost use value due to DDT and PCB contamination in the Southern California Bight'*, Report to the National Oceanic and Atmospheric Administration, Natural Resource Damage Assessment Inc., La Jolla, California.

Carson, R.T., Hanemann, W.M., Kopp, R.J., Krosnick, J.A., Mitchell, R.C., Presser, S., Ruud, P.A. and Smith, V.K. (1997) 'Temporal reliability of estimates from contingent valuation', *Land Economics*, **73**(2), 151–61.

Carson, R.T., Hanemann, W.M. and Mitchell, R.C. (1987) 'The use of simulated political markets to value public goods', *Discussion Paper 87-7*, Department of Economics, University of California, San Diego.

Carson, R.T. and Mitchell, R.C. (1993) 'The value of clean water: the public's willingness to pay for boatable, fishable, and swimmable quality water', *Water Resources Research*, **29**, 2445–54.

Carson, R.T. and Mitchell, R.T. (1995) 'Sequencing and nesting in contingent valuation surveys', *Journal of Environmental Economics and Management*, **28**(2), 155–73.

Carson, R.T., Mitchell, R.C., Hanemann, W.M., Kopp, R.J., Presser, S. and Ruud, P.A. (1992) '*A contingent valuation study of lost passive use values resulting from the Exxon Valdez oil spill*', report to the Attorney General of the State of Alaska.

Carson, R., Mitchell, R., Hanemann, M., Kopp, R., Presser, S. and Ruud, P. (1994) 'Contingent Valuation and Lost Passive Use: Damages from Exxon Valdez', *Discussion Paper 94-18*, Washington DC: Resources for the Future.

Carson, R.T., Wilks, L. and Imber, D. (1994) 'Valuing the Preservation of Australia's Kakadu Conservation Zone', *Working Paper 94-09*, University of California, San Diego Department of Economics.

Carthy, T., Chilton, S., Covey, J., Hopkins, L., Jones-Lee, M., Loomes, G., Pidgeon, N. and Spencer, A. (1999) 'On the contingent valuation of safety and the safety of contingent valuation: Part 2 – the CV/SG chained approach', *Journal of Risk and Uncertainty*, **17**(3), 187–213.

Champ, P., Bishop, R., Brown, T. and McCollum, D. (1997) 'Using donation mechanisms to value non-use benefits from public goods', *Journal of Environmental Economics and Management*, **33**(2), 151–62.

Chapman, R.G. and Staelin, R. (1982) 'Exploiting rank ordered choice set data within the stochastic utility model,' *Journal of Marketing Research*, **19**, 288–301.

Coburn, T., Beesley M. and Reynolds, D. (1960) *The London–Birmingham Motorway*, Technical Paper 46, Road Research Laboratory, Crowthorne.

Commission on the Third London Airport (1971) *Report* and *Papers and Proceedings* (9 volumes), London: HMSO.

Converse, P.E. (1974) 'Comment: the status of nonattitudes', *American Political Science Review*, **68**, 650–60.

Cooper, J. and Loomis, J.B. (1992) 'Sensitivity of willingness-to-pay estimates to bid design in dichotomous choice contingent valuation models', *Land Economics*, **68**(2), 211–24.

Coopers Lybrand and EFTEC (1996) *Cost-Benefit Analysis of the Different Municipal Solid Waste Management Systems*, Luxembourg: European Commission.

Coursey, D.L., Hovis, J. and Schulze, W.D. (1986) 'The disparity between willingness to accept and willingness to pay measures of value', *Quarterly Journal of Economics*, **102**(3), 679–90.

Cropper, M., Aydede, M. and Portney, P. (1994) 'Preferences for life saving programs: how the public discounts time and age', *Journal of Risk and Uncertainty*, **8**(3), 243–65.

CSERGE, EFTEC and Warren Spring Laboratory (1993) *Externalities from Landfill and Incineration*, London: HMSO.

Cummings, R. (1996) 'Relating stated and revealed preferences: Challenges and opportunities', in D.J. Bjornstad and J.R. Khan (eds) *The Contingent Valuation of Environmental Resources: Methodological Issues and Research Needs*, Cheltenham: Edward Elgar, pp. 189–97.

Cummings, R.G., Brookshire, D.S. and Schulze, W.D. (eds) (1986) '*Valuing Environmental Goods: An Assessment of the Contingent Valuation Method*', Totowa, NJ: Rowman and Allanhed.

Davis, J. and Whittington, D. (1997) 'A comparison of participatory group meetings and contingent valuation surveys: a case study of Lugazi, Uganda', *Economic Development and Cultural Change*, October, **46**(1), 73–94.

Davis, N. and Teasdale, P. (1994) *The Costs to the British Economy of Work-related Accidents and Work-related Ill Health*, London: Health and Safety Executive.

Davis, R.K. (1963) 'Recreation planning as an economic problem', *Natural Resources Journal*, **3**(2), 239–49.

Dawson, R. (1967) *The Cost of Road Accidents in Great Britain*, Report LR 396, Road Research Laboratory, Crowthorne.

Day, B., Dubourg, W.R., Machado, F., Mourato, S., Navrud, S., Ready, R.C., Spanninks, F. and Vazquez, M.X. (1999) 'Non-contextual values for the avoidance of episodes of ill-health: tests for the stability of benefits across national boundaries', in report by CSERGE, Agricultural University of Norway, Amsterdam Free University, Catholic University of Portugal and University of Vigo to the European Commission, Brussels.

Deaton, A. and Muellbauer, J. (1980) *Economics and Consumer Behaviour*, Cambridge: Cambridge University Press.

Department of Environment, Transport and Regions (DETR) (1998) *A New Deal for Trunk Roads in England: Guidance on the New Approach to Appraisal (GNATA)*, London: DETR.

Department of Environment, Transport and Regions (DETR) (1998) *An Economic Analysis of the National Air Quality Strategy Objectives*, London: DETR.

Department of Environment, Transport and Regions (DETR) (1998) *Quarries and Property Rights*, London, DETR.

Department of Environment, Transport and Regions (DETR) (1999) *Guidance on Methodology for Multi-Modal Study*, London: DETR.

Department of Environment, Transport and Regions (DETR) (1999) *Guidance on Provisional Local Transport Plans*, London: DETR.

Department of Environment, Transport and Regions (DETR) (2000) *Multi-criteria Analysis*, London: DETR.

Department of Health (DoH) Ad-Hoc Group on the Economic Appraisal of the Health Effects of Air Pollution (EAHEAP) (1999) *Economic Appraisal of the Health Effects of Air Pollution*, London: HMSO.

Desaigues, B. and Rabl, A. (1995) 'Reference values for human life: an econometric analysis of a contingent valuation in France', in N.G. Schwab Christe, and N.C. Soguel (eds), *Contingent Valuation, Transport Safety and the Value of Life*, Boston/Dordrecht/London: Kluwer.

Desvousges, W.H., Hudson, S.P. and Ruby, M.C. (1996) 'Evaluating CV performance: separating the light from the heat', in D.J. Bjornstad and J.R. Khan (eds), *The Contingent Valuation of Environmental Resources: Methodological Issues and Research Needs*, Cheltenham: Edward Elgar, 117–44.

Desvousges, W.H., Johnson, F.R., Dunford, R.W., Boyle, K.J., Hudson, S.P. and Wilson, K.N. (1992) 'Measuring non-use damages using contingent valuation: an experimental evaluation of accuracy', *Monograph 92-1*, prepared for the Exxon Company, USA, Research Triangle Institute, NC.

Desvousges, W., Johnson, R., Dunford, R., Boyle, K., Hudson, S. and Wilson, N. (1993) 'Measuring natural resource damage with contingent valuation: tests of validity and reliability', in J. Hausman (ed.), *Contingent Valuation: A Critical Assessment*, Amsterdam, London, New York and Tokyo: North-Holland, 91–159.

Desvousges, W.H., Smith, V.K. and Fisher, A. (1987) 'Option price estimates for water quality improvements: a contingent valuation study for the Monongahela River', *Journal of Environmental Economics and Management*, **14**(3), 248–67.

Diamond, P. (1996) 'Discussion of the conceptual underpinnings of the contingent valuation method by A.C. Fisher', in D.J. Bjornstad and J.R. Khan (eds), *The Contingent Valuation of Environmental Resources: Methodological Issues and Research Needs*, Cheltenham: Edward Elgar, 61–71.

Diamond, P. and Hausman, J. (1993) 'On contingent valuation measurement of non-use value', in J. Hausman (ed.), *Contingent Valuation: A Critical Assessment*, Amsterdam, London, New York and Tokyo: North-Holland, 3–38.

Diamond, P. and Hausman, J. (1994) 'Contingent valuation: is some number better than no number?', *Journal of Economic Perspectives*, **8**(4), 45–64.

Dillman, D.A. (1978) *Mail and Telephone Surveys – The Total Design Method*, New York: Wiley.

Dillman, D.A. (1983) 'Mail and other self-administered questionnaires', in P.H. Rossi, J.D. Wright and A.B. Anderson (eds), *Handbook of Survey Research*, New York: Academic Press.

Dillman, D.A. (1996) 'Sources of bias in contingent valuation', in W. Schulze et al. (eds), *The Contingent Valuation of Environmental Resources; Meth-*

odological Issues and Research Needs: New Horizons in Environmental Economics Series, Cheltenham: Edward Elgar, 97–116.

Dillman, D.A. (2000) *Mail and Internet Surveys: The Tailored Design Method*, John Wiley & Sons: New York.

Dillon, W.R., Madden, T.J. and Firtle, N.H. (1994) *Marketing Research in a Marketing Environment*, 3rd Edition, Boston, MA: Irwin.

Dodgson, J. and Lane, B. (1999) *The Costs of Road Congestion in Great Britain*, London: NERA.

Douglas, M. and Isherwood, I. (1979) *The World of Goods*, New York: Basic Books.

Downing, M. and Ozuna, T., Jr. (1996) 'Testing the reliability of the benefit function transfer approach', *Journal of Environmental Economics and Management*, 3(30), 316–22.

Dubourg, W.R., Jones-Lee, M.W. and Loomes, G. (1994) 'Imprecise preferences and the WTP–WTA disparity', *Journal of Risk and Uncertainty*, 9(2), 115–33.

Dubourg, W.R., Jones-Lee, M.W. and Loomes, G. (1997) 'Imprecise preferences and survey design in contingent valuation', *Economica*, 64(257), 681–702.

Dubourg, W.R. and D.W. Pearce (1998) 'The social costs of alcohol consumption: definitions, measurement, and policy implications', in M. Grant and J. Litvak (eds), *Drinking Patterns and Their Consequences*, Washington, DC: Taylor and Francis, pp. 169–88.

ECOTEC, University of Herefordshire, the Central Science Laboratory, EFTEC and University of Newcastle upon Tyne (1999) *Design of a Tax or Charge Scheme for Pesticides*, London: DETR.

EFTEC (Economics for the Environment Consultancy) (1998a) 'Review of Technical Guidance on Environmental Appraisal', Report to Department of Environment, Transport and the Regions, London, UK.

EFTEC (Economics for the Environment Consultancy) (1998b) 'Social Value of the Charitable Sector', Report to Charities Aid Foundation (CAF), UK.

EFTEC (Economics for the Environment Consultancy) (1998c) *Valuing Preferences for Changes in Water Abstraction from the River Ouse*, report to Yorkshire Water Services Ltd, Bradford.

EFTEC (Economics for the Environment Consultancy) (1999) *Economic analysis of the Machu Picchu Sanctuary*, Report to the Finnish Park Service.

Eisworth, M., Englin, J., Fadali, E. and Shaw, W.D. (1999) 'The value of water levels in water-based recreation: a pooled revealed preference/contingent behaviour model', *mimeo*, Department of Applied Economics and Statistics, University of Reno.

Englin, J. and Cameron, T. (1996) 'Augmenting travel cost models with contingent behaviour data', *Environmental and Resource Economics*, **7**(2), 133–47.

Environmental Resources Management (ERM) (1996) *Valuing management for biodiversity in British forests*, Report to the Forestry Commission, London.

Environmental Resources Management (ERM) and University of Newcastle (1997) *Economic appraisal of the environmental costs and benefits of potential solutions to alleviate low flows in rivers*, report to SW Region of the Environment Agency.

Fankhauser, S. (1995) *Valuing Climate Change: the Economics of the Greenhouse*, London: Earthscan.

Field, B.C. (1997) *Environmental Economics: An Introduction*, 2nd Edition, New York: McGraw-Hill.

Fischoff, B. and Furby, L. (1988) 'Measuing values: a conceptual framework for interpreting transactions with special reference to contingent valuation of visibility', *Journal of Risk and Uncertainty*, **1**(2), 147–84.

Fishbein, M. and Ajzen, I. (1975) *Belief, Attitude, Intention and Behaviour*, Reading, MA: Addison-Wesley.

Fisher, A.C. (1996) 'The conceptual underpinnings of the contingent valuation method', in D.J. Bjornstad and J.R. Kahn (eds), *The Contingent Valuation of Environmental Resources: Methodological Issues and Research Needs*, Cheltenham: Edward Elgar, 19–37.

Flores, N.E. (1995) 'The effects of rationing and virtual price elasticities', *Discussion Paper 95-20*. Department of Economics, University of California, San Diego.

Flores, N.E. and Carson, R.T. (1997) 'The relationship between the income elasticities of demand and WTP', *Journal of Environmental Economics and Management*, **33**(3), 287–95.

Foster, C. and Beesley, M. (1963) 'Estimating the social benefits of constructing an underground railway in London', *Journal of the Royal Statistical Society*, Series A, **126**, 46–58.

Foster, V., Bateman, I.J. and Harley, D. (1997) 'Real and hypothetical willingness to pay for environmental preservation: a non-experimental comparison', *Journal of Agricultural Economics*, **48**(2), 123–38.

Foster, V., Mourato, S., Pearce, D.W. and Ozdemiroglu, E. (2000) *The Price of Virtue: Calculating the Value of the Voluntary Sector*, Cheltenham: Edward Elgar.

Foster, V. and Mourato, S. (1998) *Testing for Consistency in Contingent Ranking Experiments*, London: CSERGE, University College London.

Foster, V. and Mourato, S. (1999) 'Elicitation format and part-whole bias: do contingent valuation and contingent ranking give the same result?' CSERGE Working Paper GEC 99-17.

Foster, V. and Mourato, S. (2000) 'Measuring the impacts of pesticide use in the UK: a contingent ranking approach', *Journal of Agricultural Economics*, **51**(1), 1–21.

Foster, V. and Mourato, S. (2001) 'Testing for consistency in contingent ranking experiments', *Journal of Environmental Economics and Management*, at www.idealibrary.com.

Foster, V., Mourato, S., Tinch, R., Ozdemiroglu, E. and Pearce, D.W. (1998) 'Incorporating external impacts in pest management choices', in W. Vorley and D. Keeney (eds), *Bugs in the System: Redesigning the Pesticide Industry for Sustainable Agriculture*, London: Earthscan.

Fowkes, T., Wardman, M. and Holden, D. 'Non-orthogonal stated preference design', PTRC conference proceedings, 21st Summer annual meeting.

Garrod, G. and Willis, K. (1996) 'Estimating the benefits of environmental enhancement: a case study of the River Darent', *Journal of Environmental Planning and Management*, **39**(2), 189–203.

Georgiou, S., Bateman, I.J., Langford, I.H. and Day, R.J. (1999) 'Coastal bathing water health risks: assessing the adequacy of proposals to amend the 1976 EC Directive', *Risk, Decision and Policy*, **4**(3), 1–20.

Georgiou, S., Langford, I.H., Bateman, I.J. and Turner, R.K. (1998) 'Determinants of individuals' willingness to pay for perceived reductions in environmental health risks: a case study of bathing water quality', *Environment and Planning A*, **30**(4), 577–94.

Gerking, S., De Haan, M. and Schulze, W. (1988) 'The marginal value of job safety: a contingent valuation study', *Journal of Risk and Uncertainty*, **1**(2), 185–99.

Gordon, F. and Risley, D. (1999) *The Costs to Britain of Workplace Accidents and Work-related Ill Health*, London: Health and Safety Executive.

Green, P., Krieger, A. and Agarwal, M. (1991) 'Adaptive conjoint analysis: some caveats and suggestions', *Journal of Marketing Research*, **28**, 223–5.

Green, P. and Srinivasan, V. (1990) 'Conjoint analysis in marketing: new developments with implications for research and practice', *Conjoint Analysis in Marketing*, 3–19.

Greene, W.H. (1993) *Econometric Analysis*, New York: Macmillan.

Greene, W.H. (1997) *Econometric Analysis*, 3rd edition, Prentice-Hall International.

Groves, R.M. (1989) *Survey Errors and Survey Costs*, New York: Wiley.

Groves, T. and Ledyard, J.O. (1977) 'Optimal allocation of public goods: a solution to the free rider problem', *Econometrica*, **41**, 783–809.

Guria, J., Jones, W., Jones-Lee, M., Keall, J., Leung, J. and Loomes, G.

(1999) *The Values of Statistical Life and Prevention of Injuries in New Zealand*, Wellington: Land Transport Safety Authority.

Haab, T.C. and McConnell, K.E. (1997) 'Referendum models and negative willingness to pay: alternative solutions', *Journal of Environmental Economics and Management*, **32**(2), 251–70.

Hamilton, K. and Lutz, E. (1996) 'Green National Accounts: Policy Uses and Empirical Experience', *Working Paper 039*, Environment Department World Bank, Washington DC: World Bank.

Hammack, J. and Brown, G.M., Jr. (1974) *Waterfowl and Wetlands: Toward Bioeconomic Analysis*, Baltimore: Johns Hopkins University Press (for Resources for the Future).

Hammitt, M. and Graham, J. (1999) 'Willingness to pay for health protection: inadequate sensitivity to probability?', *Journal of Risk and Uncertainty*, **18**, 33–62.

Hanemann, M. (1984) 'Welfare evaluations in contingent valuation experiments with discrete responses', *American Journal of Agricultural Economics*, **66**(3), 332–41.

Hanemann, M. (1991) 'Willingness to pay and willingness to accept: how much can they differ?', *American Economic Review*, **81**(3), 635–647.

Hanemann, M. (1994) *Contingent Valuation in Economics*, Berkeley, CA: Department of Agricultural and Resource Economics, University of California.

Hanemann, M. (1996) 'Theory versus data in the contingent valuation debate', in D.J. Bjørnstad and J.R. Kahn (eds), *The Contingent Valuation of Environmental Resources*, Cheltenham, UK and Brookfield, US: Edward Elgar, 38–60.

Hanemann, M. (1999) 'The economic theory of WTP and WTA', in I. Bateman and K. Willis (eds), *Valuing Environmental Preferences: Theory and Practice of the Contingent Valuation Method in the US, EU and Developing Countries*, Oxford: Oxford University Press, 42–96.

Hanemann, M. and Kanninen, B. (1999) 'The statistical analysis of discrete-response CV data', in I.J. Bateman and K.G. Willis (eds), *Valuing Environmental Preferences: Theory and Practice of the Contingent Valuation Method in the US, EU, and Developing Countries*, Oxford: Oxford University Press, 302–441.

Hanemann, M., Loomis, J. and Kanninen, B. (1991) 'Statistical efficiency of double-bounded dichotomous choice contingent valuation', *American Journal of Agricultural Economics*, **73**(4), 1255–63.

Hanley, N. (1990) *Valuation of Environmental Effects: Final Report – Stage One*, Edinburgh: Industry Department of Scotland and the Scottish Development Agency.

Hanley, N. (1991) 'The economics of nitrate pollution control in the UK', in N. Hanley (ed.), *Farming and the Countryside: an Economic Analysis of External Costs and Benefits*, Oxford: CAB.

Hanley, N., Alvarez-Farizo, B. and Bell, D. (2000) 'Valuing the benefits of bathing water quality improvements: a combined stated-revealed preference approach', *mimeo*, Institute of Ecology and Resource Management, University of Edinburgh.

Hanley, N. and Milne, J. (1996) 'Ethical beliefs and behaviour in contingent valuation', *Journal of Environmental Planning and Management*, **39**(2), 255–72.

Hanley, N., Mourato, S. and Wright, R. (2001) 'Choice modelling approaches: a superior alternative for environmental valuation?', *Journal of Economic Surveys*, **15**, 433–60.

Hanley, N., Wright, R.E. and Adamowicz, V. (1998) 'Using choice experiments to value the environment: design issues, current experience and future prospects', *Environmental and Resource Economics*, **11**(3–4), 413–28.

Hanley, N., Wright, R. and Koop, G. (2000) 'Modelling recreation demand using choice experiments: rock climbing in Scotland', Paper to Royal Economics Society conference, University of St. Andrews.

Hargreaves Heap, S.P. (1989) *Rationality in Economics*, Oxford: Blackwell.

Hartridge, O. and Pearce, D.W. (2000) 'Is UK Agriculture Sustainable? Environmentally Adjusted Economics Accounts for UK Agriculture', CSERGE-UCL, *mimeo*, University College London.

Hausman, J. and McFadden, D. (1984) 'Specification tests for the multinomial logit model', *Econometrica*, **52**(5), 1219–40.

Hausman, J. and Ruud, P. (1987) 'Specifying and testing econometric models for rank-ordered data', *Journal of Econometrics*, **34**(1/2), 83–104.

Henscher, D. (1994) 'Stated preference analysis of travel choices: the state of practice', *Transportation*, **21**, 107–33.

Henscher, D., Louviere, J. and Swait, J. (1999) 'Combining sources of preference data', *Journal of Econometrics*, **89**(1/2), 197–221.

Hicks, J.R. (1943) 'The four consumer surpluses', *Reivew of Economic Studies*, **8**, 108–16.

HM Treasury (1997) *Appraisal and Valuation in Central Government*, London: HM Treasury (the 'Green Book').

HM Treasury (1972) *Forestry in Great Britain*, London: HMSO.

Hoehn. J.P. and Randall, A. (1985) 'Demand based and contingent valuation: an empirical comparison', Paper presented at the *Annual American Agricultural Economics Association* meeting, Ames, Iowa, August 1985.

Hoehn, J.P. and Randall, A. (1987) 'A satisfactory benefit cost indicator from contingent valuation', *Journal of Environmental Economics and Management*, **14**(3), 226–47.

Hoehn, J.P. and Randall, A. (1989) 'Too many proposals pass the benefit cost test', *American Economics Review*, **79**(3), 544–51.

Horowitz, J. and McConnell, K.E. (1999) 'A Review of WTA/WTP Studies', *Working paper*, Department of Agricultural and Resource Economics, University of California.

Huang, J.-C., Haab, T.C. and Whitehead, J.C. (1997) 'Willingness to pay for quality improvements: should revealed and stated preference data be combined?', *Journal of Environmental Economics and Management*, **34**(3), 240–55.

Israngkura, A. (1998) *Environmental Valuation: An Entry Fee System for National Parks in Thailand*, EEPSA Research Report Series, Singapore.

Johannesson, M. (1995) 'The relationship between cost-effectiveness analysis and cost–benefit analysis', *Social Science and Medicine*, **41**, 483–9.

Johannesson, M. and Johansson, P.-O. (1997) 'The value of life extension and the marginal rate of time preference', *Applied Economic Letters*, **4**(1), 53–5.

Johansson, P.-O. (1991) *An Introduction to Modern Welfare Economics*, Cambridge: Cambridge University Press.

Johnson, F.R. and Desvousges, W.H. (1997) 'Estimating stated preferences with rated-pair data: environmental, health, and employment effects of energy programs', *Journal of Environmental Economics and Management*, **34**(1), 79–99.

Jones-Lee, M. (1989) *The Economics of Safety and Physical Risk*, Oxford: Basil Blackwell.

Jones-Lee, M. (1992) 'Paternalistic altruism and the value of statistical life', *Economic Journal*, **102**(410), 80–90.

Jones-Lee, M., Hammerton, M. and Philips, P. (1985) 'The value of safety: results of a national sample survey', *Economic Journal*, **95**(377), 49–72.

Jones-Lee, M. and Loomes, G. (1994) 'Towards a willingness-to-pay based value of underground safety', *Journal of Transport Economics and Policy*, **28**(1), 83–98.

Jones-Lee, M. and Loomes, G. (1997) 'Valuing health and safety: some economic and psychological issues', in R. Nau, E. Gronn, M. Machina and O. Bergland (eds), *Economic and Environmental Risk and Uncertainty: New Models and Methods*, Dordrecht: Kluwer Academic Press, 3–32.

Jones-Lee, M. and Loomes, G. (1999) *Some notes on the application of the contingent valuation approach in the valuation of health and safety*, Report for DETR, London.

Jones-Lee, M., Loomes, G., O'Reilly, D. and Philips, P.R. (1993) 'The Value of Preventing Non-Fatal Road Injuries: Findings of a Willingness-to-Pay National Sample Survey', *Working Paper WP/SRC*, Crowthorne: Transport Research Laboratory.

Jones-Lee, M., Loomes, G. and Philips, P. (1995) 'Valuing the prevention of non-fatal road injuries: contingent valuation versus standard gambles', *Oxford Economic Papers*, **47**(4), 676–95.

Kahn, J.R. (1998) *The Economic Approach to Environmental and Natural Resources*, 2nd edition, Fort Worth, TX: Dryden Press.

Kahneman, D. (1986) 'Comments by Professor Daniel Kahneman', in R. Cummings, D. Brookshire and W. Schultze, *Valuing Public Goods: An Assessment of the Contingent Valuation Method*, New Jersey: Rowman and Allenheld, 185–94.

Kahneman, D. and Knetsch, J.L. (1992) 'Valuing public goods: the purchase of moral satisfaction', *Journal of Environmental Economics and Management*, **22**(1), 57–70.

Kahneman, D., Slovic, P. and Tversky, A. (eds) (1982) *Judgement Under Uncertainty: Heuristics and Biases*, New York: Cambridge University Press.

Kahneman, D. and Tversky, A. (1979) 'Prospect theory: an analysis of decisions under risk', *Econometrica*, **47**(2), 263–91.

Kahnesman, D. and Tversky, A. (1984) 'Choices, values and frames', *American Psychologist*, **39**, 341–50.

Kanninen, B.J. (1995) 'Bias in discrete response contingent valuation', *Journal of Environmental Economics and Management*, **28**(1), 114–25.

Kemp, M. and Maxwell, C. (1993) 'Exploring a budget context for contingent valuation estimates', in J. Hausman (ed.), *Contingent Valuation: A Critical Assessment*, Amsterdam, London, New York and Tokyo: North-Holland, 217–65.

Kirchhoff, S., Colby, B. and LaFrance, J. (1997) 'Evaluating the performance of benefit transfer: an empirical inquiry', *Journal of Environmental Economics and Management*, **33**(1), 75–93.

Kling, C. (1997) 'The gains from combining travel cost and contingent valuation data to value non-market goods', *Land Economics*, **73**(3), 428–39.

Knetsch, J.L. and Davis, R.K. (1966) 'Comparisons of methods for recreation evaluation', in A.V. Kneese and S.C. Smith (eds), *Water Research*, Baltimore, MD: Resources for the Future, Johns Hopkins Press, 125–42.

Knetsch, J. and Sinden, J. (1984) 'Willingness to pay and compensation demanded: experimental evidence of an unexpected disparity in measures of value', *Quarterly Journal of Economics*, **99**, 507–21.

Kolstad, C.D. and Guzman, R.M. (1999) 'Information and the divergence between willingness to accept and willingness to pay', *Journal of Environmental Economics & Management*, **38**(1), 66–80.

Kopp, R.J. and Pease, K.A. (1997) 'Contingent valuation: economics, law and politics', in R.J. Kopp, W.W. Pommerehne and N. Schwarz (eds), *Determining the Value of Non-Marketed Goods: Economic, Psychological, and Policy Relevant Aspects of Contingent Valuation Methods*, Boston: Kluwer Academic Publishers, 7–58.

Kopp, R. and Smith, V.K. (1989) 'Benefit estimation goes to court: the case of natural resource damage assessments', *Journal of Policy Analysis and Management*, **8**(4), 593–612.

KPMG (1997) *Experience with the 'Policy Appraisal and Environment' Initiative*, London: DETR.

Krewitt, W., Holland, M., Trukenmuller, A., Heck, T. and Friedrich, R. (1999) 'Comparing costs and environmental benefits of strategies to combat acidification and ozone in Europe', *Environmental Economics and Policy Studies*, **2**, 249–66.

Krinsky, I. and Robb, A. (1986) 'Approximating the statistical properties of elasticities', *Review of Economics and Statistics*, **68**, 715–19.

Kriström, B. and Reira, P. (1996) 'Is the income elasticity of environmental improvements less than one?', *Environmental and Resource Economics*, **7**(1), 45–55.

Krupnick, A., Harrison, K., Nickell, E. and Toman, M. (1996) 'The value of health benefits from ambient air quality improvements in Eastern Europe: an exercise in benefits transfer', *Environmental and Resource Economics*, **7**(4), 307–32.

Lancaster, K. (1966) 'A new approach to consumer theory', *Journal of Political Economy*, **84**, 132–57.

Langford, I.H., Bateman, I.J. and Langford, H.D. (1996) 'A multilevel modelling approach to triple-bounded dichotomous choice contingent valuation', *Environmental and Resource Economics*, **7**(3), 197–211.

Langford, I.H., Georgiou, S., Bateman, I.J., Day, R.J. and Turner, R.K. (2000) 'Public perceptions of health risks from polluted coastal bathing waters: a mixed methodological analysis using cultural theory', *Risk Analysis*, **20**(5), 691–704.

Langford, I.H., Georgiou, S., Day, R.J. and Bateman, I.J. (1999) 'Comparing perceptions of risk and quality with willingness to pay: a mixed methodological study of public preferences for reducing health risks from polluted coastal bathing waters', *Risk, Decision and Policy*, **4**(1), 1–20.

Lanoie, P., Pedro, C. and Latour, R. (1995) 'The value of statistical life: a comparison of two approaches', *Journal of Risk and Uncertainty*, **10**(3), 235–57.

Lareau, T. and Rae, D. (1987) 'Valuing willingness to pay for diesel odor reduction: an application of the contingent ranking technique', *Southern Economic Journal*, **55**(3), 728–42.

Larson, D. (1990) 'Testing consistency of direct and indirect methods for valuing non-market goods', Davis, CA: University of California.

Lauria, D.T., Whittington, D., Choe, K.-A., Turingan, C. and Abiad, V. (1999) 'Household demand for improved sanitation services: a case study of Calamba, The Philippines', in I.J. Bateman and K.G. Willis (eds), *Valuing Environmental Preferences: Theory and Practice of the Contingent Valuation Method in the US, EU, and Developing Countries*, Oxford: Oxford University Press, 540–81.

Lave, L. (1981) *The Strategy of Social Regulation: Decision Frameworks for Policy*, Washington, DC: Brookings Institution.

Lin, B.H., Payson, S. and Wertz, J. (1996) 'Opinions of professional buyers toward organic produce: a case study of Mid-Atlantic market for fresh tomatoes', *Agribusiness*, **12**(1), 89–97.

Lind, R. (1982) *Discounting for Time and Risk in Energy Policy*, Washington, DC: Resources for the Future.

London Economics (1999) *The Environmental Costs and Benefits of the Supply of Aggregates*, London: DETR.

Loomis, J.B. (1989) 'Test-retest reliability of the contingent valuation method: a comparison of general population and visitor responses', *American Journal of Agricultural Economics*, **71**(1), 76–84.

Loomis, J.B., Gonzalez-Caban, A. and Gregory, R. (1994) 'Do reminders of substitutes and budget constraints influence contingent valuation estimates?', *Land Economics*, **70**(4), 499–506.

Loomis, J., Roach, B., Ward, F. and Ready, R. (1995) 'Testing transferability of recreation demand models across regions: a study of Corps of Engineers reservoirs', *Water Resources Research*, **31**(3), 721–30.

Louviere, J. (1988) *Analyzing Decision-Making: Metric Conjoint Analysis*, No. 67 Quantitative Applications in the Social Sciences Series, Sage University Papers, Sage Publications, Newbury Park, California.

Louviere, J. and Hensher, D.A. (1983) 'Using discrete choice models with experimental design data to forecast consumer demand for a unique cultural event', *Journal of Consumer Research*, **10**(3), 348–61.

Louviere, J., Hensher, D. and Swait, J. (2000) *Stated Choice Methods*, Cambridge: Cambridge University Press.

Louviere, J. and Woodworth, G. (1983) 'Design and analysis of simulated consumer choice or allocation experiments: an approach based on aggregate data', *Journal of Marketing Research*, **20**, 350–67.

Loewenstein, G. and Adler, D. (1995) 'A bias in the prediction of tastes', *Economic Journal*, **105**(431), 929–37.

Luce, R.D. (1959) *Individual Choice Behaviour: A Theoretical Analysis*, New York: Wiley.

Mackenzie, J. (1992) 'Evaluating recreation trip attributes and travel time via conjoint analysis', *Journal of Leisure Research*, **24**(2), 171–84.

MacRae, D. and Whittington, D. (1997) *Expert Advice for Policy Choice*, Washington, DC: Georgetown University Press.

Maddala, G.S. (1983) *Limited-dependent and qualitative variables in econometrics.*

Maddison, D. and Mourato, S. (1999) 'Valuing Different Road Options for Stonehenge', CSERGE Working Paper GEC 99-08.

Maddison, D., Pearce, D.W., Johanson, O., Calthrop, E., Litman, T. and Verhoef, E. (1996) *Blueprint 5: The True Costs of Road Transport*, London: Earthscan.

Malhotra, N.K. (1996) *Marketing Research: An Applied Orientation*, 2nd edition, New Jersey: Prentice-Hall International.

Mazotta, M. and Opaluch, J. (1995) 'Decision making when choices are complex', *Land Economics*, **71**(4), 500–515.

McConnell, K.E. (1990) 'Models for referendum data: the structure of discrete choice models for contingent valuation', *Journal of Environmental Economics and Management*, **18**(1), 19–34.

McConnell, K.E. (1997) 'Does altruism undermine existence value?', *Journal of Environmental Economics and Management*, **32**(1), 22–37.

McConnell, K.E., Strand, I.E. and Valdes, S. (1998) 'Testing temporal reliability and carry-over effect: the role of correlated responses in test-retest reliability studies', *Environmental and Resource Economics*, **12**(3), 357–74.

McDaniels, T.L., (1992) 'Reference points, loss aversion and contingent values for auto safety', *Journal of Risk and Uncertainty*, **5**(2), 187–200.

McFadden, D. (1973) 'Conditional logit analysis of qualitative choice behaviour', in P. Zarembka (ed.), *Frontiers in Econometrics*, New York: Academic Press.

McFadden, D. (1994) 'Contingent valuation and social choice', *American Journal of Agricultural Economics*, **76**, 689–708.

McFadden, D. and Leonard, G.K. (1993) 'Issues in the contingent valuation of environmental goods: Methodologies for data collection and analysis', in J.A. Hausman (ed.), *Contingent Valuation: A Critical Assessment*, Amsterdam: Elsevier Science Publishers.

Milgrom, P. (1993) 'Is sympathy an economic value? Philosophy, economics, and the contingent valuation method', in J. Hausman (ed.), *Contingent Valuation: A Critical Assessment*, Amsterdam, London, New York and Tokyo: North-Holland, 417–35.

Ministry of Transport (1963) *Proposals for a Fixed Channel Link*, London: HMSO.

Ministry of Transport (1965) *Relocation of Covent Garden Market*, London: Ministry of Transport.

Mitchell, R.C. and Carson, R.T. (1989) *Using Surveys to Value Public Goods: The Contingent Valuation Method*, Washington, DC: Resources for the Future.

Moran, D. (1999) 'After Axford: What Lessons for Environmental Valuation in the UK?', *Working Paper PA 99-01*, CSERGE.

Morgenstern, R. (1997) *Economic Analyses at EPA*, Washington, DC: Resources for the Future.

Morrison, M., Blamey, R., Bennett, J. and Louviere, J. (1999) 'A Review of Conjoint Techniques for Estimating Environmental Values', *mimeo*, University of New South Wales.

Mourato, S. (1998) 'Economic valuation in transition economies: an application of contingent valuation to Lake Balaton in Hungary', in M. Acutt and P. Mason (eds), *Environmental Valuation, Economic Policy and Sustainability*, Cheltenham: Edward Elgar.

Mourato, S. and Day, B. (1998) *Willingness to Pay for Improving Solid Waste Management in Kuala Lumpur*, Institutional Strengthening and Capacity Building, Economic Planning Unit, Prime Minister's Department, Kuala Lumpur, Malaysia.

Mourato, S., Kontoleon, A. and Danchev, A. (2002) 'Preserving cultural heritage in transition economies: a contingent valuation study of Bulgarian monasteries', in S. Navrud and R. Ready (eds), *Valuing Cultural Heritage: Applying Environmental Valuation Techniques to Historic Buildings, Monuments and Artifacts*, Cheltenham: Edward Elgar (in press).

Mourato, S. and Swierzbinski, J. (1999) *Valuing Different Management Options for Wildlife Preservation: A Case Study for the Namibian Black Rhino*, Report for CITES.

Munro, A. and Hanley, N.D. (1999) 'Information, uncertainty and contingent valuation', in I.J. Bateman and K.G. Willis (eds) *Valuing Environmental Preferences: Theory and Practice of the Contingent Valuation Method in the US, EU, and Developing Countries*, Oxford: Oxford University Press, 258–79.

MVA Consultancy, ITS Leeds University, TSU, Oxford University (1987) *The Value of Travel Time Savings*, Newbury: Policy Journals.

Navrud, S. (1992) 'Willingness to pay for preservation of species: an experiment with actual payments', in S. Navrud (ed.), *Pricing the European Environment*, Oslo: Scandinavian University Press.

Navrud, S. and Ready, R. (1995) (eds) *Valuing Cultural Heritage: Applying*

Environmental Valuation Techniques to Historic Buildings, Monuments and Artifacts, Cheltenham: Edward Elgar.

NERA (2000) *Multi-criteria Analysis: A Manual for DETR*, London: DETR.

NOAA (1994) *Oil Pollution Act of 1990: Proposed Regulations for Natural Resource Damage Assessments*, Washington, DC: National Oceanic and Atmospheric Administration, US Department of Commerce.

Nordhaus, W. and Kokkelenberg, E. (1999) *Nature's Numbers: Expanding the National Economic Accounts to Include the Environment*, Washington, DC: National Academy Press.

Norton, B. (1987) *Why Preserve Natural Variety?*, Princeton, NJ: Princeton University Press.

O'Doherty, R. (1996) 'Using contingent valuation to enhance public participation in local planning', *Regional Studies*, **30**(7), 667–78.

Olsen, J. (1993) 'Time preference for health gains: an empirical investigation', *Health Economics*, **2**, 257–65.

Orne, M.T. (1962) 'On the social psychology of the psychological experiment', *American Psychologist*, **17**, 776–89.

Parsons, G.R. (1991) 'A note on choice of residential location in travel cost demand studies', *Land Economics*, **67**, 360–64.

Parsons, G.R. and Kealy, M.J. (1992) 'Randomly drawn opportunity sets in a random utility model of lake recreation', *Land Economics*, **68**(1), 93–106.

Payne, J.W., Bettman, J.R. and Johnson, E.J. (1992) 'Behavioral decision research: a constructive processing perspective', *Annual Review of Psychology*, **42**, 87–131.

Pearce, D.W. (1994) 'Assessing the social rate of return from investment in temperate zone forestry', in R. Layard and S. Glaister (eds), *Cost-Benefit Analysis*, 2nd edition, Cambridge: Cambridge University Press, 464–90.

Pearce, D.W. (1998a) 'Cost-benefit analysis and environmental policy', *Oxford Review of Economic Policy*, **14**(4), 84–100.

Pearce, D.W. (1998b) 'Environmental appraisal and environmental policy in the European Union', *Environmental and Resource Economics*, **11**(3–4), 489–501.

Pearce, D.W. and Crowards, T. (1996) 'Particulate matter and human health in the United Kingdom', *Energy Policy*, **24**(7), 609–20.

Pearce, D.W. and Markandya, A. (1989) 'The social costs of tobacco smoking', *British Journal of Addiction*, **84**(10), 1139–50.

Pearce, D.W. and Ulph, D. (1999) 'A social discount rate for the United Kingdom', in D.W. Pearce, *Economics and Environment: Essays on Ecological Economics and Sustainable Development*, Cheltenham: Edward Elgar, 268–85.

Pearce, D.W., Whittington, D. and Georgiou, S. (1994) *Project and Policy Appraisal: Integrating Economics and Environment*, Paris: OECD.

Penning-Rowsell, E., Green, C., Tunstall, S., Thompson, P., Coker, A., Richards, C. Parker, D. (1992) *The Economics of Coastal Management: a Manual of Benefit Assessment Techniques*, London: Belhaven Press.

Plott, C.R. (1996) 'Rational individual behaviour in markets and social choice processes', in K.J. Arrow, E. Colombatto, M. Perlman and C. Schmidt (eds), *The Rational Foundations of Economic Behavior*, New York: St. Martin's Press.

Polasky, S., Gainutdinova, O. and Kerkvliet, J. (1996) 'Comparing CV responses with voting behaviour: open space survey and referendum', in Corvallis, Oregon, Paper presented at *Annual USDA W-133 Meeting*, Jekyll Island, GA.

Portney, P. and Weyant, J. (1999) *Discounting and Intergenerational Equity*, Washington, DC: Resources for the Future.

Poulos, C. and Whittington, D. (1999) 'Individuals' time preferences for life saving programs: results from six less developed countries', *mimeo*, Department of Environmental Sciences and Engineering, University of North Carolina.

Powe, N. (2000) 'Economic valuation of wetland recreation and amenity values', *PhD. Thesis*, School of Environmental Sciences, University of East Anglia.

Propper, C. (1990) 'Contingent valuation of time spent on NHS waiting lists', *Economic Journal*, **100**(400), 193–9.

Quiggin, J. (1993) 'Existence value and benefit-cost analysis – a third view', *Journal of Policy Analysis and Management*, **12**(1), 195–9.

Randall, A. (1994) 'A difficulty with the travel cost method', *Land Economics*, **70**(1), 88–96.

Randall, A. (1996) 'Calibration of CV responses: Discussion', in D.J. Bjornstad and J.R. Khan (eds), *The Contingent Valuation of Environmental Resources: Methodological Issues and Research Needs*, Cheltenham: Edward Elgar, 198–207.

Randall, A. and Hoehn, J.P. (1992) 'Embedding effects in contingent valuation: implications for natural resource damage assessment', *Staff Paper 92-14*, Department of Agricultural Economics, Michigan State University.

Randall, A. and Hoehn, J.P. (1996) 'Embedding in market demand systems', *Journal of Environmental Economics and Management*, **30**(3), 369–80.

Randall, A., Ives, B.C. and Eastman, C. (1974) 'Bidding games for valuation of aesthetic environmental improvements', *Journal of Environmental Economics and Management*, **1**, 132–49.

Randall, A. and Stoll, J.R. (1980) 'Consumer's surplus in commodity space', *American Economic Review*, **70**(3), 449–55.

Ready, R.C., Navrud, S. and Dubourg, W.R. (1999) 'How do respondents with uncertain willingness to pay answer contingent valuation questions?', *mimeo*, Department of Economics and Social Sciences, Agricultural University of Norway.

Ready, R.C., Whitehead, J. and Blomquist, G. (1995) 'Contingent valuation when respondents are ambivalent', *Journal of Environmental Economics and Management*, **29**(2), 181–96.

Reiling, S.D., Boyle, K.J., Phillips, M.L. and Anderson, M.W. (1990) 'Temporal reliability of contingent values', *Land Economics*, **66**(2), 128–34.

Reynolds, D. (1956) 'The cost of road accidents', *Journal of the Royal Statistical Society*, Series A, **119**(4), 393–408.

Riera, P. and Groves, T. (1999) 'Conditions for strategy-proofness, truthful answers and efficiency in the valuation of environmental public goods', *mimeo*, Universitat Autònoma de Barcelona and University of California at San Diego.

Roberts, K.J., Thompson, M.E. and Pawlyk, P.W. (1985) 'Contingent valuation of recreational diving at petroleum rigs, Gulf of Mexico', *Transactions of the American Fisheries Society*, **114**, 155–65.

Roe, B., Boyle, K. and Teisl, M. (1996) 'Using conjoint analysis to derive estimates of compensating variation', *Journal of Environmental Economics and Management*, **31**(2), 145–159.

Romer, A., Pommerehne, W. and Feld, L. (1998) 'Revealing preferences for reductions of public risks: an application of the CV approach', *Journal of Environmental Planning and Management*, **41**(4), 477–503.

Rosenberger, R.S. and Loomis, J.B. (2000) 'Using meta-analysis for benefit transfer: in-sample convergent validity tests of an outdoor recreation database', *Water Resources Research*, **36**(4), 1097–1107.

Rowe, R., Lang, C., Chestnut, L., Latimer, D., Rae, D., Bernow, S. and White, D. (1994) *New York State Environmental Externalities Cost Study*, Vol. 1, New York: Oceana Press.

Rowe, R.D., Schulze, W.D. and Breffle, W. (1996) 'A test for payment card biases', *Journal of Environmental Economics and Management*, **31**, 178–85.

Rowlatt, P., Spackman, M., Jones, S., Jones-Lee, M. and Loomes, G. (1998) *Valuation of Deaths from Air Pollution*, NERA, London and CASPAR – University of Newcastle.

Ryan, M. (1995) 'Economics and the patient's utility function: an application to assisted reproductive techniques', *PhD thesis*, University of Aberdeen.

Ryan, M. and Hughes, J. (1995) '*Using conjoint analysis to value surgical versus medical management of miscarriage*', Health Economics Research Unit, University of Aberdeen.

Sagoff, M. (1988) *The Economy of the Earth: Philosophy, Law and the Environment*, Cambridge: Cambridge University Press.

Samples, K., Dixon, J. and Gower, M. (1986) 'Information disclosure and endangered species valuation', *Land Economics*, **62**(3), 306–312.

Samuelson, P.A. (1954) 'The pure theory of public expenditure', *Review of Economics and Statistics*, **36**, 387–9.

Sánchez, M., Grande, I., Gil, J.M. and Gracia, A. (1997) 'Metodologías alternativas para medir la disposicion al pago de productos ecologicos', II Congreso de Economia, Navarra, Octubre.

Scarpa, R. and Bateman, I.J. (2000) 'Does a third bound help? Parametric and nonparametric welfare measures from a CV interval data study', *Land Economics*.

Scarpa, R. and Bateman, I.J. (2000) 'Efficiency gains afforded by improved bid design versus follow-up valuation questions in discrete choice CV studies', *Land Economics*, **76**(2), 299–311.

Schkade, D. and Payne, J. (1994) 'How people respond to contingent valuation questions: a verbal protocol analysis of willingness to pay for an environmental regulation', *Journal of Environmental Economics and Management*, **26**(1), 88–109.

Schulze, W.D., McClelland, G., Waldman, D. and Lazo, J. (1996) 'Sources of bias in contingent valuation', in D.J. Bjørnstad and J.R. Kahn (eds), *The Contingent Valuation of Environmental Resources: Methodological Issues and Research Needs*, Cheltenham: Edward Elgar, 97–116.

Schulze, W.D., Cummings, R.G., Brookshire, D.S., Thayer, M.H., Whitworth, R.L. and Rahmatian, M. (1983) 'Experimental approaches to valuing environmental commodities: Vol II', draft final report for *Methods Development in Measuring Benefits of Environmental Improvements*, USEPA Grant # CR808–893–01.

Schumann, H. (1996) 'The sensitivity of CV outcomes to CV survey methods', in D.J. Bjørnstad and J.R. Khan (eds), *The Contingent Valuation of Environmental Resources: Methodological Issues and Research Needs*, Cheltenham: Edward Elgar, 75–96.

Scott, A. (1965) 'The valuation of game resources: some theoretical aspects', *Canadian Fisheries Report*, iv, Department of Fisheries of Canada, Ottawa, Ontario.

Seller C., Chavas, J.-P. and Stoll, J.R. (1986) 'Specification of the logit model: the case of valuation and non-market goods', *Journal of Environmental Economics and Management*, **13**(4), 382–90.

Shogren, J. (1993) 'Experimental markets and environmental policy', *Agricultural and Resource Economics Review*, **2**, 117–29.

Slovic, P. and Lichtenstein, S. (1983) 'Preference reversals: a broader perspective', *American Economic Review*, **73**(4), 596–605.

Smith, J., Mourato, S., Veneklaas, E., Labarta, R., Reategui, K. and Sanchez, G. (1998) 'Willingness to pay for environmental services among slash-and-burn farmers in the Peruvian Amazon: implications for deforestation and global environmental markets', CSERGE/CIAT/ICRAF *Working Paper 97*.

Smith, V.K. (1984) *Environmental Policy Under Reagan's Executive Order: the Role of Benefit-Cost Analysis*, Chapel Hill, NC: University of North Carolina Press.

Smith, V.K. (1992) 'Arbitrary values, good causes and premature verdicts', *Journal of Environmental and Resource Economics*, **22**(1), 71–89.

Smith, V.K. (2000) 'Fifty years of contingent valuation', Paper presented at the Kobe Conference on the *Theory and Application of Environmental Valuation*, January 2000.

Smith, V.K. and Desvousges, W.H. (1987) 'An empirical analysis of the economic value of risk changes', *Journal of Political Economy*, **95**(1), 89–114.

Smith, V.K., Desvousges, W.H. and Fisher, A. (1986) 'A comparison of direct and indirect methods for estimating environmental benefits', *American Journal of Agricultural Economics*, **68**(2), 280–90.

Smith, V.K. and Osbourne, L.L. (1996) 'Do contingent valuation estimates pass a "scope" test? a meta-analysis', *Journal of Environmental Economics and Management*, **31**(3), 287–301.

Smith, V.L. (1979) 'Incentive compatible experimental processes for the provision of public goods', in V.L. Smith (ed.), *Research in Experimental Economics, Volume 1*, Greenwich, CT.: JAI Press, 59–168.

Smith, V.L. (1980) 'Experiments with a decentralized mechanism for public good decisions', *American Economic Review*, **70**, 584–99.

Spash, C. and Hanley, N. (1995) 'Preferences, information and biodiversity preservation', *Ecological Economics*, **12**(3), 191–208.

Squire, L. and van der Tak H. (1975) *Economic Analysis of Projects*, Washington DC: World Bank.

Srinivasan, V. and Park, C. (1997) 'Surprising robustness of the self-explicating approach to customer preference structure measurement', *Journal of Marketing Research*, **34**(2), 286–91.

Steenkamp, J.-E. (1987) 'Conjoint measurement in ham quality evaluation', *Journal of Agricultural Economics*, **38**(3), 473–80.

Steer Davies Gleave (2000) 'London Underground Customer Priorities Research', Report for London Undergound.

Steer Davies Gleave (1999) 'Bus Station Passenger Preferences', Report for London Transport Buses.

Sturtevant, L.A., Johnson, F.R. and Desvousges, W.H. (1995) *A Meta-analysis of Recreational Fishing*, Durham, NC: Triangle Economic Research.

Sudman, S., Bradburn, N.M. and Schwarz, N. (1996) *Thinking About Answers: The Application of Cognitive Processes to Survey Methodology*, San Francisco, CA: Jossey-Bass Publishers.

Sugden, R. (1999a) 'Public goods and contingent valuation', in I.J. Bateman and K.G. Willis (eds), *Valuing Environmental Preferences: Theory and Practice of the Contingent Valuation Method in the US, EU, and Developing Countries*, Oxford: Oxford University Press, 131–51.

Sugden, R. (1999b) 'Alternatives to the neo-classical theory of choice', in I.J. Bateman and K.G. Willis (eds), *Valuing Environmental Preferences: Theory and Practice of the Contingent Valuation Method in the US, EU, and Developing Countries*, Oxford: Oxford University Press, 152–80.

Sutherland, R.J. and Walsh, R.G. (1985) 'Effect of distance on the preservation value of water quality', *Land Economics*, **61**(3), 281–91.

Swait, J. and Adamowicz, W. (1996) 'The effect of choice environment and task demands on consumer behaviour', paper presented to 1996 Canadian Resource and Environmental Economics Study Group, Montreal.

Swait, J. and Louviere, J. (1993) 'The role of the scale parameter in the estimation and comparison of multi-nomial logit models', *Journal of Marketing Research*, **30**(3), 305–14.

Swanson, J. (1986) '*Demand at Regional Airports: An Interactive Model*', Proceedings of the Royal Aeronautical Society, London.

Teisl, M.F., Boyle, K.J., McCollum, D.W. and Reiling, S.D. (1995) 'Test-retest reliability of contingent valuation', *American Journal of Agricultural Economics*, **77**(3), 613–19.

Thaler, R. (1985) 'Mental accounting and consumer choice', *Marketing Science*, **4**(3), 199–214.

Thayer, M. (1981) 'Contingent valuation techniques for assessing environmental impacts: further evidence', *Journal of Environmental Economics and Management*, **8**(1), 27–44.

Train, K.E. (1998) 'Recreation demand models with taste differences across people', *Land Economics*, **74**(2), 230–39.

Tversky, A. and Kahnemann, D. (1991) 'Loss aversion in riskless choice: a reference', UNDP/UNSTAT Working on Natural Resource and Environmental Accounting, Beijing.

Tversky, A., Sattath, S. and Slovic, P. (1988) 'Contingent weighting in judgement and choice', *Psychological Review*, **95**, 371–84.

Tversky, A., Slovic, P. and Kahneman, D. (1990) 'The causes of preference reversal', *American Economic Review*, **80**(1), 204–17.

Uno, K. (1989) 'Economic growth and environmental change in Japan: net national welfare and beyond', in F. Archibuji and P. Nijkamo (eds), *Economy and Ecology: Towards Sustainable Development*, London: Kluwer.

US Department of Transportation (1982) *Guide to forecasting travel demand with direct utility assessment*, Washington, DC.

Vaze, P. and Balchin, S. (1998) 'The pilot United Kingdom environmental accounts', in P. Vaze (ed.), *UK Environmental Accounts 1998: Theory, Data, Application*, London: The Stationery Office, 7–40.

Viscusi, W.K. (1994) 'Risk-risk analysis', *Journal of Risk and Uncertainty*, **8**(1), 5–17.

Viscusi, W.K. (1998) *Rational Risk Policy*, Oxford: Clarendon Press.

Wagstaff, A. (1994) 'Health care: QALYs and the equity-efficiency trade-off', in R. Layard and S. Glaister (eds), *Cost-Benefit Analysis*, 2nd edition, Cambridge: Cambridge University Press, 428–47.

Walshe, G. and Daffern, P. (1990) *Managing Cost-Benefit Analysis*, London: Macmillan.

Wang, H. (1997) 'Treatment of "don't know" responses in contingent valuation surveys: a random valuation model', *Journal of Environmental Economics and Management*, **32**(2), 219–32.

Wardman, M. and Whelan, G. (1998) 'Rolling Stock Improvements and User Willingness to Pay', *Working Paper 523*, Institute for Transport Studies, University of Leeds.

Weber, J.-L. (1993) *Environment Statistics and Natural Resource (Patrimony) Accounting*, UNDP/UNSTAT Working on Natural Resource and Environmental Accounting, Beijing.

Whitehead, J.C. and Hoban, T.J. (1999) 'Testing for temporal reliability in contingent valuation with time for changes in factors affecting demand', *Land Economics*, **75**, 453–65.

Whittington, D., Smith, V.K., Okorafor, A., Okore, A., Liu, J.L. and McPhail, A. (1992) 'Giving respondents time to think in contingent valuation studies: a developing country application', *Journal of Environmental Economics and Management*, **22**(3), 205–225.

Williams, A. (1976) *Cost Benefit Analysis In Public Health And Medical Care*, Lund: Department of Economics, University of Lund.

Willig, R. (1976) 'Consumer's surplus without apology', *American Economic Review*, **66**(4), 589–97.

Willis, K. (1995) 'Contingent valuation in a policy context: the NOAA report and its implications for the use of contingent valuation methods in policy analysis in Britain', in K. Willis and J. Corkindale (eds), *Environmental Valuation: New Perspectives*, Oxford: CAB International, 118–43.

Willis, K.G. and Garrod, G.D. (1993) 'Valuing landscape: a contingent valuation approach', *Journal of Environmental Management*, **37**(1), 1–22.

Wonnacott, T.H. and Wonnacott, R.J. (1990) *Introductory Statistics*, New York: Wiley.

Wright, R., Hanley, N. and Koop, G. (2000) 'Choice experiments and the demand for mountaineering in Scotland', *mimeo*, Institute of Ecology and Resource Management, University of Edinburgh.

Young, M. (1992) 'Natural resource accounting: some Australian experiences and observations', in E. Lutz, *Towards Improved Accounting for the Environment*, Washington, DC: World Bank.

Glossary

Altruistic value: Altruism is the desire to secure an enhancement of the wellbeing of others. Altruistic economic value is the willingness to pay on the part of individual A to ensure that individual B secures some gain in wellbeing. Altruistic value is an example of *non-use value*.

Anchoring bias: Anchoring bias is where respondents are influenced by the starting values, or succeeding bids, used in elicitation of WTP, for example, in a bidding game or dichotomous choice elicitation format.

Axiom of transitivity: An axiom of rational choice which states that if A is preferred to B and B is preferred to C, then A should be preferred to C.

Benefit (or bid) function: A regression equation that describes the relationship between WTP and relevant factors such as characteristics of the population, the change in the non-market good or service and so on.

Benefits transfer: An approach which makes use of previous valuations of similar goods at a study site and, with any necessary adjustments, applies them to produce estimates for the same or similar good in a different context, known as the policy site. What is transferred may be a mean WTP, with or without some adjustment for changed conditions (for example, different income levels), or a benefit function (or *bid function*).

Bequest value: Bequest values measure people's WTP to ensure their heirs and future generations will be able to use the resource in the future. Bequest values are an example of *non-use values*.

Bid function: A function which relates the compensating variation measure of a change in welfare (or maximum WTP for a change in a non-market good) to changes in parameters of interest, for example, income, socio-economic and demographic factors, prices of other goods and characteristics of non-market goods.

Bid function model: A model of WTP based on direct estimation of the bid function, rather than the underlying utility function.

Bidding game: An elicitation format for WTP where respondents are faced with several rounds of discrete choice questions, with the final question being an open-ended WTP question.

Bootstrapping: A technique to create confidence intervals for mean and median WTP using any type of data (i.e. continuous, binary or interval) or results from any estimation method (i.e. non-parametric or parametric). With a data set containing N observations, the analyst creates multiple simulated data sets by sampling N times with replacement from the original set of observations. The model is re-estimated for each simulated data set to obtain a new set of parameter estimates from which estimates of mean and median WTP can be derived. These estimates can be arranged in order and 95 per cent confidence intervals defined as the values falling on the 2½th and 97½th percentiles.

Choice experiment: A form of choice modelling in which respondents are presented with a series of alternatives and asked to choose their most preferred.

Choice modelling (CM): This encompasses a range of SP techniques, including *choice experiments*, *contingent ranking*, *contingent rating* and *paired comparisons*. CM approaches describe an asset in terms of its attributes, or characteristics, and the levels that these take, and may be used to determine which attributes are significant determinants of value; their implied ranking; the value of changing them; and the total economic value of a resource or good.

Choice set: A set of alternatives presented to respondents, usually in a choice experiment context, where they are asked to choose their most preferred.

Closed-ended format: An elicitation format where respondents have to select their answer from a number of pre-specified alternatives. See *dichotomous choice* format, *referendum* format.

Coercive payment vehicles: These are payment mechanisms involving a degree of compulsion, for example taxes, rates, fees, charges or prices. May be contrasted with non-coercive instruments such as donations.

Comparative risk assessment: Method of doing risk assessment for two or more risks at the same time to determine where a given level of resources would be most sensibly allocated. A form of *cost effectiveness analysis*.

Compensating variation: The compensating variation of a price fall (rise) is the sum of money that, when taken away from (given to) the consumer, leaves him or her just as well off with the price change as if it had not occurred. Thus, initial utility is held constant.

Compliance cost assessment: An assessment of the costs of a policy (as opposed to a project) incurred by the sector which may be directly or indirectly affected.

Constant sum scale: These scales ask respondents to allocate a constant number of units (say points or money) among a set of objects according to some criterion.

Construct validity: This examines whether the relationships between measures produced by a CV study and other measures are in accordance with expectations. Examples include predictors from economic theory, and empirical regularities in the form of associations with other variables which seem intuitively correct and which hold across a large number of studies.

Constructed preferences: A view that survey responses will be 'constructed' largely as a function of how the questions are asked rather than as a function of stable underlying preferences. Constructed preferences are not therefore 'true' preferences.

Consumer surplus: The difference (or the net gain) between the price actually paid when purchasing a good or service and the price the consumer would have been willing to pay for the same good or service.

Content validity: This assesses whether the SP study asked the right questions in a clear, understandable, sensible and appropriate manner with which to obtain a valid estimate of the construct (say maximum WTP for a specific good) under investigation.

Contingent ranking: A form of *choice modelling* in which respondents are required to rank a set of alternative options. Each alternative is characterised by a number of attributes, which are offered at different levels across options. Respondents are then asked to rank the options according to their preferences.

Contingent rating: A form of *choice modelling* exercise in which respondents are presented with a number of scenarios and are asked to rate them individually on a semantic or numeric scale.

Continuous rating scale: In a continuous rating scale respondents are asked to rate an object by placing a mark at the appropriate position on a line that runs from one extreme of the criterion of interest to the other.

Convergent validity: A process of *construct* validity in which the measures obtained from a given SP study are compared with results from other SP studies to see if they produce similar answers, or answers that vary in a predicted manner.

Cost–benefit analysis: A procedure for valuing gains (benefits) and losses (costs) in monetary terms, based on individuals' willingness to pay to secure the benefit or avoid the cost and the resource costs involved.

Cost-effectiveness analysis: Evaluation of an option in terms of its cost per unit of 'output', where 'output' reflects the goals chosen (for example, lives saved).

Coverage error: The extent to which the sample frame provides a biased or unreliable coverage of the target population.

Criterion validity: The comparison of WTP estimates from a contingent valuation study with actual market or simulated market experiments. Since market prices are not available for public goods, criterion validity can generally only be tested against market prices for private goods. In this manual, criterion validity is subsumed under *convergent validity*.

Dichotomous choice: An elicitation format in which respondents are faced with only two response alternatives, such as yes/no, agree/disagree, or vote for/vote against. Sometimes a 'don't know' option is also included to avoid forcing respondents into artificially choosing one of the answers.

Direct use value: Where individuals make actual use of a resource for either commercial purposes or recreation.

Discounting: Discounting is the process of expressing future values in present value terms which allows for the comparison of cost and benefit flows regardless of when they occur. The present value of a future flow of benefit or cost will be lower than the future value because of discounting. There is no *a priori* correct way to discount future gains and losses, although *exponential discounting* is most widely used. SP techniques may be used to derive discount rates.

Distance decay effect: How WTP varies as the respondent's distance from the object in question increases.

Economic value: The monetary measure of the wellbeing associated with the change in the provision of some good. It is not to be confused with monetary value unless the latter is explicitly designed to measure the change in wellbeing, nor with financial value which may reflect market value or an accounting convention. As Freeman (1993) notes, the terms 'economic value' and 'welfare change' can be used interchangeably.

Elicitation format: The method whereby respondents are asked questions to determine how much they would value the good if confronted with the opportunity to obtain it. Possible formats include open-ended, dichotomous choice, payment card, payment ladder.

Embedding: Embedding concerns changes to two or more arguments within a multivariate utility function. For example, when we move from considering a project to preserve A to another which will conserve A plus B, we can state that the former project is perfectly embedded within the latter. See also *scope insensitivity*.

Environmental impact assessment: Systematic listing and quantification, where possible, of the impacts on the environment from a policy, project or process. Impacts may or may not be aggregated in some way.

Environmental risk assessment: A procedure for determining levels of risk and severity of events.

Equivalent variation: The equivalent variation of a price fall (rise) is the sum of money that, when given to (taken from) the consumer leaves him or her just as well off without the price change as if it had occurred. Thus, it preserves the post-change utility level.

Existence value: The value that people put on the existence of a resource, even when they have no intention of ever using the resource. Existence values are part of *non-use values*.

Expectation-based validity: A type of content validity in which SP measures are related to other constructs in a manner which is consistent with prior expectations (theoretical, intuition and empirically driven expectations).

Exponential discounting: Discounting of future costs and benefits involves applying a weight, call it α_t, to a cost or benefit in time t such that α_t is less than unity and declines with time. Exponential discounting selects a particular path for the value of α_t as defined by:

$$\alpha_t = 1/(1+r)^t,$$

where r is the discount rate. Contrasts with *hyperbolic discounting*.

External validity: Assessing the validity of SP results by reference to some yardstick outside the study, for example, the results of a different study.

Face validity: This assesses whether the CV study asked the right questions in a clear, understandable, sensible and appropriate manner with which to obtain a valid estimate of the construct (say maximum WTP for a specific good) under investigation.

Face value assumption: The assumption that (i) respondents always answer truthfully and (ii) they also answer the specific question asked.

Filter questions: Questions included at the beginning of a questionnaire in order to screen potential respondents to ensure that they meet the necessary requirements to answer the question.

Focus groups: A focus group is a discussion group by a moderator among a small group of respondents in an unstructured manner.

Free rider: An individual who benefits from the provision of a good (usually a public good) by more than he or she pays for it.

Health-health assessment: Procedure for evaluating policies in terms of health risks they reduce and health risks they increase because the costs of policy reduce incomes, some of which would have been spent on risk reduction.

Hyperbolic discounting: A form of 'slow discounting' such that the future is discounted at a rate less than that implied by *exponential discounting*.

Hypothetical bias: The possibility that SP estimates may be biased upwards due to the hypothetical nature of the payment commitment.

Incentive compatibility: The questionnaire design objective of constructing a valuation mechanism in which truth-telling and utility maximisation coincide.

Indirect use value: This arises where individuals benefit from ecosystem functions supported by a resource rather than actually using it (for example, watershed protection or carbon sequestration by forests).

Indirect utility function: A function that describes household utility (or wellbeing) usually in terms of how much utility it can derive from income, given the prices of goods and, say, the level of provision of a non-market good.

Internal validity: Assessing the validity of the results of a SP survey in terms of consistency with other features of the survey, for example, WTP should vary positively with income.

Itemised rating scale: In an itemised scale, respondents are presented with a scale that has numbers or a brief description associated with each category and are asked to select one of the categories according to some criterion. The categories are ordered in terms of the scale position.

Life-cycle analysis: Process used to evaluate environmental burdens associated with a product, process or activity by examining emissions at every stage of the life-cycle (for example, production, distribution, use and disposal).

Likert scale: A type of *itemised rating scale* where respondents are asked to indicate a degree of agreement or disagreement with statements about the object.

Meta-analysis: A statistical procedure whereby a number of different studies are treated as inputs to a wider study that seeks to explain the variability of outcomes in the individual studies. Meta-studies involve not just outcomes of the original studies (for example, mean WTP) but also the sample size, date and location of the study, the author and so on.

Multi-criteria analysis: Analysis of decisions in a context where there are multiple goals (objectives) that cannot usually be reduced to a single monetary measure. MCA seeks to identify those combinations of outcomes that are dominated by other combinations, and to show the trade-offs between the final set of potentially 'efficient' combinations.

Non-use value: The value placed on a resource by people who are not current users of that resource and who do not intend to use the resource themselves. See *altruistic, bequest* and *existence values*. It is also referred to as passive use value.

Open-ended format: A straightforward elicitation format which asks respondents to state their maximum WTP (or minimum WTA).

Option value: The value that people place on having the option to use a resource in the future even if they are not current users.

Paired comparison: In a paired comparison scale respondents are presented with two objects simultaneously and asked to select one according to some criterion. They may also be asked to indicate the strength of their preference in a numeric or semantic scale.

Payment card: An elicitation format which presents respondents with a visual aid containing a large number of monetary amounts to facilitate the valuation task.

Payment ladder: A form of payment card whereby a ladder of monetary values is presented.

Protest bid: A response to a valuation question which does not give the respondent's genuine WTP (or WTA), but either a zero value or an unrealistically high (or low) value.

QALY: 'Quality Adjusted Life Year', a remaining life year weighted by the expected quality of life in the year in question.

Rank order scale: In a rank order scale, respondents are presented with several objects simultaneously and asked to order or rank them according to some criterion.

Reference-dependent utility: An individual's utility is defined in relation to that individual's reference point, normally the *status quo*.

Referendum model: A model of questionnaire design using an elicitation format of the form 'Would you be willing to pay X?'

Reliability: This refers to the degree of replicability of a WTP/WTA measurement over time and over different SP applications.

Risk-risk assessment (RRA): Compares the risks reduced by a policy or project and asks what the risks would be if the policy was not implemented.

Sample frame population: A list of the target population from which the sample will ultimately be drawn, for example, all dwelling units in a city, all visitors to a site, all households with a telephone.

Scope: This concerns a change in just one argument of a multivariate utility function. For example, a change in the scope of a good occurs when the quantity of that good increases or decreases.

Scope insensitivity: see *scope test*.

Scope test: Tests in the processing of a SP study, or in focus groups and pretests, to see if respondents' values vary positively with an increasing quantity of the public good in question. If they do not, there is said to be '*scope insensitivity*'. One form of scope insensitivity is *embedding*.

Semantic differential scale: A type of *itemised rating scale* with seven points, the end points associated with bipolar labels (for example, very good, very bad).

Sequencing: A method of valuing a variety of goods within the same study, presenting the respondent with a series or sequence of goods in which the policy package is built up incrementally, with valuations being sought at each stage.

Stability (of values): The extent to which values remain constant over time.

Stakeholder analysis: The process of identifying groups who may be affected by a change in question, determining and monitoring their gains and losses.

Standing: A term used to describe those individuals who are affected by the change under consideration, and whose values will be considered.

Stapel scale: A type of *itemised rating scale* which uses a single key word and requires respondents to rate the object of interest on a scale generally from −5 to +5, without a neutral point.

Starting point bias: When the final valuation estimate shows dependence on the starting point used.

Theoretical validity: The consistency between WTP estimates derived from stated preference studies and underlying theoretical expectations (for example, fewer people will agree to higher price bids).

Total economic value: Total economic value of an environmental resource is made up of i) use values and ii) non-use values. Use values are composed of a) *direct use value*, b) *indirect use values* and c) *option values*, whilst non-use values are made up of a) *altruistic values*, b) *existence values* and c) *bequest values*.

Use value: The value placed on a resource by users of that resource. See *direct use value, indirect use value* and *option values*.

Utility: This is synonymous with wellbeing.

Utility difference model: An indirect utility model constructed to estimate the difference in utility that results from provision of the non-market good. This model relies on specification of the underlying utility functions and is then used to derive specific forms of *bid functions*.

Validity: Refers to the degree to which an SP study measured the intended quantity.

Verbal protocol: An approach where respondents are encouraged to think out loud and verbalise anything they might be thinking, even if trivial and seemingly unimportant, while completing a task such as answering a questionnaire.

Willingness to accept compensation: The monetary measure of the value of forgoing an environmental (or other) gain or allowing a loss.

Willingness to pay: The monetary measure of the value of obtaining environmental (or other) gain or avoiding a loss.

Index